Published by the Chicago Crime Commission, Chicago, Illinois

Library of Congress Control Number: 2007937085

ISBN-10: 0-9787471-5-1
ISBN-13: 978-0-9787471-5-2
UPC 893638001-07

The Chicago Crime Commission recognizes the following individuals as Contributing Authors of *Friend and Foe* (2007) for their individual and collective authorship, editing, input, and role in this publication:

James W. Wagner
Jeannette P. Tamayo
Linda Bond
Bruce Clorfene
Vanja Vidackovic
Katherine J. Kirby
Amy Averbuch
J.R. Davis
Arthur J. Bilek
John L. Conlon
Rocco J. deGrasse
Joseph N. DuCanto
Robert M. Fitzgerald
Gregory C. Jones

friend and foe

GRAPHIC EXHIBITS FROM THE CHICAGO CRIME COMMISSION ARCHIVES

A glimpse at citizen action, law-enforcement advancements, and crime in twentieth century Chicago.

CONTRIBUTORS

This collaborative effort would not have been possible without the tireless work and effort of the Commission's Members, staff, volunteers and others. Credit for this publication cannot be attributed to any one person, but has to be shared by many.

A special thank you to Chicago Crime Commission (CCC) staff: President James W. Wagner, General Counsel Jeannette P. Tamayo, and Program Associate Vanja Vidackovic who worked diligently on this publication. Special recognition is also deserved by Chairman J.R. Davis, Program Committee Chair Arthur J. Bilek and Committee Members John L. Conlon, Rocco J. deGrasse, Joseph N. DuCanto, Robert M. Fitzgerald, Gregory C. Jones, for their editorial assistance and, along with the Board of Directors, for their support of this publication. A special thank you to Bruce Clorfene, our copy editor. And, special recognition is also deserved by Kate Kirby, our former Executive Vice-President, and Amy Averbuch, our former research intern, who contributed to this effort during their tenure at the Commission.

A special thank you to Crime Historians Mars Eghigian, Jr. and Jeffrey Thurston for their assistance in identifying and providing information about organized crime and the CCC's history. Thank you to John Binder, author of *Images of America: The Chicago Outfit* for the use of his private photo collection. Thank you to the Chicago Tribune Archives, the Chicago Sun-Times and the Daily Herald for providing permission to reproduce many articles and photos in this publication. Thank you also to our former staff and interns, including Anthony Beckneck, Al Egan, Melissa Halik, Elizabeth Kusta, and Valencia Lee for their assistance. This publication would not have been possible without the constant assistance of our Graphic Designer and Production Artist, Linda Bond.

TABLE OF CONTENTS

FOREWORD

This Chicago Crime Commission (CCC) publication was inspired by the 2006 *Target America: Opening Eyes to the Damage Drugs Cause* exhibit held at Chicago's Museum of Science and Industry and delivered by the Drug Enforcement Administration in partnership with the CCC. The CCC supplied select materials from its extensive archives for this exhibit.

friend and foe, the title of this publication, refers to the crime fighter and the criminal and the war that is waged between the two for control of Chicago and its most valuable resources. It is the classic battle of good and evil — the battle for safety and justice over crime, violence, and unfairness. In this book you will find visuals beyond those used in the *Target America* exhibit covering organized crime, prohibition, narcotics, street gangs, citizen action, law enforcement advances, and technology throughout the twentieth century. It will provide you with only a small sample of the millions of materials that can be found in the CCC archives.

The book is not meant to be a complete history of crime, citizen action, and law enforcement in Chicago, but instead, to provide an exhibit of visual materials that highlight some aspects of that story. We hope that you will enjoy the original photographs, cartoons, headlines, lithographs, fingerprints, drawings, and information ahead.

The CCC, a not-for-profit organization, was founded in 1919 by thirty-five members of the Chicago business community and is the oldest and most respected citizens' crime commission in the nation. Today, the CCC is an active partner in programs such as Project Safe Neighborhoods and the Illinois (IIJIS) and Cook County (CCJIS) partnerships on Integrated Justice Information Systems. The Crime Commission leads the Coalition Against the Exploitation, Prostitution and Trafficking of Children (CAEPTC), the Anonymous Crime Reporting Hotline, the Business Assistance Network, the Investigative Business Advisory Service, and most recently the Hotline 888 eye on gov to accept information regarding public corruption and other illegal activities.

To learn more about the Chicago Crime Commission and to order additional CCC publications, visit www.chicagocrimecommission.org.

James W. Wagner
President

J. R. Davis
Chairman of the Board

Source: Courtesy of Chicago Tribune Archives

1850

COPS DIFFER ON VISIT OF CAPONE BEER BOSS

1929

Colonel Henry Chamberlin

Chamberlin advocated for the formation of the Chicago Crime Commission and became its first operating director in 1919. Chamberlin orchestrated the CCC's anti-organized crime campaign in 1930.

Colosimo

Torrio

"Hinky Dink" Kenna, "Bathhouse John" Coughlin, "Big Jim" Colosimo, Johnny Torrio and Alfonse "Scarface" Capone

These individuals are credited with setting the stage for organized crime activity in Chicago, and their illegal activities led to the development of the infamous Capone gang.

Although we are only able to highlight a few friends and foes for each decade, the Chicago Crime Commission reminds the public that there are many friends, and while perhaps not as famous as the criminals, they are courageous and far more impressive.

Chicago Police Force: Its Early Days
Chicago Police Force: Its Early Days

Source: Brief History of Chicago Police Department at www.chipublib.org

In the very early days of Chicago, people living in the area relied upon the U.S. soldiers stationed at Fort Dearborn for protection. Back in 1850, a citizen police force consisted of nine men. The city was divided into three police precincts with a station house in each. Station No. 1 was located in a building on State Street between Lake and Randolph streets; No. 2 was on west Randolph near DesPlaines Street; and No. 3 was on Michigan Avenue near Clark Street. In 1861, authority over the department was placed in the hands of three police commissioners, which effectively deprived the mayor of the power to interfere in the control of the police force. At this time, the title Superintendent was first used to designate the head of the department. In 1913, the superintendent, captains, lieutenants, sergeants and patrolmen became known as "policemen," and would comprise the Chicago police force. As the population of the city increased and demands upon the police force followed suit, the department responded with internal revisions.

While the threat of gangsters spread danger over the city of Chicago, fingerprinting was introduced as an innovative crime-fighting technique. In 1905 fingerprinting was introduced to the department but was not practiced until 1910, when the Illinois Supreme Court upheld fingerprints as admissible evidence. This critical technology gave hope to Chicago's police force. All fingers have friction-ridge skin that makes up an original imprint even between identical twins, proving to be a 100 percent accurate identification process.

The telephone was invented in 1876, and wiretapping became an additional and popular crime-fighting technique. In 1928, after Olmstead v. United States, the U.S. Supreme Court legitimized wiretapping, ruling that it was acceptable for police to monitor the private calls of suspected bootleggers and other criminals.

Chicago Crime Commission Is Formed
Chicago Crime Commission Is Formed

The Chicago Crime Commission was founded in 1919 after a number of well-meaning citizens tried to combat lawlessness throughout the very early 1900s without success. The futility of the attempts was because of the failure to wage a continuous war. And so, there came the incentive to create a not-for-profit, non-governmental, non-partisan group that could translate the desires of the law-abiding into terms of practical operation. Thus, the Chicago Association of Commerce recommended that the CCC be formed. Today, in 2006, the CCC consists of a membership of approximately 200 business and professional leaders.

One example of the CCC's impact in the 1920s is evidenced by the almost instant results the Chicago citizenry enjoyed with the formation of the Commission. In 1920, the Commission found an unacceptable 138 murder cases pending in the criminal court. One hundred and four defendants were at large on bail. One of the cases was eleven years old. At the insistence of the Commission, four judges were assigned to try murder cases only for a period of sixty days. At the end of that time, eighty-nine defendants were sent to the penitentiary for terms ranging from fourteen years to life. The murder rate in Chicago dropped fifty-one percent in the following year. In addition, the CCC established the first system for collecting complete records of all felony cases commenced in Cook County. The CCC also successfully advocated for an increase in the city's police force by 1,000 persons and became, along with the Secret Six, the citizens that took down Capone and his gang.

Setting the Stage for the Capone Gang
Setting the Stage for the Capone Gang

Source: Virgil W. Peterson, "Historical Background of Organized Crime Prior to 1967," published by the Chicago Crime Commission, 1979

In Chicago, the first real political machine was created by Mike McDonald, a gambling boss. In the mayoral election, McDonald demonstrated that under effective leadership the gamblers, saloon keepers and prostitution interests could be welded into formidable political power. McDonald's candidate was elected. Beginning in the late 1800s, the First Ward of Chicago was ruled politically for almost a half-century by the inimitable Bathhouse John Coughlin and Michael (Hinky Dink) Kenna. Coughlin, the proprietor of a bathhouse patronized by gamblers and race track men, was elected as alderman in 1892. Kenna, an alderman and later a ward committeeman of the First Ward ran a saloon. Above his place was a gambling establishment. In 1893, politically motivated police raids were made on gambling houses in the First Ward. This was intolerable to Coughlin and Kenna who promptly formed an organization to which proprietors of gambling houses or brothel keepers would make regular payments. Those making payoffs would be assured protection. Two lawyers, one of whom later became a judge, were placed on a permanent retainer-fee basis to represent members of the organization who might be arrested. Backed by this organization, the gamblers, procurers and thugs of the First Ward operated with virtual immunity. And it was this organization that eventually spawned the criminal organization known throughout the world as the Capone gang.

Early in the 1900s, Big Jim Colosimo, a brothel owner, became influential in the First Ward Democratic organization of Bathhouse John Coughlin and Michael Kenna. As a precinct captain, he was successful in producing votes for the machine. Colosimo prospered and he began receiving Black Hand extortion threats. The Black Hand or "La Mano Nera", consisted of over 200 of Chicago's leading Italian citizens and prominent businessmen. In 1909, the Black Hand was threatening Jim Colosimo, otherwise known as "Diamond Jim," Chicago's gambling and racketeer gangster. Colosimo had his nephew, a gunman from New York, Johnny Torrio, come to Chicago to eliminate the Black Hand gangs threatening him. Torrio had as many as ten Black Hand members killed within a decade. In 1911 thirty-eight persons were killed by an assassin known as "Shotgun Man," between Oak and Milton streets in Chicago's Little Italy. The following year, Colosimo opened a self-named restaurant, Colosimo's Cafe, at 2126 S. Wabash. Later, in 1919, Torrio opened a brothel at 2222 S. Wabash called the Four Deuces. Al Capone, Torrio's old Brooklyn lieutenant, worked there as a bartender and bouncer. This gave Capone his introduction to Chicago. In 1920, Colosimo was shot and killed and although there were strong suspicions that Torrio had arranged his murder, no suspects were ever tried for the murder. Colosimo was the first to organize disparate parts of Chicago's crime scene. After his death, his gang was taken over by Torrio, who expanded organized vice and gambling throughout Cook County. Torrio abdicated his position and moved to New York after he was ambushed and shot in 1925. Capone, who served as Torrio's principal lieutenant, took over the organization. Capone was first accused of murder in 1924. Some 500 gang murders occurred in Chicago between 1920 and 1930.

Prohibition: Alcohol Exclusion Experiment
Prohibition: Alcohol Exclusion Experiment

Prohibition took place during this decade, beginning in 1920 with the Eighteenth Amendment to the U.S. Constitution and coming to an end with its repeal on December 5, 1933. The manufacture, sale, and transport of alcohol became illegal, but possession and consumption weren't, and across Chicago, one could find alcoholic drinks with a flare of danger at "speakeasies" and underground establishments. Private bars and home breweries kept guests happy. People did become sick from the unregulated alcohol; some became blind or suffered from brain damage. "Bathtub gin" was made with industrial alcohol or various poisonous chemicals. Whiskey was available by prescription from medical doctors; over a million gallons were consumed per year through freely given, written orders. In support of further criminal activity, Prohibition agents took bribes to overlook the illegal brewing of alcohol by gangsters. Capone's criminal empire was largely built on alcohol bootlegging profits, and many believed Prohibition to be the sole cause of organized crime. It was estimated that six million dollars would be needed to enforce Prohibition laws. When Prohibition ended in 1933 only the largest breweries had survived, and the quality and variety of American beer decreased, as it became a mass-produced commodity. In the 1980s, craft brewing returned. Post Prohibition, the Capone syndicate expanded their enterprises into new areas. Gambling, prostitution, labor racketeering and eventually selling illegal drugs proved lucrative. Racketeers were pocketing over $6 million a week; beer, booze, and alky: $3,510,000; gambling house and handbooks: $1,250,000; disorderly houses, call flats, shady hotels: $1,000,000; labor rackets, bombing, arson, kidnapping: $500,000; and other crimes.

St. Valentine's Day Massacre
St. Valentine's Day Massacre

*Sources: "Graduating from Murder to Massacre – Story of Slaughter on Valentine's Day,"
Chicago Daily News, June 6, 1943 and "Valentine Day Massacre Echo Soon Will Be Silenced,"
Chicago Sun-Times, February 14, 1967*

Throughout the Prohibition Era, Chicago was a city where organized crime was rampant and Al Capone and his rival, George "Bugs" Moran, were commonly used names among citizens in Chicago's diverse neighborhoods. On February 14, 1929, an explosion of violence occurred on Chicago's north side leaving seven men murdered in Capone style. "Only Capone kills like that," stated Moran. The St. Valentine's Day Massacre brought Chicago's organized crime scene to the forefront of the city's pulse, when twenty-two gangsters were questioned, but the crimes were never solved. At 10:30 a.m. a Cadillac disguised as a police car stopped in front of a garage at 2122 N. Clark Street where six men drank coffee and made phone calls while another changed a flat tire on one of the trucks Moran used to run whiskey deliveries. Out of the Cadillac stepped four men, two dressed as police officers. Moran's gang lined up along the garage's whitewashed, north wall, believing they may be taken downtown and booked. Within sixty seconds, each one of Moran's gang members took twenty bullets. Gunpowder filled the garage as six of the victims instantly died. Three hours later in the hospital the seventh man shot whispered, "It's getting dark. So long."

Chicago's Blood Red Day
Chicago's Blood Red Day

Source: "Chicago Gangland," Chicago Daily Tribune, March 3, 1927

In 1925, prohibition-related shootings were rampant; three policemen were shot to death in one week, and on June 13, on the 5900 block of Western Avenue, sixty shots were fired killing two innocent men. Hoodlums, otherwise known as gangsters and racketeers, were making big money in Chicago this year.

CCC Urges Feds to Go After Capone
CCC Urges Feds to Go After Capone

Source: Business vs. Organized Crime by Dennis E. Hoffman

U.S. President Herbert Hoover recalls in his memoirs a March 1929 meeting with the CCC President Frank Loesch and other prominent business leaders representing the CCC:

> *"They gave chapter and verse for their statement that Chicago was in the hands of gangsters, that the police and magistrates were completely under their control, that going to the governor of the state was futile, that the Federal government was the only force by which the city's ability to govern itself could be restored. At once I directed that all the Federal agencies concentrate upon Mr. Capone and his allies. Our authority was limited to violations of income tax and prohibition laws." (Hoover, 1952)*

Chicago Police officers stand inspection along LaSalle Street near Washington Street, 1903

Source: Chicago Police Department
Reproduced with the permission of the Chicago Police Department.

UNITED STATES DEPARTMENT OF JUSTICE
FEDERAL BUREAU OF INVESTIGATION
WASHINGTON 25, D. C.

OFFICIAL BUSINESS

RETURN AFTER 5 DAYS

POSTAGE AND FEES PAID
FEDERAL BUREAU OF INVESTIGATION

Questionable Pattern

The unusual and questionable pattern presented here is classified as a whorl with meeting tracing and is referenced to a loop. The deltas are found at D^1 and D^2. The reference is necessary due to the questionable nature of the recurve in front of D^2. Over the years the Chicago Police Department submitted thousands of fingerprints to the Federal Bureau of Investigation.

Source: FBI Law Enforcement Bulletin, June 1960, Vol. 29, No. 6

First Ward Aldermen Michael Kenna (front row, second from left) and John Coughlin (front row, third from left) are with what appear to be other faithful members of the Democratic Party at an unidentified location.

Source: From the Lawrence J. Gutter Collection of Chicagoana, Special Collections, Richard J. Daley Library, University of Illinois at Chicago

Reproduced with permission of the source.

John Torrio

Source: The John Binder Collection

Reproduced with permission of John J. Binder.

At the start of Prohibition in 1920 authorities dumped this beer into Lake Michigan.

Source: The John Binder Collection

Reproduced with permission of John J. Binder.

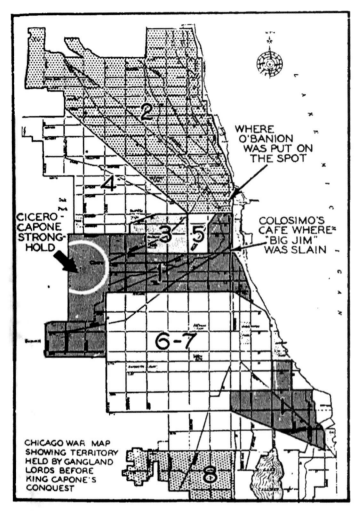

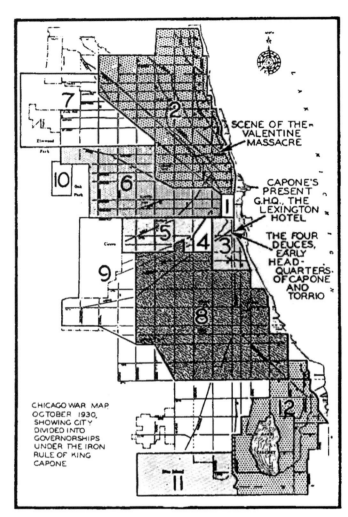

Major principalities as they appeared before the completion of King Capone's conquest are graphically shown on this war map of Chicago. (1) Capone territory; (2) North Side gang; (3) the Druggans; (4) "Klondike" O'Donnell, (5) The Gennas, Capone allies; (6-7) "Spike" O'Donnell, Joe Saltis and the Sheldon gang; (8) Joe Juliano. Map in next column shows how he conquered them all.

Map showing divisions of the Chicago monarchy with governors representing the King: (1) Jake Gusick, (2) Ted Newberry, (3) Joe Gusick, (4) Jack McGurn, (5) George Druggan, Capone ally; (6) "Klondike" O'Donnell, Capone ally; (7) Claude Maddox, (8) "Spike" O'Donnell and the Sheldon gang, with Danny Stanton in charge for the King; (9) Ralph Capone, (10) Joe Montana, (11) the old Juliano gang, (12) Joe Genaro.

Vote for Big Bill the Builder
He Cannot Be Bought, Bossed or Bluffed

CUT OUT THIS PICTURE AND HANG IT IN YOUR WINDOW

William Hale Thompson's first term as mayor was plagued with scandal and attacks from the press. When Thompson ran for a second term in 1927, cartoonist John. T. McCutcheon asked, "Will the voters look at his promises or his record?"

Source: Chicago History, Spring 1994, Chicago Historical Society

Reproduced with permission of the source.

CITIZENS GIRD TO FREE CITY OF CRIME GRIP

NEWS
HOME EDITION
MAR 21 1922

'END OF CRIME,' IS CRY OF AROUSED CITIZENS

People Urged to Join in Effort to Rid City of the Grip of Crooks.

"ONE WAY" JAILS NEEDED

Amend the criminal code of Chicago. Make our jails "one-way" institutions. Kill all forms of intimidation as you would poisonous snakes.

Wake up public sentiment to the extreme danger.

These and numerous other sentiments expressed to-day by men prominent in the city's business and civic life as necessary to end the critical crime situation in Chicago and Cook county are indications of a sentiment seemingly aroused as it has not been aroused here in years. The expressions followed heated presentation or arguments on the Chicago crime situation last night under the direction of the Chicago crime commission at the Hotel LaSalle. More than 100 representatives of thirty-four civic and industrial organizations listened to Chief Justice Kickham Scanlan, State's Attorney Crowe, Chief of Police Fitzmorris and others. The reaction to-day was vigorous.

Limit Is Reached.

"We have reached the point in lawlessness in Chicago where it and we can go no further," said John R. Magill, president of the Chicago real estate board. "It is a move in the right direction to stir up the citizens of this community to go after this lawlessness. It is timely, for it must be done. The citizens must organize to enforce the law. Every citizen, every business and professional man and woman, must awaken to the danger of the situation and take an active part in correcting it."

E. J. Phillips, president of the Rotary club of Chicago, who was unable to attend the meeting of the crime commission last night, nevertheless had a vigorous word to say about it to-day.

"It looks to me," said Mr. Phillips, "as if a great many of our laws must be changed. The present laws, especially those of the criminal code, are inadequate for a great city. Intimidation of juries and witnesses, flouting of the majesty of the law in the very courts where men are sworn to uphold the law—this is all an outgrowth of the misuse of justice, of the disregard of law and decency, of a lack of interest among our citizenry.

"All clubs and associations of men and women in Chicago and Cook county should get together to correct this condition once and for all—do it thoroughly. As far as the Rotary club of Chicago is concerned, every last man of us stands ready to do his full share, to serve on any jury to which he is called.

"But to get back to the most serious point: Our Criminal court procedure 15,000 or 20,000 persons, but for a city f 15,00 0or 20,000 persons, but for a city of 3,000,000 it is all wrong. Revise the criminal code, make it a workable code. Get away from the call jury. I for one would welcome the idea of trial by an appointive, official jury, by a body of judges or something of that sort."

Praise Judge Scanlan.

Resolutions adopted by the Chicago Association of Commerce and announced to-day commend Justice Scanlan in the following terms:

"In his charge to the special grand jury Chief Justice Kickham Scanlan courageously presented conditions that demand thoughtful consideration and intelligent, aggressive action by the law-abiding citizens of this community.

"It is, therefore, the opinion of the Chicago Association of Commerce, expressed by its executive committee, that Judge Scanlan in thus calling public attention to recent sinister developments in the administration of justice in criminal cases has performed a service of great value, deserving the commendation of the people of this city."

Hits Crooked Lawyers.

"That meeting last night sounded a keynote when Judge Scanlan said it was time for a civic housecleaning," said John M. Glenn, secretary of the Illinois Manufacturers' association. "Every citizen must put his shoulder to the wheel. He cannot pass the buck to the public officials. Everybody who wants a clean Chicago should see that the men whom Judge Scanlan terms 'vermin'—meaning crooked lawyers—are run out of the city, at least barred from the sort of practice they have been guilty of lately in our courts.

"Lack of interest by the people of the city is responsible. Wake them up. Public sentiment can run these crooks, this vermin, out of the city. Public sentiment will put the crooks into the jails and prisons and see that they are kept there.

"Make our jails and our prisons one way institutions. Criminals are let out of prison too fast. Put them behind bars and keep them there. Make punishment fit crime—something that is not being done now."

Honest Judges Needed.

The speakers in last night's meeting united in declaring that a deplorable condition had been reached in the administration of justice and that a concerted offensive was necessary. They urged that every one aid in the election of honest judges, and also serve on juries when called.

In a resolution commending the courageous actions of the state's attorney, the chief justice of the Criminal court, the chief of police and the sheriff of Cook county in making known the facts concerning the organized crime in this community, the representatives of the various organizations voted their approval of the law officers.

Source: Chicago Daily News. Reproduced with permission of the Chicago Sun-Times.

You'd never think this smiling lad bore the tough name of Scarface Al. But at that it looks as though he had merely smiled for the photographer. Al dresses well, you'll notice, but there's nothing very flashy about this get-up or any of the others he wears on the street.

Source: A page from Capone's Chicago by R.T. Enright, Victory WW2 Publishing Ltd., www.victoryww2.com

Reproduced with permission of the source.

Source: Chicago Historical Society. Reproduced with permission of the source.

July
Thirteen
1928

<u>Alphonse Caponi (alias "Scarface" alias "Al Brown")</u>

Head of a vice, gambling and beer syndicate, operating throughout
Cicero and the western suburbs, also within Chicago.

Mentioned numerous times in connection with various shootings,
sluggings and murders.

Ordered out of the City of Miami, Florida, by the police department.

Caponi and his gang of bodyguards were arrested at Joliet, Illinois,
for carrying firearms as they emerged from the train to motor back
to Chicago.

85-IT

Notes on Capone

Source: Chicago Crime Commission Archives

Al Capone:
Chicago Crime Commission Timeline
1919 – 1930

In re: Public Enemies
Re: Al Capone

File	Refer.	Date	
	Indictment Card	4/8/19	Arrested at 1438 West Madison Street as Al Brown together with his wife, Lee Lorenzo, and Jimmie Devise in connection with the killing of "St. Louis Shorty" Woeifel April 5, 1919. (Questionable)
	Indictment Card	1/27/21	As Al Brown, indicted in Case No. 23031, keeping disorderly house, etc. and bail fixed at $2000. Case No. 23032 - keeping slot machines, etc. and bail fixed at $2000.
	Indictment Card	4/14/21	Case No. 23031 (above) - plea of guilty - fined $50 and $10 costs - Judge Friend. Case No. 23032 (above) - plea of guilty - fined $100 and $10 costs - Judge Friend.
5788	Tribune	9/21/23	Suspected with George Maloney of the killing of Jerry O'Connor, George Bucher and George Meighan, "Beer runners".
7293	Report	7/14/24	Name appears as a witness before the coroner of Cook County in the killing of Joseph W. Howard (25) 335 West 29th Street, who was killed at 2300 South Wabash Avenue May 8, 1924. This Alphonse Capone has an address of 7244 Pigon Avenue and the occupation of merchant. The known Al Capone's address is 7422 Prairie Avenue.
7043	Examiner	11/12/25	Capone stays in New York because of the shooting of Sam ("Samoots") Amatuna.
	Indictment Card	7/2/26	Indicted in Case No. 40768 - conspiracy - with John Doe, Richard Roe and others to swear falsely to qualify as voters - bail $5000.
		7/28/26	Refused to sign an immunity waiver or testify before the special grand jury in the shooting of Assistant State's Attorney McSwiggin.

Source: From the files of the Chicago Crime Commission

Al Capone: Chicago Crime Commission Timeline – *Continued*

- 2 -

		7/29/26	Chief Justice Lynch dismissed complaint because of insufficient evidence.
13190	Indictment Card	7/29/26	Abe M. Eisenberg accepted as surety for $5000 by Chief Justice Lynch.
	Tribune	8/21/26	Alleged to have paid huge graft to Cicero officials.
		10/ 1/26	Indicted by the federal grand jury for conspiracy to violate the prohibition law in Cicero.
	Indictment Card	12/30/26	Indictment No. 40768 - conspiracy to swear falsely to qualify as voters - quashed by Judge Jacob Hopkins.
11654	Report	6/27/27	Al Capone, Frank Rio, Tony "Mops" Volpe, John Scalise, Tony Lombardo seen at Hawthorne Race Track. Volpe apparently the overseer for Capone.
11654	Report	7/ 5/27	Capone is the reputed big mogul of "The Ship" (gambling house), 2129 South Cicero Avenue, and Jimmie Mondi, big boss of "The Subway", 4738 West 22nd Street, "frozen out" about six months prior.
65	News	8/20/27	Jimmie Mondi, spokesman on gambling matters for Al Capone and Jack Cusick, located at 16 South Clark Street, establishing a "gambling trust" demanding 25% for "protection" to operate gambling joints.
13190	Report	8/24/27	Seen leaving the Federal Building with Tony Volpe, "Diamond Joe" Esposito, Albert Anselmi and John Scalise.
13190	Examiner	11/16/27	Capone deposed as head of gambling syndicate.
13190	Report	11/22/27	Municipal court complaints No. 800668 and
13230	Report	11/23/27	3064500 charging vagrancy and disorderly conduct filed against Capone. He was driven to the detective bureau in a large Lincoln auto by Louis Cowan "McCowan", editor of the Cicero Tribune. He was discharged by Judge Helander and drove away in the same car. Cowan returned to give bail for Tony "Little Old New York" Campagna, Sam Marcus

- 3 -

			and Frank Perry. While Cowan was in the building detective bureau officers found two loaded pistols under the seat, waited two hours for Cowan to return, then towed the car away. Cowan was later charged with carrying concealed weapons.
13190	Examiner	12/13/27	Capone left for St. Petersburg, Florida, then to Tijuana, Mexico.
13190	Examiner	12/13/27	Al Capone sought in California. Tony Lombardo, Al's closest friend and head of the Unione Siciliana, Joseph Gimpa and Michael Burtera arrested in Chicago. Richard and Harry LaSalle, bodyguards of Capone seized heavily armed in Los Angeles.
13190	Examiner	12/14/27	Capone chased out of Los Angeles after twenty-four hours and heads back for Chicago.
13190	News Tribune	12/16/27	Arrested at Joliet, Illinois, by Joliet officers as he alighted from a Santa Fe train with two pistols in his pockets. Ralph Capone, James Castor, Albert Ross, Frank Lona "Lama" and Thomas Bell there to meet him with pistols and sawed-off shotguns. All were liberated on bonds of $2500 each procured by Attorneys Nash and Ahern of Chicago.
13190	Examiner	12/18/27	Capone's home at 7422 South Prairie Avenue, surrounded by detectives waiting for him, Joseph Martin, said to be a chauffeur for Louis Cowan "McCowan", arrested armed with a pistol while going to the above address with Capone's mother.
13190	Examiner	12/19/27	Home of Joe Aiello, 2553 Lunt Avenue, guarded by police because of report that Capone planned to kill him.
13190	Tribune	1/16/28	Capone off for Miami, Florida.
13190	Tribune	2/ 5/28	Al and Ralph Capone discharged after being arrested on suspicion in New Orleans, La.
9614	News	3/ 8/28	Capone via Jack McGurn invades the north side slot machine section belonging to George

Al Capone: Chicago Crime Commission Timeline – *Continued*

- 4 -

ID	Source	Date	Description
13190	Examiner	5/17/28	"Bugs" Moran and Jack Zuta, McGurn and Nick Mastro were wounded by machine gun bullets in a smoke shop at 638 Rush Street.
			Several thousand bottles of Canadian liquor seized as it was being delivered to an office at 109 North Dearborn, Room 1004, where Al Capone and Jack Gusick are said to have their headquarters. Harry Davis, 5940 Winthrop Avenue, C. J. Doyle, 6418 South Union Avenue, Stephen Rezzonge, 1036 West 18th Street, M. A. Shank, 6802 East End Avenue, and Adolph Pfingst, 7950 Crandon Avenue, were arrested.
13190	Tribune	5/27/28	Capone "hooks up" with Cleaners and Dyers, Inc. He, with John Gusik, 7244 Luella Avenue, Maurice Cowan, 2533 Ainslie Street, Louis Cowan, Joseph Lustfield (Tom attorney of Cicero) are listed as directors. Philip D'Andrea, Frank Rio and Morris Becker took in Capone, et al to increase their inadequate police protection.
9614	Tribune	6-21-28	Capone is "slipping" in the gambling racket and is "pushing" booze and forcing the Aiellos out. John Oliveri and Joseph Salanone are killed because they infringed in Aiello-Capone booze territory.
13190	Tribune	6-24-28	Capone buys $64,000.00 home in Miami, Florida.
9614	News	7-2-28	Capone makes a hurried return to Chicago. Frankie Uale, alias Yale, shot and killed in New York from a car bearing an Illinois license. Years ago Uale helped Capone get out of a murder charge in New York. Joe Saltis fired at Uale in Chicago in 1921, when "Big Jim" Colocimo was killed and in 1924 when Dean O'Banion was slain.
13190	Examiner	7-3-28	Capone back in Chicago pitted against all other gangs seeking revenge for the shooting of Joe Oliver Joe Salamoni and "Big Jim" Murphy. Capone is lined up with Jack McGurn, Jack Cusick, Edward "Spike" O'Donnell and against Joe Saltes.

- 5 -

ID	Source	Date	Description
13190	American		Capone condemned by gangland to die.
16933	Examiner	7-3-28	Al Capone, Ralph Capone, Jack Cusick and Joe Saltis named by A. P. Madden, Chief of the Special Intelligence Unit of the international Revenue Division as income tax evaders.
14877	Examiner	7-10-28	Joseph "Peppy" Genaro, henchman of Al Capone, arrested on charges of kidnapping an election worker.
13190	Report	7-13-28	Sam Marcus, Frank Perry, Capone body guards and gunmen arrested several times for carrying concealed weapons.
13190	Examiner	8-1-28	It was reported in New York that four Capone henchmen may be indicted for death of Frank Uale. The gun used was one of an assortment bought for Capone. He was not arrested or asked for in New York.
13190	Examiner	8-2-28	Capone in Chicago to see who burned his "alky" flat plant in East Dubuque, Illinois, last week.
13190	News	8-4-28	Frank Rio, Frank Nitti, Tony "Mops" Volpe, Joe Kelly appear armed with Capone in Manganos gambling place, at 622 So. Halsted Street, where Capone lost $10,000.00.
13190	News	8-7-28	Capone moves his headquarters from rooms 408-9-10-11 of the Metropole Hotel, at 23rd & Michigan Blvd. to the Lexington Hotel, at 22nd & Michigan Ave.
14877	Examiner	8-9-28	Al Capone and Jack McGurn sought to be quizzed about the "Granady shooting."
9614	News	9-10-28	Surrounded by armed guards he pays respects to the body of Tony Lombardo.
13190	Examiner	9-13-28	Capone hunted for the death of Tony Lombardo and Tony Ferraro. Suit in Miami, Florida, to foreclose a mortgage of $30,000.00 on his home - he failed to pay 3 - $10,000.00 notes.
13190	Tribune	1-9-29	Capone directing from Florida the fight against Alderman A. J. Prignano for re-election in the 20th ward.

Al Capone: Chicago Crime Commission Timeline – *Continued*

- 7 -

13190	Post	5/17/29	Boon companion John Scalise, Albert Anselmi, Joe Guinta found dead in "prairie" two weeks ago near Hammond, Indiana. Capone and Frank Rio alias Cline sentenced to one year in Pennsylvania for carrying concealed weapons.
13190	News	5/17/29	George ("Bugs") Moran controls the liquor territory north of Madison Street to the county line. Al Capone in control south of Madison Street. Attorney E. J. O'Hara of St. Louis mentioned as the "K. M. Landis" of gangland.
13190	News	6/26/29	$50,000 offered to any attorney who would ... the release of Capone. Jack Gusick and Charles Fischetti take the money to Pennsylvania. Gusick is Capone's office man and Fischetti is a cousin. Congressman Benjamin M. Golden retained as attorney.
13190	Examiner	6/30/29	Judge John E. Walsh (Pennsylvania) refused Capone bail and to release him.
3485	News	7/ 6/29	A 250,000 gallon Capone still at 728 South Clark Street raided by Assistant Administrator George H. Hurlburt. Those present escaped through a tunnel.
9614 -5	Examiner	8/26/29	Henry Kolosky in the County Hospital shot and says he was taken for a ride by three Joe Saltis gangsters. He admits quitting Saltis and going to work for Capone as a "beer runner".
13190	Examiner	10/11/29	Capone gambling resort at 2130½ South Michigan raided. Tony "Mops" Volpe, George King and Charles Fischetti arrested. This place is across the street from Capone's headquarters in the Lexington Hotel.
13190	News	3/17/30	Released from the Pennsylvania Penitentiary at the end of three-quarters of the sentence for good behavior.
13190	Post	3/18/30	While officers were waiting at the home of Capone at 7244 Prairie Avenue for him to return from Pennsylvania they arrested Joe Montana, 914 Polk Street, Spino Amalo, 942 Polk Street, and Ralph Camardo, 806 South Loomis Street.

- 6 -

9614	Examiner	1/20/29	P. C. "Denver Blackie" Burcham, reputed Capone aid found by posse after wandering three days on desert near Wing, Texas on New Mexico line. Said kidnaped and tortured.
11654	Report	1/24/29	Before going to Florida Al Capone left Ralph Capone in charge of Cicero gambling. Later Ralph went to Florida and left Ben Markowitz and Jack Cusack in charge. Louis Cowen "McCowan" (bond signer) also left for Miami, Florida.
17252	Report	2/ 6/29	Charles Fischette (M.C.892612) cousin of Rocco Fischette (M. C. 892613) discharged for carrying concealed weapons on motions to suppress evidence by Judge Peter H. Schwabe. Both are members of the Capone gang.
		2/29	Subpoenaed before the federal grand jury investigating the Chicago Heights liquor traffic. He was in Miami, Florida and secured a stay of summons because of "bronchial pneumonia". That was found to be false and he was charged with contempt of court and released on $5000 bail.
9603	Copy of Statement	3/ 5/29	Statement of Eugene Beers taken at the Keokuk County Court House at Sigourney, Iowa, where his home is. He admits driving two beer trucks from Chicago to DesMoines in 1922 for $500 from Capone personally. In the fall of 1922 he was driving a car for Capone and the latter wanted to hire him to kill somebody but he refused. In June 1928 in Miami, Florida, Capone wanted him to kill Frank Uale of New York for $500 but he refused. Capone admitted in the presence of William Bailey, a New York gunman twenty-eight years old, "getting rid of" McSwiggin. In August 1928 William McFadden and "Stubby" McGovern and one Maloney said that Capone killed McSwiggin. He denied any knowledge of facts about the "St. Valentines Day Massacre".

Al Capone: Chicago Crime Commission Timeline – *Continued*

- 9 -

but close at his elbow was the Capone gang - Johnny Patton, who has been "the boy mayor" of Burnham for twenty-two years; Jake Guzick, hero of the Alger tale, "From Brothel Bus Boy to Racketeer First Class"; Harry Guzick, once convicted of pandering; Ralph Capone, brother of Alphonse; Frank Nitti, "the enforcer" of the Capone bombing and murder law; Hymie Levine, who graduated from the vice of the beer racket, and all the gun-toters and hoodlums on the Capone pay roll.

These and all the other Capone hoodlums will be on hand again this year, indications are, but O'Hare has taught them enough about the profitable operation of greyhound racing that he will be needed only now and again. Patton, report has it, will be "the works", but "Scarface Al" will be on the receiving end of the cash dividends. (See story in Daily News.)

News   5-2-30

Scar Face Al Capone, jail bird and brothel keeper, plans a concerted drive on the legislature this winter to legalize gambling at dog tracks. Capone has ordered his organization to raise a huge sinking fund from the profits of the tracks and other rackets. The first heavy money will be spent this fall in aiding candidates for the legislature who are friendly to the Capone brand of politics. The bulk of the sinking fund will be spent to sink opposition to the dog tracks when the legislature convenes in regular session this winter. This was the conversation bandied about last night when the Capone hoodlums opened their Hawthorne Kennel club track in Cicero. The Capone sinking fund will first be used for votes and other incidentals for Daniel A. Serritella, Capone's man in the first ward and James B. Leonardo, an Eller graduate, both of whom are candidates in the senate, in the first and seventeenth districts, respectively. In the seventeenth district the three members of the lower house are Roland V. Libonati, a republican, Charles Cola and Anthony Pintozzi, democrats. These three men have known Serritella from youth and Serritella is the spearhead of the Capone thrust for political power.
(Chicago Daily News article - May 2, 1930)

- 8 -

13190	News	3/24/30	Governor Doyle E. Carlton bars Capone from Florida and orders any sheriff to arrest him on sight.
13190	News	3/31/30	Federal injunction granted in Florida to prevent the arrest of Capone.
13190	Tribune	4/ 1/30	Joe Aiello, 2553 Lunt Avenue (Moran gang) giving occupation as real estate, Jack Zuta, James Intravia, 1125 Grand Avenue, and Jack Costa, 1160 Grand Avenue, arrested in loop in Chicago unarmed but with $4705 in cash. Jack McGurn with Louise Rolfe, Tony McGurn (Tony Accardo) arrested in Florida. She is the same woman found with McGurn in a Chicago hotel after the "St. Valentines Day Massacre".
13190	Tribune	4/ 4/30	Federal court finds $100,000 in telegraphic money orders ranging from $20 to $10,000 to and from Al Capone, A. Costa, R. Barton, Charles Fischetti (cousin), George Howlett (Chicagoan once indicted as beer runner in Wisconsin), Parker Henderson (Miami, Florida), P. A. Henderson, Jr., Mrs. P. A. Henderson, Jrs., J. C. Frisco, Sam Gusick, Bob Barton, Mrs. Mae Capone, Joe Soscione, Matthew Capone, Rocco Fischetti, Albert Capone, Tony Rich, Albert Costa, Ralph Capone and Frank Ross. Al Capone and Costa are thought to be the same. $27,400 to Costa and $16,050 to Capone.
13190	News	4/19/30	Capone plan to "seize" plumbing bureau and streets department of City Hall involving 3000 jobs and $12,000,000 annually frustrated. City Sealer Daniel A. Serritella denies the attempt.
13190	Post	4/21/30	Capone still in Florida. Joseph Corngold arrested at Lexington Hotel in a raid by investigators of the "St. Valentines Day Massacre".
13190	News	4/30/30	Capone goes to Cuba by airplane. His Hawthorne Race Track opens in Chicago under protection of an injunction granted by Judge Harry M. Fisher of the Circuit Court. E. J. O'Hara is president of the track.

Al Capone: Chicago Crime Commission Timeline – *Continued*

-10-

5-2-30   Capone completed a three day tour of Havana including a visit to the office of the Havana chief of secret police; Capone returned to Miami last night. (News dispatch)

5-8-30   "Scarface" Al Capone, age thirty, his brother John, age twenty-six, and two alleged members of his gang were arrested this afternoon at Miami, Florida, on orders of city officials. No charges were lodged against them, pending a conference. They were held under investigation.

5-9-30   Al Capone was denied an injunction restraining the police of Miami, Florida, from arresting him without a warrant by Federal Judge Halsted L. Ritter. Miami officials tell of threats received.

5-11-30   In Miami, Florida, last night, Nathan Grebstein, a real estate agent, was held in jail on a contempt of court charge growing out of his alleged offer of $5,000 from Circuit Judge Paul D. Barnes, which the jurist was to receive if he decided padlock proceedings against Al Capone's Miami Beach residence, according to news dispatches.

5-14-30   Al Capone gained his freedom this afternoon on a writ of habeas corpus after spending nearly twenty-four hours in jail in Miami. Three of Capone's companions, Nick Circella, 35, Albert Frignano, 38, former alderman of the 20th Ward in Chicago, and Sylvester Agoolia, 35, were also released. They were arrested last night attending a prize fight.

5-6-30   Tony "Mops" Volpe reputed to be an ex-convict who quit counterfeiting to become a lieutenant of Al Capone; Frank Rio reputed to be Capone's personal body guard and who recently completed a term in the Philadelphia prison for gun toting and Frank Mancuso were arrested tonight at Austin Boulevard and West End Avenue by Sergeant James Maloney and his squad of the Detective Bureau assigned to the Austin Station. It is reported that the three men were in a curtained sedan and as Sergeant Maloney approached a door opened and three pistols went clattering across the pavement. Volpe who v..s driving the car announced himself as Arthur Lo~ez, however Maloney recognized him as Volpe. Rio gave his name as James Coster, but he too was recognized by Sergeant Maloney.

-11-

5-7-30   Article appearing in the Chicago Daily News reads - "Capone gunmen seized then go free on bond. They were seized by police last night. The official plan of co-operation was demonstrated. Within half an hour they were on the street again, Rio on bonds of $900 on charges of speeding and dis—orderly conduct, and Volpe on bonds of $400 on disorderly conduct, Mancuso on bonds of $400 on disorderly conduct. The three were nabbed after a half mile chase during which they tossed revolvers out of their automobile." Under date of May 9, Commission of Police William F. Russell addressed a letter to the Chicago Crime Commission transmitting the clipping referred to, a copy of a report on the subject made by Deputy Commissioner John P. Stege and a copy of a report made by Squad Leader James Maloney showing that the men were held eighteen hours and not half an hour as reported by the Daily News. The reports of the Police show that they were booked then onl after threat of writ of habeas corpus made by Attorney Charles Horgan. The reports also show that the prisoners went through the police routine; that is, they were taken through the Detective Bureau and sent to the Bureau of Identification.

5-8-1930   Volpe, Rio and Mancuso were arranged before Judge LeRoy Fairbank inthe speeders court and their cases were continued to May 15. The continuance was asked for the purpose of having the guns examined by Coroner Bundesen to determine whether or not they oen be connected through the science of ballistics with other crimes.

5-19-30   Miami, Florida - For the third time in ten days Al Capone was arrested with Al Prignano believed to be a former Chicago alderman, as they were about to enter an American Legion boxing show. They were released after posting a $100.00 bond. Capone expects to return to Chicago the last of this week, according to press dispatches. His attorney, Vincent C. Giblin, made this announcement in asking that a master in chancery hear the testimony in the authorities action to padlock Capone's Palm Island estate as a public nuisance. Judge Paul D. Barnes granted the request on the plea that it would take some time for the defense to accumulate testimony. Giblin told the court that testimony of two witnesses

Al Capone: Chicago Crime Commission Timeline – *Continued*

-12-

Harry Read, city editor of a Chicago newspaper (Chicago Evening American) and a member of the Illinois Prison Commission, would have to be taken by deposition in Chicago. Giblin did not name the prison Commissioner, but said he and Read had visited at Capone's home recently.

5-21-30   Charges of vagrancy at Miami against Al Capone and Al Prignano were dismissed. Capone's arrest Monday night was the third since Miami adopted its "Arrest on sight" plan.

6-5-30   Miami - according to reports Capone is negotiating for hotel properties which would increase the value of his holdings there to more than one million dollars. If completed Capone will be one of the largest property owners in Florida.

6-12-30   Chicago - A complete brewery and fifty thousand gallons of beer ready for consumption and one hundred and fifty thousand gallons of mash were seized by prohibition agents under Alexander Jamie at 2108 South Wabash Avenue. The plant was controlled by the Capone booze syndicate and the seizure is the largest of its kind ever made in Chicago. There is no doubt about it being a Capone brewery and its output supplied saloons in the loop.

6-11-30   Miami - The Miami Beach residence of Capone was described as a virtual armed camp by Edward Robinson, State's witness in proceedings instituted by State's Attorney N. Vernon Hawthorne to padlock the Capone home. Robinson, whose home was close to Capone's on Palm Island, testified that he had seen men walking about the Capone grounds with pistols in their pockets or strapped to their hips. Other witnesses testified Capone is a menace.

6-14-30   Miami - Judge Paul D. Barns dismissed the State's petition to padlock Capone's Palm Island estate as a nuisance on the ground that the State did not prove its contention.

6-14-30   Miami - Capone was arrested on two warrants charging perjury a few minutes after he won a fight against Dade County, which sought to padlock his Palm Island home as a nuisance. It was charged that Capone

-13-

perjured himself in warrants he had issued for S. D. McCreary, Director of Public Safety, whom he charged with false arrest. Capone was held in total bond of $7000.

6-15-30   Miami - An attempt to steal the prosecution's evidence in the perjury charge was made. The desk, files and safe of Richard H. Hunt, special prosecutor, were ransacked and all matter pertaining to Capone's case was stolen.

6-19-30   Miami - Formal discharge of S.D. McCreary, director of public safety; admission by Scarface Al Capone that part of his previous testimony against McCreary had been untrue and complete discomfiture of Capone's counsel were the net results today of the reopening of the McCreary false arrest case before Justice of the Peace Warren L. Newcomb. Capone's testimony which lasted barely five minutes sought to correct his previous testimony.

6-28-30   Dry agents raided a bungalow distillery at 2816 S. 48th Avenue, Cicero, reputed to belong to the Capone alcohol syndicate, making 26 stills seized there in a little more than two weeks. A 300 gallon still and 8700 gallons of mash were found. Frank Long and Joseph Bruno alleged attendants were arrested.

6-30-30   Washington, D.C. - Capone has employed attorneys to make a fight to save him from sleuths of the income tax division of the Bureau of Internal Revenue investigating his financial affairs back as far as 1922. A small army of treasury agents, it was reported from Chicago, is checking the Capone bank accounts and property holdings. A report that Capone had spent several days in Washington last week in an effort to satisfy the Government was denied; but it was stated that he had sent agents to Washington.

7-8-30   Miami - An additional charge of perjury was filed against Al Capone as he awaited trial tomorrow on two similar charges. The third charge is a substitute for one of the perjury warrants quashed yesterday.

Al Capone: Chicago Crime Commission Timeline – *Continued*

-14-

7-12-30   Miami - Al Capone was acquitted of one perjury charge on a directed verdict in the Criminal Court of Judge E. C. Collins.

7-15-30   Lake Worth, Florida - W. G. Stovall, contractor, announced his company would begin clearing ground near here immediately for a $375,000.00 home for Al Capone.

7-18-30   Miami Beach, Florida - Harry T. Brundidge, a reporter for the St. Louis Star, has an interview with Al Capone at his Palm Island home relating to the murder of Jake Lingle, racketeer Chicago newspaper reporter, and crime conditions in general. (See Tribune of July 19) In another article in the same issue "Brundidge lies" says Capone.

7-24-30   A news dispatch from Youngstown, Ohio, reads - "Al Capone, who in an effort to cut in on the handbook trust when it was being organized in Chicago two years ago, has now succeeded in breaking in Mayor Joseph Heffernan of Youngstown" reported today." The announcement came when Mayor Heffernan voiced fears that the Capone Gang was attempting to get a foothold there.

8-1-30   Miami, Florida - Vagrancy charges against Capone and several companions were dismissed in the Criminal Court and the prosecution announced. No further information would be filed in the matter.

13190 Tribune 6-13-30   Capone brewery seized by federal officials at 2108 South Wabash Avenue with 100 barrels capacity daily. 50,000 gallons ready and 160,000 gallons of mash.

13190 Tribune 7-19-30   Capone brewery seized at 1421 South Wabash Avenue with 20,000 gallons capacity.

13190 Tribune 8-19-30   Capone linked with plot to assassinate Governor Doyle L. Carlton of Florida. Ann Schwartz, blonde nineteen year old Chicago girl, arrested in that connection. She has a delinquency record.

13190 News 8-22-30   Dog track at Kansas City closed. Capone is the supposed owner.

-15-

13190 Examiner 8-28-30   Capone cleared of the above assassination charges.

P D S 21 20M 9-29

D _19_

COPY OF ARREST RECORD

NAME _Alphonse Capone_

ADDRESS _7241 S 48 Ave_

AGE _24_   NATIVITY _Am_   OCCUPATION _Salesman_   MARRIED / SINGLE

CHARGE _137 Ch 38 (Carrying Con. Weapons)_   DATE ARRESTED _9/5/23_

HELD TO GRAND JURY IN BONDS OF | DATE | JUDGE

DISPOSITION _Dis_

DATE OF DISPOSITION _9/6/23_   JUDGE _O'Connell_   COURT _2_

COMPLAINANT

ADDRESS

ARRESTING OFFICERS _McGurn   Ch. Office_

Source: Chicago Crime Commission Archives

KILL TWO COPS; CITY AROUSED
JOHN HERRICK
Chicago Daily Tribune (1872-1963); Jun 14, 1925; ProQuest Historical Newspapers Chicago Tribune (1849 - 1985) pg. 1

KILL TWO COPS; CITY AROUSED

POLICEMEN SHOT DOWN BY BOOTLEG-GUNMEN

War on Gunmen to Be More Drastic; One Slain.

A page of pictures illustrating this latest Chicago gang crime — on Page 3.

BY JOHN HERRICK.

Two more policemen shot to death with gangsters' bullets brought Mayor Dever and Chief of Police Collins face to face yesterday with the stark necessity of drastic new action to combat gunmen and booze runners.

Policemen Charles B. Walsh and Harold F. Olson, as they lived, and followed the line of their duty, caused the community no concern. It took Policemen Walsh and Olson, dead; Policeman Michael J. Conway at the edge of death, and Mike Genna, notorious among the notorious Genna brothers, shot and killed, to arouse Chicago officialdom to a pitch of keen determination.

Threat of Ruthless War.

At one time yesterday, after the battle at 60th street and Western avenue in which the Genna crew showed its wanton anger at being interrupted in its business, the plan of arming police squads to go out deliberately and shoot gangsters down was seriously discussed by Mayor Dever and Chief Collins.

The mayor and the chief were seeing red. They still were seeing red when finally it was decided to give the already drastic orders more drastic activity and to give them one more try—until the next policeman is killed.

Then, if that effort to suppress gangsters is fruitless, it was admitted in the city hall, armed squads and a return to primitive methods of handing out justice are likely to appear on the streets of Chicago.

"Shoot First; Then Talk."

Chief of Detectives William Schoemaker spoke the sentiment of the Chicago police department when he said:

"Things have reached such a state in this city that a policeman daren't approach a suspicious character without having his gun in his hand. It's about time to save policemen's lives. We have reached a time when a policeman had better throw a couple of bullets into a man first and ask questions afterward. It's war. And in wartime you shoot first and talk second."

For the police department, with two less names to call at roll call last night, was seeing red, too.

Demand Gallows Quickly.

As for the two men captured after Genna's fatal wounding, State's Attorney Crowe promised last night that they would have as swift a trip to the gallows' platform as the law will permit.

The two, whom a score of witnesses have positively identified, are John Scalice, aged 25, 769 Taylor street, and Albert Anselino, aged 41, 715 Miller street.

Scalice is well known in the Italian badlands around Taylor and Halsted streets. In him the police believe they may have the slayer of Dean O'Banion, leader of another gang in the "booze racket," who was shot to death in his florist shop last November. Scalice is chief aid to "Samoots Amatuna," a power in the underworld.

Forty men, whose names would make a fair roster of the Sicilian sector of the bootleg trade, were brought in by the police last night and questioned by State's Attorney Crowe and his assistants. Search was made among them for the fourth man in Genna's gang of yesterday, the one man who escaped.

Question Genna's Sweetheart.

Two women were questioned by the state's attorney's office. One was Germaine Triest, 18, 2619 North Halsted street, said to be a former manicurist at the Sherman hotel and Genna's sweetheart. The other was Anna Varanovich, 3603 West 53d street, who was mentioned in a statement by Scalice. Both said they knew nothing about the killing.

Washington Bell, colored, Genna's chauffeur, also was taken into custody for questioning. He, too, knew nothing. As for Scalice and Anselino themselves, they shook their heads, yawned calmly, and remained mute. They had never seen each other before, they maintained brazenly, and said they had been job hunting and looking for a boarding place when the flivver squad caught them.

At the conclusion of a session of many hours Mr. Crowe stated that the case against Scalice and Anselino was complete.

"Not only is it complete," he declared, "but it is one of the most open and shut I've ever seen. I promise to bring these men to immediate justice."

Tomorrow morning the evidence will go before the grand jury. An indictment is looked for before nightfall.

POLICE MEET GUNMEN

It has been many a day since Chicago saw a slaying comparable to the one that began yesterday morning when the auto load of gunmen—Genna, Scalice, Anselino, and the unknown man—passed the car containing Policemen Walsh, Conway, Olson, and William Sweeney at 47th street and Western avenue.

The policemen were members of detective bureau squad No. 8, assigned to the Chicago Lawn station. They were touring their district, cruising north on Western avenue, when the car of gunmen came in sight, going at a good speed.

Genna Identified in Car.

As the Genna car flashed by one of the policemen remarked on the occupants.

"There's a bunch of hoodlums," he said.

Then Policeman Conway, in charge of the squad, spied Genna. From the direction the gunmen were going, they might have been heading toward some one of the railroad yards in the southwest part of the city to convey a fresh load of alcohol.

"We'll follow 'em and see what they are up to," Conway decided.

Quickly, at the intersection of 47th street, the bureau car made a turn and set out in pursuit. Policeman Olson at the wheel rang the gong, but the sound only made the flying car a block ahead go faster.

Truck Blocks Genna's Car.

The detectives shot southward. The Genna car raced ahead. Faster and faster, tearing down the street car tracks, dodging traffic, with the gong ringing and the horn burring out its orders to stop went the pursuers. The bureau car touched 73 miles an hour and crept up on the machine ahead. Both cars were large and swerved dangerously on the wet pavement.

Fifty-ninth street was passed with the detectives still behind. Then a truck made a sudden swerve into the path of Genna and his men. The driver, the unknown man whom the police are still hunting, tugged at the wheel. There was a scream of brakes. The big car skidded around in a half circle, jumped the right hand curb

Article continues from previous page.

and came to rest against a lamp post, its nose facing northeast.

Police Halt Near Gunmen.

Policeman Olson, too, tugged at his wheel. Another set of brakes clamped down and the detectives' car swung and slid to a halt a few feet away, the radiator heading due west.

Genna, Scalice, and the other two were out of their car and behind it by the time the detectives had stopped. The four policemen, ready with words instead of guns, opened the doors of their car to get out.

"What's the big idea? Why all the speed when we were ringing the gong?" they wanted to know.

Olson First to Be Hit.

Policeman Olson had one foot on the step of the auto. There was a roar and a flame from the back of the Genna car. Scalice was peering over the barrel of a repeating shotgun. Smoke drifted from the muzzle. Patrolman Olson, less than two years on the force, crumpled to the ground. His jaw was almost torn away by the slugs.

There was another blast from the muzzle waving back and forth in front of Scalice. Patrolman Walsh clutched his breast. It was riddled with bullets.

Sweeney and Conway had their guns out then. Crouching in the tonneau, they fired at the figures behind the other automobile.

Anselino Begins Firing.

Walsh and Olson were down. A gun barrel jutted out quickly from the other car. Anselino's hand was on the trigger. Anselino's finger jerked quickly.

Policeman Conway, leader of the squad, groaned once. His shirt over his heart was torn and the red stained it as he fell in a heap.

Policeman Sweeney kept on firing. He got out of the car. The gunmen ran. They dashed into a vacant lot next to the Tourist garage at 5940 South Western avenue, where amazed employés had stared at the battle. They still carried their shotguns. Later the police found that two repeating shotguns and four sawed-off shotguns had been in the car.

Gun Falls Genna.

After the gunmen ran Policeman Sweeney. He was still shooting. The gunmen gained the alley running north and south between Western avenue and Artesian avenue. Genna was last. As his companions turned into a passageway beside the house at 5941 Artesian avenue Genna turned and pointed his shotgun full at Sweeney.

He pulled the trigger, but there was no explosion. Sweeney fired quickly and his bullet struck Genna in the leg. The gangster stumbled after his comrades through the passageway.

Genna rounded the house, which is occupied by Mrs. Eleanor Knoblauch, with Sweeney hard after him, still firing.

Dives Through Window.

Desperately the gunman looked for refuge and spied a basement window. Smashing the glass with his shotgun he dived through, with bullets from the policeman's gun smacking after him.

While Sweeney was winning himself the record of a hero, two other policemen, both off duty, were coming to help in the chase. Policeman Albert Richert of the Brighton Park station was riding on a Western avenue car. He reached the intersection of 60th street and Western avenue in time to see the gunmen take flight, and to see Sweeney pounding in pursuit.

Jumping off the car he took up the chase.

At almost the same moment Mrs. Ellen Oakey looked from her window at 2434 West 60th street. Excitedly she called to her husband, "George, look, there's a shooting."

Policeman George Oakey is 60 years old and white haired. He sits, nights, at the outer desk in the state's attorney's office.

Before his wife knew it, he was downstairs and in the street. In the vacant lot he found a gun one of the fleeing gangsters had dropped. Together Oakey and Richter panted up to the back door of the cellar into which Genna had thrown himself. Together they put their shoulders to the door and kicked it until it burst open. As they entered they fired at Genna lying on the floor. In Genna's hand was a blue steel revolver, manufactured in Spain but using .38 caliber cartridges. The Spanish revolver barked. Then Genna fell back. Policeman Sweeney, Oakey, and Richert rushed upon him. They found no wounds except that from Sweeney's first bullet. But the bullet had severed an artery and Genna was weak from loss of blood. Carrying him out, they summoned an ambulance.

Companions Rush to Store.

Genna's companions in the meantime had run down Artesian avenue to 59th street. What happened to the driver of the car the police are still trying to learn. What Scalice and Anselino did, they learned from Edward Issigson, owner of a dry goods store at 59th and Rockwell streets.

Hatless and out of breath, Scalice and Anselino rushed into his store demanding whether he had any caps for sale.

Issigson turned the gangsters away and they ran down 59th street to Western avenue. Word had spread to the surrounding police stations that a shooting had taken place. Policemen Thomas Cohen, Edward Hayes, and Michael Stapleton of the West Englewood station were sent in haste with the district flivver.

They came in time to see two hatless, panting men boarding a Western avenue street car. Giving chase, they overtook the car at Talman avenue. Fists flew for a minute before their captives were subdued. They found later they had caught Salice and Anselino.

Employés of the nearby garage volunteered their services. Walsh, Olson, and Conway still were lying where they had fallen, so swiftly had one event followed another. Walsh and Olson were rushed in automobiles to the German Deaconess hospital. They died there within a few minutes. Conway was taken to St. Bernard's hospital, where it was found his chest had been badly injured. Late last night he was fighting for life and the surgeons said he had only a slim chance of living.

Kick Is Dying Gesture.

The police ambulance came for Genna. Carefully he was lifted into it for his trip to the Bridewell hospital. Blood which could not be stopped was pouring from his leg. He was growing weaker. But as they laid him on the stretcher he lifted his good leg and kicked the man who was helping him full in the face, "Take that you ——," he said and fell back. He died shortly afterward from loss of blood and his body was taken to Donovan's morgue.

Policemen Conway and Sweeney were ordered promoted to be sergeants for the bravery displayed by them in the battle, and out of his personal fund Chief Collins sent checks for $200 to the families of Conway, Olson, and Walsh, as emergency relief pending the payment of benefits from pension and city funds to which they are entitled.

Orders were given by Chief Schoemaker which dispatched five detective squads with orders to arrest all members of the Genna, the Torrio, and the Caponi gangs.

The license of the gangsters' car was traced to Frank Marino, 72 West 22d street. The address is one of Torrio's headquarters. Here Lieut. Leonard Bush and his men arrested Johnny Patton, known as the "Boy mayor" of Burnham, and James Cusick, notorious vice lord, two of Torrio's most powerful aids; Robert L. Rose, 13591 Brandon avenue; Matt Wallace, 4117 South Michigan avenue, and Robert McCullough, 4728 Michigan avenue. A hunt was started for Marino, who, it is believed, may have been the driver of the Genna car.

Brother Seeks Revenge.

As Scalice and Anselino were being questioned by Chief Schoemaker and Capt. John Stege at the New City station, Policeman John Olson, brother of the slain detective, entered the room.

"I'm going to shoot my brother's murderer," he cried, and only prompt intervention prevented him from carrying out his threat.

State's Attorney Crowe, with his assistants, Robert McMillan and Emmett Byrne, came to the station the minute the Shepherd trial was out and began the preparation of their case against the killers.

One theory on which the police are working attempts to link the Genna gang and their car with a shooting which took place earlier in the day, and which was laid to the smoldering feud which brought about Angelo Genna's death.

Five men, about 8:30 o'clock, or an hour or so before the detectives sighted the murder car, lay in wait in an alley between Sangamon and Morgan streets and ambushed an automobile going east on Congress street. The poured a volley into the passing car from shotguns and are believed to have wounded at least two of the car's occupants.

The man in the car returned the fire and drove away. Their five assailants thereupon ran to a waiting car and escaped. Two of this party also were believed to have been wounded. At Green street and Jackson boulevard, witnesses said, the car with the five men stopped long enough to let out two men, seemingly wounded, who staggered to an alley. Then the car drove away southward.

Police Bullets Fell Man Who Shoots When Quizzed

Police bullets won a revolver battle early this morning when Gus Singer, 28 years old, 2246 Carver street, was shot and probably fatally wounded by Policemen Thomas Creighton and John Sweeney of the Shakespeare station. The shooting occurred at North avenue and Wood street after Singer and a companion had opened fire upon the policemen, who attempted to question them.

Source: Courtesy of Chicago Tribune Archives

Figures and Scenes of the Gun Battle in Which Two Policemen and Gangster Were Slain

GANGSTERS KILL POLICEMEN. Lieut. Albert Winge (at left) questions John Scalice and Albert Anselino, members of gang which slew two policemen, and wounded a third.

GENNA'S CAPTORS. Policeman Albert J. Richert (left) and Sergt. William Sweeney. The latter fired the shot that ended gunman's life.

SLAIN. Policeman Charles B. Walsh, father of three small children, killed in Genna battle.

ALSO KILLED. Policeman Harold F. Olson, 25 years old and unmarried, was slain in the gangster affray. He is shown with his mother, who lives at 6508 S. Rockwell street.

CROWE QUIZZES KILLERS. The state's attorney (at the right) visits cell where John Scalice (center) and Albert Anselino were taken after their capture. They were with Genna during the gun fight with police pursuers.

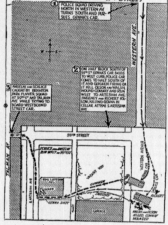

LINE OF BATTLE. Diagram charts course of gunmen and police pursuers. The oblong at the bottom gives the detail of action wherein the policemen and Genna were killed.

FATHERLESS. These are the children of Policeman Walsh, killed in the gangster fight. Their home is at 10723 Cottage Grove avenue.

WOUNDED. Michael J. Conway, promoted to sergeant of police, for bravery in Genna fight.

PAYS WITH LIFE. Mike Genna, gangster, slain after he and companions had killed policemen.

GENNA LEAPS THROUGH WINDOW. Wounded in the leg by a shot fired by Policeman Sweeney, Mike Genna hurled himself through this basement window.

GENNA WAS CORNERED. When he sprang through the window he landed in this basement at 5941 Artesian avenue. There policeman Sweeney followed and captured him.

GANGSTERS' ARSENAL. Policeman Albert Richert, who helped trap Genna, examines repeating and sawed off shotguns found in a vacant lot near the place where the gangsters' car crashed.

GENNA'S PAL. Miss Germaine Triest, 2619 N. Halsted street, slain gunman's sweetheart.

WHERE POLICE AND GUNMEN FOUGHT. The gangsters' car is shown wrecked against the post and headed north after skidding completely around. The police car is in the foreground in the street. After the crash the gunmen fired and then fled through the vacant lot.

POLICE WHO SEIZED FLEEING GUNMEN. Left to right: Thomas Cohen, Edward Hayes, Michael Stapleton, and John Stege, captain of detectives. Stege lauds the trio for their capture of two of Genna's companions.

Source: Courtesy of Chicago Tribune Archives

Chicago Daily Tribune (1872-1963); Jun 24, 1928; ProQuest Historical Newspapers Chicago Tribune (1849 - 1985) pg. 5

GRAFT PLOT ACED TO 1922 U. S. AGENTS

Company Outgrowth Convicted Drug Firm

Shirley laboratories, fake toilet and perfume concern through which prohibition agents are to have obtained $100,000 in was known to the prohibition as far back as 1922 to company formed for the of diverting government al-into bootleg channels, it was last night by federal agents. the Shirley Laboratories as the Val Dona Drug The concern went out of to that year when, as a cor-it was indicted in connec-illegalities in handling its alcohol, and in the trial of was fined $1,000 and costs. was created the Shirley The government agents the prohibition agents' it was simply a change of and that that fact must have in record in the prohibition en-office.

Holds Largest Permit.

for more than five years imme-following this change of name, show that this crooked held the largest permit issued government to any concern in west for the withdrawal of alcohol.

same set of officials involved in company graft charges were involved in the charges the Val Dona Drug company Samuel J. Weinberg, who the title of sales manager for the Laboratories, also was in-in the charges against the Val company.

and Roy C. Swanson, officials, were convicted of con-to violate the prohibtion law before Federal Judge Fred on Friday. They face two federal prison. It was through investigation of the diversion of 100,000 gallons of alcohol Weinberg, Swanson, and others to discoveries of the huge the prohibition department in with it.

"Little Black Book."

been making over-to the government to supply "his black book" in which he records of all these graft pay-exchange for some mitiga-of the two years' imprisonment him. He says it con-evidence in each trans-guilt, even down to the de-of the banknotes in which payment was made.

issued by the prohibition to the officials of the Laboratories allowed them to gallons a month. They government grain alcohol, the official prohibition poisoning process, for 80 gallon. This was tax free and in furtherance of the al-conspiracy on which they approximately $3 a

officials say the Shirley through the connivance of crooked prohibition agents, di-practically every gallon of al-it withdrew. Assuming they the Shirley company had di-its alcohol from the time it out of the Val Dona Drug it must have diverted, in a more than half a million into bootleggers' hands.

Amazed, Says Anderson.

amazed that a permit to ob-alcohol for any purpose was ever

Chicago Gangster Defies Miami to Oust Him

Al Capone's Palm Island estate, which he is reported to have purchased for $64,000 despite warnings of the Miami police that he will find the city an unhealthy place. The high stone wall has been added since Capone purchased the place.
[Pacific and Atlantic Photo.]

issued to the officials of the Shirley Laboratories," said Assistant U. S. District Attorney Daniel Anderson, in charge of the graft inquiry. "The change from the Val Dona company to the Shirley company was apparently one in name only."

Ben Black, who pleaded guilty to the conspiracy charges of which Weinberg and Swanson were convicted, was the man who redistilled the alcohol and then redistributed it for gin making purposes. He operated stills at 4927 Prairie avenue; 2112 Prairie; 1822 Indiana avenue, and 3726 Cottage Grove avenue.

The government men say that Black in his recooking activities helped to slake the thrist of many and many a Chicago gin drinker. For if he recooked and resold only the 100,000 gallons charged by the government it was enough to supply some 2,000,000 pints of gin.

May Collect $740,000.

Assistant District Attorney Anderson points out that the government may be able to collect the $100,000 bond of the Shirley officials and that it also may be able to collect a penalty of $6.40 for each gallon diverted, or $640,000.

The federal investigation shows that the thirty allegedly crooked prohibition agents collected $1 for each gallon which was diverted. And the agents doing the investigation say they now know where 80 cents of each dollar went and that they believe the other 20 cents went to "prohibition officials both in Chicago and Washington."

Al Capone (in bathing suit with towel thrown over his shoulder) watching a boxing match near the water at Miami Beach.
[Pacific and Atlantic Photo.]

NOTHIN' LIKE TRYIN'

Source: Chicago Daily News
Reproduced with permission of the Chicago Sun-Times.

Loop Beer War Held Cause of Kolosky "Ride"

Even. Post   4/26/29

An attack of one of Al Caponi's beer hustlers is the opening shot in a new gang war over bootlegging priviliges which may be expected to take a further toll unless the prohibition department steps in to curtail the activities of beer runners.

This warning was sounded today by Pat Roche, chief investigator for the state's attorney as he questioned Henry Kolosky, who was taken for a ride yesterday and dumped from a machine near Summit. Kolosky, who was reported dying, named three aids of Big Joe Saltis as his assailants.

The investigator said that gang leaders like Danny Stanton, Jack Gusick and George ("Bugs") Moran have had another "falling out" over the supply of beer to the loop. Beer is being forced on loop speakeasies and saloons by all factious at $55 a barrel, Roche said.

"I am not interested in the prohibition angle," Roche said, "but I am interested in stopping the killings. A one-legged prohibition agent on a bicycle could stop the delivery of beer to the loop. The beer is usually driven to the loop betwen 5 o'clock and 7 o'clock in the morning."

Source: Chicago Evening News
Reproduced with permission of the Chicago Sun-Times.

SAYS ONE AGENT COULD CLEAN UP WITHIN HALF DAY

Believes New Beer War Is Impending; Plans to Fight Evil.

TELLS GANG ACTIVITY

"A one-legged prohibition agent, riding a bicycle, could dry up Chicago's loop in half a day—provided he were honest."—Pat Roche, chief investigator for State's Attorney Swanson.

Roche made this statement today as he began an inquiry into a story told by Harry Kolosky, who said he had forsaken the Joe Saltis beer syndicate to drive a beer truck for "Scarface Al" Capone.

Kolosky was found near Argo, suffering from a fractured skull. He said he had been taken for a ride by two men, slugged and thrown from the automobile. Roche was of the opinion that the Kolosky attack might be the opening of a new beer war.

Demands Halt on Crimes.

"I'm not interested in enforcing the prohibition law or in drying the loop," Roche said, "but I am interested in stopping the murders that are caused by the prohibition situation.

"And if the prohibition agents don't get busy I will.

"There was a split on the south side three weeks ago," Roche continued. "Danny Stanton, who has been acting the tough guy for the Capone outfit since "Scarface Al" went to jail, had a falling out with Frank McErlane and Joe Kaufman, who have been peddling beer in the Englewood district.

Has Corps of Men at Work.

Roche revealed that he has had a corps of undercover men at work on the prohibition situation for the last three weeks.

"The south-side situation, an argument over territory and prices, is only one phase of what is going on," Roche said. "The shooting of George Maloney in front of the Pershing hotel also has something to do with the strained relations between Stanton and McErlane.

"There is a lot of dissatisfaction in the loop, both among the beer racketeers and the proprietors of speakeasies.

"The speakeasy owners are being forced to take the syndicate's beer, whether they want it or not, and the price is $55 a barrel. A lot of the speakeasy owners have wanted to sell near-beer, but the syndicate insists they take the $55-a-barrel beer.

"I have been too busy over here to fool with the prohibition situation, but I am being forced into it.

Delivering Beer In Loop.

"The Capone-Moran syndicate has been delivering beer into the loop, usually about once a week, between 5 and 7 o'clock in the morning. Stanton has been serving as the 'muscle man' for the Capone gang at the behest of Jack Guzick.

"Early Saturday morning I sent twenty-five men into the loop in an effort to seize the syndicate's trucks. The beer usually flows into the loop fifteen or twenty truckloads at a crack. But the syndicate sent spies —men riding in roadsters carrying Indiana and Michigan licenses—and they spotted my men and the beer didn't come in, I have since learned, until about 3 o'clock in the afternoon."

Roche also revealed that he tapped the wires at George Moran's headquarters at 192 North Clark street and that some "interesting conversations" had been heard.

Calls Gang Peace Genuine.

A genuine peace exists between the Moran and Capone gangs, according to Roche. In addition to maintaining joint headquarters at 127 North Dearborn street, members of the two gangs—Moran, Ted Newberry, Paul Morton, "Mops" Volpe, Frank Nitti, Frankie Rio, Jack and Harry Guzick—are wont to gather several times a week at a south side hotel for friendly poker games.

Another development since Capone's incarceration has been the return to power in the beer racket of the south side O'Donnell gang. The family, through the efforts of Percy, the redoubtable "Spike's" younger brother, has regained its old footing and its beer trucks once more are rumbling through south side streets.

Daily News
Aug. 26, 1929

Source: Chicago Daily News. Reproduced with permission of the Chicago Sun-Times.

POLICE HUNT FOR 2 SUSPECTS IN STREET MURDER
Chicago Daily Tribune (1872-1963); Sep 17, 1929; ProQuest Historical Newspapers Chicago Tribune (1849 - 1985)
pg. 5

POLICE HUNT FOR 2 SUSPECTS IN STREET MURDER

Victim in Financial Straits, Widow Declares.

(Picture on back page.)

Two men known to police only as "Joe" and "Angelo" were being sought by the police last night for a possible clew to the killing of Peter Pulizzi, 29 years old, who was shot yesterday at the wheel of his automobile at Taylor and Lytle streets. The two men were seen with Pulizzi at the Zep café, Lake and Howard streets, Elmhurst, last Saturday night and police believe that they alone know the motive for the killing.

Pulizzi, who lived at 1437 South 59th court, Cicero, had no gang connections so far as police could learn and their only theory of the murder was that, badly in need of money, he was trying to "muscle in" as a racketeer or alcohol peddler in the Italian district in the vicinity of Taylor street and Racine avenue. A bank book found in his pocket, showed that he had a balance in the First Italian bank of only $5.75 and his widow, Anita, told police that he had been in financial straits recently.

Pulizzi was slain as he was driving west in Taylor street, and although police could find no witnesses they were able to reconstruct the killing. Two street car motormen saw the automobile swerving in the center of the street. Suddenly it stopped, and Pulizzi leaped from it, an automatic pistol clutched in his hand. He collapsed in the middle of the car tracks.

He had been shot once in the right side and twice in the back and a fourth bullet had struck the right front door of his car. All three wounds were high in the body, above the height of the back of the automobile seat.

Tony Rio, a barber at 1243 Taylor street, near where Pulizzi fell, said he heard three shots, but did not see Pulizzi's slayers. Police believed that the slayers had ridden past Pulizzi's car farther up the street and fired into it as they passed.

Pulizzi's widow, questioned by Capt. Matthew Zimmer at the Maxwell street station, said he had not been in the alcohol business or any other business since he sold his half interest in the Zep café to his partner, Frank Primilio, several months ago. He left home yesterday morning at 10 o'clock, two hours before he was slain.

Lieut. Edward Balata of the Maxwell police said Pulizzi had been arrested by him in a raid on a flat a short time ago, and that at that time he had had no police record. A rent receipt for a basement flat, which was found in his pocket, started police on a search for the flat to learn whether Pulizzi had been operating a still there.

Source: Courtesy of Chicago Tribune Archives

WHERE CICERO MAN WAS KILLED AS HE LEFT AUTO, PISTOL IN HAND.
Crowd at Taylor and Lytle streets, where Peter Pulizzi of 1604 South 51st court, Cicero, was shot down before he had a chance to reply to assailant's fire. *(Story on page 5.)*
[TRIBUNE Photo.]

[TRIBUNE Photo.]
JUDGE IS WELCOMED BACK TO BOYS' COURT.
Left to right: George W. Dixon, A. J. Whipple, and John J. Phelan congratulating Judge Francis B. Allegretti on transfer.
(Story on page 5.)

KILLED IN FIGHT.
Peter Pulizzi, Cicero, slain as he leaps from auto, pistol in hand.
(Story on page 5.)

Source: Courtesy of Chicago Tribune Archives

Graduating from Murder to Massacre—Story of Slaughter on Valentine's Day

News 7-6-43

(Eleventh of a series on the fate of the "Heat Boys," otherwise called Chicago's public enemies, as framed against the sometimes dramatic, often fantastic, backgrounds of gangland's prohibition era.)

BY CLEM LANE.

The heirs of Dion O'Banion found life a short and fearsome affair. And never more fearsome than on St. Valentine's day, Feb. 14, 1929, when Capone gunnen lined up seven men in a garage at 2122 N. Clark st. and sprayed the seven with machine guns.

TED NEWBERRY.

There had been snow flurries that morning as the mailmen made their rounds, their loads made heavier by the lovers' missives.

In the Clark st. garage seven men had gathered. The word was that George "Bugs" Moran and Ted Newberry, leaders of the North Side gang, would be along about 10:30 o'clock that morning.

Cozy Breakfast Scene.

Four of the men were gathered about an electric plate on which bubbled a pot of coffee. A box of crackers and a half dozen cups, a half-emptied bottle of cream, completed the breakfast layout. A fifth man mumbled to himself as he wrestled with the wheel of a truck. The other two alternated in use of the telephone.

The front door of the garage opened, and in walked two men in police uniform, carrying machine-guns, followed by two in civilian attire, carrying sawed-off shotguns.

"Nuts," said one of the breakfast group. "A pinch."

The seven were rounded up, they were ordered to face the north wall, their hands in the air. As they stood facing its whitewashed surface, hands flashed up and down their clothes, frisking them for weapons. The frisking ceased.

Behind them in a line stood the four men, the "policemen" with machine guns at each end, the two men with sawed-off shotguns in the center.

The policemen looked at each other, there was a nodded signal

and the machine—gunner at the left turned his gun much as if he were a gardner spraying a row of bushes.

A Scientific Massacre.

His gun swept left to right, head high. The machine-gunner at the right aimed a little lower, sweeping right to left, the bullets cutting into the necks and shoulders of the seven men against the white wall. Back again along the row of men swept each of the tommy guns, this time along two lines below the previous marks. And then a third time across the knee joints and lower.

To the right of the victim's lineup were John May, 1249 W. May st., a $50-a-week mechanic, and Dr. Reinhardt Schwimmer, an optometrist who had started playing cousin to the gangsters in search of a thrill.

May, incredulous first, then terror-stricken, that he, a working stiff with no gang pretensions, a married man with a family of seven was about to die, turned to plead for his life, but the chattering stream cut short his plea, beheading him.

Some Nice Play Acting.

The killers looked for a moment at the writhing bodies, shrugged and turned away. Out the front door they went, the two civilians, their hands in the air, preceding the two men in police uniform. A nice bit of play-acting, simulating two policemen arresting two hoodlums.

Into a Cadillac car, which resembled a squad car, went the four. The fifth man at the wheel pressed the accelerator, there was a whine as the car went into high, and off it went.

The driver sped to an alley garage at 1723 N. Wood st., not far from the Circus Cafe, hangout for Claude Maddox, alias "Screwy Johnny" Moore; Tony Accardo, alias Joe Batters; Tony Capezio and some more of the Capone mob's allies.

The "coppers" shed their uniforms. The five went their separate ways.

All was now hustle and alarm at the Clark st. garage as word reached police that the gangs had graduated from murder to massacre.

Lives, But Won't Talk.

Six of the men were dead. In addition to May and Dr. Schwimmer, they were Pete Gusenberg, a criminal that Moran had picked up to bolster his armed forces; Albert R. Weinshank, owner of the Alcazar Club, 4207 Broad-

and dyeing firm; Adam Heyer, alias Snyder, alias Hayes, who had rented the massacre garage for the S.M.C. Cartage Co., and James Clark, Moran's brother-in-law and a noted gunman.

The seventh man, Frank Gusenberg, brother of Pete and just as tough, was found still living. He was hurried to the Alexian Brothers hospital. The police sought to question him in his conscious moments, but he died, refusing to talk.

What about Moran and Newberry? They were nearing the garage when they saw the tableau of police making arrest and had departed forthwith, Newberry to flee the city, Moran to take sanctuary in a hospital whence came word from him: "Only Capone kills like that."

City Gets Excited.

Chicago, as is its custom under the circumstances, became aroused. There was talk of a reward of $100,000 for the apprehension of the killers. The City Council voted $20,000 for such a reward, but spent it on something else when the heat died down. There were vehement statements from civic leaders. Where was "Scarface Al" Capone? In Florida. At Miami. Deputy Police Commissioner John Stege was in Florida, too. Police Commissioner William F. Russell, in revealing that Stege was returning to Chicago to take charge of the investigation, issued a remarkable statement.

"I believe the deputy commissioner will have some interesting information on the massacre," said Russell. "When he read the papers he probably looked up Al Capone, who, I understand, also is in Miami, and more than likely obtained information that will aid him in the inquiry."

State's Attorney John A. Swenson instructed police captains to close all speakeasies, bawdy houses and gambling joints.

Some Gents Disappear.

Police learned that several men who had rented front rooms in rooming houses across from the massacre garage had disappeared coincident with the slayings.

"Machine Gun" Jack McGurn and a personable blonde, Louise

Rolfe, were found at one of the city's swank hotels. McGurn was identified by witnesses as one of the killers. So was Rocco Fannelli. The state never got around to trying them. Nor was anyone else ever tried for the murders.

JACK McGURN.

McGurn, on his seizure, pointed out that, had he been associated with the men killed they would have recognized him immediately had he stepped into the garage and would have seen through the police hoax at once. He denied any part of the killing. History vindicates him.

A fire in the Wood st. garage led to the discovery that the Circus gang had dismantled and sought by fire to destroy the car used to carry the killers to the scene.

Daily News Gets First Clue.

The first real clue came when The Daily News suggested to Dr. Herman N. Bundesen, then coroner, that he have his ballistics expert, Col. Calvin Goddard, check a machine gun found after a man in St. Joseph, Mich., had killed a policeman in resisting a traffic arrest.

Dr. Bundesen's staff had carefully saved the bullets—the number taken from each of the bodies ranged from 22 to 50. These were compared with test bullets fired from the machine gun found in Michigan.

"That was one of the machine guns used in the massacre," said Col. Goddard.

Eventually the possessor of the machine gun was captured. He was Fred "Killer" Burke, a Missouri desperado. He is now in a Michigan penitentiary.

Long afterward, the names of two of the other killers were learned. They were Gus Winkler, later the proprietor of a thriving

Article continues on next page.

Source: Chicago Daily News, June 6, 1943. Reproduced with permission of the Chicago Sun-Times.

Article continues from previous page.

North Side beer business, and Fred Goetz, who had fled his native Chicago in his youth to continue his crime career elsewhere. Both men subsequently were shot to death in Chicago.

Gang Imports Gunmen.

The Capone gang had to have men not known to Chicago gangsters. Claude Maddox, originally from St. Louis, arranged for the importation of Burke, Winkler and Goetz. Several other hoodlums have been named from time to time as the fourth killer, but there hasn't been sufficient corroboration to make any of those named a logical selection.

What led up to the massacre? After O'Banion had been shot to death, "Two Gun Louis" Alterie, O'Banion's closest friend, issued a loud challenge. Then he took himself off to his ranch out West. Maxie Eisen, who had made a bundle in his association with O'Banion, went to Europe. This Eisen, not to be confused with the Eisen who thumped fish peddlers, returned to Chicago years after and is now reported living a hand-to-mouth existence.

Perhaps the toughest of O'Banion's gang were Moran, Earl Wociechowski, alias "Little Hymie" Weiss, and Vincent "The Schemer" Drucci. John Torrio and Al Capone, after O'Banion's death, wouldn't turn over O'Banion's cut, so the latter's gang opened war on John and Al.

Fail to Kill Capone.

They tried to kill Capone, but missed because he wasn't in his car when they let fly at it. They shot Torrio, but he recovered and, after a jail sentence, fled the city. They broke up the Genna gang, killing two of the Gennas and Sam "Samoots" Amatuma.

Public clamor caused a group of politicians to seek to arrange a truce. Weiss, Drucci and Moran met Capone, Tony Lombardo and Frank "The Enforcer" Nitti in a downtown hotel—the guns were checked in the lobby. The North Siders are said to have demanded that Anthony "Mops" Volpe be put on the spot for them before they would agree to peace.

"I wouldn't do that to a yellow dog," said Capone.

The peace meeting broke up. A few days later at high noon the North Side sent a caravan of cars loaded with gunmen down 22d st. (now Cermak rd.) in Cicero, spraying the Hawthorne Hotel, the Capone headquarters, with bullets. McGurn, then with the North Side mob, was one of the machine-gunners. The raid, while spectacular, was a flop in gang results—the only ones wounded being a couple of innocent bystanders.

Michigan av. Battle.

This was followed by a gun battle in Michigan av. No casualties resulted, but Weiss and Drucci were seized nearby, waiting for the customary streetcar.

Joe Saltis, who had made a loose alliance with the North Side gang, was on trial for the murder of John "Mitters" Foley, who had been trying to peddle beer in Saltis territory. Attorney W. W. O'Brien, who was defending Saltis, left the courtroom with "Little Hymie" and three of the North Siders to drive the few blocks to Schofield's flower shop, the spot across from Holy Name Cathedral where O'Banion had been killed.

As they alighted at the flower shop, a machine-gun began its chatter from a second floor window of a rooming house nearby. Weiss and Paddy Murray were killed. The lawyer and the other two were wounded but recovered.

Policeman Kills Drucci.

Drucci and Moran were left as North Side gang leaders. Drucci, called "The Schemer" because of his cunning, had sought to carry on the political activities that had kept police from interfering with O'Banion's activities.

Report had it he was on his way to kidnap a Democratic alderman when a police squad seized him and Henry Finklestein.

In the squad car en route to the station Drucci started an argument that ended when Policeman Daniel Healy, now a captain, shot Drucci to death.

Moran took over the gang's leadership and brought in Jack Zuta and Barney Bertsche, a couple of smart operators, to help him run things. Joe Aiello lined up with the new alliance. A truce was declared, giving the North Siders a free hand north of Madison st., the Capone-ites to have the territory lying south.

The Aiello alliance proved a slight error, for it was in this sector that the fighting broke out. Lombardo, head of the Unione Siciliana, was shot to death in front of the Morrison Hotel one afternoon, followed by the end of the truce, followed by more shootings, followed by the St. Valentine's day massacre.

(Tomorrow: The end of the North Side gang—the stories of Jack Zuta, Joe Aiello, and George "Bugs" Moran.)

The St. Valentine's Day Massacre

Source: The John Binder Collection. Reproduced with permission of John J. Binder.

Where Gang Massacre Search Center

This picture, looking west in North avenue from Honore street, was made today by a Journal cameraman Figure No. 1 indicates 1837 West North avenue, where Pasqualino Lolordo lived some months ago before he moved to 1921 West North avenue, where he was killed early in January. No. 2 points to the Circus cafe, where two suspects in the Moran gang murders were picked up. No. 3 shows 1859 West North avenue, a vacant building, the address given by one, Rogers, who rented the garage at 1723 North Wood street, where the burning auto was found last night

in "Little Sicily"

The garage at 1723 North Wood street.

The block where St. Valentine's Day Massacre suspects were picked up, and the location where the burning auto used in the massacre getaway was found.

Source: The Chicago Journal. Reproduced with permission of the Chicago Sun-Times.

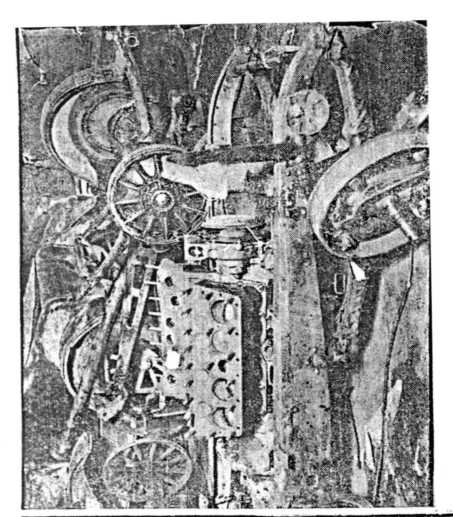

CAR WHICH POLICE BELIEVE WAS MACHINE USED BY GANGSTER SLAYERS

Source: Daily News, Chicago, February 1929. Reproduced with permission of the Chicago Sun-Times.

Gangland is hard on automobiles. Above is the car in which Philip Gnolfo, alky peddler and extortionist of Chicago's Little Italy, was slain with machine guns. Below is a car found at Maywood, Ill., after being dynamited. It is believed to be the getaway car used after the St. Valentine Massacre.

Source: A page from Capone's Chicago by R.T. Enright, Victory WW2 Publishing Ltd., www.victoryww2.com
Reproduced with permission of the source.

All Chicago gasped at the ruthless murder of Bugs Moran's hardboiled gang, but when the bodies were hauled away Al Capone was left in peace, and Bugs ducked for Minnesota to hide for his life. Two of the slayers who left death behind them in the garage on St. Valentine's Day, wore the uniforms of policemen. The evidence is that whoever planned this astounding crime intended to "put on the spot" at least ten members of the gang which was then challenging Capone's supremacy. Three of the men, including Moran, escaped by good fortune and have thus far dodged gang death.

Source: A page from Capone's Chicago by R.T. Enright, Victory WW2 Publishing Ltd., www.victoryww2.com
Reproduced with permission of the source.

A general without an army was Bugs Moran, shown here with his wife, after seven of his men were lined up and filled with hot lead.

Source: Photo and caption from Capone's Chicago by R.T. Enright, Victory WW2 Publishing Ltd., www.victoryww2.com
Reproduced with permission of the source.

Valentine Day Massacre Echo Soon Will Be Silenced

By Earl Moses

The dingy garage on N. Clark St. that was the scene of the St. Valentine's Day Massacre 38 years ago soon will be razed to make way for a high-rise apartment building for the elderly.

Old-timers may recall that it was cold on the morning of Feb. 14, 1929, and snow swirled in the street. Inside the S. M. C. Cartage Co. garage at 2122 N. Clark, seven men who were soon to be corpses went about their tasks.

John May, a former convict and a mechanic, was changing a flat tire on one of the trucks that George (Bugs) Moran and his gang had used to run the rot-gut whisky that was the elixir of Prohibition Era massacres.

Four hoodlum types milled about a bubbling coffee pot and the other two men busily made telephone calls.

The Seven Inside

Besides May, there was James Clark, Moran's brother-in-law; Adam Heyer, a muscleman and manager of the cartage firm; Dr. Reinhardt Schwimmer, an optometrist who got his kicks from associating with gangsters, and had been brought along by Heyer; the Gusenberg brothers—Pete and Frank—gang-war veterans who had been enforcers, for the old Dion O'Banion gang,

whose mantle Moran now wore, and Albert R. Weinshank, operator of a North Side speakeasy—the Alcazar Club.

And there was the one survivor of the carnage — Weinshank's big police dog, High Ball.

Moran and one of his lieutenants, Ted Newberry, were on their way to the garage with a load of hijacked liquor when, about 10:30 a.m., a Cadillac touring car with a bell on the side—identical to those used by Chicago detectives—stopped in front of the garage.

Five Strangers Arrive

Two men in police uniforms alighted, revolvers drawn followed by two other men in plainclothes—one carrying a submachine gun wrapped in newspapers. A fifth man remained at the wheel of the big car, its engine idling.

When the strangers entered the garage, the seven men inside were not unduly alarmed. Just another police raid, they thought. They would be taken downtown, booked, fingerprinted, released on bond, and their cases later "fixed."

Warlords' Monument

So they dutifully turned their backs to line up along the garage's whitewashed, north wall to await the inevitable frisking, their hands in the air.

The stillness suddenly

erupted in a blaze of gunfire. The executioners methodically swung their weapons back and forth, raking each of their victims with at least 20 slugs.

Within perhaps 60 seconds the dingy garage was transformed into a monument to the supreme effrontery of the gangland warlords to an ordered society.

As the acrid fumes of gunpowder wafted to the rafters of the newly created shrine, silence returned — except for the cowed yelping of High Ball, who was chained to a truck.

When the Chicago police routinely investigated the report of a shooting, they found six of the victims dead.

Frank Gusenberg, miraculously, was still alive.

He crawled toward Policeman Clarence J. Sweeney, who knew the Gusenbergs when they were boys, and had arrested them on several occasions.

"It looked like a battlefield," said the late Dr. Herman N. Bundesen, then coroner.

Sweeney took Gusenberg to Alexian Brothers Hospital and asked him who had shot him. "Nobody shot me," replied the dying thug. "It's getting dark, Sarge," he gasped. "So long."

He died three hours after the massacre.

Moran and Newberry

A crowd gathered in front of garage at 2122 N. Clark on Feb. 14, 1929, after police arrived to remove the bodies of six slain members of the Bugs Moran gang.

showed up at the garage shortly after the shooting, but kept on driving when they saw all the policemen. The next day, a reporter found Moran and questioned him about the massacre.

"Only Capone kills like that," he said.

The murders never were solved. But, as an epilog, 22 gangsters who were questioned in the investigation later died violent deaths.

Al Capone, who was in Florida at the time, eventually went to prison for income-tax evasion.

Come April or May, the old two-story brick building—now a warehouse—will be razed. In its place, the Chicago Housing Authority will erect a 100-unit apartment building for the elderly.

Few, except curiosity seekers, will bemoan the eradication of the monument.

The massacre did have this effect: It jarred a somnolent citizenry and officialdom from their lethargy and triggered a cleanup campaign by city and federal lawmen.

Chicago Gangland The True Story of its Murders Its Vices, and Its Reprisals
James O'Donnell Bennett
Chicago Daily Tribune (1872-1963); Mar 3, 1929; ProQuest Historical Newspapers Chicago Tribune (1849 - 1985) pg. G1

Chicago Gangland ⁜ ⁜

Gennas Bring Blood-Red Day of Sixty Shots

(This is the fifth article of a series on the gangsters of boozedom and what they have done to Chicago. In previous installments Mr. Bennett has told the stories of Dean O'Banion, Johnny Torrio, and other notorious hoodlums.)

By James O'Donnell Bennett.

MORNING of June 13, 1925, in Chicago.

A day of shifting showers and sunshine.

Pavement out Western avenue way—in the 5900 block—wet and slippery, which is a factor in the morning's doings because it brings death to two innocent men and to one of the wickedest and most dangerous men that ever bogus prohibition developed.

A blood-red day, therefore, for leading gangsters of boozedom.

It has passed into crime annals as "the Day of the Sixty Shots."

As a matter of fact, more than sixty shots were fired, but sixty bullet holes were found in the car of the innocent men. So "sixty" served.

Amid the sunshine and rain of the "the Day of the Sixty Shots" Police Detectives Michael J. Conway, William Sweeney, Charles B. Walsh, and Harold F. Olson are touring their district in a detective bureau car. Within a week three policemen have been shot to death by gangsters of boozedom. It is a time for keeping sharp lookout. Conway, Sweeney, Walsh, and Olson are good men and true; no suspicion that they are in cahoots with gangsters and racketeers. They have been assigned by the central detective bureau to Chicago Lawn station. Just now they are cruising north on Western avenue. Near 47th street an automobile containing four men passes them on its way south. One of the policemen, with a sixth sense for instant identification, mutters:

"There goes a bunch of hoodlums"—hoodlums being the general term for the gangsters and racketeers of boozedom.

Death Stalks the Gennas.

Conway, who is in command, looks up alertly and sees in the approaching car Mike Genna, one of the six Genna brothers from Marsala in Sicily, of whom one or another has been a pest to the police and of use to evil politicians for at least half a decade. Only 19 days before this cloudy June day of 1925 Brother Angelo had been killed in one of the battles of boozedom; Brother Mike's turn is to come today; Brother Tony is to die twenty-six days from now, the whisper, "Get the Cavallero" on his lips. The lads from ancient Marsala, which has been making wine from the days of antiquity, have made big money in "alky

GANGSTERS' ARSENAL

Policeman Albert Rickert, who helped trap Mike Genna, examining repeating and sawed off shotguns found in a vacant lot near the place where the gangsters' car crashed prior to the slaughter.
[TRIBUNE Photo.]

cooking" in Chicago, but it will be seen that their occupation is not without its disconcerments.

No wonder Conway is interested when he spies Brother Mike in the approaching automobile.

"We'll follow 'em and see what they're up to," said Conway.

The Fatal Swerve.

Officer Olson is at the wheel of the bureau car. Swiftly he turns and heads southward. Pursuit for twelve blocks at seventy-three miles an hour begins. Gong ringing, horn roaring, the bureau car creeps up on the suspect car, which is desperately increasing its speed. Both cars are large and they swerve dangerously on the wet pavement. At 59th street the inevitable happens. A truck swerves into the path of the pursued car. Amid screaming of brakes pursued and pursuers come to a halt, the hoodlums' car first jumping the right hand curb and slamming against a lamp post; the bureau car swings and slithers to within a few feet of it. Both cars belch armed and angry men.

"What's the big idea?" the policemen clamor. "Why all the speed when we were giving you the gong to stop?"

A roar of flame and slugs is the reply. Officer Olson falls dead, almost the whole of his jaw torn away by the slugs. Poor chap, he has been only two years on the force and he leaves an aged mother, who is a deaf mute, and four young brothers.

Then another blast of fire and slugs. Officer Walsh falls dead, his breast riddled with bullets and the left side

of his face torn away by the homemade, soft lead slugs used by the gangsters. He leaves a widow and three small children.

Now a third blast and Officer Conway falls—not killed, but terribly wounded. Blood is gushing from his right breast.

And Sweeney Plunges On.

Officer Sweeney is firing rapidly throughout this terrific fusillade, he remains unwounded and unafraid. He drives the gangsters out of their car and from behind their car. He pursues them across a vacant lot next to the Tourist garage at 5940 Western avenue, out of which rush dumfounded employés to stare at the running fight. Sweeney is gaining on Mike Genna, who is the last of the fleeing men. He turns and points his shotgun full at Sweeney. He pulls the trigger. There is no report. Brave Sweeney is saved. He plunges on, still firing. One of his bullets hits Genna in the leg. He stumbles, recovers himself, lurches on, spies a basement window in the house at 5941 Artesian avenue, dashes his shotgun through the glass and plunges after the gun. Sweeney's bullets still spattering after him.

Now unexpected help drops off a passing street car and pops out of a house.

An Old Fire Horse Starts.

Officer Albert Rickert, just happening to be passing 60th street on a Western avenue car, jumps from the car, jumps to his duty and joins Sweeney in pursuit of Mike Genna.

Source: Courtesy of Chicago Tribune Archives. *Article continues on next page.*

Article continues from previous page.

The True Story of Its Murders Its Vices. and Its Reprisals

ON TRIAL FOR THEIR LIVES

"George!" calls Mrs. George Oakey, at almost the same instant. "George! Look! There's a shooting!" She has been drawn to a window of her home at 2434 West 60th street by the noise of the shots, and it is to her husband, 60 year old George Oakey, who is night officer on duty at the state's attorney's office, to whom she is calling.

She does not have to call twice.

Before Ellen Oakey can stop her white haired George he is clattering down the stairs. He gallops after Genna like an old fire horse when the alarm sounds. He and Rickert and Sweeney reach the basement at 5941 Artesian avenue into which Genna has hurled himself. They burst open the door and find the gangster lying on the floor, a blue steel Spanish revolver in his hand. He is dying, bleeding to death from one of Sweeney's bullets which has severed an artery in the leg.

He fires one last shot at his captors but hits none of them; then falls back, almost lifeless. He is carried out. An ambulance comes. As one of the attendants is doing his best to ease him on to the stretcher, Mike Genna snarls, "Take that, you——," lifts his good leg, and kicks the attendant in the face.

A few minutes later he is dead and the ambulance changes its destination from the Bridewell hospital to Donovan's morgue.

Sweeney and wounded Conway, and Oakey have won their sergeancies.

* *

Hatless and in Flight.

Meanwhile Genna's three companions are in flight. Two of them—John Scalisi and Albert Anselmi—are overhauled as they are boarding a Western avenue car at 59th street by a hurry up detail from West Englewood station. Hatless and panting, they had rushed into Edward Issigson's dry goods store at 59th and Rockwell streets. They wanted to buy caps, but Issigson turned them away. The third man was never captured.

Death and the devil having taken charge of Mike Genna, it remained for the law to deal with Anselmi and Scalisi, and the law took not so much its own way about that as bowed to the ways of the gangsters and their highly paid lawyers. There were trials and retrials to the number of three and in two years and ten days after Officers Harold Olson and Charles Walsh were killed Albert Anselmi and John Scalisi were free to resume their activities in boozedom. That they did.

* *

See How the Feuds Interlock.

The police believe that Mike Genna, Anselmi, and Scalisi were on murder bent hours before they were signalled to halt in Western avenue by the gong of the bureau car in which Officers Conway, Sweeney, Olson, and Walsh were cruising their district. In November, 1924, Dean O'Banion, leader of the north side gangsters of Chicago boozedom, had been killed as a result of quarrels and double crossings between his gang and the south side gang of John Torrio and the west side gang of the Genna brothers. In January, 1925, an automobile which north side gangsters supposed Al Capone, chief co-criminal of Torrio, to be rid-

John Scalisi, left, and Albert Anselmi as they appeared in court for the third trial growing out of the killing of the two detectives. In this trial the jury acquitted the gunmen on the grounds that they had only defended themselves against unwarranted police aggression.
[TRIBUNE Photo.]

ing in—but he was not—was riddled with shotgun slugs and Capone's chauffeur was wounded in the back. Capone promptly bought a new car and had it completely equipped with bullet proof glass. A few days later John Torrio was shot down by north side gangsters, as related in chapter III.

* *

Plot and Counterplot.

And so it went from month to month, year in and year out—reprisals and counter reprisals, killings and attempted killings, crossings and double crossings, dishonored checks, unpaid bills for booze, hijacking of one gang's loads of illicit liquor by gangsters supposed to be allied with the hijacked gang, but turning traitor to it. Invasion, too, of one another's territory—the practice known as "muscling in"—and hatreds bubbling and boiling over between affiliated gangs who

could not remain true to one another for the simple reason that there is no *more arrant bosh than the old saying* about "honor among thieves."

Thus 1925 wore along into May, and on May 26 came the killing of Angelo Genna, described by Mrs. Genevieve Forbes Herrick as "youngest and toughest of the Genna boys." It was the familiar story of "a big touring car with four passengers, a chase, the running down of the victim, the firing of a dozen slugs into his body"—and another gang "mystery" made the front page.

What with the attempts by gangsters in five months of 1925 to kill such conspicuous gangsters as Capone and Torrio, and what with the actual killing of so active and pitiless a villain as Angelo Genna, the reprisal score was running heavily against the Torrio-Capone-Genna gangs.

Source: Courtesy of Chicago Tribune Archives. *Article continues on next page.*

Article continues from previous page.

WHERE POLICE AND HOODLUMS FOUGHT

The gangsters' car is shown wrecked against a lamp post and headed north after skidding completely around. The police car is in the foreground. Following the crash, gunmen and police engaged in a bloody and deadly gun battle. Then the gangsters fled through the vacant lot near 59th street and Western avenue.
[TRIBUNE Photo.]

Were They Trailing Moran?

One police theory is that early on the morning of June 13, 1925—the "Day of the Sixty Shots"—Genna, Anselmi, and Scalisi had been out scouting for George "Bugs" Moran, O'Banion's successor in the leadership of north side boozedom, but, though shooting Moran's car full of holes, had missed their man. This theory was given worth by the finding, a few days later, of a slug riddled automobile, the ownership of which the police traced to Moran.

Another theory is that the killers were seeking Tony Kissane, who was wrestling with the Gennas for the control of west side boozedom, and who had been heard to threaten that he would "clean out the whole Genna tribe." The awed whisper among the neutrals dwelling in the Genna stronghold around Taylor and Halsted streets was that a good start toward fulfillment of the threat had been made when Angelo, "youngest and toughest of the Genna boys," was shot down.

* *
Why the Gong Was Important.

The significant point in the mention of that early morning scouting is that part of the defense of Anselmi and Scalisi was that they thought they were being pursued in Western avenue not by police but by rival gangsters. That is why the detail as to whether the pursuing police were or were not pounding the gong of the bureau car became important. As is usual in trials of gangsters there was some contradictory evidence as well as a suspicious changing of testimony by witnesses who had become frightened. In fact, before the end of the three trials of Anselmi and Scalisi for the murder of Olson and Walsh the fact that when Olson fell dead he fell before a blast from a repeating shotgun in the hands of Scalisi seemed to become quite an inconsequential detail. Also lost in the shuffle of legalistic chicanery and bluff which disgraced all three trials was this bit of color which I extract from contemporary accounts:

"There was another blast from the muzzle waving back and forth in front of Scalisi. Patrolman Walsh clutched his breast. It was riddled with bullets."

Italy Wanted Anselmi.

Anselmi was as desperate a character as Scalisi, and was known to the Italian police as such. On Sept. 11, 1923, an Italian court issued a warrant against him for attempted murder, and on Nov. 27 of the same year a warrant for operating with a band of outlaws. In September, 1924, he fled from Sicily and entered the United States illegally. Coming to Chicago, he joined his compatriots, the Gennas, who, like him, were born in old Marsala.

The usual hullabaloo of insensate talk by officialdom followed the slaying of Olson and Walsh. Chief of Detectives William Schoemaker utterly lost his head and emitted this:

"We have reached a time when a policeman had better throw a couple of bullets into a man first and ask questions afterwards. It's war. And in wartime you shoot first and talk second."

The effect of such wild utterances was—as the three trials of Anselmi and Scalisi proved—to put thousands of citizens—thousands of possible veniremen—in an "Iz zat so?" frame of mind, which worked terribly against the orderly and effective administration of justice.

Caw! Caw! Caw!

State's Attorney Crowe also scurried to the main deck with language. He promised the reporters that the prisoners would "have as swift a trip to the gallows platform as the law will permit." He called for "forty judges to sit in criminal cases for the next few months." He demanded that they give up their summer vacations, "as I am going to do, in the interest of public duty in the face of a crisis."

As for Anselmi and Scalisi, they yawned with boredom when questioned through an interpreter, shook their heads, and said nothing save that they never had seen each other before and had been "out looking for work" and "looking for a boarding place."

The trials of Anselmi and Scalisi were fraught with scandal. Before the first trial began gangdom threatened prospective witnesses for the state by telephone and in anonymous

letters. On June 15, two days after the killing. Officer Sweeney was threatened by telephone. On Oct. 12, fifteen days before the actual taking of testimony in the first trial began, Sweeney's home was bombed. The loss to his father, who owned the house, is $7,500.

On June 16 an unknown gunman fired two shots into State's Attorney Crowe's outer office from a doorway and escaped.

* *
Thousands for Defense.

By June 19, $50,000 of a defense fund of $100,000 had been raised by allied gangs working under Capone and the four surviving Gennas, the Cicero gamblers contributing heavily. Some honest but ignorant Sicilians were cajoled, or bludgeoned, or blackmailed into contributing to this fund on the plea that the good name of the Sicilian colony of Chicago was at stake. The real reason for gangdom's solicitude for the accused gunmen was apprehension that its power would go to pieces unless its killers were protected. They were protected all right.

From the forcing of contributions came a long train of dreadful events which are here epitomized.

Sammy "Samoots" Amatuna, underworld leader, was killed because he refused to make a second contribution.

So was Henry Spingola, whose sister Lucille Angelo Genna had wedded in the presence of 3,000 guests who partook of a wedding cake that was 12 feet high and weighed 2,000 pounds. Spingola had contributed $10,000 to the defense fund for the first trial but when asked for the same amount for the second had tried to compromise on $2,000.

So were Augustino and Antonio Morici, Sicilian grocers, who sold sugar and yeast to the Genna gangs of alcohol makers.

Tito Schipa Weeps.

So was Vito Bascone, fish dealer, wine merchant and opera fan, over whose death Tito Schipa, tenor of the Chicago Civic Opera company, wept, saying: "We were close friends. This is sad news!"

Source: Courtesy of Chicago Tribune Archives.
Article continues on next page.

Article continues from previous page.

Gangland: The True Story of Chicago Crime

By James O'Donnell Bennett.

DODGING THE CAMERA

So was Joe Calabriese, one of a large family with a long, black record.

So was Edward Bardello, known as "the Eagle."

And so, by one of the dainty ironies of life and death, was Orrazio Tropea, who was known as "the Scourge" and who was one of the principal collectors of the defense fund.

One of Crowe's sunkist prophecies the day after the killing was that the accused would be tried in thirty days.

But on June 23, fifteen days after the killing, the defense obtained a postponement to Aug. 17, which invalidated Crowe's prophecy by more than a month.

Worse, far worse, was to come.

What came affects you personally as a reputable citizen brought up on the tradition that trial by jury is a main bulwark of the general social order.

* *

Where All This Hits You.

If you are a banker and do not like to see your guards shot down, if you are a storekeeper and do not like to see your clerks shot down, if you are a law abiding citizen and do not like to see policemen shot down when they are trailing notoriously lawless men, or if you are a householder and fear to remove the chain when you open your front door after nightfall, then a brief high spotting of the scandals of these three trials ought to interest you, for it will show you how the chicanery of lawyers, the sluggishness of judges, and the weakness of jurors have reduced that traditional bulwark to an extremely frail and undependable prop.

* *

Remember, Now—This Is 1925.

Here, then, are the high spots:

The first trial opens Oct. 5, 1925, with the effort to get a jury.

By Oct. 15, 235 veniremen have been questioned and four more have been accepted as jurors. On that date Assistant State's Attorney Gorman says, "It is surprising how many high class men who come into the jury box talk themselves out again."

On Oct. 16 Venireman Enos Tope, 446 North Lawler avenue, Chicago, is refused as juror because he has contributed to law enforcing organizations. For fifty-five minutes by Judge Brothers' clock the lawyers for the gangsters try to have Mr. Tope dismissed for cause, but to no avail. Finally they have to use a peremptory challenge.

By Oct. 20, three weeks have been consumed in the effort to complete the jury.

On the same day Attorney O'Donnell of the defense is accused of giving whisky to attachés of the court. The clerk of the court and three custodians of the jury are discharged after confessing. O'Donnell laughs it off.

Not until Oct. 26 is the jury completed.

On Oct. 27 the actual trying of the case begins.

On Oct. 28 Anselmi and Scalisi are identified over and over again and under oath as the killers.

Scalisi and Anselmi, Genna gangsters, trying to dodge the camera as they were brought back from the state penitentiary to face a new trial. They were convicted of killing Olson, but were acquitted on the charge of killing Walsh. [TRIBUNE Photo.]

On Oct. 31 State's Attorney Crowe says publicly, "I am convinced that Anselmi and Scalisi are also the O'Banion killers." Nothing came of that declaration.

By Nov. 1 the homes of two jurors are under police guard owing to the receipt by their relatives of letters threatening the jurors' lives.

On Nov. 2 Attorney Patrick H. O'Donnell of the defense, a white haired bravo of the bar, shouts in court. "The witness"—he means Francis Zolfano, the Genna brothers' bookkeeper and cashier in their alky cooking and bootlegging trade, "will prove indisputably that Mike Genna paid $8,000 monthly to the police for protection. I offer to prove that for six months he met 300 policemen per month and had cordial and direct business relations with them, and that

there were 200 of the policemen from the Maxwell street station, two squads from the central detail and one squad from the state's attorney's office." Crowe shouts back that O'Donnell's charge is "a vicious effort to scandalize the police department." Asked what he will do if Mayor Dever and Chief of Police Collins make a formal demand on him for the evidence of his charges, O'Donnell roars, "They can both go to hell!"

On Nov. 6 O'Donnell's charges are sustained, for Chief Collins says, "I am convinced that there were grafting policemen on the Gennas' pay roll. There are some 185 policemen attached to Maxwell street station and at least 170 are to be given new berths." They were.

* *

Source: Courtesy of Chicago Tribune Archives. Article continues on next page.

Article continues from previous page.

"Killing Policeman No Crime."

On Nov. 6 the defense sets up its case, which Lawyer Michael Ahern epitomizes thus:

"If a police officer detains you, even for a moment, against your will, and you kill him, you are not guilty of murder, but only of manslaughter. If the police officer uses force of arms, you may kill him in self-defense and emerge from the law unscathed."

That presentation of the law gives rise to the phrase, "Killing a policeman no crime."

On Nov. 11 the jury finds Anselmi and Scalisi guilty of manslaughter and fixes their punishment at 14 years in prison. As the verdict is read both prisoners smile. Crowe blows up and in demanding prompt trial of Anselmi and Scalisi for the murder of Policeman Walsh—this first trial has been for the murder of Policeman Olson, you must remember —says:

"I hope to God that then we have a jury of decent, God-fearing men and that they will do their duty and hang these killers."

"What do you know of decent people?" shouts Attorney Nash of the defense.

"I associate with them," Crowe replies, "and not with gangland, as you do."

Then something weird happens. Out of complete silence come silent words. Mrs. Myrtle Olson, aged, deaf mute mother of the slain policeman, is asked her opinion of the verdict. "The verdict," her moving fingers say, "is a blow to justice."

While Nash and Crowe are squabbling, Judge Brothers breaks in with, "I'll set the case charging the murder of Walsh for next Monday."

That means Nov. 15, 1925, for "next Monday" is only four days distant.

* *

Now You Are in 1926.

As a matter of fact this second trial does not begin until Feb. 7, 1926.

On Feb. 10 Venireman Orval W. Payne, 502 South 7th avenue, Maywood, explaining why he is unwilling to serve as juror, says to Judge Brothers, "I would have to carry a gun the rest of my life if I serve and found the two guilty. It isn't always healthy to bring in a verdict of guilty. Pressure is brought to bear on families." Furore in the courtroom; judge shocked; Payne dismissed.

By Feb. 21, 246 veniremen have been refused as jurors and only four accepted.

On March 2, William A. Lockwood, credit manager of Darling & Co., 4201 South Ashland avenue, Chicago, is reprimanded by the court for trying to keep Charles E. McKibben, one of his employés, out of jury service.

On March 3 the jury is completed.

On March 4 the actual trying of the case begins.

On March 10 two witnesses swear that Mike Genna fired on Olson and Walsh before they fired on him.

On March 18 Anselmi and Scalisi are acquitted of the murder of Walsh. Taken back to jail—for they still were being held on the 14 year sentence for the killing of Olson—they, in the words of an onlooker, "leaped for joy. They shouted. They danced about each other. And they embraced many times." "The verdict," said Chief Collins, "is a disgrace to Chicago."

On May 3 the men are taken to Joliet to serve the 14 year sentence for killing Olson.

On Dec. 23 the Illinois Supreme court grants a new trial on the grounds that if the men are guilty of murder the fourteen year sentence is "but a mockery of justice," and if they are guilty of manslaughter only, then it is "an injustice."

By Jan. 25, 1927, Anselmi is out on bail in the sum of $25,000. So is Scalisi by Jan. 27.

* *

And Now 1927.

On June 9 the third trial begins. This date is two years—less four days —after the killing of Olson and Walsh.

On June 14 and 15 more than one hundred veniremen pass through the jury box, not one qualifying as juror.

On June 22 Scalisi takes the witness stand and acknowledges that he fired on Olson and Walsh—once.

On June 23 the jury finds Anselmi and Scalisi not guilty on the ground that they had only defended themselves against unwarranted police aggression.

Let the Widow Walsh sum up for a gang ridden community. "There's nothing more to be done," she said. "My husband, his friend were killed by these men who now have a crowd waiting to shake their hands. I give up."

POLICE HERO

Sixty-year-old George Oakey, then a night officer at the state's attorney's office, joined in the pursuit of the fleeing Genna, and for his work was promoted to a sergeancy.
[TRIBUNE Photo.]

Have you caught from these five chapters the fact that during the red years of boozedom the only power that successfully fought gangsters was not the law but other gangsters? So it was on the north, south, and west sides of Chicago and in the county villages. It was so when the O'Banion gangs fell out with the Genna gangs and the Torrio gangs fell out with the O'Donnell gangs. The only punishments gangdom really feared were the ferocious punishments inflicted by gangdom. What those punishments were and how the men who meted them out were incredible combinations of ferocity, foppishness, and childishness will be unfolded next Sunday.

Source: Courtesy of Chicago Tribune Archives.

Source: Chicago Historical Society. Reproduced with permission of the Chicago Historical Society.

THAT BED OF ROSES——

Source: Chicago Evening Post, January 6, 1920. Reproduced with permission of the Chicago Sun-Times.

1930

1939

Frank J. Loesch
*Source: Business Vs.
Organized Crime*

Col. Robert
Isham Randolph
*Source: Business Vs.
Organized Crime*

Al Capone
*Source: Capone's Chicago by R.T. Enright,
Victory WW2 Publishing Ltd.,
www.victoryww2.com*

FRIEND

FOE

Frank J. Loesch

Loesch was the president of the Chicago Crime Commission from 1928 to 1937 and led a delegation of prominent businessmen to meet with U.S. President Herbert Hoover on March 19, 1929. This meeting set in motion a movement against Al Capone involving federal authorities and Chicago's business elite. Loesch was also a member of the Secret Six.

Robert Isham Randolph

Randolph, a major supporter of the Chicago Crime Commission, led the Secret Six into battle against Al Capone and his gang. He was the only self-acknowledged member of the Secret Six and thus, was approached by Capone who wanted to set up a meeting. Capone met with Randolph in order to try and make a deal with the citizenry of Chicago. By this time, the Secret Six and the Chicago Crime Commission were doing serious damage to his gang and their illegal activities.

Al Capone

Al Capone, known as "Scarface," led the Outfit in Chicago in the 1920s and was finally imprisoned in the early 1930s. His gang was perhaps the most famous organized crime ring ever to operate in the nation.

Although we are only able to highlight a few friends and foes for each decade, the Chicago Crime Commission reminds the public that there are many friends, and while perhaps not as famous as the criminals, they are courageous and far more impressive.

CCC Names Public Enemies: Capone #1
CCC Names Public Enemies: Capone #1

Determined to end Al Capone's activities, the Chicago Crime Commission influenced government action by enlisting the support of the press and the public by creating the Public Enemies List. The list, a compilation of Chicago's organized criminal elite, was sent to newspapers and to local criminal-justice officials. "List 28 As Public Enemies" headlined the *Chicago Tribune* front page in April 1930, and Public Enemy Number One was Capone. Other well-known and notorious gangsters on the list included Tony "Mops" Volpe, Ralph Capone, Frank Rio, Jack "Machine Gun" Demore, James Belcastro, Rocco Fannelli, Lawrence Mangano, Jack Zuta, Jack "Greasy Thumb" Guzik, Frank "Legs" Diamond, George "Bugs" Moran, Joe Aiello, Edward "Spike" O'Donnell, Joe Saltis, Frank McErlane, Vicent McErland, William Niemoth, Danny Stanton, Myles O'Donnell, Frank Lake, Terry Druggan, William "Klondike" O'Donnel, George "Red" Barker, William "Three Finger Jack" White, Joseph "Peppy" Genero, Leo Monoven, and James "Fur" Sammons.

The Secret Six
The Secret Six

Source: Business vs. Organized Crime by Dennis E. Hoffman

In 1930, Col. Robert Isham Randolph went to lunch with five of the wealthiest and most influential men in Chicago, including Julius Rosenwald, Major George A. Paddock, Edward E. Gore, Samuel Insull, and Frank J. Loesch. These men were to become known as the Secret Six. They agreed to put up their own money to form a fund to combat Al Capone and his gang. To carry out their plan, the Secret Six employed investigators, undercover men, special prosecutors, guards, and other technical personnel. They guaranteed protection to witnesses in cases involving organized crime figures. They acted as a supplementary investigating and prosecuting force, aiding the police, the Cook County State's Attorney, and other official law enforcement organizations. They even opened a speakeasy in order to secure evidence. As most of the members of the Secret Six were also involved in the Chicago Crime Commission, these two groups worked in partnership to bring down Capone and his gang.

Capone Wants To Make A Deal With Chicago's Citizens
Capone Wants To Make A Deal With Chicago's Citizens

Source: Business vs. Organized Crime by Dennis E. Hoffman

In February 1931, Al Capone requested a meeting with Secret Six member and Chicago Crime Commission backer Col. Robert Isham Randolph. Randolph agreed to meet with Capone. According to the *Randolph Scrapbooks IV, 1921-1946*, part of their discussion went like this:

Capone: ......"Colonel, what are you trying to do to me?"

Randolph: ...."Put you out of business."

Capone: ......"Why do you want to do that?"

Randolph: ...."We want to clean up Chicago, put a stop to these killings and gang rule here."

Capone: ......"Colonel, I don't understand you. You knock over my breweries, bust up my booze rackets, raid my gambling houses, and tap my telephone wires, but yet you're not a reformer, not a dry. Just what are you after? ...Listen, Colonel, you're putting me out of business. Even with beer selling at $55 a barrel, we didn't make a nickel last week. You know what will happen if you put me out of business? I have 185 men on my personal payroll, and I pay them from $300 to $400 a week each. They're all ex-convicts and gunmen, but they are respectable businessmen now, just as respectable as the people who buy my stuff and gamble in my places. They know the beer, booze, and gambling rackets – and their old rackets, rackets that sent them to the can. If you put me out of business, I'll turn every one of those 185 respectable ex-convicts loose on Chicago."

Randolph: ...."Well, Al, to speak frankly, we are determined to put you out of business. We are burned up about the reputation you have given Chicago."

Capone: ......"Say, Colonel, I'm burned up about that, too. Chicago's bad reputation is bad for my business. It keeps the tourists out of town. I'll tell you what I'll do: If the Secret Six will lay off my beer, booze, and gambling rackets, I'll police this town for you – I'll clean it up so there won't be a stickup or a murder in Cook County. I'll give you my hand on it."

Randolph refused to cut a deal and drank another glass of Capone's beer.

Al Capone Convicted of Income Tax Evasion
Al Capone Convicted of Income Tax Evasion

As a result of powerful citizen action, led by the Chicago Crime Commission and the Secret Six, in 1931 Capone was convicted of income tax evasion and was committed to Alcatraz. Frank (The Enforcer) Nitti succeeded Capone as head of his gang.

Chicago Mayor Anton Cermak Shot
Chicago Mayor Anton Cermak Shot

Source: graveyards.com – copyright 1996-2002, Matt Hucke

Born in Bohemia and emigrating to the United States as a child, Anton J. Cermak eventually worked in the coal mines near Joliet, Illinois and then came to Chicago when he was only sixteen. He worked with the railroad as a brakeman and a teamster. He became active as a Democratic precinct worker, and organized a group called the United Societies for Local Self Government apparently made up of mainly thieves, prostitutes and gamblers. In 1902 he became a state legislator and was able to earn over seven million dollars in real estate using his knowledge of government land-purchase plans.

Cermak became Chicago's mayor on April 7, 1931. The Chicago mob considered him an enemy because of the protection Cermak gave to his friend, a labor organizer named Roger Touhy. In 1932, Cermak sent a special squad of police officers to raid Frank Nitti's headquarters. One of the officers shot Nitti during the raid, but he survived. Cermak went to Florida to secure Federal Funds for a bankrupt Chicago. On February 15, 1933 he made a public appearance with President-elect Franklin D. Roosevelt and was shot and killed by an Italian marksman, Guiseppe Zangara. It has never been confirmed that Cermak, rather than Roosevelt, was the target, but some believe that Capone ordered his death in retribution for the shooting of Nitti. Other reports note that Zangara stated after the shooting, "Well, I got Cermak," which may imply that he was either attempting to kill Roosevelt, or that he succeeded in his mission.

Union Falls Under Domination of Capone Gang
Union Falls Under Domination of Capone Gang

Source: Virgil W. Peterson, Historical Background of Organized Crime Prior to 1967, 1979.

In the 1930s the Capone gang had succeeded in having its designated representative elected President of the International Alliance of Theatrical Stage Employees and Motion Picture Operators. As a result, 125,000 members of this union fell under the control of Capone gangsters who then extorted millions of dollars from the motion picture industry. This is the start of Chicago's organized crime infiltration in the unions. The unions provided a ready-made voting population, providing traditional organized crime with incredible political power. In future years, organized crime would be linked to numerous unions, including the Teamsters, the Laborers, the Hotel Employees, and others.

La Cosa Nostra: Its Beginnings
La Cosa Nostra: Its Beginnings

Source: Virgil W. Peterson, Historical Background of Organized Crime Prior to 1967, 1979.

J. Richard (Dixie) Davis, attorney for Dutch Schultz, stated that following the murder of Salvatore Maranzano (a gang leader in New York) in 1931, Charles "Lucky" Luciano took over the leadership of the Unione Siciliana, which he erroneously called an "international secret society." Luciano, he said, changed the Unione from a federation of Italians into a close-knit national organization affiliated with criminal mobs of other national origin. The system of underworld cooperation between gangs, regardless of ethnic background, spread from coast to coast.

Three decades after the Maranzano murder, Joseph Valachi gave still another version of the significance of the killing. Valachi stated that Joseph Masseria had decreed a death sentence on anyone in the United States who had originated from the locality of Castellamarese del Golfo, Sicily, Maranzano's home town. Thus, the bitter warfare that raged in 1930 and 1931 between the two groups of the Italian-Sicilian underworld was known as the Castellarmarese War. One group was led by Joseph Masseria and the other by Salvatore Maranzano. Out of this conflict there evolved a rigidly-structured nationwide organization called La Cosa Nostra, in which membership was restricted to full-blooded Italians. The members were divided into five families (gangs) in New York City.

Chicago's Own Crime Laboratory Division
Chicago's Own Crime Laboratory Division

Source: "Scientific Experts at Work on Actual Cases in Police Department's New Crime Laboratory," Chicago Daily Tribune, November 21, 1938.

For law enforcement efficiency and accuracy, additional patrol cars were added to the force in 1929, and that same year Chicago's police department collaborated with the *Chicago Tribune* and installed one-way radio transmitters in five squad cars. In 1932, centralized switchboards facilitated efficient communication so that call-box queries were received at the six divisional headquarters instead of at each station. Around the corner was the Chicago Police Department's acquisition of the Crime Laboratory Division, owned and operated by Northwestern University since 1930. In 1940 the police department purchased the laboratory for $25,000 and moved it to its new quarters of 10,000 square feet at 1121 S. State Street. The Chicago Police Scientific Detection Laboratory's first director was Fred Inbau. Inbau also served as the Assistant Chairman of the Chicago Crime Commission, and thus, the Commission played an active role in working to support the crime lab expansion efforts. With the facility consisting of two chemical labs, a photography room and dark room, a machine shop, ballistics room, microscopy lab, a documents examiner room, lie detectors and research library, the opportunities to convict Chicago's gangsters and other criminals increased.

THIS COMPLETES THE PHOTO

Yesterday we printed a photograph of six sunny boys taking the air and anything else they want at Atlantic City. The big, smiling chap in the light suit (second from the right) was cut out. We're introducing him to-day. He's Enoch ("Nocky") Johnson, a dapper duke with the smile of a sheik. Johnson is G. O. P. boss in the environs of Atlantic City. On the right is "Scarface Al" Capone, Chicago gang czar, who has a strangle hold on booze rackets in Chicago, Florida and points north, south, east and west. It was "Scarface's" frequent visits to At-lantic City that caused the New York **Evening Journal** to investigate rum and vice conditions there. He is now doing a stretch because the "Philly" police didn't like him running around their town with a "gat." Also in the group are David Palter (second from left) and Charl. T. Green, between Capone and Palter, "high pressure" men. Palter admitted paying $65,000 to avoid a year v cation in Atlanta penitentiary after being convicted mail fraud.

Source: New York Evening Journal, January 22, 1930

Al Capone (above) taking his leisure at his luxurious Miami Beach, Fla., home, which is shown on the upper right. On the right deputies are pictured removing sacks of liquor seized in a raid on the pretentious establishment in March, 1930.

Source: Daily Times, Chicago
Reproduced with permission of the Chicago Sun-Times.

27TH MAN SLAIN IN NEW YORK'S 1930 GANG WARS

TOM PETTEY

Chicago Daily Tribune (1872-1963); Apr 7, 1930; ProQuest Historical Newspapers Chicago Tribune (1849 - 1985)
pg. 9

27TH MAN SLAIN IN NEW YORK'S 1930 GANG WARS

Drug and Rum Mobs Fight While Police Reminisce.

BY TOM PETTEY.

[Chicago Tribune Press Service.]

New York, April 6.—[Special.]—A dapper little man in a brown suit sat humped over a steering wheel like a racing driver last night. He was John Imperale, gangster, but he was not going anywhere in his automobile as he had a bullet hole in his head.

Imperale belonged to the narcotic mob and his death this morning in a Brooklyn hospital bed was relatively unimportant. The reason he has a paragraph at the top of this story is because John Imperale was gangland's twenty-seventh victim in the metropolitan area since Jan. 1.

It's Done Quietly in Most Cases.

Most of gangland's readjustment work in the five boroughs has been done quietly. There has been a neat spacing of "jobs" and only on one occasion has it been found necessary to eliminate two overly ambitious racketeers on the same night. There has been two or three brief flareups in the newspapers but the police department always has acted promptly to provide more interesting data for the crime writers—stories about the gangs having been broken up years ago in this city.

In the meanwhile the alcohol ring, the beer runners and the narcotic mobs have been settling their own unemployment and territorial problems by a process of inconspicuous elimination.

How They Die in New York.

The manner of passing of these 27 gangsters as revealed by police reports provides an interesting sidelight on the New York technique. Footnotes on the deaths of several of the leaders follow:

Jim Tinerello, high in the "alky" world, died behind a pine barricade in a lumber yard and was buried in a bronze coffin.

William "Baron" Simpson, old time rough and tumble fighter, stepped out of an East river alleway into a pound of lead.

Guiseppe "Clutching Hand" Piraino, who aspired to alcohol kingdoms beyond the Brooklyn bridge, stepped from his doorway to fill his lungs with spring air and got them filled with bullets.

Gabriel Nucci, leader of a Greenwich Village gang, wandered across a territorial line and kept right on to a cemetery.

Frankie Dunn, the beer baron, stood too long on the sidewalk admiring his new purchased ten story office building and a machine gun in a passing automobile mowed him down.

Statistically the elimination of the twenty-seven gangsters without benefit of police took place as follows:

Shot from ambush while seated at steering wheel, 6.

Taken for a ride, 4.
Killed in bed, 2.
Killed in lumber yard, 1.
Slain on sidewalk while waiting [on the spot], 5.
Killed in doorway while leaving homes, 4.
Slain in park, 2.
Killed in "conference," 3.

Nine of the local gangland's executions took place during the last six weeks in the quiet borough of Brooklyn. The racketeering privileges on the docks still is an unsettled problem and the narcotic murder yesterday indicates that there still are some wrin-

kles in the trade to be ironed out across the river.

Three Informers Dead.

In the boroughs of Manhattan and the Bronx the alcohol and beer trade appears stable, but gang warfare has accounted for the deaths of three "informers" or state witnesses in less than twelve weeks, and two "mob" killings have been traced to gambling rackets. At least four of the Manhattan gang murders had an indirect connection with the speakeasy trade.

The common or private homicide rate has been climbing almost as rapidly as the gang killings, and many of them if not actually linked with gangland are on the edge. During January and February there were thirty homicides in New York City.

Source: Courtesy of Chicago Tribune Archives

April 23, 1930

Subject: Well known gangsters, criminals
and police characters.

1. In the program of the Chicago Crime Commission is this
paragraph:

2. "Preparation of a list of known criminals and systematic re-
lentless procedure against them in every legal way. These men
are public enemies and should be treated accordingly."

3. To carry this ~~part of the program into forceful effect re-~~
quires co-operation on the part of all law enforcing agencies
and includes:

   A. Vigilant watchfulness and arrests, B. Court action, C. Deportation of criminal aliens, D. Investigation to determine
   whether personal property taxes have been paid by these
   persons. E. Investigation of the status of their Real
   Estate holdings and the taxes paid thereon. F. Inquiry as
   to whether or not they have paid their United States
   Income taxes. G. Raids on disorderly houses controlled by
   them. H. Raids on gambling houses, night clubs, dog tracks,
   etc., in which they are interested or which they frequent.
   I. Inquiry to determine their political affiliations and
   publication of the facts. J. Publication of business and
   residence addresses, business affiliations and such information as may be developed regarding banking connections
   and other financial interests.

4. The purpose is to keep the light of publicity shining on
Chicago's most prominent well known and notorious gangsters
to the end that they may be under constant observation by
the law enforcing authorities and law abiding citizens
apprized of the hazard to be encountered in dealing with those
who are constantly in conflict with the law.

4. Appended hereto is a partial list of the most notorious in the
files of the Chicago Crime Commission. These men are a continuing menace to the peace and dignity of the community and
every legal effort should be made to bring about a termination
of their criminal activities by vigorous, systematic, relent-
less procedure against them.

                              FRANK J. LOESCH
                              President

In re: Chicago's Well Known Gang
          Leaders and Gangsters.

The following is a partial list of Chicago's most prominent
well known and notorious gangsters:
Alphonse Capone alias "Scar face Capone" alias "Al Capone"
alias "Al Brown", Tony ("Mops") Volpe, Ralph Capone, Frank
Rio alias "Frank Kline", alias "Frank Cline" Jack Demore
alias "Jack ('Machine Gun') McGurn" James Belcastro, Rocco
Fannelli Lawrence ("Dago Lawrence") Mangano, Jack Zuta,
Jack Gusick Frank Diamond, George ("Bug") Moran, Joe Aiello,
Edward ("Spike") O'Donnell, Joe ("Polack Joe") Saltis, Frank
Mc Erlane, Vicent McErlane, William Niemoth, Danny Stanton,
Myles O'Donnell, Frank Lake, Terry Druggan, William
("Klondike") O'Donnel, George ("Red") Barker, William "Three
Finger Jack" White, Joseph "Peppy" Genero, Leo Mongoven,
James "Fur" Sammons,

   The above list represents persons who are constantly in
conflict with the law.

BIRTH OF THE PUBLIC ENEMIES

THE TERM "Public Enemy" was first coined by Frank J. Loesh, president of the Chicago crime commission.

In late 1930, the commission urged an extensive crackdown on gangland after Lingle's murder. Loesh prepared a list of 28 of Chicago's most notorious gangsters and announced that henceforth these men were public enemies and should be treated as such and dealt with accordingly.

Judge John H. Lyle took up the challenge and issued vagrancy warrants against 26 of the named, two had been killed meanwhile, and directed the police to bring them all before the bar of his court. Once there he set bail at $50,000.

The 26 named on the crime commission list were:

(1) ALPHONSE CAPONE, alias Scarface, the worst of them all.

(2) RALPH CAPONE, brother of Al and his chief lieutenant.

(3) TONY "MOPS" VOLPE, a Capone bodyguard.

(4) FRANK RIO, another Capone bodyguard, who was his chief's companion for a year in a Philadelphia prison, where both had been sent for carrying concealed weapons.

(5) JAMES "KING OF THE BOMBERS" BELCASTRO, West Side hoodlum, bomber and labour racketeer.

(6) JACK DeMORE, alias Machine Gun Jack McGurn, the chief gunner of the Capone gang.

(7) DAGO LAWRENCE MANGANO, West Side gambling house keeper.

(8) JACK GUZIK, business manager for the Capone syndicate.

(9) FRANK DIAMOND, Capone gunman.

(10) GEORGE "BUGS" MORAN, leader of the North Side gang.

(11) JOSEPH AIELLO, head of seven brothers comprising the notorious Aiello clan, also of the North Side gang.

(12) EDWARD "SPIKE" O'DONNELL, a beer peddling boss on the South Side.

(13) POLACK JOE SALTIS, South Side beer chief.

(14) FRANK McERLAND, accused of several murders.

(15) VINCENT McERLAND, gangster brother of Frank.

(16) DANNY STANTON, Capone beer hustler and labour racketeer.

(17) WILLIAM "KLONDIKE" O'DONNELL, West Side beer peddler and labour racketeer.

(18) MYLES O'DONNELL, brother of Klondike, also a labour racketeer.

(19) FRANKIE LAKE, one of the first beer barons.

(20) TERRY DRUGGAN, of the lawless Druggans, partner of Frankie Lake.

(21) JAMES "FUR" SAMMONS, ex-convict, beer runner.

(22) GEORGE "RED" BARKER, ex-convict, the chieftain of the Capone labour racketeers.

(23) WILLIAM "THREE FINGERED" JACK WHITE, former convict, Capone labour agent.

(24) JOSEPH "PEPPY" GENERO, south suburban beer hustler for Capone.

(25) LEO MONGOVERN, former bodyguard for Bugs Moran.

(26) ROCCO FANNELI, hoodlum in the bloody 25th ward.

The phase "public enemies" caught the imagination of the American people, receiving widespread publicity. Newspapers emblazoned it across the front pages. The term was used for titles of books and movies. The crime commission reported that it "stirred the entire nation into action and gangdom began to feel the backlash of an aroused citizency."

Caught in the round-up were many important gangsters. Three Fingered Jack White was returned to prison for killing a policeman in 1924. Danny Stanton was extradited to Wisconsin to face a murder charge. James "Fur" Sammons was returned to the penitentiary to complete a sentence for murder. Extradition proceedings began against Tony "Mops" Volpe and James Belcastro. Jake Guzik was charged with income tax evasion.

Further lists were issued and by 1934, the crime commission was able to report that since 1930, 15 public enemies had been convicted, nine had died, one was awaiting deportation, eight were on trial, and the rest were "on the run because of the existence of various warrants against them."

The Chicago Crime Commission releases its first and famous Public Enemies List.

Source: Chicago Crime Commission Archives

After becoming the operating director of the Chicago Crime Commission in 1919, Henry Barrett Chamberlin supervised the CCC's staff, reported on the administration of criminal justice agencies in Chicago, and edited the CCC's journal Criminal Justice. Chamberlin orchestrated the CCC's anti-organized crime campaign in 1930.

Frank J. Loesch, the CCC's president from 1928 to 1937, led a delegation of prominent Chicago businessmen to meet with President Hoover on March 19, 1929. This meeting set in motion a movement against Al Capone involving federal authorities and Chicago's business elite. Loesch held joint memberships in the CCC and the Secret Six.

Samuel Insull, a public utilities magnate, broke a stalemate among six businessmen meeting at the Mid-Day Club in 1930. The men couldn't decide whether or not Chicago's organized crime problem warranted direct action until Insull pledged his financial support to start the Secret Six.

Julius Rosenwald, a great philanthropist and merchant, donated $25,000 to the Secret Six. Rosenwald held memberships in several private crime-fighting groups, including the CCC, the Secret Six, the Committee of Fifteen, and the Citizens' Committee to Enforce the Landis Award.

Source: Business Vs. Organized Crime by Dennis E. Hoffman

When he led the Secret Six into battle against Al Capone in 1930, Robert Isham Randolph sought to improve Chicago's reputation before the start of the 1933 World's Fair. Randolph was the only self-acknowledged member of the Secret Six.

Edward E. Gore, a public accountant, held joint memberships in the CCC and the Secret Six. Gore served as president of the Chicago Association of Commerce in 1922 and as president of the Chicago Crime Commission from 1926 to 1927. Like Paddock, Gore belonged to the Sons of the American Revolution.

George A. Paddock, a lawyer-turned-stock-broker, belonged to both the CCC and the Secret Six. Paddock was an extremely skillful fund-raiser, chairing the CCC's finance committee for ten years. Paddock founded the American Legion in Evanston, Illinois, and served as the president of the Sons of the American Revolution.

Al Capone, a major participant in the rampant violence and lawlessness that plagued Chicago in the 1920's, was the primary target of the Secret Six and the Chicago Crime Commission.

Source: Business Vs. Organized Crime by Dennis E. Hoffman

NEW SLAYINGS TO BEER FIGHT

McGurn Seized Again as Gangland Figures Are Sought by Squads.

TWO OTHERS MAY DIE

A police roundup of hoodlums was launched again today as they sought the machine gunners responsible for the Fox Lake beer war massacre last night in which three Chicago gangsters were killed and a woman was wounded.

Gunmen of the Capone and the Aiello-Zuta-Moran mobs were the ones the police were seeking principally, and one of the first to fall into their hands was Jack McGurn, corporal of the Capone machine-gun squad.

Charles Joey, a companion of McGurn; Frankie Foster, a north side hoodlum, and Izzy Alderman, identified as a minor figure in the rackets, were others gathered in.

Six Slain Over Week-End.

The Fox Lake killings during the night brought the death toll of gangsters to six in the last forty-eight hours, three other men dying in street executions.

McGurn had walked out of Criminal court only ten minutes before he was nabbed by Sergeants John Foley and Fred Hinkens. He had obtained another continuance of an old gun-toting charge and was driving at 22d street and Damen avenue when Foley and Hinkens grabbed him and oJey.

McGurn tried to talk himself out of the jam, but was taken to the station, where Capt. John Stege said he was not wanted for questioning in the Fox Lake affair.

He was booked on an open charge while his attorneys were scurrying around to get a writ of habeas corpus for his release.

Lieut. William Cusack and his squad saw three cars of gangsters in 22d street this afternoon and gave chase. In one of them, they said, was Frank Diamond and four other "hoods." Foster and Aldermen were alone in the other machines. Diamond and his companions got away, but Foster and Alderman were seized.

Lay Killings to Beer War.

The Fox Lake killings were laid today to a beer war that has been brewing between the Capone gang and the followers of Aiello, Zuta and Moran. Coupled with the massacre was an outbreak of killings here and in Detroit, which led Capt. Stege to believe another war is on for control of the Union Siciliane throughout the country.

"Joe Aiello disappeared ten days ago," said Stege, "and when a hoodlum of that prominence goes into the basement, trouble is brewing."

The finding of the bullet-torn body of an unidentified man in an alley at 495 Milwaukee avenue and the death of a victim of Sunday's gun play in Washington square today brought the ganglan: death toll to six within forty-eight hours.

Separate Gangs Involved.

The fact that the three men slain and the fourth man wounded in the Fox Lake massacre, which occurred early yesterday in Manning's hotel near Fox Lake, were all members or leaders of separate gangs was one of the chief puzzles to the authorities.

George Druggan, who was wounded, probably fatally, has taken over most of the territory in which his more notorious brother, Terry, made his fortune in beer.

Sam Pellar, who was slain, was one of the Eller militia, was once a bodyguard for Hymie Weiss, and lately had been playing about the fringes of the Capone camp.

The other two men slain were Joe Bertsche, a safe-blower, an ex-convict; brother of Barney Bertsche, and lately active in west side beer circles, and Micky Quirk, who quit a job as an express truck driver to join "Klondike" O'Donnell's mob and to wind up in the big money and the big headlines as a machine gunner's victim.

Mrs. Vivian McGinnis, wife of Arthur McGinnis, a Chicago attorney, was the fifth victim of the shooting at Manning's hotel. She may recover.

Druggan is known to have run afoul of the Capone beer interests both in Chicago and Cicero. He and henchmen of "Scarface" Al Capone, the jailbird and brothel keeper, have clashed several times in the section south of 18th and Halsted streets and Druggan is known to have muscled in his beer in several speakeasies in Cicero, which is territory claimed by Ralph Capone.

Lake County Competition.

Then there is the theory that the beer situation in Lake county may have accounted for the shooting. The Aiello-Zuta-Moran gang has long had an interest in the summer beer trade in the Fox Lake resort region. They have a headquarters at Grass Lake, about five miles from the scene of the massacre. Druggan and his allies, who once operated extensively in Dupage county, might have had designs on the lucrative beer business which Moran and a Lake county native, Ray Pregenzer, have been enjoying for several years.

Moran's machine gunners would have had but a few minutes' run if they were the ones who staged the massacre. Frank Quirk, a brother of the slain Mickey, was found at Cassidy's resort, the Moran gang headquarters, shortly after the shooting, another factor that indicated the Moran gang might have had no share in the multiple killing.

Union Guard Theory.

A third theory on which the authorities were working was based on information that union chieftains, alarmed at the threat of invasion by gangsters whose rackets were bringing them less money than heretofore, formed a defense squad.

The squad, backed by a $100,000 jackpot, the authorities were told, was made up of four former service men, men without gang alliances or criminal connections and backed by the moral suasion that the gangsters they were fighting were enemies, not only of union labor but of society at large.

A fourth theory, advanced by Chief Stege, held that Bertsche might have been the target of the machine gunners.

news
6-2-30

Source: Chicago Daily News, June 2, 1930. Reproduced with permission of the Chicago Sun-Times.

6,000 SALOONS PILE UP CASH FOR HOODLUMS

15,000 Regular Outlets Dispense 75,000 Gallons of Alcohol.

2,000 HANDBOOKS OPEN

Six million dollars a week for Chicago's racketeers—for the Capones, Aiellos, Gusicks and Morans.

Six million dollars a week as the war chest whence comes the money that corrupts politicians, police and prohibition agents.

Six thousand speakeasies doing business as usual. Two thousand handbooks running unmolested. At least 2,000 disorderly houses going their shady way.

And thirty-nine racket murders this year and none of them solved.

The slaying of Alfred ("Jake") Lingle, Chicago Tribune reporter, has prompted The Daily News to make inquiry as to just how much money is at stake in the control of the booze, vice and gambling rackets.

The results of the inquiry are printed herewith—with the figures in all cases on a conservative basis.

Revenue of Gangland.

The information was gathered from widespread sources on the strict understanding that no names would be quoted as authority. Here are the weekly figures of the money which goes to the racketeers:

Beer, booze, alky	$3,510,000
Gambling houses and handbooks	1,250,000
Disorderly houses, call flats, shady hotels	1,000,000
Labor rackets, bombings, arson, kidnapings and other crimes	500,000
Total	**$6,260,000**

There are 6,000 speakeasies operating normally in Chicago. At election times when votes and campaign contributions are needed the number goes skyrocketing up beyond the 10,000 mark, as high, according to some prohibition officials, as 12,000, but in the normal week of the average month some 6,000 speakeasies, where draft beer, whisky and gin may be had, are operating.

These speakeasies average, men in the racket say, six barrels of beer and two cases of whisky a week.

Boost Price of Beer.

The racket beer costs $55 a barrel, although Harry Gusick and Hymie Levine, the white slavers who are now collecting for "Scarface Al" Capone in the loop, have hiked the price to $60 a barrel. But the average price throughout the city is $55 a barrel.

Whisky costs the saloonkeeper, where the major mobs are in control, $90 a case. These same spots also peddle gin, and many of them peddle the concoction known as yockey-dock, or Polish pop, a synthetic whisky with alcohol as its base and so differentiated from the "moon" sold in some beer flats, which is a distilled liquor

Including the 6,000 speakeasie there are some 15,000 places in the city which are outlets for alcohol. Drug stores which peddle gin, cigar stores which peddle gin, beer flats with gin or the yockey-dock (alcohol colored with caramel) and sometimes flavored with bourbon essence.

By and large, the speakeasies, drug stores, gin mills, not to mention the peripatetic bootlegger who operates in some of the apartment house and hotel districts average five gallons of alcohol a week. And there are 15,000 outlets of this kind. That's 75,000 gallons of alcohol a week.

The best grain alcohol is almost unknown to the Chicago bootleg trade, despite assurances from druggists and other bootleggers. The stuff being sold is corn sugar alcohol, run through a column still to rid it of nauseous odors, and selling to these outlets at an average of $6 a gallon.

Table of Income.

Here's a table—based on a week:

Beer—6,000 places, 6 barrels a week, at $55 a barrel	$1,980,000
Booze—6,000 places, 2 cases a week, $90 a case	1,080,000
Alcohol, gin, yockey, etc., 15,000 places, 5 gallons a week, $6 a gallon	450,000
Total booze bill	**$3,510,000**

Of course, this isn't all profit. But beer can be made at $7 a barrel—

that's a spread of $48 a barrel for profits, protection and the hiring of gunmen such as killed Jake Lingle.

Real Whisky? Never!

Whisky such as the major mobs sell is far from being the real Canadian. The practice is to cut it three ways, using one-third Canadian; one-third 90-proof alcohol, one-third water—and not always distilled water.

Canadian whisky, up to the recent ban on exports to the United States, cost a large operator about $45 a case. Twenty-four pints equal three gallons. For the new Capone case, then, figure $15 as the cost of the whisky base, alcohol 90 cents or a dollar and the bottles twice as much, or about $20 a case cost at the most for stuff that the loop speakeasy operator is forced to pay $90 a case for.

Big Alcohol Profits.

The alcohol situation is even more murderous, so far as profit is concerned.

Operators of any size figure they can make moonshine alcohol—distilled from corn sugar—at 60 cents a gallon. The topside cost would be $1 a gallon. And the prices to the 15,000 outlets range from $4 a gallon up to $8 and $9.

Of course, there are politicians, policemen and prohibition agents to "take care of," but the profits are large enough to do that.

There are about fifty large gambling spots around town, luxurious affairs for the high-class trade, that bounce hither and yon, now in a hotel, now in a residence, now here, now there. These average a net of about $5,000 a week.

Two Thousand Handbooks Flourish.

There are at least 2,000 handbooks in Chicago. By that it is meant places where racing service—the Central News Service, owned by Mose Annenberg—can be had. There are at least 10,000 places in Chicago where a bet can be placed on the horses—cigar stores, barber shops, news stands—and there are other thousand agents, ranging from a smart office boy on up, who will run to the nearest handbook with a wager and receive for his service 5 cents on each dollar bet.

The 2,000 handbooks net an average of about $500 a week each. They have to make big money, for Annenberg's racing service, a monopoly enforced by the police, charges them from $35 a week up as high as $125, depending on the size of the place for the service, which includes the morning line, the jockeys, the post line and the call of the race.

Source: Chicago Daily News, June 13, 1930. Reproduced with permission of the Chicago Sun-Times.

Chicago Daily Tribune (1872-1963); Sep 26, 1930; ProQuest Historical Newspapers Chicago Tribune (1849 - 1985) pg. 1

2 CENTS PAY NO MORE!

Chicago Daily Tribune
THE WORLD'S GREATEST NEWSPAPER

FINAL EDITION

VOLUME LXXXIX.—NO. 231 C   FRIDAY, SEPTEMBER 26, 1930.—48 PAGES   **   PRICE TWO CENTS

CAPONE ALLIES SEIZED BY U. S.

Harry and Sam Guzik Held on Tax Charge

(Pictures on back page.)

Harry and Sam Guzik, brothers of Jack Guzik, one of the 26 public enemies named by the Chicago crime commission, were seized last night by agents of the special intelligence unit of the bureau of internal revenue on warrants charging violation of federal income tax laws. The two are aligned with Jack in his activities as business manager of the Capone beer and liquor interests.

A chauffeur for the Guziks was arrested by a squad from the detective bureau and held incommunicado.

Harry Guzik is said to be collector for Capone interests in the loop. Although no warrant has been issued for him in the campaign of State's Attorney Swanson against hoodlums through the vagrancy act, he has been sought by the police with his brother, Sam, for prosecution under the act.

Convicted as Pander; Pardoned.

Harry achieved notoriety in 1923 when he was convicted as a pander. With his wife, Anna, he was found guilty of selling a country girl to the vice system. They were freed through pardons by former Gov. Small before they began serving their sentences. Since then Harry has risen in the Capone ranks to the most important post under that of his brother, Jack. Sam Guzik, the police say, is a lieutenant of Harry. The two have been shadowed for three weeks by Agents C. L. Converse and N. E. Tessem. Twice they eluded capture by the nimble maneuver of dodging out secret exits as the agents guarded other exits.

Captured in Cafe Speakeasy.

Last night the agents trailed the pair to a restaurant at 1215 South Wabash avenue, said to be one of the headquarters of Capone's gang. The brothers were seated at a table in the rear of the restaurant, a speakeasy, when the agents entered.

As the two Guziks were taken prisoner Harry asked, "What do you want us for?"

"Income tax," Converse replied.

"O, I thought you was vagin' us," Harry said with a sigh of relief.

Converse explained that since the drive on hoodlums under the vagrancy act a new word has been coined in gangdom. The word is "vagin'," which means that a gangster is being sought on a warrant in the new campaign.

Chauffeur Also Seized.

The chauffeur who was arrested is Robert Burton. He gave his address as 2128 South Wabash avenue. The arrest was made while Burton was seated in a car near the restaurant where the Guzik brothers were seized.

Harry and Sam were taken to the bureau of internal revenue, where they were questioned. Agents refused to reveal whether the men are wanted for failure to file income tax schedules or for making fraudulent returns. The agents also refused to name specific amounts.

The brothers are to be arraigned before United States Commissioner Edwin K. Walker this morning. Converse said that the government would ask high bonds for the men. The evidence against the pair will be presented to the federal grand jury and will not be released until indictments are returned, the agents said.

Notifies Police of Arrests.

Following the questioning, Converse notified Chief of Detectives Norton that he had the men in custody. He said that the police could have an opportunity to take the Guziks if they were wanted. Harry and Sam Guzik were not listed in the 26 vagrancy warrants issued recently for "public enemies" by Municipal Judge John H. Lyle, although Jack Guzik's name was well up on the list.

Other hoodlums taken by Converse and his squad and indicted after the presentation of income tax evidence

(Continued on page 2, column 5.)

PROMINENT VAGRANT IN HIS TROPHY ROOM

Source: Courtesy of Chicago Tribune Archives.   *Article continues on next page.*

Article continues from previous page.

FEDERAL AGENTS CAPTURE TWO OF GUZIK BROTHERS

(Continued from first page.)

by United States Attorney George E. Q. Johnson are Terry Druggan, Frankie Lake, Frank Nitti, and Ralph Capone, who was convicted. Politicians indicted on income tax charges include Assessor Gene Oliver, also convicted, and Lawrence C. O'Brien.

From this federal contribution toward cleaning up Chicago Converse declared that the Guzik brothers have more to worry about as a result of the government action than they would have if sought on vagrancy warrants. The Guzik family is completed by a fourth brother, Joe Guzik, handbook operator, who is not wanted by the government at present, Converse said.

Earlier in the evening Pat Roche, chief investigator for the state's attorney, and Special Assistant State's Attorney Charles F. Rathbun, in charge of the Lingle murder investigation, swooped down on Calumet City in a series of raids. The investigators found vice dens sandwiched between rows of speakeasies, they said. All were deserted and gave evidence of a hasty evacuation. No arrests were made.

Willie Jackson, sought as one of the owners of the machine guns used in the St. Valentine's day massacre, was arrested in Niles last night by Sergt. Daniel Madigan of Roche's staff. Jackson was taken to the office of the investigators while they were making the Calumet City raids. In their absence he was not questioned and was placed in a cell in the detective bureau.

The guns used in the massacre were sold by Peter Von Frantzius shortly before the seven Moran gangsters were shot. They were traced a year ago to James Shupe and Jackson, owner of a roadhouse on the River road in Schiller Park.

VICE RING AGENTS SEIZED BY GOVERNMENT.
Harry Guzik (left, seated) and Sam Guzik, brothers of Jack Guzik, Capone lieutenant and public enemy. Harry was pardoned by former Gov. Small after his conviction as a pander. *(Story on page 1.)*

Source: Courtesy of Chicago Tribune Archives.

Chicago Daily Tribune (1872-1963); Sep 26, 1930; ProQuest Historical Newspapers Chicago Tribune (1849 - 1985) pg. 1

Chicago Daily Tribune

THE WORLD'S GREATEST NEWSPAPER

FINAL EDITION

2 CENTS PAY NO MORE!

VOLUME LXXXIX.—NO. 231   C   FRIDAY, SEPTEMBER 26, 1930.—48 PAGES   ✱ ✱   PRICE TWO CENTS

CAPONE ALLIES SEIZED BY U. S.

RAIDERS FIND POLICE FILE IN GANG HANGOUT

Secret Paper Lists 31 for Arrest.

Hidden under a pillow in a south side hotel, reputed to be a Capone gang hangout, a secret police department list of thirty-one hoodlums scheduled for arrest was found by federal agents yesterday. Besides the name of each gangster, racketeer, or pander appeared the names of a policeman or policemen who had arrested him before and who will be expected to do so again, the next time serving a new vagabond warrant.

The government agents were searching for Frank Nitti, Capone bookkeeper and treasurer, who is under indictment for income tax evasion. Believing that Al Capone, his brother, Ralph, and the golfbag gunman, Sam Hunt, might also be found, A. P. Madden and Clarence Converse of the special intelligence unit, bureau of internal revenue, led the raid which took them through the five story Carleon hotel at 2138 South Wabash avenue.

Find Secret Police Document.

From top to bottom the agents and two detective bureau squads roamed the place, encountering 12 men and a bevy of women, but no gangsters. Working down from the top floor, Converse, however, finally arrived at room 204. Within lay Tony Tagenti, a Capone bondsman, who said he was suffering from the influenza.

Converse slid his hand beneath Tagenti's pillow searching for a gun, and withdrew the folded police memorandum.

He scanned it a moment with Police Lieut. Walter Storms.

"Where did you get this?" Converse asked Tagenti.

"I don't know a thing about it," said Tagenti. "This is my office here, but I didn't even know that thing was around."

Ryan Tells of Document.

Converse took the document to the detective bureau, where Deputy Chief Ryan said it was a copy of a memorandum he had dictated on Sept. 18 and of which he had ordered four copies made. Two of these copies, Ryan said, were for his own office, one for Chief Norton and another for the newly formed vagrancy bureau, Acting Commissioner Alcock's own department for the elimination, by way of the rock pile, of Chicago's public enemies and undesirables.

Ryan said his two copies were safe. He declared he had taken one to Chief Norton who directed him to give it and the remaining copy to Attorney William Luthardt, head of the vagrancy bureau. Last night Norton displayed little interest in the list.

"I don't know what kind of a list it is," he said, "and I know damn well it isn't my list." Chief Norton denied that Converse had even given him the list seized in the raid, but the government man said he placed it in Norton's hands.

Nobody Wants Prisoners.

While the detective bureau was seething with talk of the discovery Tagenti and the eleven other men taken from the hotel were fingerprinted and left in cells without being questioned. Converse said he did not want the prisoners and Lieut. Storms approached Chief Norton for instructions.

"If the government men don't want them, turn them out except those with records," said Norton.

Tagenti and nine others then went their way while Milton Edwards and Frank Bell, the former once fined for disorderly conduct and the latter charged with burglary, were held. Forty-five minutes later they, too, were released on bonds.

Planned for the secret information of the police department, awaiting the time when the vagabond warrants were ready for issuance, the list of hoodlums had never been posted at the detective bureau.

The Secret Memorandum.

Following is the confidential list, just as it was prepared, with the names of the policemen scheduled to make the arrests following those of the hoodlums to be arrested:

"DETECTIVE BUREAU.

"Sept. 18, 1930.

"Memorandum from the deputy chief of detectives to the chief of detectives:

"Subject: Well known racketeers and gunmen. Following is a list of well known racketeers and gunmen for whom vagrancy writs may issue:

"Mike Heitler, alias 'Mike De Pike,' racketeer and pander.—Lieuts. Byrnes and O'Brien, D. B. [detective bureau].

"Nick Kramer, beer runner and pal of Joe Saltis.—Sergt. Roza, D. B.

"James Joyce, beer runner and pal of Joe Saltis.—Sergt. Tom Curtin, D. B.

"Sol 'Solly' Vision, racketeer and pander, pal of Jack Zuta.—Lieut. Andy Barry, D. B.

"Albert Ruggio, racketeer and gunman.—Officer W. Carney, D. B.

"Sam Kaplan, racketeer and gunman.—Lieut. [Phil] Carroll, D. B.

"Martin O'Leary, racketeer and gunman.—Officer A. Mahoney.

"George Vogel, alias Legge, racketeer and beer runner—Sergts. Murphy and McSwiggin [father of the murdered assistant state's attorney].

"E. Cook, alias Butch, racketeer and beer runner—Sergts. Murphy and McSwiggin.

"John Began, racketeer and beer runner—Sergt. Kakacek, 21st district.

"Ernest Fontana, beer runner—Officer Frank Fuerst, D. B.

"Thomas Abbott, racketeer and stickup man [now thought taken for a ride]—Officer T. Lamie, D. B.

"Joe Fiore, racketeer and stickup man—Officer E. Piesta.

"Rocco Rocuna, racketeer and stickup man—Capt. James Fleming, 32d district.

"Jack Sopkin, racketeer and stickup man—Lieut. McGinnis.

"Frank Panio, beer runner—Sergt. Roy Crane, D. B.

"Frank Berman, racketeer and stickup man—Officer J. Kerch, 36th district, and Officer Tom Alcock, D. B. [nephew of the acting commissioner].

"Ralph Scala, beer runner and racketeer—Officer William O'Donnel, Maxwell.

Source: Courtesy of Chicago Tribune Archives.   *Article continues on next page.*

Article continues from previous page.

" James Pelcere, racketeer and stick-up man—Officer William O'Donnel.

" Steve Oswald, racketeer and beer runner—Sergt. Roza.

" Nick Valeta, racketeer and gunman—Officer T. Lamie.

" Max Eisen, labor racketeer—Officer Mahoney.

" William Diggs, labor racketeer and arrested with gun—Officer Helster. [Diggs is a brother-in-law of the slain Big Tim Murphy.]

" Mike Carrozza, labor racketeer—Drury and Howe, D. B. [Carrozza is president of the street sweepers' union.]

" William ' Dutch ' Emmerling, racketeer and bomber—Sergt. Roza.

" Dan McGeoghegan, racketeer—Lieut. Walter Storms. [McGeoghegan was once under sentence of death with Henry 'Midget' Fernekes for murder.]

" William 'Bubs' Quinlan, Saltis racketeer and hoodlum—Sergt. McFadden.

" Dominick Nuccio, racketeer and gunman for Capone—Lieut. Andy Barry.

" Paul Swain, racketeer and beer runner—Sergt. Ray Kilgore, 29th district.

" Harry Brown, alias ' Frisco Dutch,' racketeer—Lieutenants Byrnes and O'Brien.

" Red Bolton, racketeer and beer runner—Lieut. William Cusack, Des Plaines."

The federal raid was the result of undercover information gained through several weeks' observation by Converse, ace of the internal revenue intelligence investigators. Disguised in corduroy trousers, slouch hat, and worn work shirt, Converse had posed as a " gandy dancer," or track laborer, in the Carleon hotel neighborhood and had the opportunity to learn that Nitti, wanted under a delinquent income tax indictment, frequented the place.

Yesterday Chief Madden Converse, and four or five of Madden's agents went to the detective bureau and obtained Chief Norton's consent to use two police squads under command of Lieut. Storms for surrounding and searching the hotel.

$55,725 IN REWARDS.

Rewards totaling $55,725 are offered for information leading to the arrest and conviction of the slayer of Alfred Lingle. Of the $25,000 reward offered by The Tribune, $10,000 will be paid to any person who will give confidential information identifying the slayer of Lingle. All information should be sent to the headquarters established by State's Attorney Swanson in room 503 Temple building, 77 West Washington street. Telephone State 3729.

About 2 p. m. the agents and squads reached the hotel. Two policemen and a federal agent were placed in front, a similar trio in the rear, and more squads were posted on the roof. Chief Madden covered the lobby himself and Converse, Storms, and the others began the systematic search of the thirty-five rooms. The rooms were tenanted by more than thirty women.

The room where Tagenti was lying appeared to be an office for the hotel, which, Converse says, is owned by Dennis Cooney. Cooney was not present, and no records could be found which would disclose the ownership. At the telephone switchboard downstairs was tacked a cardboard list of girls' names, an index, apparently, to the whereabouts of others who could be called in.

Serritella Arrives on Scene.

While the hubbub attending the transfer of the prisoners to the bureau was at its height, City Sealer Dan Serritella and Attorney Tyrell Richardson arrived.

Converse and Madden have been seeking Nitti for some weeks. A raid last week on the Lexington hotel, 22d street and Michigan avenue, the reputed headquarters of the Capone gang, was staged when evidence reached the government that Nitti was hiding there. No gangsters were seized.

Source: Courtesy of Chicago Tribune Archives.

DAILY TIMES, CHICAGO, SATURDAY, FEBRUARY 21, 1931

CAPONE
PUBLIC ENEMY NO. 1
How Much Longer Can He Get Away With It?

Yesterday Mr. Doherty painted Dion O'Banion as Chicago knew him, and told of his abrupt departure from the business of selling flowers and hijacking booze.

Three of "them Sicilians" he didn't like came into his florist shop, across from the Holy Name cathedral—and while one of them shook the hand that had shaken the life out of so many, the other two handed O'Banion the works. One gave him the mercy shot—to make sure he was dead. Then they ducked.

By EDWARD DOHERTY

FOR days after O'Banion's erasure from Chicago gangland, all one heard was what a swell guy he had been, how good he was to his folks, how nice he was to his wife, how many people he had helped, and how much his coffin and all the other funereal doo-dads cost.

Talk of his private cemetery, conversation about his crazy itching trigger finger, whispers about his safe-cracking and drunk-rolling days, were taboo.

No! No! Them devilish wops had killed the best guy on earth—now get together and give them the works.

O'Banion, shortly before he died, had blasted "them Sicilians."

His followers took him at his word and vowed to blast them, each one looking like a commercial map filled with red dots.

O'Banion Followers
Stage Greatest Funeral

There was a truce, for a few days. The boys had to expend their grief before they took vengeance. They had to see the earth fall on the coffin before they went gunning for the murderers. The main thing was to give Dion the greatest funeral any Chicago white man ever had. After that—the limit.

So they got a coffin for him. They bought it in Philadelphia and shipped it by fast express. And it was said to have cost $10,000.

I can't tell you whether it was a better coffin than the one Rudolph Valentino used in his last appearance. I didn't see it. But from all accounts it was an exquisite silver-gray box grand enough even for such a wonderful fellow as O'Banion.

And there were solid gold candlesticks, I'm told, with the regulation angels on them, and soft lights, and Dion's face fixed pretty by a sorrowing undertaker, and music that expressed the grief of all the family and friends—and crowds and crowds and crowds.

Dion was exhibited to the vulgar gaze for two or three days—and so insatiable was the curiosity of Chicago citizens to look upon the angelic countenance that the police had to keep order among them.

The cardinal refused to let Dion's intimates bury him with the rites of the church or to place him in consecrated ground.

The body was taken from Sbarbaro's undertaking rooms and borne to the unconsecrated part of Mt. Carmel cemetery.

There were more than 100 funeral cars in the procession. There were hundreds of private cars. There were twenty-six truckloads of flowers.

There were gun guys aplenty. If there was one gunman in Chicago who wasn't present at the funeral chapel or the grave, it was because he was sick or out of town or busy hijacking.

All the big-shots might be seen there and some of them were weeping like kids. There were enough gangsters present to give any city gangrene.

By a sort of mutual agreement none of the hoodlums wore their side arms —well, each had but one gun with him during the long ride out to the grave yard. After the body was lowered into the earth they got the rest of their equipment from their gun bearers— those youngsters who stood in the background during the reciting of prayers.

—well, each had but one gun with him during the long ride out to the grave yard. After the body was lowered into the earth they got the rest of their equipment from their gun bearers— those youngsters who stood in the background during the reciting of prayers.

Fully 5,000 Citizens
Attended Funeral

Fully 5,000 citizens of Chicago attended the funeral, the newspapers declared, and among them were some of the high and mighty of the town.

How O'Banion would have laughed if he could have seen the turnout!

O'Banion, petty thief, clumsy peter man, unscrupulous killer, buried as though he had been a hero!

The widow put up a costly monument to "My Sweetheart," but the cardinal caused it to be taken down.

But the gang gave him another monument—a pile of Sicilian bodies. And no doubt, O'Banion would have got more of a kick out of that if he could have known.

One Louie Alterie, a lippy guy who called O'Banion his best pal, wished to meet at State and Madison sts., the busiest corner in the world, the cowards who had killed "poor Dion."

Article continues on next page.

Source: Chicago Daily Times. Reproduced with permission of the Chicago Sun-Times.

Article continues from previous page.

It was a typical gang introduction and farewell.

O'Banion fell with five bullets in him, one in his head—and as he lay on the floor one of the three bent over him and gave him the so-called mercy shot—the shot in the head that excuses all lesser wounds.

I can't say whether or not Mike Merlo got his flowers. The men who had come to buy them didn't wait. They were outside in a few seconds, and speeding down the street in one of a dozen or more cars that had been hanging around the shop, waiting to make good the get-away.

Capone, Torrio, Frankie Yale were all mentioned in the investigations that followed. But nobody went to jail.

(Copyright, 1931)

Tomorrow's installment deals in part with the funeral of O'Banion, which was at once the sensation and the scandal of Chicago, and the brash words of one Louis Alterie, at present out west "for his health."

HALF-WORLD JARGON

A gangster's pal understands him, perhaps, but the rank and file of honest, home-loving citizens wouldn't know what he was talking about. Here's a key:

Weeded: Loot from which one has taken more than his share.

"By the time we get back the stuff's weeded."

Kosher: One above reproach.

"Trust him—he's kosher."

Labor-skate: Union racketeer.

"Joe's making big dough now. He's a labor skate."

Shakester: One who extorts.

"He's shakester for a labor-skate."

Lifeboat: Pardon, parole or commutation of sentence.

"Take the rap and we'll buy you a lifeboat."

McCoy or McMann: Genuine bonded liquor.

"You guys don't even know a McMann when you taste it."

Woody: Crazy.

"Never trust a woody. You'll get jammed."

Meshuka: Insane.

"He's used snow till he's meshuka."

Noble: Armed guard for scabs.

"So two nobles hold the labor skates off till the bulls come."

Sister-in-law: A hoodlum's second choice woman when he has two working for him.

"His broad don't squeak when he starts with the sister-in-law."

The State st. florist shop where Dion O'Banion's career came to an end. The picture was made a few minutes after the murder. James Genna, the last of the five Genna brothers, from whom O'Banion hi-jacked liquor, is shown in the inset.

What it was all about—bootleg brew. Here's a Capone beer layout raided in the Loop.

A Capone beer layout raided in the Loop.

Source: Chicago Daily Times

CHARGES CAPONE PUT UP $260,000 TO AID THOMPSON

Loesch Avers Bargain for Gangdom "Rights."

How much did Scarface Al Capone contribute to Mayor Thompson's campaign fund four years ago?

The sum contributed in the primary was $50,000, according to Judge John H. Lyle, who is combating the Thompson-Capone forces in the present campaign. But Frank J. Loesch of the national and Chicago crime commissions said yesterday that Capone contributed a total of $260,000 in the primary and election campaigns to insure the election of Thompson.

The deal, according to Mr. Loesch and the records of this investigation, was that Capone should have the undisputed right to run houses of prostitution and gambling houses, to operate slot machines, and control the sale of beer and booze in all the territory of the city south of Madison street."

Mayoralty Practically Purchased.

Mr. Loesch began his investigation as a special assistant attorney general and continued it as first assistant state's attorney and during the year he was so engaged he said he heard considerable about Capone's relations with Thompson. The mayoralty was practically purchased at that time with money taken from prostitutes and with booze and slot machine profits, the Loesch archives allege.

"Homer Galpin was then head of the Thompson organization and he fled from Chicago and remained away more than eighteen months to avoid being questioned before the grand jury," said Mr. Loesch yesterday in a message from Washington. "He is still away, fearful of being questioned about the money accepted by the Thompson machine. We wanted to know how much of Capone's money was given to Thompson and Galpin to Boss Morris Eller of the Bloody Twentieth ward. Galpin is still away, not daring to return."

Staff Recalls Alleged Deal.

The history of the Capone-Thompson deal, as recalled by the Loesch staff, was as follows:

"State's Attorney Crowe and Sheriff Graydon had control of the county, outside Chicago, and Capone's field of operations was limited to that territory while Dever was mayor. Capone had brothels, slot machines and liquor rights. A huge amount of money was needed to defeat Dever, who was honestly trying to stop crime and prevent gang rule.

"'Money was ladled out to Thompson workers from a bathtub in the Hotel Sherman, filled with packages of $5 bills,' committeemen declared.

"Thompson was elected and immediately Capone took over the south side, with all privileges. His man Mondi opened a gambling joint on Clark street, south of Madison street. Crowe was still state's attorney. Capone took over beer territories from the Saltis and O'Donnell gangs. The slot machine racket later involved the indictment of six police captains. Capone got more than the $260,000 back.

Fights to Retain Crowe.

"Then Crowe was a candidate for reëlection as state's attorney, and Thompson was anxious to keep him in office, saying publicly, 'Another state's attorney might indict me.' Thompson wanted to reëlect his faithful ward committeemen, including Eller. On primary day Octavius Granady, only oponent of Eller, was killed.

"The public was aroused and the Loesch investigating staff was given authority to proceed. The Thompson officials were swept out of office, including Crowe, but the power of Thompsonism remained and Capone flourished until recently, when Loesch and Lyle joined forces to wage war on him."

The Loesch reports show that Capone, in the second year of Thompson's present administration, started encroaching on territories north of Madison street and the Valentine day massacre resulted. So powerful was Capone that police captains who would not grant him every concession were banished, according to investigators for Loesch.

GANGDOM IS CAMPAIGN ISSUE

AL CAPONE.

MAYOR THOMPSON.
[Photo by Hearst's Evening American.]

Frank J. Loesch charges that the Capone gang contributed slush funds totaling $260,000 to elect Thompson mayor in his last campaign. Judge Lyle says Capone has put up $150,000 in this campaign.

Capone, Sentenced, Faces More Woe
Chicago Daily Tribune (1872-1963); Feb 28, 1931; ProQuest Historical Newspapers Chicago Tribune (1849 - 1985) pg. 1

Capone, Sentenced, Faces More Woe

GETS 6 MONTHS IN JAIL; BLOW TO GANG POWER

U. S. Works on His Income Taxes.

(Pictures on back page.)

George E. Q. Johnson, federal district attorney, marked the opening of his second term by scoring the conviction of Al Capone yesterday as the eighth of his successful prosecutions of personages in the Chicago politico-crime alliance.

JUDGE WILKERSON.

Promptly following the sentencing of Capone to six months in the county jail for contempt of court the news trickled out of Mr. Johnson's offices that Capone is confronting only the first of his troubles with the government. It was reported, quite unofficially, that income tax investigators are completing the network of evidence which will result in the indictment of Capone. If Mr. Johnson maintains the "100 per cent" standard of successful convictions thus far achieved, Capone is regarded as a certainty for Leavenworth penitentiary.

Gangster Power on Wane.

That the wane of gangster authority in Chicago is apparent appears in the legal processes now at work. Judge Wilkerson, in sentencing Capone to jail for six months, indicated that this sentence should begin before July.

Before the release of Capone at Christmas time federal authorities believe an indictment will be returned charging the gang boss with failure to account to Uncle Sam for enormous illicit profits.

So far United States Attorney Johnson's income tax war against the hoodlums has set the "100 per cent standard." His war upon hoodlums has had these results:

RALPH CAPONE, sentenced to three years in prison.

FRANK NITTI, serving eighteen months in prison.

JACK GUZIK, sentenced to five years in prison.

SAM GUZIK, indicted, and HARRY GUZIK, scheduled to be indicted.

TERRY DRUGGAN, pleaded guilty, not sentenced.

FRANKIE LAKE, pleaded guilty, not sentenced.

This evidence that the Capone gang is skidding from its pinnacle was augmented yesterday by the ruling of Secretary of Labor Doak, who held that Tony [Mops] Volpe, another of Al's captains, must be deported.

Not only hoodlums but public officials have been gathered in the tax net. County Assessor Gene Oliver is under a three year sentence; State Representative Lawrence C. O'Brien must serve eighteen months. Contractors who fattened on sanitary district largess in the days of President Tim Crowe are indicted but not tried.

The power of the United States government to deal with the Capone gang and effect its gradual disintegration, authorities believe, has been demonstrated.

How Capone Was Sentenced.

The sentencing of Capone terminated a dramatic scene in the courtroom of Judge Wilkerson and the judgment came at the end of a 15 minute oral decision of the court which permitted of no doubt as to its conclusion.

The chief public enemy knew his fate even before his counsel, Benjamin P. Epstein, had concluded his final address to the court, for Judge Wilkerson sharply cut off the attorney at frequent intervals and assailed Capone's failure to take the stand and state the facts of his illness in Florida two years ago. An admittedly false affidavit made after this illness obtained a stay of Capone's appearance before the federal grand jury from Jan. 12 to Jan. 20, 1929.

Gangster Shows Anxiety.

The gangster, attired in a flashy brown suit, having worn blue and gray, respectively, the first two days, nervously shifted his position as the court recited the decision with vehemence.

"Upon the record as it stands in this case there is nothing the court can do but adjudge the respondent guilty as charged in the information," said the court. Clerk Joseph O'Sullivan and Bailiff Frank Otto arose and approached the bench, heralds of bad news for Capone.

Capone sat motionless, with rapt countenance, like his attorneys. Silence fell over the crowded courtroom and Judge Wilkerson continued:

"And as punishment for the contempt, the respondent shall be confined in the Cook county jail for a period of six months."

Length of Term a Blow.

Capone appeared stunned by the length of the sentence, but he pulled himself together, smiled broadly, and began chewing his gum. "If the judge thinks it's correct, he ought to know," he said as he left the courtroom. "You can't overrule the judge."

Judge Wilkerson recited the facts in the case, how Capone, on March 11, 1929, made an application for postponement of his appearance before the grand jury in a series of liquor violation cases and submitting at that time an affidavit stating:

"'That the respondent was then under professional treatment, and from Jan. 13, 1929, had been suffering from broncho-pneumonial pleurisy, with effusions of fluid in the chest cavity, and for six weeks had been confined to his bed at his home on Palm Island and had been out of his bed only for ten days last past.

Dangerous to Leave Florida.

"'His physical condition was such that it would be dangerous for him to leave the mild climate of southern Florida and go to Chicago, and that to do so would entail a grave risk of a relapse, which might result in his death from recurrent pneumonia.'

"The doctor [Kenneth Phillips] said he did not pay much attention to the affidavit when it was dictated by the lawyer. There is no contention, however, by the respondent, that he did not understand the allegations of the affidavit. On the contrary, he adopted it and sent it to Chicago to be used for the purpose indicated. Aside from the opinion of the doctor as to what was the matter with the respondent there were certain averments of fact in the affidavit which could not have escaped the attention of any one who had given casual consideration to the language.

"Dr. Phillips' testimony, of course, must be considered in the light of the telegram he sent to Dr. Omens [Capone's Chicago physician], in which he characterized the sickness of the respondent as not serious."

 Article continues on next page.

Article continues from previous page.

Not Confined to Bed.

The court then reviewed the testimony of Capone's two nurses, Ann Fagan and Nora Hawkins, both of whom left the Capone house by the last week of January. He recalled that against the testimony of these nurses that Capone did not leave his bed while they were there, "the evidence established beyond all possibility of doubt that during the month of February the respondent was not confined to his bed."

"The evidence shows during that period," he continued, "frequent attendance at the race track, shows trips in an airplane, shows a boat trip, and, taking all of this evidence, it is perfectly clear that, after at least the second of February [the airplane trip to Bimini], it could not be truthfully stated that he was confined to his bed, and that the statement made on March 5 that he had been out of bed only ten days last past was glaringly false."

Failed to Obey Court.

Referring to the false representation to the court for a postponement, Judge Wilkerson said:

"The point in this case is the effect of conduct of that kind upon the administration of justice. The situation would not have been changed, is not changed, by the action the court took with reference to the document. The point is that instead of obeying the process of the court, this affidavit, which contained false statements, was made and presented.

"The court deals with litigants, witnesses and jurors in only one way, and that is through the process of the court, and when that process is issued it is to be respected, it is to be obeyed, it is not to be trifled with, it is not to be flouted."

Attorney Epstein attempted to show that Capone was without knowledge of the facts stated in the affidavit and colloquy ensued between him and the court:

EPSTEIN—It is fundamental in the law of contempt that before one can be charged with a contemptuous act he must be shown to have had knowledge of the acts on which the contempt charge is predicated.

THE COURT — The affidavit was prepared in a law office, with a doctor and the respondent present.

EPSTEIN—He testified before the grand jury that he did not read it.

THE COURT—He hasn't said it here. He adopted it and defended it in this proceeding. The whole attitude of the defense has been an attempt to defend the truth of the affidavit, thus aggravating the offense.

No Word from Capone.

The defense attorney declared that the only positive testimony to the effect that Capone attended the races during February had been discredited, and Judge Wilkerson replied:

"The respondent has said nothing on this subject. In response to the rule entered here he has vouchsafed no information to the court as to whether he went to the races."

An ironic smile played upon the features of the judge as Attorney Epstein declared:

"There is no exertion in sitting at the races in that warm, tropical climate. As a matter of fact, physicians down there prescribe it."

Defense a Lost Cause.

The attorney asserted that the United States attorney's office didn't know what to do with Capone when he came here, that the Volstead act [Capone testified as to booze conditions] provided immunity for one testifying before the grand jury. Apparently realizing that the defense was a lost cause, he continued:

"Surely, your honor, the fact that the assistant district attorney admitted that Capone's appearance was not urgent, and the fact that he did appear on the date set by your honor, should have some weight in mitigation."

Prosecutor Jacob Grossman declared that the fact of Capone's ultimate appearance was not material, and he referred to the sentence of Harry F. Sinclair to six months for contempt.

"That charge grew out of the shadowing of jurors," he said. "The evidence showed that Sinclair had nothing to do with the shadowing, and that even the jurors were unaware of the attempt. None was shown to have been approached or intimidated.

"The Supreme court held that the tendency of the act must be considered. If people can do as they please, soon the processes of the court will be nullified, the business of the court thrown into confusion, and the court itself held in contempt."

Judge Wilkerson overruled a motion for a new trial, but granted a supersedeas, with Capone's $5,000 bond to stand, permitting an appeal. He declared, however, that he was restricting the ordinary provisions of a supersedeas in order that the case might be disposed of by the end of the court term, July 1. Unreasonable delay, he said, would destroy the effect of the punishment.

Only thirty days was permitted for the filing of a bill of exceptions, which means, according to the prosecutors, that the case will be disposed of by the April term of the Circuit Court of Appeals. Since wide discretion is permitted federal judges in contempt matters, there being no statutory limit on the fines and sentences that may be imposed, it is believed that Capone's chances of a reversal by the Appellate court are slight.

The gangster must appear again before Judge Wilkerson on Monday, when the order will be entered and a new bond provided. On Wednesday he is scheduled to appear before Judge Frank Padden of the Criminal court on a vagrancy charge.

Ready for Vagrancy Trial.

"I shall be very glad to try Capone on the vagrancy charge," said Assistant State's Attorney Harry Ditchburne yesterday. "He has had no legitimate occupation for years, and I believe that in view of his record, we can make a good showing against him."

However, because the Three Fingered Jack White murder case, scheduled for Monday, is to go ahead, Prosecutor Ditchburne said the Capone vagrancy case will have to be continued.

United State's Attorney Johnson gave full credit to Mr. Grossman for his successful prosecution of the Capone case, and praised the manner in which the trial was conducted by Judge Wilkerson.

Sheriff William D. Meyering issued the following statement:

"Custody of Al Capone for six months does not present any serious problem. The Cook county jail has a set of rules which apply equally to all federal prisoners committed there. These rules will not be changed because of the presence of Capone. He probably will be a tractable prisoner, especially after he finds that he is being treated just like any other prisoner. He will not be abused, neither will he be glorified."

Source: Courtesy of Chicago Tribune Archives.   *Article continues on next page.*

[TRIBUNE Photo.]

FALL OF PUBLIC ENEMY SEEN IN SIX MONTHS' PRISON SENTENCE. Rogues'
gallery picture of Al Capone, who was ordered imprisoned six months for contempt of court
by Judge James H. Wilkerson yesterday in the United States District court.
(Story on page 1.)

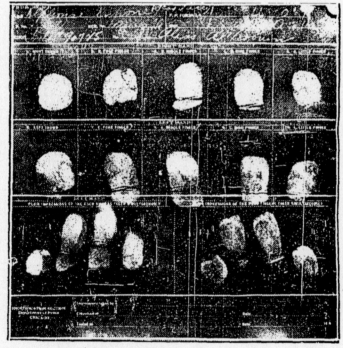

[TRIBUNE Photo.]

FINGERPRINTS OF FALLEN GANGLAND CHIEF.
While he was in the federal court Al Capone was arrested
as a vagrant and taken to the detective bureau, where the
usual methods were employed to enable his identification in
the future.　　*(Story on page 1.)*

Source: Courtesy of Chicago Tribune Archives

PUBLIC ENEMY HEARING IS SET FOR MARCH 20

AL CAPONE made another public appearance today—this time in the Felony court. He showed up on time, attracted a huge crowd and walked out within half an hour, because his vagrancy case was put over until March 20. He left as he came, escorted by a large police guard.

Perhaps the feature of the whole show was the avidity of the crowd in the courtroom and about the building. They pushed and shoved to get a squint at him.

Called by All His Aliases

"Al Brown, Alphonse Capone or Scarface Al," a clerk with a sense of dramatics boomed, as he called the case. Capone, shielded by his attorneys, Michael Ahern and Miles J. Devine, moved up to the bench.

After some dickering between Asst. State's Attys. Ditchburne and Brown, and the defense, it was agreed to continue the case.

"I have a motion to quash the evidence ready now, but I'll hold it until that time," Atty. Ahern said.

"Well, you can change it to apply to a new complaint then," Ditchburne said. "We will offer an amended complaint at that time. I can't go ahead with the case now because of the White case."

"The new complaint," added Mr. Ditchburne, "will include Capone's conviction in Philadelphia for carrying a concealed weapon."

Scramble to Get in Picture

Asst. State's Atty. Mast broke in to ask the proper name for the gang chieftain, calling attention to the three names on the original complaint.

"My client's name is Alphonse Capone," Atty. Ahern said, pronouncing the name to rhyme with stone, "He wants it understood he is not Al Brown, Scarface Al or anything else but Alphonse Capone."

This seemed to end the matter and newspaper photographers begged for a shot of Capone before the bench. There was a mad scramble of other persons to get in the picture with Al.

Crowd Disappointed Again

Those who missed the gangster as he came in and were waiting to see him as he left were disappointed, for he was led to a prisoner's elevator that took him to the first floor in the rear where he jumped into his own auto and sped away, followed by two squad

CAPONE WINS VAG STAY

Al Capone, gentleman of the underworld, steps into his swanky sedan after a court appearance. These petty harassments are such a bore.

(DAILY TIMES Photo)

cars. A third roared away a few moments later to catch up.

Capone was perfectly at ease. He was dressed in a blue chinchilla overcoat over a gray ensemble, which included hat, suit, spats and shirt. There was no pin in his solid blue tie, but a huge diamond shone on his left little finger.

Throws Crowd Off Scent

Flanked by 15 detectives, Capone, followed a few steps behind by Jack McGurn, had entered by the rear door of the Criminal court building.

The crowd that surged around the building was thrown off the scent momentarily by his avoiding the front door. A bureau squad car drove up to the front entrance and the crowd milled around it. At the same time, Capone was entering at the rear.

The building was guarded by the squad car details which had accompanied Capone from the Lexington hotel. Lieut. William McCarthy was in command.

Capone ascended to the fourth floor on a crowded elevator, Sergts. Daniel Healy and Roy Van Herik standing on each side of him. Van Herik signed the complaints on all of the vagrancy warrants issued for public enemies by Judge Lyle last September.

Clubwomen in Audience

A crowd, which soon became almost unmanageable, and which consisted largely of women, tried to break in the anteroom of the court.

A delegation from the Wicker Park Women's club, headed by Mrs. William E Padden, sister-in-law of the judge, was among them.

The crowd milled about the courtroom trying by various stratagems to

see the gang leader. Police were obliged to use force to keep the curious in order.

In the anteroom Capone posed for newspaper photographers with Asst. State's Atty. Mast. He was fingerprinted again before he went into the courtroom.

Charge Capone Gang Uses Poisoned Bullets

Washington, March 4 (AP).—A story of open-faced gangster activities, far-flung governmental corruption and wholesale liquor law violations was unrolled today before the senate.

Drawn from the files of the Wickersham commission by a senate resolution, the testimony spread through surveys of prohibition conditions in Illinois, New York, New Jersey, Louisiana and Colorado. Only in the latter state was dry law enforcement termed "satisfactory."

Some highlights in the mass of data were:

A gangster map of Chicago.

The names of 330 alleged Chicago "racketeers," 113 of them now 6 4 with each listed under such heading as "dynamiter and bomb thrower," or "booze and beer."

The reported discovery of "large quantities of poison tipped bullets," in the reputed headquarters of the Al Capone outfit.

SOLONS PROBE "U" RUM

Lansing, Mich., March 4 (AP).—Investigation of liquor conditions on the University of Michigan campus has been started by a house committee pledged to secrecy until it has rendered its report.

TIMES MAR 4 1931   MAR 4 1931

Chicago Daily Tribune (1872-1963); Jun 15, 1931; ProQuest Historical Newspapers Chicago Tribune (1849 - 1985) pg. 1

Capone, in Trap, Ponders Guilty Plea

TWICE INDICTED GANG CHIEF MAY GIVE UP BATTLE

Calls on Lawyers to Advise Him.

(Picture on back page.)

Al Capone's fate was in the hands of his lawyers yesterday. It was reported that he was considering payment of his debt to society without a fight—that pleas of guilty were being pondered by the gang leader and his attorneys on both the federal indictments that have been returned against him in the last few days.

One indictment charges Capone with the evasion of $215,000 in income taxes and the other charges him and 68 of his men with a ten year beer conspiracy in which they are alleged to have taken in gross receipts of $200,000,000.

The reports were that Capone was giving his lawyers some good reasons for entering pleas of guilty, and that, on the other hand, the lawyers and some of Capone's allies were pointing out certain dangers attendant on such pleas.

Johnson Declines Comment.

District Attorney George E. Q. Johnson, under whose direction the investigation of Capone was conducted, refused yesterday to discuss any possible compromises by the government.

Whatever Capone's decision, it will have to be made by tomorrow when he is to be arraigned before Federal Judge James H. Wilkerson on both indictments.

If Capone decides to face juries and is convicted on both the prohibition and income tax indictments, which the prosecutors regard as likely, he is liable to a maximum penalty of thirty-four years in prison and fines totaling $90,000. It is reported that this has caused the gangster to consider pleading guilty.

Concurrent Terms Probable.

On the other hand, lawyers are agreed that the government cannot hope for such a sentence and that the prison terms on the various counts will in all probability be made to run concurrently. As one government lawyer pointed out, " the charges against Capone involve only the tax laws and prohibition. He is not charged with murder as no doubt he ought to be."

It is reported that it is Capone's desire to plead guilty with the understanding that he is to serve a prison sentence, though not too long a one. A term of less than five years is his hope, it is said.

This was the punishment imposed on Jack Guzik, one of Capone's chief lieutenants, for income tax fraud, but the Guzik sentence followed conviction by a jury and Capone is said to feel that if he pleaded guilty he could do no worse than Guzik and might do considerably better despite his nationwide bad reputation.

Three Years for Brother Ralph.

His brother, Ralph Capone, after a trial lasting three weeks, was sentenced to three years in prison for income tax fraud. Under the various counts with which he was charged the sentence could have been twenty-two years. At the time the Ralph Capone sentence was the most severe in the history of income tax fraud cases. Then came the Guzik case, lasting two weeks. Guzik faced the possibility of an eighteen year sentence. He was given five years which still remains the record sentence for income tax fraud throughout the United States.

Government prosecutors say that if Capone elects to fight and is convicted he can stall off his passage through the portals of Leavenworth prison for at least two years. It is known that District Attorney Johnson has been hopeful throughout the long investigation that Capone could be gotten to prison before the Chicago World's Fair of 1933.

If Capone offers to plead guilty the district attorney's office will be confronted with the question: Capone in prison now for four or five years, or Capone to prison two years hence for a longer term.

Dangers in Guilty Plea.

There is danger for Capone, however, in a plea of guilty, it was pointed out, and it was to cogitate these points that the gang chief's lawyers forsook their golf games yesterday.

The problem was outlined thus: If Capone pleads guilty to the beer conspiracy indictment, he will leave his 68 co-defendants in the lurch. The

(Continued on page 4, column 1.)

AND CHICAGO IS ABOUT TO LOSE ITS BAD REPUTATION

Source: Courtesy of Chicago Tribune Archives. *Article continues on next page.*

Article continues from previous page.

CAPONE, IN U. S. TOILS, PONDERS GUILTY PLEAS

Twice Indicted Gang Chief May Give Up the Fight.

(Continued from first page.)

apparent fear of the gang chief and his advisers is that these 68 men will also rush in with pleas of guilty in an effort to save themselves and in so doing may disclose information about murders and other crimes incident to the beer business which have so far been mysteries.

Another danger in pleading guilty, according to government officials, is that if Capone starts making any admissions or his co-defendants start telling the truth about his liquor activities, the government may be able to reindict him on many specific charges under the Jones law. This law permits a five year sentence and a $10,000 fine for each specific violation of the Volstead act.

Meets Legal Advisers Today.

One of the battery of attorneys which is weighing the questions involved in the situation said that Capone will meet with his legal advisers this morning to decide whether to follow his inclination and plead guilty or give heed to the suggestions of some of his lawyers that he has a chance to beat the income tax charge and later plead guilty to the prohibition indictment, getting off with a year or two on the latter. Capone was said to have spent yesterday in a retreat in Michigan.

It was learned that among those with whom he is consulting is the law firm of Nash and Ahern. Attorneys Thomas D. Nash and Michael J. Ahern have liberated several of Capone's men charged with murder, among them John Scalisi and Albert Anselmi, who killed two policemen in a daylight gun battle.

Attorney Ahern admitted he had received a call for aid from Capone, but said he did not know whether he would respond.

Indicate He Has Money.

That Capone, who is only 32 years old, might have plenty of money to live in luxury after a stretch of several years in Leavenworth was indicated yesterday from two sources. This information seemed to belie some of the statements made by federal authorities that Capone is nearly broke.

The Associated Press carried a dispatch from Washington reporting that "an offer of several millions" was made by attorneys for Capone in an effort to settle the gangster's income tax troubles. This offer the government turned down.

Also, information reached government agents here that as late as last March Capone purchased $1,000,000 worth of Liberty bonds and that a few weeks ago he bought $500,000 of the recent issue of $800,000,000 of treasury bonds. It was also learned that he has established a trust fund at a New York bank for the care and education of certain of his relatives.

Round Up the Co-defendants.

While Capone was pondering what to do when he appears before Judge Wilkerson tomorrow, government agents and the city police had begun the task of rounding up his 68 co-defendants in the beer conspiracy case on bench warrants issued from the federal court.

Acting Police Commissioner Alcock has assigned a number of policemen to work with government operatives in arresting all the men named in the indictment with Capone. Alcock's detectives will participate in the questioning of every one arrested and will be ready to follow up confessions that might lead to the solutions of many murders, such as the Valentine day massacre, the machine gunning of Joe Aiello, and the slaying of Scalisi, Anselmi, and their fellow murderer, Joe Giunta.

Assistant State's Attorney Charles J. Mueller, in charge of the special grand jury investigation of the police department, said he will be on hand, too, ready to take proper action if any evidence is obtained of bribes paid to policemen or other officials.

LEGAL STAFF WHICH CONDUCTED THE FIGHT AGAINST GANG CHIEFTAIN.
Left to right, seated: Dwight Green, assistant district attorney; George E. Q. Johnson, United States district attorney; Jacob Grossman, assistant. Standing: George C. Dawson, assistant, and William J. Froehlich, assistant attorney general.
(Story on page 1.) [Acme Photo.]

Chicago Daily Tribune (1872-1963); Jun 18, 1931; ProQuest Historical Newspapers Chicago Tribune (1849 - 1985) pg. 14

Source: Courtesy of Chicago Tribune Archives

GANG MACHINE GUN ROARS; ONE SLAIN BY SLUGS
Chicago Daily Tribune (1872-1963); Jun 19, 1931; ProQuest Historical Newspapers Chicago Tribune (1849 - 1985) pg.1

GANG MACHINE GUN ROARS; ONE SLAIN BY SLUGS

Outbreak Is Laid to Beer Rivalry.

(Picture on back page.)

Two men were shot, one fatally, in an attempted wholesale assassination by machine gunners in front of a saloon at 1137 West 69th street last night. Two other men who police say probably were the intended targets of the gunmen escaped injury, as did a family of three persons whose automobile, caught in the line of fire, was hit five times by machine gun slugs.

The victims of the would be murderers are James Janis, 32 years old, 5514 Blackstone avenue, a brakeman employed as a part time bartender in the saloon, and Thomas Norton, 30 years, 7039 Throop street, a steamfitter. Janis was riddled twelve times by slugs and taken to the Englewood hospital, where he died early this morning. Norton was wounded in the left thigh and cut about the face and hands by flying glass shattered by bullets.

Blame Beer Rivalry.

Detectives laid the machine gunning to beer rivalry on the south side. One report was the shooting might have been a signal of the return of Joe Saltis, "retired" southwest side beer czar, to the racket. In any event, the inspiration is believed to have been in the purchase of "wrong beer" by the saloon.

Norton and Janis were sitting in the automobile of William Conway, 6842 South Racine avenue, in front of the saloon. Conway and his brother, George, 6751 South May

street, reputed owner of the resort, were sitting in front of the butcher shop next door at 1139 West 69th street.

Out of the east approached a touring car. As it neared the saloon it slowed down. Suddenly there was a roar and a stream of bullets sprayed the Conway car. At this moment the automobile of Clyde W. Bennage, 6723 Green street, eastbound, came in the line of fire, cutting off the targets of the assassins.

Auto Hit; No One Hurt.

Bennage's machine was pierced at the front, windshield and center, but he, his wife and their son, Earl, 7 years old, escaped unscathed. As Bennage's machine passed beyond range the foiled gunmen sent three bullets toward the Conways, the missiles piercing the butcher shop door behind them.

William Conway took Norton to St. Bernard's hospital. Later he and his brother appeared at the Englewood station for questioning. They offered no motive for the shooting.

Since the middle of April, when Edward Fitzgerald, alleged follower of Frank McErlane, was killed, several harmless shootings have been reported on the south side. They were charged to a feud between the McErlane and "Spike" O'Donnell beer outfits.

Report New Gang Formed.

Another theory on the shooting being investigated involves an upstart gang of beer boys led by Dan McGeoghegan, once condemned to the gallows but eventually freed. The story is that McGeoghegan recently organized a beer outfit in the Chicago Lawn territory and is now poaching on the south side sections controlled by McErlane and Saltis.

McGeoghegan, it is said, has won two of O'Donnell's aids to his camp, Joe Cainski and George Larson, and is prepared, with a following of desperadoes, to carry on deadly war against his established rivals. The recent shooting troubles on the south side, which until last night shed no blood, originated, it was said in McGeoghegan's entry into the beer field. Incidentally Cainski and Larson were seized early Tuesday morning after the former's car was found bullet riddled at 83d and Bishop streets.

Two Shot by Machine Gunners in Beer War Renewal—Mercury Climbs to 90 on Year's Hottest Day

[TRIBUNE Photo.]

TWO IN CAR WOUNDED BY MACHINE GUNNERS.
Policeman Samuel Morris looking at bullet riddled auto in which James Janis and Thomas Norton were shot in front of 1137 West 69th street. *(Story on page 1.)*

Source: Courtesy of Chicago Tribune Archives

12,000 GALLONS OF ICED BEER SEIZED IN RAID

Furtive Truck Driver Leads U. S. Agents to Well-Stocked Garage.

Nearly 12,000 gallons of iced beer ready for delivery for the week-end trade, valued at approximately $20,-000, retail price, was seized today by prohibition agents in a raid on a Capone-Guzik-Fusco delivery station in the rear of 2636 Calumet avenue.

James Calloway, an aid to Bert Delaney, an old beer maestro for the Capone outfit-and himself under indictment with "Scarface Al" for conspiracy to defeat the dry laws, was seized after an automobile chase punctuated by revolver shots. Two of Calloway's aids escaped. The beer was confiscated and the plant placed under guard.

Furtive glances by the driver of an ice truck, apparently deeply interested in noting whether he was being watched, precipitated the raid. Two agents under Elliott Ness, assistant to W. E. Bennett, chief of special agents, were cruising the south side when the actions of the iceman aroused them. They followed him until he drove into a big double garage in the rear of the Calumet avenue address.

After waiting a moment they rushed the place. Three men dashed out a side door. Two of them got away, but the agents were lucky in enlisting the aid of a passing flivver squad car from the Stanton avenue station, in which rode three policemen. They immediately gave chase to one of the fugitives, who halted when a couple of bullets had whistled past his ears. He was Calloway.

Returning to the garage, the agents found 362 large barrels and ten half barrels of beer, part of it loaded on a three-ton truck, said to be owned by the World Motor Service Company, the trucking division of the Capone-Guzik-Fusco combine. All the beer was iced and ready for delivery.

Calloway was trapped with Delaney and two other men April 12 by Ness when the four returned to a huge Capone brewery at 3136 South Wabash avenue the day after it had been raided and boldly tried to cart away all of the equipment. An indictment for conspiracy in connection with this raid is pending.

Source: Chicago Daily News, June 26, 1931

Reproduced with permission of the Chicago Sun-Times.

BUT THE CHORUS REMAINS.

[Pittsburgh Post-Gazette.]

Al Capone in Hands of Judge Today

Chicago Daily Tribune (1872-1963); Jul 30, 1931; ProQuest Historical Newspapers Chicago Tribune (1849 - 1985) pg. 1

Al Capone in Hands of Judge Today

CHIEF OF GANGS WAITS DECISION ON PRISON TERM

Sentence to Follow Final U. S. Evidence.

(Picture on back page.)

The fate of Al Capone will rest today with Federal Judge James H.

JUDGE WILKERSON

Wilkerson, who will decide on the length of the prison term the gang leader must serve at Leavenworth on his pleas of guilty to two indictments.

Whether Judge Wilkerson will sentence Capone immediately or take the case under advisement, is a matter for speculation, but the government will conclude its statement of evidence as to income tax dodging and conspiring against the prohibition laws before the end of today's session.

May Go to Prison Tomorrow.

If Capone is sentenced immediately and remanded to the custody of the marshal, he will be locked up in the county jail over night and taken to prison tomorrow night with a regular consignment of convicts. It is possible that Judge Wilkerson will order the gangster started on his way for the penitentiary at once.

Capone has pleaded guilty to eight counts of violating the income tax laws in attempting to evade payment of $215,080 on an income of $1,038,000 over a five year period, and to a blanket conspiracy charge in connection with his reputed $20,000,000 a year beer business.

Maximum Penalty Discounted.

He is subject to a possible maximum penalty of thirty-two years' imprisonment and fines of $80,000 on the income tax counts and two years'

imprisonment and a $10,000 fine on the conspiracy charge. However, the magnitude of the punishment that might be imposed is regarded by the federal prosecutors as immaterial, for the gangster is pleading guilty and precedent decrees comparatively short sentences in such cases.

The highest sentence of record in an income tax case where the defendant pleaded guilty was two years. The highest of record where the defendant was found guilty by a jury—the case of Jack Guzik, Capone gangster—was five years and a day. Taking these facts into consideration, it is regarded as unlikely that Capone will receive a sentence of more than three years and a fine of $10,000.

He Hopes to Serve 11 Months.

The federal building and other quarters have been buzzing with rumors that Capone will have to serve little more than a year, because of the operation of the federal parole laws and the time off allowed for good behavior. A rumor being circulated among lawyers representing Capone hoodlums in the federal courts is that the gang leader is confident he will have to serve only eleven months.

Thomas S. Rice, a member of the New York state crime commission, writing in the Brooklyn Daily Eagle, said of Capone:

"What sentence he receives will be a gross fraud upon the public unless, at the time it is imposed, the newspapers make clear that Capone will be entitled to apply for a parole at the end of the first third of his sentence, and should be at liberty within two to four months after he files his application."

Getting Out Is Different.

Officials here point out, however, that any federal prisoner may apply for parole when he has served one-third of his sentence, but that getting out is a different matter. These officials say that the federal parole board at Washington seldom acts on an application—and certainly would not in the case of the notorious Al Capone—without consulting the prosecuting attorney.

United States Attorney George E. Q. Johnson has declared he would never recommend parole for a gangster, and in view of his three year struggle to rid Chicago of Capone, it is considered unlikely that he would make an exception for the most notorious gangster of them all.

It is also possible, lawyers said, that Capone will be sentenced in such a manner as to circumvent the parole

(Continued on page 10, column 2.)

FATE OF CAPONE RESTS IN HANDS OF JUDGE TODAY

Sentence Is to Follow Final U. S. Evidence.

(Continued from first page.)

possibilities. If he were sentenced to three years in the penitentiary on one or more of the felony counts, the sentences to run concurrently, and a year and a day each on three other felony counts, these sentences to run consecutively, the total sentence would be three years and three days, but Capone would not be eligible for parole after a year and a day. He would not be eligible until he had served four months of the third term.

Case of Brother Ralph.

Capone's brother, Ralph, was sentenced in this manner by Judge Wilkerson. Ralph received a total prison sentence of three years and three consecutive jail sentences of one year each. The defense on appeal objected to this, contending that it rendered void the parole provisions, but the Appellate court ruled that the manner of sentence rests with the District court.

Six days a month would be allowed Capone for good behavior, if he were sentenced to three years in prison, so that he would have to serve approximately 29 months, assuming a parole were not forthcoming, on a straight sentence of that length.

Another possibility is that Capone, in addition to a penitentiary sentence, will be placed on probation for a stated period, to begin upon his release from prison.

Say Gangs Dread Probation.

This was done by Federal Judge Walter C. Lindley in sentencing "Machine Gun Jack" McGurn, Capone henchman. Federal officials declare that hoodlums dread probation almost as much as a prison sentence, because of the drastic provisions of the federal probation laws.

Even after the expiration of the stated probationary period, and at any time within the period to which the defendant might originally have been sentenced, he is subject to arrest if caught violating any federal or state law. Moreover, he may be taken before the court and resentenced to the maximum of his original possible punishment.

In Capone's case this would mean if at any time within thirty-four years he were caught violating the law—say, carrying a gun—he could be arrested and sentenced to thirty-four years, less his original sentence.

Due in Court at 10 A. M.

Capone yesterday was reported holding final conferences with his hoodlum retainers at the Lexington hotel, while federal officials were putting the finishing touches on their summary of the evidence.

Capone is to appear in court at 10 o'clock this morning, and the prosecutors, Dwight H. Green, for income tax, and Victor E. La Rue, for the conspiracy charge, will make their statements to the court. The principal government agents in each case are expected to be called, and at the conclusion of the testimony District Attorney Johnson will make his recommendations to the court.

Government agents from all branches of service will be on hand to handle the crowds expected at the federal building. Chief of Detectives John Norton has delegated a squad of ten policemen, under Lieut. William McCarthy, to report to Charles Nagle, assistant custodian of the building.

[TRIBUNE Photo.]

GANG CHIEF TO BE SENTENCED TODAY. Al Capone, who will learn penalty he must pay for defrauding government and violating prohibition act when he appears before Judge James H. Wilkerson. *(Story on page 1.)*

Source: Courtesy of Chicago Tribune Archives

COPS DIFFER ON VISIT OF CAPONE BEER BOSS

(DAILY TIMES Photo)

Here's Policeman Sylvester Stock aboard the beer truck captured at 18th and State sts. by Sergt. John Coughlin.

Joe Fusco, indicted as Al Capone's beer boss, was and was not at the S. State st. police station last night. Take your choice.

Joe was there—according to Lieut. Thomas Geary.

Joe wasn't there—according to Capt. John Prendergrast. Even if he were, the captain said, the police did not know he is wanted by Uncle Sam.

Be that as it may, a big truck, loaded with 21 barrels of beer worth $1,115 on the retail market, was at the station. And today the government had it.

The conscientious action of Sergt. John T. Coughlin, newly assigned to the district, who seized the truck, caused quite a confusion. It was the first time that any one of the thousands of beer trucks which have rumbled through the Loop had been parked at the station.

The story told was that Fusco, hot and bothered about such a breach of faith, had gone to the station and spoken his mind. Then Dennis Cooney, Capone's vice lord of the south side, appeared and spoke his. But it was of no avail.

In the meantime, the two men taken with the truck, Joe Bue, 29, of 3836 Wentworth ave., and John Radia, 26, of 4236 Ellis ave., were held as federal prisoners.

Source: Chicago Daily Times, July 14, 1931

Reproduced with permission of the Chicago Sun-Times.

Chicago Tribune (1872-1963); Jul 31, 1931; *ProQuest Historical Newspapers Chicago Tribune (1849-1985)* pg. 14

Source: Courtesy of Chicago Tribune Archives

CAPONE 'DEAL' RULING TODAY
Chicago Daily Tribune (1872-1963); Jul 31, 1931; ProQuest Historical Newspapers Chicago Tribune (1849 - 1985) pg. 1

CAPONE 'DEAL' RULING TODAY

JUDGE REFUSES TO BE BOUND TO EASY SENTENCE

Gangster Seeks to Drop Guilty Plea.

(Pictures on back page.)

Al Capone was informed by Federal Judge James H. Wilkerson yesterday that "it is utterly impossible to bargain with a federal court."

The gangster's hopes of escaping with a two or three year sentence through an arrangement with the government were shattered, and his attorneys quickly moved to change their pleas from guilty to not guilty on the income tax evasion and booze conspiracy indictments against Capone, who is No. 1 on the list of public enemies.

The motion to back out on the pleas of guilty, which can be done only with the court's permission, was continued for consideration until 2 p. m. today, when the judge will rule as to whether Capone may withdraw his plea and go to trial or be sentenced on his plea as it stands.

Capone Stalks Into Court.

The porcine Capone stalked into the courtroom at 10 o'clock in the morning, beaming with the visible assurance that "everything was all set," that the prosecutors would say a few words to the court and he would be sentenced on the terms which he had accepted to plead guilty.

The arrogant manner had gone when the gangster slipped stealthily away with his attorneys at 3 o'clock in the afternoon. The collar that had been white and fresh in the morning was wilted, and his greasy hair was disarranged by the nervous mopping of his brow during the colloquy at the bar. The ear to ear grin was displaced by a sullen countenance as he slunk from the courtroom at the conclusion of the afternoon session.

Gang Chief's Hopes Upset.

The dramatic upsetting of all that Capone had confidently expected came after Defense Attorney Michael Ahern made a statement to the court at the opening of the afternoon session. He explained that the pleas of guilty were entered into after conferences with District Attorney George E. Q. Johnson and with the understanding that recommendations as to punishment would be made to the court.

Mr. Ahern also asserted that the agreement was entered into with the approval of the United States attorney general and an assistant secretary of the treasury. Attorney Ahern was prompted in this explanation by a statement from the bench during the morning, in which Judge Wilkerson set forth in unequivocal language that he was not bound by any understanding between counsel.

Court Refuses to Be Bound.

Judge Wilkerson repeated at the afternoon session that, although the court could not be bound by an understanding between the prosecutor and the defense, it was the court's right and duty to hear such recommendations as the government wished to make.

"But we cannot start a hearing in which there is an understanding that the court is bound as to the judgment. It will impose by the recommendations of the district attorney," said Judge Wilkerson.

"There have been some unfortunate things in connection with this case. There have been some publications which were contemptuous in character, and tending to bring the administration of justice in the federal court into disrepute They have even gone so far as to announce in advance what the period of punishment would be.

"It is time for somebody to impress upon this defendant that it is utterly impossible to bargain with a federal court."

Judge Is Emphatic.

Judge Wilkerson leaned forward over the bench as he made this assertion, and his eyes glinted with feeling. He was apparently referring to articles published at the time of Capone's pleas of guilty that the government had "made a deal" with the gang chief, and that the punishment would be two and one-half years in the penitentiary.

Attorney Ahern informed the court that the approval of the agreement between counsel by the attorney general and an assistant secretary of the treasury was of paramount importance in the decision to plead guilty.

"We were led to believe that the recommendations would be approved by the court." he said. "That department (treasury) has the power to compromise both civil and criminal liability in income tax cases. This constituted an inducement to us. Unless we had been confident that the court would act according to the recommendation agreed upon the pleas of guilty never would have been entered."

United States Attorney Johnson, whose triumphant campaign with the income tax prosecutions against hoodlums and crooked politicians was to have been climaxed with the sentencing of Al Capone, was manifestly distressed with the turn of events. Soft spoken and mild of manner, the federal prosecutor, who seldom participates personally in court proceedings, was crushed against the bar with Capone and the other counsel in the only vacant space—six feet square—in the courtroom.

What Mr. Johnson had to say was frankly and straightforwardly put. "It seemed very desirable on the part of the officers of the government who are charged with this responsibility," he said, "that, if we could avoid the hazards of a trial, this defendant might at an early date be imprisoned in the penitentiary."

Dispels Hopes for Defense.

Any hopes entertained by the defense counsel of prevailing upon Judge Wilkerson to accept their terms of pleading guilty were quickly dispelled by the court. As Attorney Ahern reached the end of his opening remarks, telling of his former belief that judgment would be entered according to the district attorney's recommendations, Judge Wilkerson frequently cut him short. The following colloquy ensued:

MR. AHERN—The recommendation of the district attorney was not only with respect to the duration of the punishment but to the punishment on each count, and he agreed to recommend that all penalties on each count run concurrently.

THE COURT—You have not any doubt that I stated the law correctly this morning, have you, as to the duty of the court in the imposition of sentence on a plea of guilty?

Lawyer Replies to Court.

MR. AHERN—I draw a distinction between the act of a court in imposing penalties and the act of a court in prejudging a case. Now the defendant here, by a plea, would prejudice his own case on the facts. If the court would follow the recommendation of the district attorney as made, and if we could have the assurance of the court——

Source: Courtesy of Chicago Tribune Archives.   *Article continues on next page.*

Article continues from previous page.

Judge Wilkerson interrupted the lawyer and fairly snapped at him: "Suppose the court does not agree with that."

MR. AHERN—Well, then, that is what I was coming to, if it please the court.

THE COURT—Certainly it is an unheard of thing in a criminal proceeding, that anybody, even the court itself, could bind the court to the judgment which is to be entered after the hearing.

MR. AHERN—Well, as I say, I make a distinction, and I can conceive well, of course, that a court cannot bind itself to enter judgment on the ▓▓▓; but when a defendant enters a plea, he himself decides the facts.

Refuses to Be Bound.

THE COURT—The court will listen, as I said this morning, to the recommendation of the district attorney. The court will listen to the recommendation of the attorney general. Whether it adds anything to that of the district attorney is not material, because the district attorney is an officer of this court. But the thing that the defendant cannot think—must not think—is that in the end—the recommendations of the attorney general and of secretary of the treasury, all considered—the court is bound to enter judgment according to those recommendations.

The defense and government counsel crowded closer to the bench and the audience swayed forward in an effort to hear what was going on. Capone shifted his weighty bulk from one foot to another and mopped his face with a soaked handkerchief.

"Not in Court's Power."

Judge Wilkerson continued: "Now it is well settled—a party who makes that kind of agreement with the officers of the government is not without protection. But it is not for the court to carry it out. The executive officers have the pardoning power.

"As far as these income tax prosecutions are concerned, the executive officers have the power to compromise both the civil and criminal liability, but they cannot transfer to the court the duty of putting upon the record a judgment which does not represent the sober conclusion of the court as to what the record requires."

MR. AHERN [now speaking hopelessly]—Well, it may be that the matter was overstressed, but in any event, if it please the court, the defendant feels that there has been a serious misapprehension of the whole matter, and that——

Discusses Question of Judgment.

THE COURT—When you were here the last time, when this case was continued, you commenced to argue to the court as to what the judgment should be. You seemed then to regard it as an open question upon which the court was to exercise its judgment.

MR. AHERN—I might say, if it please the court, that I did that upon the suggestion of somebody else. It was not my better judgment, but I do not care to go into it.

THE COURT [with finality]—Well, I do not think there is any misunderstanding about it, about the law here, and there can be no misunderstanding about the situation.

Judge Wilkerson then indicated that he had apprehended the intention of the defense to withdraw the pleas of guilty. He observed that if the hearing were opened and the district attorney made a showing of his evidence, there being a possibility that the court would not follow his recommendations, the 'government's case might be seriously affected on a change of plea.

MR. AHERN—Well, I will make a motion now, if it please the court, before the government attempts to introduce any evidence, to withdraw the pleas.

THE COURT—What is your attitude, Mr. District Attorney?

Johnson States U. S. Stand.

MR. JOHNSON—It would be impossible for the government to present its case and then permit a withdrawal of the pleas. For that reason we feel the motion should be disposed of now. And I further feel, your honor, that I owe it as a duty to the court, and as a duty to the defendant's counsel, to make a statement here of the facts that led up to the United States attorney's saying he would make a recommendation in this case.

Mr. Johnson spoke excitedly and his hands trembled as he addressed the court. His statement was as follows:

"After the first indictment was returned in this case, which was returned at an earlier date because it was necessary to avoid the running of the statute of limitations, in some way unknown to me the defendant became acquainted with the fact and advised his counsel.

Confers with Defense Counsel.

"The defendant's counsel then asked me for a conference, which was held, and I advised counsel that there would be further indictments. However, I did not advise counsel as to the nature of the offenses under investigation.

"Then, after the final indictments were returned, a number of conferences were held with the defendant's counsel. The head of the intelligence unit came here from Washington and participated in those conferences and I reported them to my superiors in the department of justice.

"The United States attorney stated to the defendant's counsel that he had sought the permission of the court to make a recommendation. The suggestions for recommendation made by the defendant's counsel were not agreeable to the government. They sought a much shorter recommendation than the government's counsel was willing even to suggest to the attorney general.

"But these conferences reached a stage where I stated to the defendant's counsel that I had conferred with my superiors in the department of justice, and with permission of the court, I was prepared to make a recommendation, the full information of which I imparted to him.

"The defendant's counsel inquired of the United States attorney what the attitude of the federal judges had been towards recommendations which the United States attorney had made. I stated to him that in the few instances where I had had occasion to make a recommendation to the court, and where the court found upon a hearing that I had faithfully represented the facts as they were, the courts in those cases had followed my recommendation.

"I think I owe this further duty to the court and to the defendant's counsel, to say that if they had not understood that I would make the recommendation, I do not believe they would have pleaded guilty."

Asks for Communication.

Judge Wilkerson interposed to ask the federal prosecutor whether he had the communication from the attorney general with him.

"Are you willing to let the court see the communication?" he asked.

"Yes, your honor, I will let the court see it. But in giving this to the court, I should add that there is one minor—not one minor, but one further—recommendation," Mr. Johnson replied.

"I assume," said the court, "that like all departmental communications, they relate to government business and are privileged."

MR. JOHNSON—Yes, your honor.

THE COURT—And of course should not be disclosed unless presented to the court for action.

Agrees to Present Document.

MR. JOHNSON—Yes—well, I will present it to the court.

THE COURT (smiling)—And I shall so treat them, because all these communications are privileged, and should not be disclosed unless presented formally for action, and if you have no objection I shall look at them.

The handing of this communication to Judge Wilkerson occasioned much speculation, but questions as to its contents were futile. It was conjectured, however, that it made reference to the length of sentence to have been recommended for Capone.

Attorney Ahern then took up the colloquy with the court, a discussion on his motion to withdraw the pleas.

MR. AHERN—I never doubted what the court's attitude would be. My impression was at the time that we had these conferences and up to the time that the plea was entered that the court would acquiesce in the recommendations of the district attorney.

THE COURT—Well, you never had any conferences with the court and nobody had any right to make any such assumption for the court.

Reason for Plea, Lawyer Says.

MR. AHERN—Well, I thought I had, and if I had not had that belief I would not have recommended a plea of guilty in these cases.

The defense lawyer then disclosed another agreement with the prosecution which he said was entered into and which disclosed Capone's fear of being put upon the witness stand for the first time in his life. Mr. Ahern said:

"There is one other thing I want to say to the court—I did not want to say it—but at the time, or long before the plea was entered, I attached a condition with the district attorney, and that was, we thought at the time, that no evidence would be adduced.

"We never contemplated offering any in mitigation and it was expressly stipulated by me as a condition of the plea that the defendant should be asked no questions."

Source: Courtesy of Chicago Tribune Archives. *Article continues on next page.*

Article continues from previous page.

This statement referred to Judge Wilkerson's remark during the morning session that if the defendant sought leniency he should be prepared to answer all questions put by the court concerning the charges he had confessed.

A possible dispute between the defense counsel and Mr. Johnson was precluded by the interruption of Judge Wilkerson as the prosecutor replied to Mr. Ahern.

"Now, we are getting into details that I do not care to go into," remarked the judge. "That was between you."

In further explaining his view of the case Judge Wilkerson said:

"It is an unqualified plea, as the record stands. It may be withdrawn on a proper showing. It does not appear here that there is any question about the propriety of this recommendation that the district attorney is to make. That is not unusual; it is done in criminal cases every day. He understands, of course, that while courts receive and give weight to such recommendations, sometimes things transpire at the hearing which make it impossible for the court to follow the recommendations.

Johnson's Attitude Asked.

"Your plea was not induced by any representation which the district attorney is not carrying out in good faith. He is doing everything he told you he would do, and the court is doing everything that he had the right to tell you that the court would do."

Mr. Johnson was asked whether he would consent to the withdrawal of the plea.

"If the court please," he replied, "I would have to take the position that I am not objecting if upon my statement the defendant has been misled or mistaken in any way. But I would not want to take the responsibility of consenting without conferring with the attorney general."

"Very well," said the court, "I will take this motion under advisement, and dispose of it tomorrow afternoon at 2 o'clock."

Capone Appears Shocked.

The next remark seemed to be a shock to Capone, who had turned from the bench and started away. He stopped short and stared at his attorneys when Judge Wilkerson said: "In the meantime, the defendant is remanded to the custody of the marshal." This meant the lockup for the gangster, who has been at liberty on bonds of $50,000.

But Judge Wilkerson withdrew the order remanding Capone to custody until 2 o'clock today when Attorney Ahern declared the defendant had been out on bail and that he has a wife and child. Judge Wilkerson explained that he thought he was doing something for the protection of the defendant, in view of the guards who accompanied him to and from the building.

"If somebody chooses to attach guards to him, may it please the court, that is their business," said Attorney Ahern. "I don't believe the defendant is requesting those guards."

Judge Wilkerson indicated that he would consent to a withdrawal of the guilty plea only upon a proper showing of the necessity. The courts in such instances, federal prosecutors declare, allow a withdrawal only when it appears that the pleas of guilty were entered through ignorance or inadvertence, or through the holding out of some false hope or inducement.

The Outlook for Gangster.

If the gang chief is not permitted to change his plea, Judge Wilkerson may impose whatever penalty he chooses under a possible maximum of thirty-four years' imprisonment and fines totaling $90,000. If a change in plea is allowed and Capone goes on trial he faces the virtual certainty of conviction. The government has not lost a single income tax prosecution, and its investigators declare that the Capone case is as strong as any of the others.

If convicted, he would be subject to the same possible maximum penalty. Jack Guzik, Capone business manager, was sentenced to five years in the penitentiary on his conviction of tax fraud. Capone, in addition to the tax evasion charges, is under indictment for conspiracy to violate the prohibition laws, which carries an additional maximum penalty of two years and $10,000.

Reason for Prosecutor's Stand.

One of the reasons attributed as causing District Attorney Johnson to agree to a recommendation if Capone would plead guilty was the aim to get him into the penitentiary as soon as possible. It has been the prosecutor's prime objective to rid Chicago of Capone before the World's Fair in 1933.

If the gangster goes on trial, it probably will be in September, early in the fall term of court. If convicted, his case would be disposed of by the Circuit Court of Appeals during the spring, and the Supreme court would have time to act on his petition for a writ of certiorari the next fall, or little more than a year from now. All propositions of law involved in the case have been upheld by the Circuit Court of Appeals, so that Capone would have slight chance on an appeal.

Crowd Wait To See Hoodlum.

The crowds at the federal building in the morning craning their necks for a glimpse of the hoodlum king, exceeded those which came during Capone's trial for contempt of court last spring. Capone was escorted from his hotel by a squad of police under Lieut. William McCarthy. He was driven into the mail tunnel entrance of the federal building on Adams street. Thousands awaited his arrival, and the crowds were there again at 2 o'clock.

The court room was filled to capacity, although no one unknown or bearing convincing credentials was allowed to pass through the improvised gate in the court corridor. The federal grand jury filled some of the benches in the rear, and there were many wives and other relatives of federal officials and employés—the usual privileged few.

"Jake" Factor in Court.

John [Jake the Barber] Factor, was in the court room when Capone entered. The former Halsted street hair cutter was there trying to get a writ of habeas corpus in fight to escape extradition to England as a swindler.

Judge Wilkerson heard Factor's attorneys and continued the case until this morning. He heard half a dozen routine motions before taking up the Capone case, and then adjourned it promptly after reading his own statement.

Capone listened intently and exhibited grave concern during the brief morning session as Judge Wilkerson read his statement, making it plain that he was not bound by any agreement. The gangster was accompanied by his lawyers, including, besides Mr. Ahern, Leopold B. Melnick, to his suite in the Lexington hotel, where they discussed their plans during the noon recess.

The gang chieftain was on his way out of court thirty minutes after the afternoon session opened, surrounded by a cordon of police as he escaped the curious crowds by taking an elevator. He appeared glum over the prospects of a trial or a sentence with no strings attached.

The government agents who developed the cases against Capone were in the court room, prepared to summarize their evidence had they been called upon. A. P. Madden, head of the intelligence unit, which handles all tax fraud cases, was there with Frank Wilson, ace investigator of the intelligence unit from Washington.

Young Eliot Ness, the special prohibition agent who with a half dozen others gathered the evidence on which Capone and 68 of his henchmen in the beer business were indicted, was also there.

Besides Mr. Johnson, the prosecution staff in the court room included Assistant United States Attorneys Victor E. La Rue, Dwight H. Green, Jacob Grossman, Samuel G. Clawson, and Special Assistant Attorney General William J. Froelich. However, the court, Mr. Johnson, and Attorney Ahern did all the talking.

The indictments against the chief public enemy charge attempts to evade payment of $215,000 in taxes on an income of $1,023,000 for 1924 and 1929 inclusive and conspiracy with 68 of his henchmen to violate the dry laws for ten years.

Source: Courtesy of Chicago Tribune Archives.

Capone Faces Long Term as Judge Refuses to Sanction Bargain with Government—Flyers Reach Istanbul

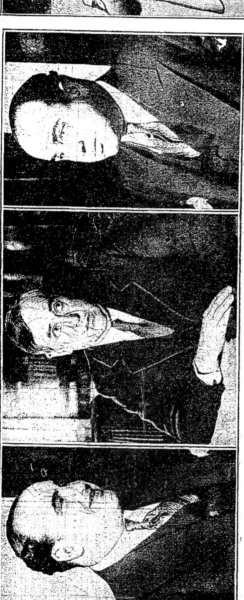

SMILE FADES FROM GANG CHIEFTAIN'S FACE AS JUDGE BLASTS HIS HOPE OF BEING GIVEN SHORT TERM IN PRISON. At the left is Al Capone, his face wearing a smile similar to the one which appeared upon it as he entered court. At the right is Capone as he appeared after the smile faded from his face when he realized his predicament. In the center is Judge James H. Wilkerson, wearing the stern expression he assumed when he announced he could not be a party to any agreement with Public Enemy No. 1.

[TRIBUNE Photo.]

(Story on page 1.)

AFTER THE BLOW FELL. Al Capone, subdued and making furtive effort to hide face as he left court.

[TRIBUNE Photo.]

(Story, on page 1.)

EXPLAINS STAND.
U. S. District Attorney George E. Q. Johnson says superiors approved terms.

(Story on page 1.)

Source: Courtesy of Chicago Tribune Archives

Chicago Daily Tribune (1872-1963); Oct 18, 1931; ProQuest Historical Newspapers Chicago Tribune (1849 - 1985) pg. 2

Judge Wilkerson's Instructions to Capone Jury

In his charge to the jurors in the Capone case Judge Wilkerson first instructed them that they had nothing to do with fixing punishment. He gave them the general rules of law applicable to criminal cases and said that in this case the averments in the indictment might be established by a chain of facts or circumstances "strong enough to exclude to a moral certainty every reasonable hypothesis of innocence."

He then enumerated the 23 counts in the indictments and, summarizing them, said:

"Now you will see that with reference to the tax for each year different charges have been made. With reference to each of these counts, however, the question for you is to arrive at a conclusion as to whether or not the averments of that particular count have been established by the prosecution in this case. When you have done that you have completed your duty in the case.

Defines Court's Province.

"The entry of the judgment upon the different counts, in case there should be a conviction here, the determination of the questions relating to the relation of those counts one to another, also that they charge the same or different offenses, is one for the court.

"You will see in each one of the counts certain averments of dates and amounts and numbers. It is not necessary for the government to prove in this case the precise amount of tax for each year as stated in the indictment.

"So far as the counts which charge a willful failure to file a return are concerned it is sufficient if the government establish a gross income of such an amount that under the law the defendant was obliged to file the return. In the counts charging an attempt to evade and defeat the tax, it is sufficient if the government establishes an amount of taxable income sufficient so that the defendant was obliged to pay a tax."

The court then explained the law on gross and net incomes, stating that losses incurred in trade or business were deductible, losses from fire, storm, shipwreck, etc., but no mention was made of gambling losses, which was the chief item of the Capone defense.

Income from Illegal Sources.

On the point of income from illegal occupations the court said:

"If you believe from the evidence that the defendant had a gross income of $5,000 or over during any of the calendar years 1924, 1925, 1926, 1927, 1928 and 1929, the mere fact that the defendant derived all or a portion of said income from illegal occupations or illegal sources . . . did not exempt him from making a return stating specifically the items of his gross income and the deductions and credits allowed.

"In a case in which the jury find that no books of account were kept, that there were no memoranda preserved of transactions by the defendant, that there were no bank accounts, that there was no record kept of money which comes in and goes out, the existence of a net income requiring a payment of a tax by the taxpayer is a fact which may be established by a chain of facts and circumstances. . . .

Evidence to Be Considered.

"Now in this case in arriving at a conclusion upon such question of fact in the case you may consider all the facts and circumstances which have been shown here in evidence.

"You may consider the evidence relative to the activities of the defendant in the places in Cicero. You may consider the evidence relating to the living by the defendant at the two hotels, the Metropole and the Lexington; the manner in which he there lived.

"You may consider the evidence with reference to the moneys which were transmitted from Chicago to the defendant in Florida. You may consider the evidence relating to the expenditures of money by the defendant in Chicago and in Florida. You may consider the facts relating to the connection—if you find from the evidence beyond a reasonable doubt that there is such a connection—between the defendant and the business which was conducted under the name of Guzik.

"View Evidence as Whole."

"You can't look at this case piecemeal. You must look at the evidence as a whole. You must consider each fact in relation to all of the other facts, and so viewing the case arrive at a conclusion whether each one of the essential elements of these indictments have been established to your satisfaction beyond a reasonable doubt.

"Unless it has been proved by competent legal evidence beyond a reasonable doubt that the defendant had a gross income of $5,000 or over you cannot convict him of the offense of willfully failing to make an income tax return, and unless it is proved by competent legal evidence beyond a reasonable doubt that the defendant had a net taxable income you cannot convict him of the offense of willfully attempting to evade or defeat the tax or the payment thereof.

"The mere failure to file a return does not in itself constitute an attempt to evade or defeat the tax. The failure to file the return may be a step in the attempt to evade or defeat the tax. Such failure to file must be considered in connection with all the facts and circumstances of the case.

"The mere failure or omission to do some act or perform some duty is not an attempt to do a specific thing. As I have explained to you, such a failure may be a part of a general plan for a general program."

Takes Up Mattingly Letter.

Judge Wilkerson then took up his discussion of the so-called "confession letter" written by Lawrence P. Mattingly, an income tax attorney for Capone, in which Mattingly stated that Capone might be assumed to have had a total income of $266,000 for the years involved.

This letter was introduced into testimony along with oral statements that Capone had referred questions to Mattingly in conferences with internal revenue agents. The defense attorneys, however, denied the authority of Mattingly to speak for Capone and the validity of the introduction of his written statement. Judge Wilkerson's carefully worded instructions on the exact weight to be given the Mattingly letter follow in part:

"The statements of a duly authorized agent may be proof against the principal the same as if he had conducted in person the transaction in which the statements were made. The agent stands in the place of the principal and acts for him and in his behalf. The statements, however, are not to be considered as the acts of the principal unless they are made pursuant to the authority conferred upon the agent by the principal.

First Point to Determine.

"You must first determine whether or not the statements of Mattingly were within the scope of his employment and were made while he was carrying on the work for which he was employed.

"If you find that under the evidence before you Mattingly had no authority to state his opinion as to the amount of defendant's income, you will disregard the statement of Mattingly as to his opinion as to the amount of income.

"But if you find that under the power of attorney and the authority, if any, given at the interview in the revenue agents' office, considered with all the other facts and circumstances shown here in evidence, Mattingly was employed to get together information and to make an estimate and give his opinion thereof to the bureau, then the fact that Mattingly made a statement as to what his opinion on that subject was is a fact to be considered by you with all the other facts and circumstances in this case.

The "Corpus Delicti" Explained.

"During the trial and in the arguments of counsel you have heard used the phrase a number of times, 'corpus delicti'—body of the crime. On that subject I charge you that proof of a charge in criminal cases involves the proof of two distinct propositions: First, that the act itself was done, and, second, that it was done by the person charged and by none other.

"In this case the proof that a crime has been committed involves proof that as to the evasion counts of the indictment the defendant had an income of the kind which required him to pay a tax. And as to the other count, that he had a gross income of the kind which required him to make a return.

"Now, that fact, that the defendant was bound to pay the tax, or that he was bound to make the return, may not be established by the extrajudicial confession of the defendant unsupported by other evidence. That element of the case is not established by admissions of the defendant, unless such admissions are corroborated by other proof of the corpus delicti.

"The corroborating circumstances must be such that, taking the evidence as a whole, the jury is satisfied beyond a reasonable doubt that the crime has been committed."

Capone Waiting for Jury to Decide His Fate

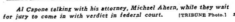

Al Capone talking with his attorney, Michael Ahern, while they wait for jury to come in with verdict in federal court. [TRIBUNE Photo.]

Federal Judge James H. Wilkerson, who heard case.

Source: Courtesy of Chicago Tribune Archives, October 18, 1931. Article continues on next page.

Article continues from previous page.

Chicago Daily Tribune (1872-1963); Oct 18, 1931; ProQuest Historical Newspapers Chicago Tribune (1849 - 1985) pg. 2

G. E. Q. JOHNSON MAKES EFFECTIVE CONVICTION PLEA

Appeals to Jury to Hold Up U. S. Tax Law.

District Attorney George E. Q. Johnson made what was generally considered an effective plea for Al Capone's conviction to the jurors, nine of whom have served before on grand or petit juries in the federal courts and all but two of whom come from small towns and farms.

Mr. Johnson was earnest, so much so that he was almost evangelical at times, clenching his fist, shaking his gray head, clamping his lean jaws together as he bit into the evidence and tore into the defense theories of its meaning and lack of strength.

Objects to Charge of Unfairness.

The prosecutor objected particularly and with vehemence to the defense charge that the government was unfair, that it was riding beyond the law, trying to "con" the jury, and acting because of public clamor.

As to the weight of the evidence that Capone had a taxable income, the prosecutor said that the government considered this so strong from a civil standpoint that it would go ahead and assess and collect on the specific amounts shown in this trial.

"Gentlemen of the jury, counsel for the defense has used a very ugly word in referring to this prosecution," Mr. Johnson began. "They have charged that the government would endeavor to 'con' a verdict from the jury. You have been present, many days during this trial, and I am sure you must have been impressed with the sincerity of my assistants in presenting the evidence.

"Counsel also has sought to characterize this prosecution as frivolous. Every morning thousands of unmarried men and unmarried women go to their daily work. These people pay their share of the government's requirements—an income tax on everything they make in excess of $1,500. There is no more important function of the government, except the emergency of war, than the enforcement of the revenue laws.

Importance of Revenue Laws.

"If the revenue laws cannot be enforced, then government will fail; the army and navy will be swept aside; our courts and all our institutions fall, and our civilization will revert to the chaos of the middle ages."

"Who is this man who has become such a glamorous figure? Is he the little boy from the Second Reader who has found the pot of gold at the end of the rainbow that he can spend money so lavishly? He has been called a Robin Hood by his counsel. Robin Hood took from the strong to feed the weak.

"Did this Robin Hood buy $8,000 worth of belt buckles for the unemployed? Was his $6,000 meat bill in a few weeks for the hungry? Did he buy $27 shirts for the shivering men who sleep under Wacker drive?

"Let us look at his background. We first see him as a bartender at Coney Island. Next he appears at Colosimo's and later, through the testimony of Hickory Slim the Dice Man, he is betting on the races on 22d street, with Johnny Torrio.

"In 1924 he has risen in affluence and power. He buys a $4,500 car and has a prosperous gambling establishment in Cicero, the profits of which were $300,000 for that year. If you say he had only an interest of 8¾ per cent, as Mr. Fink contends, then his income that year was $24,000.

"In 1925 the Rev. Mr. Hoover, that sincere man, a minister of the gospel, and other members of a civic organization, formed a raiding party and visited this place on Derby day. Mr. Ahern said the raiding pastor had better be tending to his own business, but that raid, gentlemen, sprang from the highest motives of citizenship.

Discloses His Real Nature.

"It was here that the defendant disclosed his true identity in flesh and blood. It was a natural impulse to protect his property, the source of his income. 'I own this place,' he said.

"The records show that this place had netted a profit of $200,000 since the first of the year at that time, and the profits for 1926 were $515,000. During this raid, we see Charles Fishetti, whose name appears all through this case, sneaking out the back door with the $10,000 bankroll after talking to the defendant.

"And this raiding pastor should have called in the police! I'll tell you why it was necessary for them [the civic organization] to act; and that's the little notation 'Town' and '$6,000' in the books of that place. That money went to the Cicero town police. That's why the civic organization didn't call in the police. Where were the police when Bragg, that courageous man, was beaten up, his nose broken, by the mob outside the place?

United States Attorney George E. Q. Johnson, who directed prosecution of Capone.

"Let us see how the halo of mystery and romance fits upon the brow of this defendant. Does he ever appear in a reputable business? Did he keep any records, such as an honest citizen keeps? Was there a single instance of contact with reputable business except when he purchased his Florida home?

"He attempted the 'perfect crime,' but slipped up in two instances, once in indorsing a check from the gambling house profits and again in using Guzik checks in Florida.

"They [Capone's attorneys] pictured this defendant as being prosecuted because of public clamor," Mr. Johnson said in closing. "Can you imagine the federal court considering a case which was the result of clamor?

"The United States attorney was never more sincere or more determined in the five years that he has been in office than he is in this case in which the facts cry out a violation of the law.

"This case has been presented with high purpose and honesty in every step."

Source: Courtesy of Chicago Tribune Archives, October 18, 1931.

Chicago Daily Tribune (1872-1963); Oct 25, 1931; ProQuest Historical Newspapers Chicago Tribune (1849 - 1985) pg. 2

JOHNSON READS GANGDOM'S DOOM IN CAPONE FATE

Prosecutor Commends His Aids in Case.

Twilight of organized gangdom in Chicago was forecast by United States District Attorney George E. Q. Johnson yesterday after Al Capone was sentenced. Smiling happily, the prosecutor thanked his assistants and all others who had been instrumental in the conviction of the gang chief.

In a short statement he gave especial thanks to the intelligence unit of the internal revenue bureau.

"At the conclusion of the trial of the Capone case I feel that it is due from me to say that the people should have a deep appreciation of the service rendered by the intelligence unit in the case." the statement read in part. "It should inspire confidence to know that men like Frank Wilson of the intelligence unit, who has been directly in charge of the investigation, should serve the government for small compensation with such great ability and fidelity."

Praises Chief of Unit.

Prosecutor Johnson gave particular credit to Elmer L. Irey, chief of the intelligence unit in Washington, Mr. Wilson and the assistant prosecutors who conducted the case, and to the revenue agent in charge, C. W. Herrick, and his chief deputy, Lew Wilson.

Informally the prosecutor said, "I believe this is the beginning of the end of gangs as Chicago has known them in the last 10 years. Capone is the last of the outstanding leaders now living. Those remaining are merely lieutenants."

Mr. Johnson declined to comment specifically on the court sentence.

Federal Officials' Comment.

The following comments were made by assistant district attorneys and other federal officials:

DWIGHT H. GREEN, income tax expert who handled the opening statement for the prosecution—I believe Capone was given a fair and impartial trial. The sentence of the court speaks for itself. Personally I feel fine over the case.

WILLIAM J. FROELICH—I have no particular comment to make. I am not unhappy over the conclusion.

SAMUEL G. CLAWSON—In regard to the Capone trial, such a matter is like any other business. After laboring for several months it is nicer to have those labors bear some fruit. Naturally I am pleased. To say otherwise would be ridiculous. It was a fair trial. I noticed Capone took it on the chin when the sentence was imposed. He smiled but said nothing.

JACOB I. GROSSMAN—Well, I have no comment to make. It was just another case. On the court action I have nothing to say. As to future cases, we will just keep plugging along.

ROBERT NEELY, acting collector of internal revenue—Credit for the successful prosecution belongs to George E. Q. Johnson. Now, since the criminal charges have been disposed of, I am proceeding vigorously to force collection of the tax that has been imposed on Alphonse Capone and his wife, Mae Capone. We will do all possible to collect the tax penalty, and fine, amounting to $137,328.

Tribune artist's sketch of scene in Judge Wilkerson's court yesterday when Al Capone learned his fate. Left to right: United States Marshal H. C. W. Laubenheimer, Capone hearing sentence, and Judge Wilkerson on bench. [TRIBUNE Photo.]

COST OF PLACING CAPONE IN PRISON IS SET AT $130,000

The drive to put Capone behind bars cost the United States government about $130,000 his prosecutors estimated yesterday. The investigation alone—long months of tedious and meticulous work leading to an indictment—brought an expenditure of approximately $100,000, involving, as it did, the services of most of the ace agents of the special intelligence unit, bureau of internal revenue.

Capone must bear the expenses of the trial, Judge Wilkerson ordered. Items among these include the mileage and daily witness fees of $4 for 35 men and women from Miami, Fla., who came to tell of Capone's luxurious life on his Palm Island estate, A number of other witnesses were under subpoena, although they were not called to the stand. These included Gangsters John Torrio of Long Island and Louie La Cava of Pittsburgh.

The cost of the jury was calculated at $200 per day. More than 50 Chicago witnesses were kept under subpoena and Capone must pay their daily fees. Elmer L. Irey, chief of the intelligence unit, came from Washington for the case and a number of his agents from such distant points as Baltimore and Boston were with him. There is also the time spent by the court and the salaries of prosecuting attorneys to be reckoned. All in all, the total cost of the trial was set at from $25,000 to $30,000.

PROSECUTORS AND JUDGE WHO CAUSED CAPONE DOWNFALL

The staff of prosecutors which brought about conviction of Capone. Left to right: Samuel G. Clawson, Jacob I. Grossman, U. S. Attorney G. E. Q. Johnson, Dwight H. Green, and William J. Froelich, after sentence was pronounced. [TRIBUNE Photo.]

JUDGE JAS. H. WILKERSON. [TRIBUNE Photo.]

Source: Courtesy of Chicago Tribune Archives

CAPONE IN JAIL; PRISON NEXT
Chicago Daily Tribune (1872-1963); Oct 25, 1931; ProQuest Historical Newspapers Chicago Tribune (1849 - 1985) pg. 1

CAPONE IN JAIL; PRISON NEXT

TRIP TO LEAVENWORTH IS ORDERED TOMORROW

One Day Is Granted to Seek Stay of 11 Year Sentence.

Justice moved to a swift and stern conclusion for Al Capone, yesterday. Federal Judge James H. Wilkerson sentenced the tax dodging gang chief to eleven years' imprisonment, fined him $50,000 and denied an appeal bond.

It was all over in twenty minutes. Capone's lawyers, pleading in vain to save their client from immediate confinement. At 10:30 Capone was jostled into the United States marshal's lockup, where he was finger printed. At 11 he was locked in a detention cell in the county jail, while his attorneys scurried around the federal building.

Barring a last minute stay from the Circuit Court of Appeals, Capone is to be taken to Leavenworth penitentiary tomorrow night. Meanwhile, he will remain a prisoner in the jail.

Most Severe Tax Sentence.

The gangster's sentence is by far the highest ever imposed for violation of the income tax laws. The previous record was five years and a day imposed upon Jack Guzik, a Capone gangster. The Capone sentence calls for 10 years' service in Leavenworth penitentiary and one year in the county jail, together with the payment of fines totaling $50,000 and the cost of the trial, which is estimated at $30,000.

Capone can escape paying this total assessment of $50,000 by serving thirty days after his sentence expires and then taking a pauper's oath. But if he takes such an oath, and is found to have assets, perjury charges will ensue.

The fine imposed was the maximum possible. The maximum imprisonment possible was seventeen years. Ten days a month are allowed at Leavenworth for good behavior, so that Capone will have to serve six and two-third years. Five days a month are allowed for good behavior at the county jail. Thus his prospective total imprisonment is seven and one-half years.

Prosecutors Are Jubilant.

United States Attorney George E. Q. Johnson, his assistants and the agents of the intelligence unit who investigated the case, were jubilant. Congratulations were in order. The three year campaign to put Al Capone behind the bars had come to a triumphant close, and Capone, they said, was through in Chicago.

Capone struggled to appear good natured about his fate. A sickly, forced smile betrayed his concern, but he tried to be genial when reporters asked how he felt about the sentence.

"I'd like to say something, boys, but what can I say?" he asked. Later, in the county jail, Capone burst into a fit of temper when confronted by photographers.

As he stood before Judge Wilkerson at the bar, his hands clasped behind his back and a white bandage wrapped around a cut on his trigger finger, Capone glanced appealingly from one lawyer to another. His half grin was repeatedly forced, and when it was all over he grasped Attorney Albert Fink's hand and beamed. "You've done all you could," he said.

Defense Motion Overruled.

Judge Wilkerson, who has told Capone "it is utterly impossible to bargain with a federal court," began the proceeding by summarily overruling Capone's motion for arrest of judgment. The defense lawyers had sought to preclude the execution of judgment, alleging that the counts in the indictment were insufficient.

"It is my opinion that the averments in these counts are sufficient to comply with the constitution and the motion will be denied," said the court.

Capone was sitting unconcerned at counsel's table, wearing a neat looking, dark purplish suit, dark figured tie, and white shirt. His lawyers, Mr. Fink and Michael J. Ahern, had rushed to the bar, making sure that the record showed an exception to the court's ruling.

Judge Imposes Sentence.

"Let the defendant step to the bar," said the court.

Capone stalked forward, with United States Marshal H. C. W. Laubenheimer at his side. Mr. Johnson and the four prosecutors who assisted him gathered around. The court read the statutes covering the income tax offenses of which Capone was convicted, including the maximum penalties. The courtroom, filled from the jury box to the last seat in the spectators' gallery, was stilled.

"It is the judgment of the court," began Judge Wilkerson, "that on count one [a felony count charging income tax evasion for the year 1924] the defendant is sentenced to imprisonment in the penitentiary for a period of five years, and to pay a fine of ten thousand dollars and all costs of the prosecution."

Gang Chief Does Not Flinch.

Capone did not flinch, nor did his lawyers. At least five years was expected, and there was hope that the other sentences would be made to run concurrently. The court continued:

"On count five [a felony count charging tax evasion for 1925] the defendant is sentenced to five years in the penitentiary and to pay a fine of ten thousand dollars, together with all costs of the prosecution.

"On count nine [a felony count charging tax evasion for 1927] the defendant is sentenced to five years in the penitentiary and to pay a fine of ten thousand dollars, together with all costs of the prosecution.

"On each of counts thirteen and eighteen [misdemeanor counts charging failure to file returns for the years 1928 and 1929] the defendant is sentenced to one year in the county jail and to pay a fine of ten thousand dollars, together with all costs of the prosecution."

Capone Stares at Judge.

Capone stared intently at the court, apparently hoping for that much loved word, "concurrently."

"The sentence on counts one and five," the court went on, "is to be served concurrently. The sentences on the other counts are to be consecutive and cumulative.

"The defendant is under sentence of this court on a charge of contempt [for feigning illness to evade a federal grand jury summons]. He was sentenced to six months' imprisonment in the county jail on the 8th of April, 1931. The sentence on counts one and five may be applied in such a way that he will receive credit for the service of the contempt sentence.

"That same thing is applicable to count thirteen, but not to count eighteen. But the contempt sentence and count thirteen are not to run consecutively, but consequently. The felony sentence will be concurrent, first with the six months' contempt sentence, and after that with the sentence of one year on the misdemeanor count.

"The result is that the aggregate sentence is eleven years and fines aggregating $50,000."

Capone for the first time appeared uneasy, but quickly regained his composure and shook hands with Attorney Fink. Mr. Ahern was busy.

"Now, count eighteen on the misdemeanor," said Ahern, "will your honor have that run first and have the remainder of the sentence run afterward?"

"No," said Judge Wilkerson. "That sentence could not be served in the penitentiary. He is to serve first on the felony counts and then on the misdemeanor."

MR. FINK—If the felony counts are reversed by the Appellate court, he will have to serve two years?

THE COURT—Two and a half. The contempt sentence runs concurrently with the felony count but not with the misdemeanor.

Ahern's Plea Turned Down.

Then Mr. Ahern began pleading for the right to serve the misdemeanor count first, whether or not bail were allowed.

Source: Courtesy of Chicago Tribune Archives.   Article continues on next page.

CAPONE IN JAIL; PRISON NEXT

TRIP TO LEAVENWORTH IS ORDERED TOMORROW

*Article continues from
previous page.*

"He will serve the felony counts first," said the court.

"But suppose," said Mr. Ahern, "he is admitted to bail by some court having jurisdiction and still wanted to serve count eighteen—he could not serve it under your order?" (The defense strategy was to keep Capone out of the penitentiary, hoping to defeat the felony counts on appeal.)

Judge Wilkerson turned to District Attorney Johnson:

"You understand what the sentence is and you present your order, and it is ordered that the marshal take custody of the defendant."

Defense Asks an Appeal.

Mr. Ahern presented a petition for an appeal, accompanied by an assignment of errors and provision for a writ of supersedeas.

"I will grant an appeal without allowing the supersedeas," said the court.

MR. FINK—I might call your honor's attention to the fact that your honor has not got the power to deny the application—to deny the supersedeas. We have perfected our appeal. The writ of error is ipso facto a supersedeas in felony and capital cases. However, your honor perhaps knows more about it than I do.

THE COURT—Motion for a supersedeas is overruled and application for bail is denied. You will only be required to give a cost bond on appeal. That will be $250. The defendant will go to the custody of the marshal.

Capone Remains for Discussion.

Marshal Laubenheimer took Capone by the arm and started to lead him away, but the colloquy at the bar was resumed and Capone was permitted to remain awhile.

MR. FINK—Is it in contemplation that the marshal will take him to Leavenworth now or await the disposition of the writ?

THE COURT—After I make the order, it is for the marshal to execute it.

MR. FINK—But I think that you might instruct the marshal not to take him to Leavenworth until such times as we have a chance to present our matters to the Circuit Court of Appeals.

THE COURT—I think he probably would not take him to Leavenworth until Monday in the regular course.

THE MARSHAL—I am ready to go tonight. [The defense lawyers stood aghast, turning first to Capone and then to the court.]

THE COURT—All right. You may prepare the order.

Defense Fights for Bail.

MR. AHERN—Now, my understanding of the law is that when we have perfected our appeal it per se operates as a supersedeas.

THE COURT—That is not my understanding. [Mr. Ahern began citing authorities.]

"That does not entitle the defendant to bail," said the court." Under our practice here, I presume the marshal is always to execute the order of the court unless the court grants a supersedeas.'"

MR. AHERN — But your honor's order is inconsistent; it is contrary to law.

THE COURT—I have nothing to add.

MR. AHERN—But your honor has the authorities in the library, why don't you look them up?

THE COURT — [Smiling ironically and visibly out of patience]—You certainly don't presume to tell this court what to do?

MR. AHERN — I merely wanted your honor to look up the authorities.

THE COURT—I have nothing to add.

Gives Chance for Appeal Bond.

Judge Wilkerson then instructed Marshal Laubenheimer to hold Capone in Chicago until tomorrow night, giving the defense attorneys an opportunity to apply to the Circuit Court of Appeals for an appeal bond.

Mr. Fink and Mr. Ahern said they were undecided as to what course to take tomorrow, their first opportunity to appeal to the higher court. The appeals court was not sitting yesterday.

"We may seek an appeal bond and we may decide to let them take him away to prison and go ahead with our appeal," the lawyers said. "We can get the appeal docketed in about two weeks. At any rate, nothing will be done over the week-end."

A majority of the Appellate court must be sitting to hear the defense application. This would be two of the three judges. In all probability two of the judges will be present tomorrow, but whether they will overrule Judge Wilkerson in the matter of bond is doubtful. Ordinarily the court follows the judge below in such matters, it was said.

More Trouble for Al.

Marshal Laubenheimer took Capone away and there was a rapid exodus from the courtroom. A deputy collector of internal revenue met Capone in the corridor. "Read this," he said, handing the gangster a slip of paper.

Capone took it, and glanced inquiringly at the deputy. Then he read, and gloom spread over his face. It was a jeopardy assessment for delinquent taxes, tying up all his property. The process called for $68,664 in taxes, penalties and interest from Capone and for the same amount from his wife, Mae, for the years 1926 to 1929, inclusive, making a total of $137,328.

Robert E. Neely, acting collector of internal revenue, meanwhile had drawn up papers preparatory to seizure of Capone's safe deposit boxes and telephoned the collector at Miami Beach, Fla., to attach Capone's home.

A battery of photographers stalked the gangster up to the eighth floor of the federal building, where he was taken to the marshal's lockup and finger printed.

Capone Taken to Jail.

Then a taxicab was summoned by Deputy Marshals William G. Thompson and Eric Glasser and Agent J. M. Sullivan of the intelligence unit. They took Capone to the county jail.

As Capone stood in the hallway at the north entrance to the jail, waiting for the door to the cell inclosure to open, reporters again crowded around him. The gangster was visibly in a bad temper by this time.

"It was a blow below the belt," he told the newspaper men, "but what can you expect when the whole community is prejudiced against you? I've never heard of any one getting more than five years for income tax trouble, but when they're prejudiced what can you do even if you've got good lawyers?"

The door swung open and Capone entered the inclosure.

Climax to U. S. War on Gangs.

The sentencing of Capone furnished a dramatic climax to the income tax campaign launched three years ago by federal authorities against gangsters and grafting politicians. The prime objective throughout the drive, as one gangster after another was brought to justice, was to rid Chicago of Capone before the World's Fair. About $100,000 was expended in the nation-wide investigation of Capone's financial affairs, and the trial, which lasted ten days, added many more thousands to the cost.

After indictments charging Capone with income tax fraud and conspiracy against the dry laws had been returned last June, he attempted to bargain with the government and escape with a light sentence. He pleaded guilty with the understanding that the government would make a recommendation as to punishment.

But Judge Wilkerson refused to be bound to any agreement, told Capone he could not bargain, and permitted the pleas of guilty to be withdrawn. Capone still faces the liquor conspiracy charges, but the government is no longer concerned over them.

Huge Expenditures Proved.

Capone's defense in the tax trial was that he had no taxable income, that his losses in gambling dissipated his winnings. But the government linked him with various Cicero gambling dives, and then recounted his expenditures—$100,000 to furnish a $40,000 home; $12,500 automobiles, $27 shirts in dozen lots, $135 suits by the half dozen, thousands of dollars for Chinese rugs, cakes, macaroni and jewelry. A jury chiefly composed of residents of small towns found him guilty on five of 23 counts.

Judge Wilkerson's sentence makes it impossible for the federal parole regulations to operate in Capone's case. A prisoner is eligible for parole upon the completion of one-third of his sentence. But Capone cannot be paroled on the first felony term of five years because the second runs consecutively. He must serve a minimum of 1 year and eight months on the second before becoming eligible for parole, and by that time, or at the end of six years and eight months, he would be released under the good behavior allowance.

The prosecution, headed by District Attorney Johnson, included Dwight H. Green, Samuel G. Clawson, Jacob I. Grossman and William J. Froelich. The agents who made the case, almost the entire force of the intelligence unit in Chicago, were headed by A. P. Madden of the Chicago office and Frank Wilson, ace of the national unit, who came here from Washington.

PUTTING OFF THAT COLD PLUNGE

Source: Chicago Daily News. Reproduced with permission of the Chicago Sun-Times.

The Alcatraz Island prison facilities are shown in this aerial photo taken in the 1920s.

Source: The John Binder Collection
Reproduced with permission of John J. Binder.

Al Capone's Fingerprints

Source: Chicago Crime Commission Archives

1.Paul Ricca(36)/2.Sylvester Agoglia   3.Charles Luciano(35)/4.Meyer Lansky(30)   5.John Senna(29)/6.Harry Brown(43)   Photo dated 4/19/32

Source: James W. Wagner Collection.   Reproduced with permission of James W. Wagner.

Chicago Mayor Anton Cermak (below left) was shot in the abdomen in February 1933 at Bayfront Park in Miami while attending a rally for President-elect Franklin D. Roosevelt. He died three weeks later. Many believe that Giuseppe Zangara (right) was not aiming at FDR but at Cermak, and was sent by the Chicago mob as retaliation for the shooting of Nitto. • Ed Kelly (below right) succeeded Cermak as Chicago mayor. He retained the office until 1947 and posed no serious threat to Nitto's operation.

Source: Eastland Memorial Society Collection
Reproduced with permission of the source.

Source: Images of America: The Chicago Outfit by John J. Binder.
Reproduced with permission of John J. Binder.

Chicago Daily Tribune (1872-1963); Nov 21, 1938; ProQuest Historical Newspapers Chicago Tribune (1849 - 1985)
pg. 26

Chicago Daily Tribune
THE WORLD'S GREATEST NEWSPAPER

MONDAY, NOVEMBER 21, 1938.

Scientific Experts at Work on Actual Cases in Police Department's New Crime Detection Laboratory

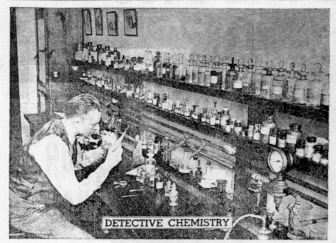

DETECTIVE CHEMISTRY

Working in front of his racks of chemicals Edwin O'Neill restores erased writing on a suspected document. By his method fumes are blown through the tube in his hand, turning the erased ink red.

HANDWRITING EXPERT

Enlarged photographs of words in threatening letter are compared with other specimens of suspected person's script by Ardway Hilton. The enlargements can also be used in court to point out similarities to jury.

BALLISTIC PHOTOGRAPHY

Special camera and apparatus for photographing bullets. A murder weapon can be identified by comparing enlarged photographs of scratches left on fatal bullet with those on test bullet fired from suspect's gun.

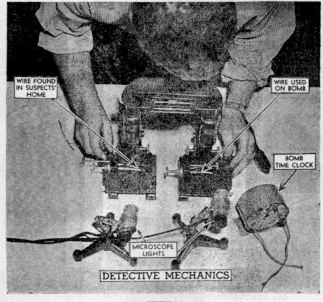

DETECTIVE MECHANICS

Charles M. Wilson examining two pieces of wire which resulted in conviction in Illinois mine bombing. Through comparison microscope he sees two wire surfaces side by side, and can show they came from same piece.

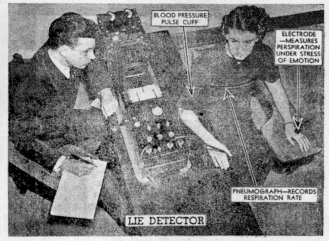

LIE DETECTOR

Using an office employe as a model, Paul V. Trovillo demonstrates use of the polygraph or lie detector, which was developed at the laboratory. It tests truthfulness by recording physical reactions to questions.

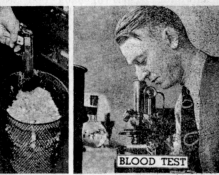

BLOOD TEST

Firing test bullet into basket of cotton.

Through microscope Edwin O'Neill studies stains found at scene in hit-run auto case to identify them as human blood.

Fred E. Inbau, director of the laboratory.

Source: Courtesy of Chicago Tribune Archives

1940

1949

Source: Chicago Crime Commission Archives

Virgil W. Peterson

From 1942 - 1970, Virgil Peterson was the Operating Director of the Chicago Crime Commission. Peterson gave invaluable testimony at the (U.S. Sen. Estes Kefauver D-Tenn.) hearings on organized crime in interstate commerce in the 1950s and was known for many years as the foremost expert on organized crime, not only in Chicago, but across the country. Peterson was a prolific communicator and authored numerous publications on organized crime and other prevalent crime issues of the day. He was credited with bringing about the enactment of critical criminal justice legislation, bringing together press and law enforcement intelligence across the nation on organized crime and for significantly upgrading the administration of justice in Cook County.

Source: John Binder Collection

FOE

Frank Nitti

Frank Nitti took over leadership of Capone's gang and expanded the gang's operations when the Great Depression and the end of Prohibition came about. He expanded gambling, small-time bootlegging, juice loans, and local labor racketeering. A Chicago police detective shot Nitti three times after ordering Nitti to get up against a wall. Nitti, however survived, and in 1943 he committed suicide.

Although we are only able to highlight a few friends and foes for each decade, the Chicago Crime Commission reminds the public that there are many friends, and while perhaps not as famous as the criminals, they are courageous and far more impressive.

Capone's Retirement
Capone's Retirement

Source: Images of America: The Chicago Outfit by John Binder.

In 1940, after Capone's prison sentence of seven and one-half years for income tax fraud was served, he spent most of his time lounging at his various vacation homes sunning, eating, and sleeping. Considered past his prime, Capone was thought to have burned out. Some suspect that he was suffering from syphilis. For a legendary man, this was not an ending that most would have predicted. He was still receiving a cut of the profit from his syndicate heirs and claimed to not remember much of the Chicago gang wars.

Frank Nitti: Outfit Expansion, Indictment, Suicide
Frank Nitti: Outfit Expansion, Indictment, Suicide

Sources: Mars Eghigian and Images of America: The Chicago Outfit by John Binder.

After Capone, Frank Nitti took over. He had a difficult job since the Great Depression hurt the income of the gang, and the end of Prohibition was the end to their most prized and fruitful business. Nitti had to deal with numerous gangsters who expected "jobs" at a time when gang proceeds were drastically declining. To deal with this, Nitti extended operations, moving into expanded gambling (mostly horse racing), small-time bootlegging, non-gambling-related "juice loans," and local labor racketeering. He soon controlled many of the heavily Irish labor unions. In 1934, Nitti brought the various people involved in organized crime into one gang with the help of many of Capone's men, basically forming "the Outfit." Nitti also understood the need to stay out of the spotlight so, from around 1933, to well into the 1940s, the Outfit was practically left alone by law enforcement. However, in 1942, led by Virgil W. Peterson, a former FBI man, the Chicago Crime Commission continued to effectively monitor and address the Outfit. During World War II the Outfit got involved in counterfeiting ration coupons for gas and other items.

The Outfit's primary players during the Nitti years were Paul "the Waiter" Ricca, Tony Accardo, Claude Maddox, "Tough Tony" Capezio, Louis Campagna, Sam "Golf Bag" Hunt, Willie Heeney, Rocco DeGrazia, Jimmy Emery, and Frank LaPorte.

Frank Nitti committed suicide in 1943 when he was indicted in a case involving the extortion of money from the Hollywood film studios. Many believe that Nitti also had cancer and was not a well man at the time of his suicide.

Paul Ricca and Tony Accardo
Paul Ricca and Tony Accardo

Source: Images of America: The Chicago Outfit by John Binder.

Paul "The Waiter" Ricca spent his early days during Prohibition as Frank Nitti's understudy and by the mid-1930s as his underboss. Tony Accardo began his life of crime as a teenager, getting involved with the "Circus Gang" and then joining Capone's gang in 1929. Accardo was likely working as an assistant to Jack McGurn, committing some of the major Prohibition-Era murders, then as body guard to Capone, and eventually as underboss to Ricca after Nitti died. Accardo took over in 1944 as acting boss when Ricca fled the country because of a murder indictment. During the Accardo years, there was an expansion of "street tax" activity. In addition to the usual gambling activities, street tax was collected from professional jewel thieves and robbers and from other criminal sources, particularly when the Outfit was not interested in operating the activity themselves. Accardo served as the boss or chairman of the board for the Chicago Outfit until his death in 1992, having the longest career of any U.S. mobster.

Breakthrough Practices & Equipment
Breakthrough Practices & Equipment

Sources: "Invisible Thumbprint Checks Bad Checks," Chicago Daily News, August 11, 1949.
"Scientific Traffic Control" by L.J. McEnnis Jr., National Law Enforcement Review, August 1949.

Lucky for Capone, the progression of law-enforcement technology was slow until he began his retirement. In 1942, dependable communication between law-enforcement officers was revolutionized when all squad cars were equipped with two-way radios. Electric megaphones were available to law officials for directing traffic, calming panic, and guiding rescue work. Due to the fact that 39,969 people were killed in auto accidents in 1941, officers began receiving modern, scientific traffic-control and accident-investigation training. This training included traffic engineering, safety education, driver licensing, chemical testing for intoxication, testing to determine automobile speed from skid marks, and practical photography. In 1946, the Motorcycle Police Officer position grew to include tending heavy traffic, restraining the thoughtless driver, handling emergencies, and controlling pedestrians. In 1946, fingerprinting was expanded and currency-exchange businessmen adopted the system of invisible fingerprinting for all clients as a safeguard against fraud. That same year the National Law Enforcement Review concluded that public safety depended upon the mobilization of police equipment and proposed compact safety units. These mobile crime laboratories were equipped with an operating room, photography department, radio tower, chemical and fingerprint lab, and enabled police to deal with asphyxia, suicide and attempted suicide, vehicle and falling accidents, and other general cases. In 1947, proposed compulsory and universal fingerprinting came before the U.S. House Judiciary Committee, requiring all adults to be fingerprinted, and stating that law-abiding persons everywhere should welcome its enactment for their own protection.

A Police Officer's Legend
A Police Officer's Legend

Sources: "Chicago Police Scandals," Atlantic Monthly Company, 1960.
"Criminal Justice", Journal of the Chicago Crime Commission, April 1944, No. 71.

During this decade, while technology increased, law-enforcement practices came under examination. Police officers, expected to offer diplomacy, heroism, and tragedy in a day's work, were now in the public eye. The common use of the night-stick or police-club became obsolete as offensive and defensive self-defense methods were practiced daily. Officers were expected to accomplish their ends without wounding or killing criminals. Law-enforcement-officer practices came under scrutiny, when in 1944, the Chicago Crime Commission noted numerous instances where justice failed to appropriately practice the laws of arrest, search and seizure. The Commission stated that evidence had been improperly obtained, and under Illinois law should be inadmissible. The Commission published a manual in February, 1944 to assist law-enforcement officials in complying with the arrest, search and seizure Illinois law. Appointments to the Chicago Police Department were also questioned that year. Politicians, many times affiliated with racketeers and hoodlums in gambling, vice, or other illicit enterprise had been highly influential in the placement of men in the police department. Political control over the Chicago Police Department was even thought to explain unlawful killings of innocent people by some law-enforcement officers.

Narcotics, Alcohol & Crime
Narcotics, Alcohol & Crime

Source: The Narcotic Addict In Chicago prepared by Mary J. McCormick under
the sponsorship of John E. Babb, Sheriff of Cook County.

As early as the 1940s the increase in Chicago's crime rate pointed to narcotics and alcohol use. Out of 563 narcotic offenders, 432 used heroin, thirty-six used marijuana, five used cocaine, two used opium, and four used morphine. Another eighty-four used a combination of the listed drugs. In 1948, the Institute on Adult Delinquency named chronic alcoholism as the number-one cause of crime. Referral centers for those on parole was the recommendation of the American Red Cross.

Stonewall Clark: Wrongly Imprisoned
Stonewall Clark: Wrongly Imprisoned

Source: History of the Chicago Crime Commission.

In 1949, Chicago Crime Commission investigation, evidence, and testimony proved the innocence of Stonewall Clark. After serving over twenty years for a murder he did not commit, Clark was released from prison. His famous defense attorney, Clarence Darrow, had entered a guilty plea. Clark wrote to the CCC in 1947 requesting assistance, at which time CCC officer and Northwestern University Professor of Law, Fred E. Inbau, furnished legal services gratuitously. On the day of Clark's release from prison in 1949, he visited the CCC offices to express his appreciation for the efforts, which had brought about his freedom.

PLEASE POST

FRANK R. NITTO
WANTED
$1,000 REWARD

September 27, 1930

A Reward of $1,000 will be paid by the *Citizens' Committee for Prevention and Punishment of Crime* of the Chicago Association of Commerce for information leading to the arrest of FRANK R. NITTO, alias FRANK NITTO, alias FRANK NITTI, Capone gangster and fugitive from Justice, for the arrest of whom warrant is in the hands of the United State Marshal for the Northern District of Illinois.

The information with reference to this man should be communicated to A. P. Madden, head of the United States Intelligence Unit, Room 587 Federal Building, Chicago, Illinois, Tel. Harrison 4700, Extension 392.

DESCRIPTION

Age	35 to 40
Height	5 ft. 4¾ in.
Weight	About 145 lbs.
Complexion	Swarthy
Eyes	Dark
Hair	Dark, fairly heavy, usually combed smooth and parted on right side
Italian	Usually well dressed

FINGER PRINTS
31 M M 14

Source: Mars Eghigian, Jr. Collection. Reproduced with permission of Mars Eghigian, Jr.

Source:
John Binder Collection

Reproduced with permission of John J. Binder.

This photo shows Frank Nitti very late in his career. Nitti was in ill health when he took his own life and, according to information in some circles, was suffering from cancer. This helps explain his action, which was rather unusual for a gangster. During that era, many victims of cancer committed suicide rather than live in prolonged pain.

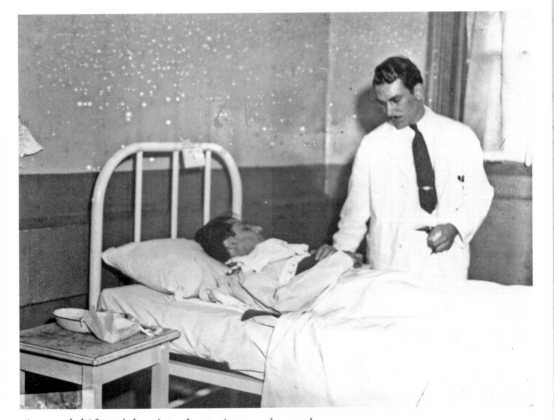

A wounded Nitto (above) in the city's prison hospital.

Source: Chicago Historical Society. Reproduced with permission of the Chicago Historical Society.

(From left to right, top row) Frank Nitti (possibly), Al Capone, Paul Ricca, Anthony Accardo and Ralph Capone at Ricca's wedding in January 1927.

Source: Photo provided by the Drug Enforcement Administration.

Paul Ricca and Louis Campagna.

Source: John Binder Collection. Reproduced with permission of John J. Binder.

This image of Tony Accardo is taken from a very early (probably mid-1920s) line-up photo. Although he might never have spent a night in jail due to a criminal conviction, it appears that Accardo was arrested and held overnight at least twice.

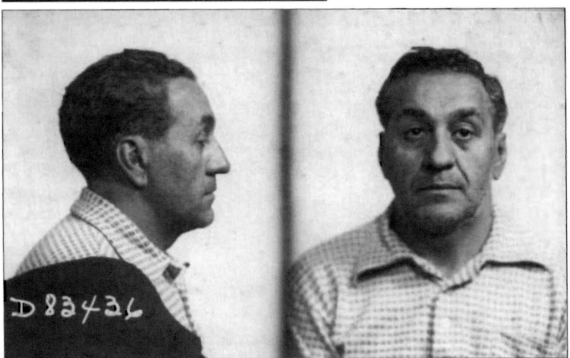

Unusual for a top gangster of this period, Accardo is not wearing a suit or tie in this Chicago Police Department mug shot. He is also sporting what looks to be more than one day's worth of facial hair, indicating that he did spend at least a night in jail on this occasion, probably in September 1943, based on evidence uncovered by organized crime researcher Jeff Thurston.

Source: John Binder Collection

Reproduced with permission of John J. Binder.

What 'Heat Boys' Are Doing Today

Saltis Is Broke and Al Capone Is Sick, but Roundup Finds Old Gangs Are Still on the Make.

(First of a series on the current activities of Chicago's public enemies against the sometimes dramatic, often fantastic, background of the prohibition era.)

News 6·23

BY CLEM LANE.

What's become of the "heat boys?"

The court appearance of Joe Saltis, who is broke, and several others of those listed in 1930 and 1931 as public enemies by the Chicago Crime Commission has prompted a survey to determine how the 56 men so named had fared with the passing years.

Investigators for The Daily News found almost at once that many persons were much more willing to talk than in the days when gang guns were sounding with vicious frequency.

The lapse of time and the additional information have provided perspective. The picture of the gang wars can now be seen whole.

For the benefit of those who came in late, it might be mentioned that the underworld termed the public enemies the "heat boys" because publication of their names by the Crime Commission had turned "the heat," official and otherwise, on them.

ALPHONSE CAPONE.

The current word on the first 14:

Alphonse Capone, the original Public Enemy No. 1. Capone is a victim of paresis. The disease has left him slightly negative in the noggin. Since his release from federal penitentiary where he served seven and one-half years for income tax fraud, he has spent most of his time on his estate at Palm Island, Fla., with some summer trips to Long Beach, Ind.,

and the Wisconsin North Woods. He owns a summer home on Little Martha Lake near Mercer. How Capone's heirs continue to carry on will be detailed in later articles.

Anthony "Mops" Volpe, one of the first Capone gunmen. The government ordered him deported but Italy said: "No, thanks," so he's still here, living in North Austin, with a handbook in the 3800 block on Broadway and a piece of one in Cicero. Chief topic of conversation: his ailing stomach.

Ralph Capone, elder brother of Alphonse. Got on the list chiefly through that relationship; never too heavy in the mob; served three years for income tax violation; hangs his hat in the Knickerbocker Hotel and at 4300 Marine dr.; operates a charged water business at 116 Hubbard st. and has some cigarette vending machines.

Frank Rio, Capone's one man dog. Sentenced with Capone in Philadelphia on that strange gun-toting arrest. Died of a heart attack in his Oak Park home in February, 1935. A story later on his fantastic negotiations in behalf of Capone at the time of the Lindbergh baby kidnaping.

"Machine Gun Jack" McGurn, born Vincent Gebhardi. A boxer of some skill, he swapped the gloves for a machine gun and became a tommy man, first for the North Side mob, later for Capone.

Shot to death Feb. 15, 1936, in a bowling alley at 803 Milwaukee av. by three men who left no forwarding address. There's a good yarn to be told later in this series about the Wild West raid he led one noon on syndicate headquarters in Cicero.

James Belcastro, the "king of the bombers." Belcastro hired out as a pineapple planter and went in for other forms of skulduggery at rates not too high; has a handbook over a poolroom on Roosevelt rd. just east of Ashland av.

Rocco Fannelli, Belcastro's brother-in-law and chief aid. Now handles the games in Belcastro's handbook, where his brother, George, is manager.

"Dago Lawrence" Mangano, a protege of "Diamond Joe" Esposito, who went in for mayhem, alky and gambling. He is now running a book, wire service spot and a layoff joint for the syndicate on the second floor at 57 E. Chicago av., has a summer home on the Fox River near McHenry, Ill.

LAWRENCE MANGANO.

Jack Zuta, a crafty, soft spoken schemer who got his start as a West Side brothelkeeper and later became the brains of the Aiello-Moran North Side mob; shot to death by a band of gunmen who caught him Aug. 1, 1930, on the dance floor of a crowded Wisconsin resort; his death followed published suspicion that he plotted the death of Alfred "Jake" Lingle, Chicago Tribune reporter, but the records he left behind caused more of a furor than Zuta ever did in life.

Jack Guzik, Capone business manager. Guzik got his start as a call boy in a bawdy house; ran houses in Burnham and the 22d st. district; became supervisor of the syndicate's Loop interests; did time for income tax; still active in the mob, with a handbook near Wabash av. and Lake st.

Frank Diamond, born Francis Maritote. Under federal indictment in New York with the other members of the Capone syndicate's board of directors in the million-dollar movie shakedown; lives at 26 N. Long av. Diamond's activities with the other board members will be told later.

George "Bugs" Moran, North Side gang leader. He went into the booze racket when he got out of the penitentiary in 1923; now serving time in Cook County Jail for gun toting and forging travelers' checks; claims to have forsaken the rackets for an oil well. More in succeeding articles about Moran's escape from the St. Valentine's Day massacre and other gang killings. And some of those he staged.

Joe Aiello, the business man who plotted to succeed Capone. He was shot to death the night of Oct. 23, 1930, when caught in cross-fire from two machine gun nests. Details forthcoming of his plan to seize the Unione Siciliana, of his alliance with Moran and Zuta, of the traitors' banquet, with a footnote on what became of the $23,000 he had with him when he died.

Edward "Spike" O'Donnell, ex-convict, beer hustler and fixer. Fresh out of the hospital after an attempt was made to kill him, Spike has resumed his custom of giving open air conversational concerts on street corners; something about O'Donnell's activities in and out of the paving business.

(Tomorrow: What's new with Terry Druggan, Frank Lake, William "Klondike" O'Donnell and the others of the first public enemies.)

THE CHICAGO DAILY NEWS, WEDNESDAY, JULY 7, 1943.

'Bugs' Moran — One of Few to Wage War with Al Capone, and Live

Teamed with Jack Zuta as Alky Partner

(Twelfth of a series on the fate of the "Heat Boys," otherwise called Chicago's public enemies, as framed against the sometimes dramatic, often fantastic, backgrounds of gangland's prohibition era.)

BY CLEM LANE.

George "Bugs" Moran, now serving a year's sentence in the Cook County jail for forging money orders, is one of the few "heat boys" who waged major war on the Capone syndicate and lived to tell of it.

"BUGS" MORAN.

Twenty years ago Moran was released from the penitentiary. He allied himself with the North Side gang, then blossoming forth under the leadership of Dion O'Banion.

Thirteen years ago Moran saw the last North Side opposition to Capone crumble when in short order Jack Zuta and Joe Aiello were shot to death as Dion O'Banion was shot to death.

Just Escaped Massacre.

In between "Little Hymie" Weiss had been killed by gangsters and Vincent "The Schemer" Drucci had been shot down by a policeman, and there were others, including the seven men who died on St. Valentine's Day in 1929.

Moran escaped the massacre by an eyelash, as He escaped other attempts upon him. One reason he may have escaped is that Moran gave as good as was sent —witness his attacks upon the Gennas, his attempt to kill Johnny Torrio, his participation in the raid on Cicero and some coroner's cases that were never officially solved.

The St. Valentine's Day massacre would have chased a more sensitive soul than Moran out of Cook County, but it wasn't long after that that the city saw Moran

blossoming forth into partnership with Joe Aiello and Jack Zuta, with Barney Bertsche, an old con man, and Billy Skidmore, long the "fix" between politicians and racketeers, sharing office space at 127 N. Dearborn st. with the Moran-Zuta-Aiello combination.

Recall Lingle Death.

A truce had been made with the aid of politicians between the North Side gang and the Capone syndicate. While Moran's faction held forth in Loop offices, the Capone headquarters were at various hotels in the neighborhood of 22d st. and Michigan av.

But a little more than a year after the massacre, in April and May, 1930, the Moran-Zuta-Aiello mob was complaining that the police were pushing them around, that the Capone syndicate wasn't living up to its deal and was cutting in on their preserves.

Then on June 9, 1930, Alfred "Jake" Lingle, Chicago Tribune reporter, was shot to death in the Randolph st. underpass leading to the Illinois Central. Lingle was a close friend of both Police Commissioner William F. Russell and of "Scarface Al" Capone, and it transpired that he had become a power in underworld manipulation.

Laid at Zuta's Door.

Out of the hullabaloo of charges and countercharges that filled the air after Lingle's assassination there came word that the wily Zuta had staged the killing of Lingle in a deliberate attempt to bring "heat" on both police and Capone. He succeeded inasmuch as Russell was removed as police commissioner and the lid was slammed on the city.

Parenthetically it might be said that long afterward Leo Brothers, a St. Louis hoodlum who had been doing odd jobs in Chicago, was convicted of the Lingle slaying.

It was long common Chicago gossip that Brothers was "railroaded," but in all justice it must be said that the men who prosecuted Brothers insist, both on and off the record, that if Brothers didn't fire the shots that killed Lingle, he was present in the tunnel and not by accident.

Had Little in Common.

Moran, Zuta and Aiello, the North Side triumvirate, had little in common but their willingness to break the law to make a dollar. Moran was an old-time h'ist man, a simple person who had long made a living by taking a revolver and shoving it at someone with a demand for his money. Boot-

legging seemed a much more respectable career.

Zuta was a short, plump creature, soft spoken and a trifle oily as to manner. He got his start operating a chain of second-rate bawdy houses in the Warren av. police district. As a brothel operator, he had learned the system of greasing police and politicians. Like Moran, the alky and beer rackets provided a step up.

For Aiello, the racket was a step down. Joe Aiello was head of a numerous clan that included his five brothers and about 40 close kinsmen.

Join in Genna Attack.

He had an importing and a commission business in Randolph st., a bakery on the Near North Side, holdings in real estate and other lucrative enterprises.

The rise of the Gennas and the wealth they amassed seems to have affected Aiello and his business partner, Tony Lombardo. That Aiello and O'Banion joined hands to attack the Gennas is evident in retrospect. Tony Aiello, a brother of Joe's, was identified in one of the Genna killings, but the sluggish movement of the Cook County law enforcement machinery stymied the case.

Lombardo allied himself with Capone in an effort to freeze out Aiello. The newspapers reported it as a war for control of the Unione Siciliana, whereupon respectable citizens, including Former Judge Bernard P. Barasa would protest that the Italo-American National Union, the Unione's successor, was a highly respectable fraternal society.

Slain on Loop Street.

Nevertheless, Tony Lombardo could be found regularly in the union's offices near Madison and Dearborn sts. and he had just left those offices the afternoon of Sept. 7, 1928, when gunmen stepped up to him in Madison st., between Clark and Dearborn sts. and pumped lead into him. Aiello's stock ran high after that daylight assassination in the heart of the Loop.

His attempt to get Capone and take over the Chicago rackets will be told tomorrow in the story of Albert Anselmi and John Scalise.

After Lingle's death and the heat it engendered, Zuta was

JACK ZUTA.

seized by the police and questioned at headquarters at 11th and State sts. As he rode through the Loop toward his North Side hotel, Capone gunmen, led by Ted Newberry, who had thrown in his lot with the syndicate, tried to kill him. Lt. George Barker, an able policeman who has since died, fought off the gunmen, but one of the

Article continues on next page.

NEWS
JUL 7 1943

Article continues from previous page.

THE CHICAGO DAILY NEWS, WEDNESDAY, JULY 7, 1943.

'Bugs' Moran — One of Few to Wage War with Al Capone, and Live

Capone bullets killed a streetcar motorman.

About a month later, on Sunday night, Aug. 1, 1930, the Capone gunmen trailed Zuta to the Lake View Hotel at Deerfield, Wis., a resort town about 25 miles west of Milwaukee.

Zuta was standing on the dance-room floor, shoving nickels into a mechanical piano. The rear door of the bar room adjoining the dance pavilion, was opened and in strode six men, guns in hand. One of the six took charge of the bar room, the other five marched into the pavilion. Two had machine guns, two had sawed-off shotguns, the other a brace of automatic pistols.

As the leader sang out "There he is," Zuta made a dive for shelter behind the piano. The five gunmen ran toward him. One gunman slowed up long enough to toss a 7-year-old boy out of range. The five closed in on Zuta.

Greater Nuisance Dead.

As the dancers fled screaming, the gunmen cut loose, scores of bullets and slugs tearing into Zuta's body.

Then, as a hint to the remaining dancers who cowered against the wall, they fired a couple of bursts into floor and ceiling.

Then they walked, at not too rapid a pace, to two waiting automobiles.

Zuta dead was as much of a nuisance as Zuta alive. He left behind him various notes and records, some which, although quite innocent, took on a sinister aspect in juxtaposition with his racket records.

Gunmen Ambush Aiello.

Moran had gone into hiding up in Lake County. As indicated, Moran's prowess as a gunman caused hesitation in the Capone ranks, but Aiello's record was that of one who hired his gunmen.

On the night of Oct. 31, 1930, almost three months after the slaying of Zuta, the Capone gunmen ambushed Aiello and killed hml. Aiello had sneaked back into Chicago to arrange his affairs. He wanted, too, to raise a considerable sum for an extended stay in Mexico.

With $23,000 in his pocket and transportation to Mexico, Aiello summoned a cab to the home of his partner Pasquale Prestogiacomo, 205 N. Kolmar av. Pasquale, known as Patsy Presto, had been in the firm when Lombardo and Aiello were partners.

Staggers Around Corner.

For the first time in 10 days Aiello stepped out of doors as he followed the driver to the cab. A window slid up in a second floor apartment, directly across the street. There was a flash and then the drumming of machine gun fire.

Aiello screamed as a bullet caught him. He started to run and was staggered by another blast. Half crawling, half staggering he rounded a corner into a court only to be met by a third burst of machine gun fire from a third floor apartment at 4518 West End av.

Aiello was taken to Garfield Park Hospital. He was dead, with two score machine gun bullets in his body. When the coroner's investigators arrived, they inventoried his possessions. The $23,000 had disappeared. Those who took it had thoughtfully left $6.25 in his clothing.

Who Can Blame Him?

The death of Zuta, followed by the death of Aiello, broke up the North Side gang. Moran for a time confined his activities to Lake County where with Leo Mongoven, he dabbled in slot machines and other rackets.

He's interested now, in the oil business in the Illinois field. As soon as he gets out of jail, which will be along about Nov. 1, he's through with Chicago, he says.

Who, checking the coroner's records, can blame him?

Tomorrow: The Traitors' Banquet, the death of the torpedoes, Scalise and Anselmi.

Al Capone: Legend of His Life Fizzles Out

News 7943

(Fourteenth of a series on the fate of the "Heat Boys," otherwise called Chicago's public enemies, as framed against the sometimes dramatic, often fantastic, backgrounds of gangland's prohibition era.)

BY CLEM LANE.

There's a touch of anticlimax in Al Capone being on hand as of July 9, 1943 — something like hearing that Gen. Custer didn't die in that last stand, that he's playing third base for the Pittsburgh Pirates.

AL CAPONE.

For Capone, the original Public Enemy No. 1, the first and foremost of the "heat boys," became a legend years ago, a legend wreathed in the gun smoke of gang wars, a legend of prohibition millions, illicit power, of the chatter of machine guns, of X marks the spot, the one-way rides, of murder and massacre.

Now to have him a doddering paretic, the periods of lucidity growing less frequent, a shadow now in the Wisconsin North Woods or again at Palm Island, Fla., just doesn't make a fitting end to the legend.

Properly, for the sake both of art and justice, he should have died in the electric chair or under the flaming guns of a spectacular assassination.

Alphonse Capone was born Caponi in Naples, Italy, Jan. 17, 1899. His father brought the family to the United States when Capone was 5 years old, settling in Brooklyn, where he opened a barber shop. Capone quit school when the study of fractions in 5th grade proved too much for him.

Street gamin, poolroom hanger-on, petty thief, apprentice pander, it was in those days his youth that Capone got the jagged scar that marked the left side of his face and give him his sinister-sounding nickname. When Capone came to prominence, he started a story that he had got it fighting with the famed Lost Battalion in France.

Here Are Facts.

The fact is that the nearest he got to the Army in the first World War was registration for the drafting of 18-year-olds. The scar was inflicted in a knife fight with one Frank Callucci in Fifth av., between Union and President sts. Callucci is still in Brooklyn, occasionally being picked up as a "vag."

After the war Capone drifted to Chicago, and scraped up an acquaintance with Johnny Torrio, who had come West some eight or nine years before. The killing of "Big Jim" Colosimo moved Torrio into front rank and by 1924 when Capone was first accused of murder, the Brooklyn lad had become Torrio's right-hand man, his ostensible occupation being that of male madame of the notorious Four Deuces bawdy house at 2222 S. Wabash av. Capone had adopted the name of Al Brown.

The murder was that of Joe Howard, shot to death May 8, 1924, in Hymie Jacobs' saloon at 2300 S. Wabash av. by a man he greeted with a "Hello, Al." Capone surrendered a month later. The witnesses, of course, couldn't identify him.

Little-Known Figure.

Capone to that time had been a little-known figure, although the police had marked his rise in racket circles, his growing power not alone in Chicago, but in Burnham and in Cicero and other west suburbs.

After Torrio fled Chicago, following his attempted assassination and his hasty retreat to the Lake County jail, Capone became the No. 1 man of the rackets and the guns barked more briskly than ever.

The syndicate was battling the North Side gang led by Hymie Weiss, "Schemer" Drucci and "Bugs" Moran; it was lending a hand to its allies Frank McErlane, Joe Saltis and Ralph Sheldon in their battles with "Spike" O'Donnell and other Southwest Side beer hustlers; it was warring with "Klondike" O'Donnell and assorted West Side mobs.

Events of 1926.

The year 1926 saw the killing of Assistant State's Attorney William H. McSwiggin and two gangster pals, followed by a lid-clamping and farcical investigation; the North Side gang machine gun raid at noon on Capone headquarters in Cicero; the prohibition indictment of 79 persons, headed by Capone and Joseph Z. Klenha, president of Cicero, and Ted Svoboda, the town's chief of police; the killing of Weiss in front of Holy Name Cathedral; shootings in downtown streets, and the announcement that the gangs had signed a peace agreement.

Oh, yes, and the dropping of vote fraud charges involving the election in Stickney, which the McSwiggin grand jury had voted against Capone.

Early in January, 1927, the body of Theodore Anton, owner of the Anton Hotel in Cicero where the Capone gang often made its headquarters, was found buried in quick lime in prairie land in Burnham. A bullet in the head had caused death.

That wasn't a gang murder but a personal job on the part of Capone. Slightly in his cups at a gang celebration, Capone whipped out a pistol at a remark of Anton's he took as an insult and shot the hotelkeeper.

The police answer to that was to raid "The Ship," a Cicero gambling house Capone owned.

In March, an attempt was made to kill Capone in Hot Springs, but he eluded his assassins by leaping down a mountain trail.

Dog Tracks Blossom.

The summer of that year saw the dog tracks blossoming forth in Cook County, with Eddie O'Hare brought on from St. Louis by Capone to run things for the syndicate.

In the fall of that year Joe Aiello tried his hand against Capone, setting up, the police said, a machine-gun nest in a room in a Loop hotel across the street from "Hinky Dink" Kenna's cigar store, where Capone was a frequent visitor.

Aiello was seized and thrown into a police cell next to which some Capone gangsters had been conveniently housed. They kept Aiello awake throughout the night, telling him what they planned to do with him. On his release, Aiello fled the city, and Capone announced, too, that he was departing.

As soon as Al lit in Los Angeles, the police grabbed him and shoved him on a Chicago-bound train. Chicago police said they'd catch him on the first bounce, but he sneaked off the train at Joliet and into the hands of the police. He was fined $2,500 for gun-toting.

In 1928 a nice quiet time was had by all, except Tony Lombardo, head of the Unione Siciliana, shot down in Chicago's Loop, and Frankie Uale, alias Yale, slain in New York by guns which Capone had purchased in Florida.

Capone was conveniently in Florida when his machine-gunners staged the St. Valentine's Day massacre in February. He was summoned to federal authorities and a month later. That was of the income-tax hunt A. P. Madden and the the intelligence unit of nal revenue bureau.

A Triple Slaying.

Then came the killing Guinta, Albert Anselmi Scalise at the traitors May 7, 1929.

The triple slaying treachery that caused him petrate it did something pone.

Nine days later he was seized with Frank Rio by Philadelphia police. The next day he and Rio were sentenced to a year in prison for gun-toting.

Capone told Philadelphia authorities he had just come from concluding a three-day meeting with George Moran and other Chicago gangsters, presumably Jack Zuta and Joe Aiello, at Atlantic City. The meeting was to put an end to Chicago gang wars, Capone said.

There was something about that Philadelphia arrest that wasn't quite kosher, the underworld decided. It looked as if Capone wanted no part of the rackets, at least temporarily.

Capone was released in March, 1930, and returned to Chicago. There was an abortive attempt on his part to seize some of the unions with the aid of Mike Carrozzo, but publicity halted the drive.

That Lingle Killing.

The start of the income-tax drive by Madden's intelligence unit sleuths brought about the conviction of Al's brother, Ralph. There were the slayings of Capone's friend, "Jake" Lingle, and the breakup of the North Side opposition with the slaying Jack Zuta and Joe Aiello.

Capone was riding high.

But back in 1929 he had been cited for contempt for his failure to appear promptly in response to a federal subpoena.

On Feb. 27, 1931. Federal Judge

Article continues on next page.

Source: Chicago Daily News, July 9, 1943. Reproduced with permission of the Chicago Sun-Times.

Article continues from previous page.

James H. Wilkerson found Capone guilty of contempt and sentenced him to six months in Cook County jail.

Hit in Indictments.

In June Capone was hit in two indictments—one for income-tax evasion, a second in which he and 68 of his aids were accused of a huge beer conspiracy. The federal administration wanted to show it was doing the right thing by the prohibition law, according to gossip about the U.S. Courthouse.

Capone, stuck on the income tax, offered to plead guilty to both indictments. The report was that in return for his plea of guilty, he would be given a sentence of but two and a half years in prison. Then it could be said he had been sent to jail for violating the prohibition law.

Judge Wilkerson hadn't been reckoned with. He refused to be a party to the deal. The guilty pleas were withdrawn and Capone went on trial. He was accused of defrauding the government of $215,000 through failure to pay taxes on an income of $1,036,654 for the years 1924 to 1929.

A few days after the trial opened, Madden's intelligence unit agents seized Philip D'Andrea, close friend of Capone's as

PHILIP D'ANDREA.

he left the court-room with the gang chief. He was found in possession of a revolver. For that, he was later given six months in jail.

At the time it was reported the gun was simply for protection of Capone. Now it can be said definitely there was a harebrained plot on to kill Judge Wilkerson.

Parade of Witnesses.

There was a long parade of witnesses as little by little the government built up its case. The jury found Capone guilty on Oct. 17 and on Oct. 24, Judge Wilkerson sentenced Capone to 10 years in the penitentiary and a year in jail, plus $50,000 in fines.

He was held in the County Jail until May, 1932, when his last appeal was denied by the Supreme Court, and then sent to the federal penitentiary at Atlanta.

It was while he was held in the County Jail pending appeal that Capone sent Frank Rio to Hopewell, N.J., to talk with Col. Charles A. Lindbergh about the kidnaping of the Lindbergh baby. Madden, head of the government agents who had built the income tax case against Capone, was at work in Hopewell on the Lindbergh kidnaping.

Sought His Freedom.

Rio dwelt on the Capone influence in the underworld, telling Lindbergh and Madden that if Capone were allowed his freedom temporarily, he could effect the baby's return within 24 to 48 hours. This was in April.

Six weeks before Capone himself had said: "I know a lot of people who might be valuable in finding the child. There's nothing I can do here behind the bars, but I'm pretty sure there would be if I could get out for a while."

Capone's offer was refused.

Sent to the 'Rock.'

On Aug. 22, 1934, Capone was removed from Atlanta to Alcatraz Island penitentiary off San Francisco—"The Rock"—where the government keeps the toughest of its tough prisoners. From time to time word drifted out of Capone quarrels with other inmates, including one in midyear 1936 when he was stabbed by James C. Lucas, a Texas bank robber.

On Jan. 7, 1939, he was transferred to Terminal Island prison at Los Angeles, there to finish out his sentence. Granted time off for good behavior, he served seven years, six months and two weeks.

He was released to his family at Lewisburg, Pa., federal prison Nov. 16, 1939. He was taken to Baltimore for treatment by specialists in syphilis.

Gets Cut of Profits.

Since then he has spent his time mostly at his estate on Palm Island in Florida, varied by trips to Long Beach, Ind., and to the Wisconsin North Woods.

His heirs in the syndicate still give him a cut of the profits.

Capone, those who have talked with him recently say, doesn't seem to remember much of the Chicago gang wars—or anything else. Just a feeble animal, liking the sun, food, sleep.

What a lousy ending for a legend.

(Tomorrow: The Capone sydicate today—last of the series.)

Source: Chicago Daily News, July 9, 1943

Engineer designing circuits for Motorola two-way radios, Chicago, 1940.

© 2007, Motorola, Inc. Reproduced with permission.

Motorola two-way radio police customer, Berwyn, Illinois, USA, circa 1941.

© 2007, Motorola, Inc. Reproduced with permission.

Motorola two-way radio research and production, Chicago, 1942.

© 2007, Motorola, Inc. Reproduced with permission.

Source: International Industries, Inc. as published in the National Law Enforcement Review,
September, 1946, Volume 1, Number 3.

124

Fellowship Students receive field work in accident investigation.

Source: Evanston Police Department

Reproduced with permission of the Evanston Police Department.

Illinois State Police crime lab on wheels, with a complement of state troopers on inspection day.

Source: Illinois State Police
Reproduced with permission of the Illinois State Police.

Motorcycle Officer riding the Indian, hydraulic-controlled, spring frame, bike.
Source: National Law Enforcement Review, August, 1946, Volume 1, Number 2.

Invisible Thumbprint Checks Bad Checks

The system of invisible fingerprinting suggested as a safeguard against vote frauds is already protecting businessmen who cash checks for strangers.

More than half the city's 500 currency exchanges and nearly 200 retail stores and saloons now use the device to identify persons seeking to cash personal checks.

So successful has it been at reducing forgeries that the Canler Corp., distributor for the service, now guarantees all its clients against loss.

How It Works

This is how the system works:

A stranger seeking to cash a check is asked to put his thumbprint beneath

It's Biggest Value

Although 45 forgery convictions have been credited to the invisible print system in the last three years, Morris J. Kilmnick, president of Chicago Currency Exchange Association, says its biggest value is in discouraging forgeries.

'Our members have found that a man is a pretty safe bet once you get his fingerprint,' Kilmnick said. 'Criminals just don't want to leave their mark.'

He said currency exchanges had found very few honest citizens who objected to being printed with the colorless ink.

Source: Chicago Daily News
Reproduced with permission of the Chicago Sun-Times.

As he accepts Union League's 1965 Distinguished Public Service Award, Chicago Crime Commission Director Virgil W. Peterson receives a standing ovation from an audience of over 300, including Chicago Superintendent of Police Orlando W. Wilson, Cook County Sheriff Richard B. Ogilvie, Chicago Crime Commission President William B. Browder, and State's Attorney Daniel P. Ward.

Source: Chicago Crime Commission Archives.

The Long Arm of the Law
Reprinted through the courtesy of the Chicago Daily News.

Source: Chicago Daily News
Reproduced with permission of the Chicago Sun-Times.

Your Banker and
LIQUOR LAW ENFORCEMENT

By FRANK C. RATHJE, President of
the American Bankers' Association

Well known leader in banking field suggests advisability of closer cooperation with police

I AM CONVINCED law enforcement agencies in any community—particularly the municipal police—would find it advantageous to team up with the banker. He is a component part of that vast institution commonly termed "private industry," but he also functions as an ex-officio public servant, vitally interested in law and order, prosperity and community welfare in general.

How? Take as an example the liquor law enforcement. As a whole, the liquor business has kept itself remarkably clean since the repeal of prohibition, but human nature being what it is, bad spots develop here and there in every city. The big ones are known to the police and can eventually be handled, but the small, casual violations are the things which undermine the public's respect for the law, and these are hard to catch. However, close attention, on the part of the banker, to the matter of leases made with retail liquor

Frank C. Rathje, President, The American Bankers' Association

dealers would serve the two-fold purpose of protecting property owners and the community. In most states, the owners of real estate are held responsible for their own or their tenants' operations wherever liquor sales are concerned and penalties for violations are heavy and liability for injury high. The banker, through loans, trusteeships, and so forth, has a voice in a large proportion of real estate operations. He is a good judge of character through long years of credit work. He has at his service sources of information on the business histories of individuals. In the matter of liquor dealers, he can sense potential trouble and apply preventative measures long before the police even know of the impending arrival of questionable individuals in the liquor business in their neighborhood. Convince your banker of the importance of a careful screening of all applicants and he will pass the word on, impressively, to renting agencies and landlords. I cannot say how far your local banker will go in working with you— nor can I assure the banker of an enthusiastic welcome from police officials. But this much I can state—here is an opportunity for mutually advantageous cooperation.

Another place where police and bankers could work together is in the matter of slum control and slum clearance. The police know the pest spots of crime incubation. They know where undesirable conditions lead to juvenile delinquency, to the deterioration of neighborhoods, to the destruction of values. It may be everyday knowledge to them, yet have escaped the notice of the banker. It might be a smart move on the part of the police authorities to force these matters on the attention of bankers and insurance companies. Two chances of three, something could and would be done.

A completely cordial relationship between the banker and the police—a thorough understanding of local problems, needs, improvements—make of the banker a stronger advocate of more adequate financial support of police work. This is well worth consideration, as the operations of any law enforcement agency are limited by the size of the budget. Get the banker interested in the means and methods of proper law enforcement. He knows the incalculable value of reputation to the individual or to the community. He knows the devastating results of rampant crime on the commercial growth of any town or city. Make him part of your inner, family circle on what's being done to hold down crime and maintain the good reputation of your city. When he is allowed to see actual results, he will gladly champion necessary costs. It is up to you to show him.

8

Source: National Law Enforcement Review, July, 1946, Volume 1, Number 1.

DOPE-RING MEMBER SLAIN BY SHOTGUN ASSASSINS
LEFT: Coroner A. L. Brodie examines the automobile of Carl Carramusa, 37, in which he was shot to death last night in front of his home at 837 N. Lawndale av. before the eyes of his 15-year-old daughter.
RIGHT: He examines shotgun holes in auto's windows.

SUN PHOTOS.

Source: Chicago Sun, June 22, 1945
Reproduced with permission of the Chicago Sun-Times.

Table 13

Population, Size and Racial Composition of
Four Areas having the highest Number of
Narcotic Offenders

| Area | Square Mile | Population | | | Per Cent Negro |
		Negro	White	Total	
28	4.6875	65,519	94,843	160,362	40.9
35	1.3252	76,421	2,324	78,745	97.0
38	1.6421	113,374	1,183	114,557	98.9
40	.8901	56,178	678	56,856	98.8

Table 14

Volume and Density of Population in 1940 and
1950 in Four Areas having the Highest Number
of Narcotic Offenders

| Area | Square Mile | 1940 | | 1950 | | Per Cent Increase |
		Population	Density	Population	Density	
28	4.6875	136,518	29,124	160,362	34,105	17
35	1.3252	53,124	40,088	78,745	59,429	48
38	1.6421	103,256	62,880	114,557	69,762	11
40	.8901	52,736	59,247	56,856	63,872	8

* Size in square miles and 1940 figures on Area population and density are
taken from Local Community Fact Book of Chicago, Edited by Wirth and
Berner, University of Chicago Press. 1949.

Chicago area narcotic figures

Source: Crime Prevention Bureau of Illinois

DEATH VERDICT FOR 2 KILLERS IN $4 ROBBERY
Chicago Daily Tribune (1872-1963); Jun 5, 1927; ProQuest Historical Newspapers Chicago Tribune (1849 - 1985)
pg. 9

DEATH VERDICT FOR 2 KILLERS IN $4 ROBBERY

The death penalty was voted by a jury in Judge Emanuel Eller's Criminal court yesterday afternoon for Stonewall Clark, 20 years old, and Ernest Holt, 19 years old, both colored, who were found guilty of murdering Robert Levy while robbing him in his grocery at 1443 Fulton street. Both defendants are ex-convicts.

The crime for which the men will go to the gallows unless a new trial is granted on June 18, netted them only $4. On Dec. 22, 1926, they entered Levy's grocery shortly before 7 o'clock and demanded that he give them the contents of the cash register. When he refused, Holt is alleged to have shot him.

Identified by Widow.

Assistant State's Attorneys Harold Levy and Emmet Byrne, who prosecuted the case, had to depend on the identification of the bandits made by Mrs. Anna Levy, the widow, and a repudiated confession by Holt. The widow, however, who was standing in the rear of the store when her husband was murdered, could not be shaken in her identification.

"I am glad the murderers of my husband are to get the proper punishment," was the comment of the widow, who was in court with her 4 year old daughter, Shirley. It was on the child's birthday that the father was shot down.

Fifteenth Death Penalty.

The death verdict makes the fifteenth such penalty obtained by Prosecutors Byrnes and Levy since they have specialized in prosecuting murder cases.

Holt was paroled from Pontiac reformatory on Sept. 21, 1926, after serving 2 years of a burglary sentence, and Clark was paroled from the same institution where he had been sentenced on a larceny indictment. He also has served other minor sentences.

DIES AS RESULT OF FALL.

Stephen Peterson, 70 years old, 6725 South Green street, died in the county hospital yesterday of a fractured hip received last week when he fell in his home.

RADIO BOSSES STICK BY THEIR GUNS; REFUSE K. C. CHANGE FOR WGES

Washington, D. C., June 4.—[Special.]—In accordance with its announced determination not to modify the reallocation of frequencies and power output order which becomes effective on June 15, the federal radio commission today denied the appeal of radio station WGES in Chicago for assignment to a more favorable band.

Yesterday the commission denied a similar petition for station WJAZ, also in Chicago.

WGES, which is to be transferred in the order from its old frequency of 950 kilocycles to 1,240 kilocycles and must divide its time on the air with station WEDC, also in Chicago, requested that the 920 kilocycle frequency be assigned to it. The station also protested at the terms of the order which will compel a reduction in its power output from 1,000 watts to 500.

EXPECT POLICE TO SEND IN $2,050 FOR IRONSIDES

Charles A. Brown announced yesterday that approximately $2,050 would be added to the mayor's Old Ironsides button fund on Tuesday, when the receipts from forty-one police stations are due. A check for $50 was received yesterday from the Irish-American society, and an order of buttons was sent to the Proviso High school. The committee will send a delegation of girls to Hammond, Ind., on June 14 to sell Old Ironsides buttons to the crowd expected to hear President Coolidge's address.

Commander A. G. Dibrell reported that the Save Old Ironsides committee had placed $25,000 worth of pictures on sale, and that another order of pictures would arrive this week.

CORONER'S JURY DISAGREES.

Eau Claire, Wis., June 4.—(P)—A third adjournment, without reaching a verdict, was taken last night by the coroner's jury investigating the murder of Harold Munson, 27, in a ditch a few yards from the back door of his farm home, a mile from the village of Eleva.

Source: Courtesy of the Chicago Tribune Archives

1950

Tony Accardo – *Source: John Binder Collection*

1959

Dr. Lois Higgins

Source: United Press

U.S. Senator Kefauver

Source: Chicago Sun, August 8, 1951

FRIEND

U.S. Senator Estes Kefauver

Kefauver led the United States Senate Committee that investigated organized crime in interstate commerce. He worked closely with the Chicago Crime Commission when devoting time to the gambling syndicate, the wire service, and the survivors and heirs to the Capone gang.

Dr. Lois Higgins

Dr. Higgins took the first Chicago policewomen's exam offered in twenty years. Of 1,119 women, only ten were hired with Higgins on that list. She was well-known for solving the Schwenke "baby farm" case where a married couple was selling babies and later for her work as the Chief Executive Officer of the Illinois Crime Prevention Bureau.

Although we are only able to highlight a few friends and foes for each decade, the Chicago Crime Commission reminds the public that there are many friends, and while perhaps not as famous as the criminals, they are courageous and far more impressive.

Tony Accardo and Sam Giancana

Source: John Binder Collection

FOE

Tony Accardo

A teenage Accardo began his life of crime as a member of the Circus Gang and then joined up with Capone in 1929. Allegedly, he was responsible for many of the Prohibition era slayings. He became body guard to Capone, underboss to Paul Ricca, and then, eventually served as the chairman of the Outfit. Accardo had the longest career of any U.S. lead mobster until his death in 1992.

Sam Giancana

Giancana became the boss of the outfit in 1957 when Accardo decided to step down from the day-to-day operations and become the chairman. Giancana reported to Accardo and also received counsel from Paul Ricca. His very public and erratic behavior, along with growing law enforcement pressure did not please Accardo and he was, in effect, fired. Wisely, he decided to leave the country. Upon his return he was murdered.

United States Senate Committee Joins Forces With CCC
United States Senate Committee Joins Forces With CCC

In 1950, the United States Senate Committee investigating organized crime in interstate commerce came to Chicago and asked the Chicago Crime Commission for assistance. The CCC supplied investigators and subpoena servers while working closely with Senator Estes Kefauver. The committee under Kefauver followed the suggestions of the Crime Commission and devoted much time to the gambling syndicate, the wire service, and in general, the survivors and heirs of the Capone gang.

Tony Accardo and Sam Giancana
Tony Accardo and Sam Giancana

Source: Images of America: The Chicago Outfit by John Binder.

According to John J. Binder, author of *Images of America: The Chicago Outfit*, in the 1950s the Outfit was at its peak:

> *"their gambling and vice activities included clubs and casinos on Rush Street (in the heart of the old North Side cabaret district), in Cicero, and on the Strip in south suburban Calumet City, which was nationally renowned. The Outfit also ran wide open in west suburban Lyons and along Milwaukee Avenue in the suburb of Niles, at the northwest tip of the city, where Eddie Vogel's firm Apex Amusement was located."*

The Outfit controlled unions, gambling and striptease clubs, and many taverns were forced to use Outfit-supplied coin-operated machines, such as juke boxes and cigarette machines. Its biggest move in the 1950s was its investment in casino gambling outside of Chicago, e.g., investing in a hotel casino in Cuba and helping to build the Strip in Las Vegas. In the 1950s the Outfit controlled crime families in Milwaukee and Madison, Wisconsin, Rockford and Springfield, Illinois, and Kansas City, Missouri. It had a major presence in Los Angeles and other areas of California. It spoke for all crime families west of the Mississippi River on the national commission of La Cosa Nostra. In 1957, Accardo stepped down from the day-to-day operations of the Outfit and Sam Giancana succeeded him. Giancana, however, still reported to Accardo (and Ricca) for counsel. A number of years later, in the mid-60s, Accardo, in effect, fired Giancana due to growing law enforcement pressure on the Outfit and Giancana's very public and erratic behavior. Once relieved of his duties, he left the country. When he returned, he was murdered. Many in the upper tiers of the Outfit from Prohibition days died from natural or other causes by this time, so the higher ranking members of the Outfit were beginning to change.

Juke Box Racket
Juke Box Racket

An exhaustive study completed by the Chicago Crime Commission in 1954 detailed the fact that far too many juke-box distributorships and operating routes were in the hands of powerful organized crime leaders. Testimony given by the CCC's Operating Director Virgil Peterson to a U.S. Senate Committee provides an example of the kind of information contained in the report: Peterson explained, "Meyer Lansky, an original member of the Frank Costello group, is one of the big gambling racketeers of the country with operations in several sections of the country. In New York he has been in the juke-box distributing business. There were strong indications that Lansky's juke-box operations in New York had some connection with similar juke-box distributing activities of the Capone gang in Chicago. In fact, one company with which he was connected at one time had the same financial backing as the financial backing of a company operated by Jack Guzik's son-in-law in Chicago." This confidential report was provided to several branches of the U.S. government in many sections of the country.

CCC Calls For End To Police Kickbacks
CCC Calls For End To Police Kickbacks

After receiving numerous complaints from citizens, in 1954 the Chicago Crime Commission conducted an investigation into a towing racket involving Chicago police officers steering business to firms and receiving kick-backs. The Chicago Police Commission then conducted their own internal investigation and formed a new administrative unit to supervise towing records and eliminate the racket exposed by the CCC.

CCC Wants Liquor Licenses Revoked
CCC Wants Liquor Licenses Revoked

In 1955, the Chicago Crime Commission conducted a survey of teenage gang activities in taverns located in three police districts and recommended that the police commissioner revoke the liquor licenses of twelve taverns.

The Walkie Talkie & The Security System
The Walkie Talkie & The Security System

Sources: "New School Vandal Weapon," Chicago American, September 23, 1958.
"Super Security Program In City Schools Cuts After Hours Crime," LEAA Publication.

Advancements in law-enforcement technology continued into the 1950s. In 1952, the walkie-talkie telephone was gaining professional acceptance and was used for two-way, car-to-car communication. In 1957, the telephoto transmission of photographs, fingerprints, and other data was developed. In 1958, the electronic detection device was piloted for the protection of all Chicago public schools after hours. Microphones were hooked up with telephone wires leading to a control panel at the nearest police station. When sounds or voices were picked up at the station, squads were dispatched to the school. The additional ability to pinpoint the section of the school that was being vandalized would result in saving the city thousands of dollars of damage annually. The development of these electronic "watchmen" offered great promise for the future of technology advancement in law enforcement.

The Illinois Crime Prevention Bureau
The Illinois Crime Prevention Bureau

Source: Crime Prevention Bureau Publication.

The examination of crime, particularly focusing on narcotics, led to the formation of the Narcotics Program of the Illinois Crime Prevention Bureau. In 1949, the Bureau opened on LaSalle Street in Chicago's downtown. Led by Dr. Lois Higgins, the Bureau was formed to crusade against narcotics peddlers and addicts, and to coordinate efforts between police agencies from the local to the state level. For fourteen years, Dr. Higgins headed the Bureau after a long personal history of criminal justice affiliations. In 1937, Dr. Higgins, among 1,119 other women, took the first policewomen's exam offered in twenty years. She was among the only ten women hired and was assigned to the sex and homicide division, the only woman among twenty-six men. She also developed the first training program for Chicago policewomen. Dr. Higgins grew up in Chicago and eventually studied social work on a scholarship at Loyola University. She became a social worker in the old Women's Court of the Chicago Municipal Court. She broke the Schwenke "baby farm" case in 1942, where a married couple was found guilty of running an unlicensed home for, and selling, babies. She was a member of the Illinois Association of Chiefs of Police and the International Association of Chiefs of Police, was president of the International Association of Women Police, and served as Executive Director of the American Law Enforcement Officers Association until 1980. The Bureau was eager to cooperate with all groups to reach its goal. It believed that the involvement of law enforcement, courts, medical physicians and psychiatrists, sociological, medical and legal researchers, legislature, educators, civic, fraternal and welfare community organizations, congressional affiliates, and the Illinois Department of Public Welfare would lead toward the elimination of narcotics peddlers and addicts. The Illinois Crime Prevention Bureau closed its doors in 1963.

The Kefauver Story... In Chicago

Probe Links Mobsters to Politicians

By Estes Kefauver
(United States Senator)

CHAPTER 4.

If the Senate crime committee had gone no further than Chicago in its quest, it could have written a complete report-in-miniature on the picture of nationwide criminal and political corruption. For practically every example of rottenness found anywhere in the United States was duplicated in the capital of the Capone mob.

Chicago remains the jungle of criminals who walk in the footsteps of Al Capone.

Virgil Peterson, operating director of the Chicago Crime Commission and former FBI agent, traced the history of the Chicago mob from the days of Big Jim Colosimo, who "had risen to power and influence through the operation of a string of brothels."

On May 11, 1920, Big Jim was bumped off. Peterson noted that there always had been suspicion that the bodyguard imported by Colosimo from New York, Johnny Torrio, had engineered the killing. Torrio succeeded Colosimo as Chicago's underworld lord.

He, in turn, imported as his bodyguard a cold-blooded little killer from New York's Five Point Gang, a then obscure, scarfaced hoodlum of 23 named Al Capone.

For four years, Torrio enjoyed a bloody reign in Chicago, waxing high on the profits of prostitution, gambling, beer and booze. But after Torrio was the victim of an ambush which almost cost his life, he lost his nerve and abdicated in favor of Capone.

RULE IS EFFECTIVE

With Greasy Thumb Guzik as his paymaster and business adviser, and such stalwarts as Frank Nitti, Paul (The Waiter) Ricca, Louis (Little New York) Campagna and the Fischetti

Jake Guzik (above), Capone mob paymaster and business adviser, and Anthony Accardo (right) are reputed to be heirs to Scarface Al's syndicate. Both men were reluctant witnesses before Kefauver quizzers.

Ricca and Anthony Accardo wield great influence.

Although the Capone and other mobs, in the process of getting rich on the wire service, "policy wheels" and similar "quiet" rackets, have soft-pedaled bloodshed, the undertone of violence still is there. A brutal example was the murder in September, 1950—still unsolved—of former police Lt. Drury before he could appear as a witness before our committee.

CASE OF GILBERT

A wave of suspensions and resignations by high-ups in the police department followed our investigation of great wealth accumulated

Paul Ricca   Frank Nitti

by a number of Chicago police captains.

The most highly publicized case was that of Capt. Daniel A. Gilbert, referred to by Chicago newspapers as "the richest cop in the world." Gilbert was serving as chief investigator for the state's attorney's office of Cook County, and also was the Democratic candidate for sheriff.

Capt. Gilbert, a well dressed, breezy figure told us he estimated

and Charles (Cherry Nose) Gioe, alias Joye.

The three, along with a pack of other Chicago, New York and West Coast mobsters, were sent to the penitentiary in 1943 to serve 10-year sentences on conviction of conspiracy to extort huge sums from the movie industry by threatening to call a strike of a gangster-controlled union. After Ricca, Campagna and Gioe had served only about one-third of their sentences, efforts to secure their paroles were successful.

However, Ricca and Campagna also were in trouble with the federal government on charges of income tax evasion. The claims had to be settled before the gangsters could be paroled. At this point, the mob stepped in, and there ensued events as strange as a dime novel.

The attorney called in to settle the tax case was Eugene Bernstein. Many years ago, Bernstein had been with the Internal Revenue Bureau. When he obtained his law license and left the bureau, he specialized in tax cases. He accumulated a list of clients that read like the blue book of the Capone syndicate.

With information obtained with Accardo's help, he was able to effect a settlement with the government. Campagna's case was settled for $90,371.49; Ricca's for $36,146.50, and accumulated interest brought the total settlement for the two cases to approximately $190,000. This was approximately $322,000 less than the original deficiency claims.

Anyway, the next question was how to raise the money.

Source: Chicago Sun-Times, July 29, 1951. Reproduced with permission of the Chicago Sun-Times.
Note: Bottom half of this article is on the next page.

Note: Upper section of this article is on the previous page

brothers as his lieutenants, Capone was able to rule effectively. The infamous St. Valentine's Day massacre of Feb. 14, 1929, was an example of how Capone dealt with opposition.

In 1931, however, Capone was cut down by Uncle Sam on an income-tax evasion charge and was sent to prison. Frank Nitti succeeded him, but in 1943, facing prosecution on an extortion charge, Nitti was found dead under circumstances that indicated he had committed suicide.

Since then, the mob—known to this day as the Capone syndicate —has been run pretty much by a "corporation," in which Guzik,

his net worth was approximately $360,000, and that dividends on stocks and bonds he currently held were bringing him in about $42,000 a year.

I remarked to him, "People don't understand how you get hold of all that money." Whereupon, the captain began explaining to us all the details of his badge-to-riches story.

There was a little "honest gambling" on the side, but mostly it was done through investments in stocks and bonds.

It was about two weeks after this that the voters of Cook County registered their disapproval of Gilbert by defeating him at the polls.

LAWYERS STEP IN

In Chicago, too, we gathered evidence of a disturbing phenomenon that we found repeated in other large cities: The active participation in gang affairs by a certain element of lawyers, accountants and tax consultants.

One fascinating story was the net of strange circumstances surrounding the parole from the federal penitentiary at Leavenworth of three Capone syndicate gangsters, Ricca, Louis Campagna,

Bernstein returned to Chicago. Almost immediately, he said, strangers started walking into his office and leaving packages of bills, usually wrapped in paper, in amounts varying between $10,-000 and $20,000.

ASKED NO NAMES

When the first batch of bills came in, Bernstein told us (in what seemed to be a masterpiece of understatement) he was "taken aback." The procession of strange men bearing currency continued until the needed total of $190,000 had been brought in.

Q—"Did you ask their names?"

A—"I wouldn't think of asking their names, because it made no difference to me . . ."

When all was settled, Bernstein went to Leavenworth again to see the boys out of the penitentiary. At the Kansas City airport, Tony Gizzo, the mobster and alleged Mafia chieftain, met them.

We ran up against a stone wall when we sought to learn from Ricca and Campagna — and later from Accardo—who might have put up the $190,000. "Why I would be glad to find out who did that for

Source: Chicago Sun-Times, July 29, 1951

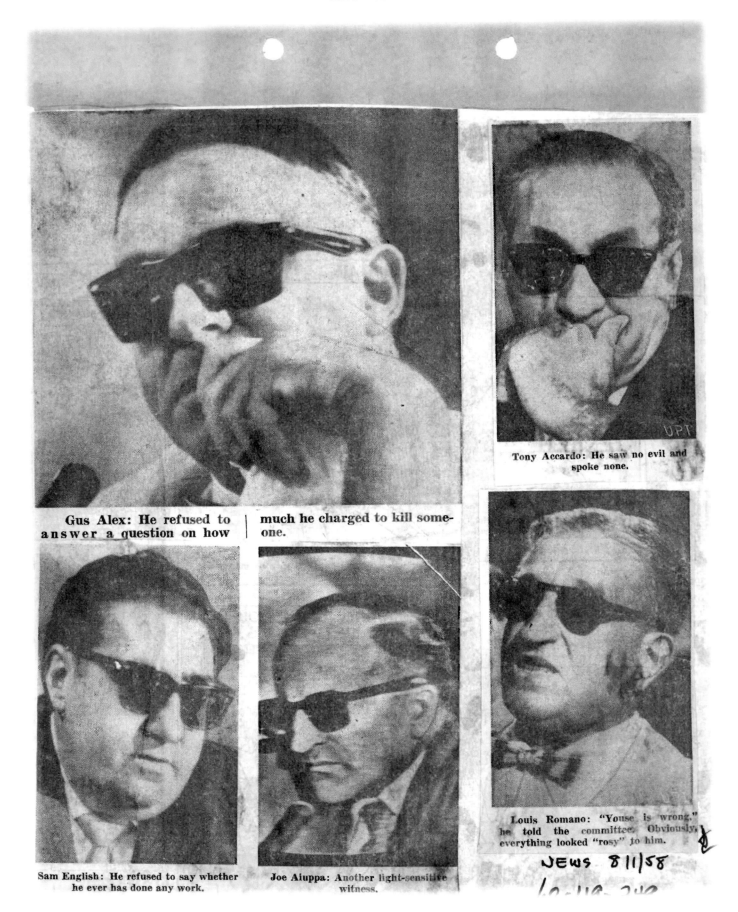

Gus Alex: He refused to answer a question on how much he charged to kill someone.

Tony Accardo: He saw no evil and spoke none.

Sam English: He refused to say whether he ever has done any work.

Joe Aiuppa: Another light-sensitive witness.

Louis Romano: "Youse is wrong," he told the committee. Obviously, everything looked "rosy" to him.

NEWS 8 11/58

Source: Chicago Daily News. Reproduced with permission of the Chicago Sun-Times.

Twin City Witness

Roland Schaefer (right) identified as the head of the Lakeside Specialty Co., in East Chicago, looks over a paper Tuesday as he sits with his attorney, Stanley Clinton of Chicago, at the witness table before the Senate Rackets Committee. The witness refused to tell whether he made "payoffs" to officers in the city and county government. (AP Wirephoto)

SAM (MOONY) GIANCANNA   FRANK ZIZZO   TED PETERS

Source: Hammond Times, Hammond, Indiana, June 10, 1959
Photos used with permission of the Times of Northwest Indiana.

A Cook County State's Attorney's policeman is at work during a periodic Chicago gambling raid on July 31, 1951.

Source: John Binder Collection. Reproduced with permission of John J. Binder.

30 YEARS AGO: A MASSACRE IN A BEER WAR
ROBERT WIEDRICH
Chicago Daily Tribune (1872-1963); Feb 14, 1959; ProQuest Historical Newspapers Chicago Tribune (1849 - 1985)
pg. B12

30 YEARS AGO: A MASSACRE IN A BEER WAR

How Moran Gang Died —and Why He Didn't

BY ROBERT WIEDRICH

The machine gun barked, its slugs tearing into the backs of the seven men.

Once, twice, and then a third time its muzzle swung the length of the concrete garage wall, spewing flame, blasting a crscendo of leaden hate.

The bullets cut and slashed thru flesh and bone, the scream of the ricochets harmonizing with the cries of

Al Capone

the victims as their bodies twisted and buckled under the sledge hammer blows of the heavy caliber slugs.

Day of Hearts, Flowers

That was St. Valentine's day, 1929—a day of love, a day of hearts and flowers.

It also was a day of the Chicago style blood bath, the day the Capone mob graduated from mere murder to massacre.

When the last thunderous echo of the machine gun had died in the rafters of the garage at 2122 N. Clark st. and the acrid stench of burned gun powder rose toward the roof of the one story building there was really only one survivor in the charnal house —a whimpering police dog.

One of the seven lived for a little while, but when police asked him who had done the shooting, he snarled, "Nobody."

Exit: Beer Competition

That was the infamous St. Valentine's day massacre, the day most of George [Bugs] Moran's gang was blasted out of the beer business.

Yet, in an era when some people were killed merely

George [Bugs] Moran

for looking the wrong way, there really was nothing personal in this slaughter—it was strictly a matter of business, call it prohibition gangster economics if you will.

As best as can be determined, the multiple slayings were intended to eliminate the Moran gang's competition to the beer peddling efforts of Al Capone's syndicate on the north side.

The Capone gang had acquired exclusive beer rights on Chicago's south side thru the device of a dozen or so murders.

Change in Occupation

There was no reason to doubt the same method wouldn't work in a north-ward expansion. It did.

Moran, frightened by the mass killing, turned to other vocations—burglary, robbery, and confidence game.

Thirty years have passed. The scene of this economic execution remains much the same, tho.

The old red trolley cars that used to rattle past the narrow building on the west side of Clark street have given way to propane powered buses. But the rooming houses and shops that crowd the street are still as drab and rundown as they were that blustery winter day when Chicago acquired a reputation for death.

Bullet Scars Remain

There's a storage company now in the building and an extra floor has been added to the one story structure.

The bullet scars are still on the wall.

To the north of the building is an old four story room-

Dr. Reinhardt H. Schwimmer

ing house with its bulging bay windows from which residents looked down on the aftermath of violence as the blanket shrouded bodies were loaded into ambulances.

The rusting iron balconies of the building are like a grotesque caricature of the old world.

A somber, four story weather stained gray stone building stands to the south.

On that day 30 years ago, the members of the Moran gang were gathering in the garage headquarters which housed the trucks used to haul the beer to Moran's clientele.

Scout Garage for Week

Across the street in a rooming house three men paced the floor, periodically peering thru the tattered lace curtains that screened their view of the street.

The men had been there a week. They were the advance scouts of the execution squad.

They did their work well.

Six members of the Moran gang entered the garage. Then a seventh man arrived, Albert R. Weinshenk, a night club operator and a partner of Moran in a cleaning and dyeing business.

Weinshenk bore a close resemblance to Moran. The lookouts apparently mistook him for the gang leader and the executioners got the signal to move in.

2 Disguised as Cops

Moments later an auto resembling a squad car drew up in front of the garage. Four men, two in police uniform, got out and walked into the Moran headquarters.

Inside, the appearance of the police uniforms caused little concern — the Moran gang was accustomed to routine arrests.

Police Re-enact St. Valentine's Day Massacre

[TRIBUNE Photo]

With detectives acting as the victims, police are pictured in a re-enactment of the St. Valentine's day gangland massacre in a garage at 2122 N. Clark st. 30 years ago.

The gangsters were ordered to line up against the wall. They complied, expecting to be frisked for weapons.

As they faced the wall, one of the civilian attired men quickly ripped away the wrap-

Adam Heyer [left], James Clark [center], and Al Weinshenk.

ping of a package he carried.

It was the machine gun, the weapon which was to authoritatively bring an end to free enterprise in the sale of beer to Chicago's thirsty citizens.

100 Bullets Fired

Moran's boys didn't have a chance.

The machine gunner used the tool of his trade with deadly accuracy.

When the last of the victims had slumped to the floor, he fired a final torrent of bullets into their sprawled bodies.

The staccato tattoo of the machine gun had delivered Al Capone's Valentine to Moran. It had taken a hundred or more bullets to do it.

Here is the death honor roll of the Moran gang:

Frank and Pete Guesenberg, brothers and two of Moran's beer hustlers; John May, onetime safe blower; James Clark, Moran's brother-in-law; Adam Heyer, owner of the cartage company using the garage; Weinshenk; and L. Reinhardt H. Schwimmer, an optometrist.

Calmly Walk Away

Schwimmer, a pathetic man who liked to associate with

Frank Gusenberg [left], John May [center], and Pete Guesenberg.

hoodlums, got more glory than he eypected. He died, too.

Frank Guesenberg lived briefly. He died without identifying the gun squad.

The slayers walked calmly to their car and drove away. No one has ever been tried for the murders.

The massacre had a few side effects which the mobsters hadn't reckoned on.

It aroused a wave of civic indignation which caused officials to put the heat on the gangsters who, for all practical purposes, were running Chicago.

As for Moran, who reportedly missed the execution by five minutes, he moved on to other climes.

He never returned to large scale bootlegging. He'd had his warning.

On Feb. 25, 1957, Moran died in Leavenworth penitentiary, where he was serving a bank burglary sentence. His death was attributed to lung cancer.

Source: Courtesy of Chicago Tribune Archives

April
Ten
1957

Mr. Timothy J. O'Connor   Re: <u>Leon Marcus murder</u>
Commissioner of Police
Room 505, City Hall
Chicago 2, Illinois

Dear Commissioner O'Connor:

    I received a telephone call on April 9, 1957 from an
individual who stated that he has a relative whom he has
been trying to get out of the mob. This man did not
give his identity, but stated that the Leon Marcus killing was perpetrated by top men from the mob, and he
named the mob's killers as <u>Mike Jelly</u> alias <u>Mike Spazes</u>
or <u>Spazie</u>; one <u>Tietz</u> who lives in Oak Park; Marshall,
and Milwaukee Phil.

    I am sure you are thoroughly familiar with Milwaukee
Phil Alderisio, who has long been known as a gunman for
the syndicate. It is presumed, although this individual
did not so state, that Marshall may be Marshall Caifano.
This information is forwarded to you for your appropriate
consideration.

    This informant also stated that the murder of Seymour
H. Kreda in Skokie, Illinois was based on mob muscle.
He stated that if the police would thoroughly question
Glen Rodkin, Kreda's partner, he could give information
which would throw light on the killing.

                Sincerely yours,

                Virgil W. Peterson
                Operating Director

VWP:JMS

Thermo Fax to

CHICAGO CRIME COMMISSION

APR 1 1 957

Route to

17-2924-55

Source: Chicago Crime Commission Archives

Throughout its history, the Chicago Crime Commission has supplied intelligence received from the public to law enforcement.

Motorola two-way radios on parade, Chicago, Illinois, USA, 1955.

© 2007, Motorola, Inc. Reproduced with permission.

Motorola two-way radio production, Chicago, 1956.

© 2007, Motorola, Inc. Reproduced with permission.

Motorola Handie-Talkie portable radio, civil defense exercise, Evanston, 1950.

© 2007, Motorola, Inc. Reproduced with permission.

Motorola Handie-Talkie portable radio, civil defense planning, 1959.

© 2007, Motorola, Inc. Reproduced with permission.

Mother of Two Leads Chicago's Battle Against Dope Menace

OAN BECK

Chicago Daily Tribune (1872-1963); Jul 16, 1951; ProQuest Historical Newspapers Chicago Tribune (1849-1985) pg. A1

Mother of Two Leads Chicago's Battle Against Dope Menace

Lois Higgins Is Expert on Rising Peril

[First of a series of three articles about Chicago's vicious narcotic problem and a woman who is helping solve it.]

BY JOAN BECK

A 13 YEAR OLD BOY is arrested for stealing to buy heroin. A 17 year old girl of good family turns prostitute to get money for dope. Boys are initiated into the use of narcotics in high school washrooms. The average age of addicts has dropped from 37 to 24 since 1946; of Chicago's estimated 7,500 addicts, 3,000 to 3,500 are under 21.

Chicagoans lose 60 million dollars a year in crimes traceable to dope users. About 95 per cent of all addicts turn to crime to obtain the $5 to $40 they must have every day to buy dope.

These are the facts, the facts of Chicago's growing narcotic menace.

What can a Chicago woman do to fight it?

Washington Witness

Dr. Lois Higgins, petite, dynamic director of the crime prevention bureau and attractive mother of two children, has done so much to fight the dope problem that twice she has been called to Washington to testify before congressional investigating committees.

Last March she outlined Chicago's vicious dope problem to the house ways and means committee. Recently she told the senate's crime investigating committee [and a whopping TV audience] how the crime prevention bureau is mobilizing all of Chicago's law enforcing agencies into a war against dope and dope peddlers.

"The increase in dope addiction, particularly among younger people, has reached shocking proportions," Dr. Higgins emphasized. "It's like a forest fire. It can break out anywhere and it spreads as fast as fire."

Knows Problem Fully

Dr. Higgins—who has seen dope addiction snowball into a national problem in her 14 years as Chicago policewoman and social worker—knows every tragic part of the narcotic problem. She knows there is no one cause, no one answer.

The weapons she coördinates against narcotics include the judicial, legislative, psychological, medical, sociological, law enforcement, and educational forces of Chicago, Cook county, and Illinois.

Drug addiction as a criminal problem among younger persons is largely a post-war, big city menace, Dr. Higgins explained to the senate investigators.

She quoted a Chicago police captain who said 60 per cent of crimes in his district—one of Chicago's worst—are committed by narcotics addicts. Last year 4,437 persons were arrested by Chicago police for violating narcotic laws; almost as many—4,185—have been arrested in the last seven months.

Post-War Increase

Until the Harrison narcotic law of 1915 made selling narcotics illegal without a license for medical purposes, addicts could buy enough heroin and cocaine for four to 10 days' use for 35 cents in a corner drug store.

With these supplies cut off, addicts were forced to obtain drugs illegally from peddlers, who make huge profits and now are often associated with national crime syndicates and international narcotic rings. For example, morphine sells legitimately for about $18 an ounce [437½ grains]; peddlers sell it to addicts for from $1 to $8 a grain.

Seeking an expanding market after World War II, peddlers began to prey on children and teen-agers as a rich, untapped source of new income.

Dr. Higgins also suggested that part of the tremendous post-war increase in drug addiction may possibly be communist inspired. She noted the communist government of China recently offered 500 tons of opium for export, enough to make 25 to 35 tons of heroin and give illegal dope peddlers profits running into billions of dollars.

How Peddler Operates

The professional peddler contacts children in soda fountains, alleys, cars parked near schools, on street corners; urges them, "Try it just for fun. It'll make you feel swell." Often first samples are given away.

Boys and girls take their first smoke or shot "to get a thrill," "to satisfy curiosity," "to be one of the gang," as young addicts explain later. Teen-agers particularly feel the insecurity, lack of self-confidence, desire for adventure, and defeatist attitudes which characterize a majority of persons who become addicts.

Once a young person becomes addicted, the vicious cycle of stronger drugs, larger doses begins, usually progressing from smoking marijuana to snuffing heroin to mainlining speedballs [shooting a mixture of cocaine and heroin directly into the veins].

Law enforcement agencies estimate that 95 per cent of addicts obtain drugs illegally and commit crimes to get the money.

One authority estimated that an addict must steal $40 to $70 a day to sell in exchange for an average day's supply of drugs. Others tell of fences operating openly near schools where children can bring stolen goods.

"One of the easiest ways to earn drugs is for the addict to turn peddler himself," continued Dr. Higgins. "A few years ago most peddlers didn't use the stuff themselves; today it's common."

Addiction Spreads

Once addiction starts in a neighborhood, a housing development, a teen-age group, a school, it's likely to spread. Usually it goes from husband to wife, sister to brother, boy friend to girl friend, even from parent to child.

"Addicts always try to make addicts of those nearest and dearest to them," Dr. Higgins said. "It's not because the addict loves the other person so much. But he knows that if someone else craves drugs as he does, two of them together stand a better chance of obtaining narcotics."

Drug addiction in itself is not a crime. Selling or possessing narcotics without a license is. But drug addiction almost inevitably leads to crime.

Chicago's most urgent crime problem is drug addiction, it was disclosed at a meeting of leading Illinois law enforcement officials called to study crime prevention in September, 1949, by James Doherty, crime reporter of THE CHICAGO TRIBUNE.

At Doherty's suggestion, the heads of all Chicago law enforcement agencies, the board of education, and the United States district attorney's office set up a crime prevention council, with the crime prevention bureau as its acting agency and Crime Prevention, Inc., an organization of private citizens, as its supporting arm.

Policewoman Lois Higgins, also a lecturer in criminology at Loyola university, was assigned to the bureau as assistant director by Police Commissioner Timothy J. O'Connor. She became acting director in July, 1950, and director last December. Her first job: To mobilize Chicago in a war against dope—public crime problem No. 1.

Tomorrow: Can you guard your children against Chicago's dope menace?

Source: Courtesy of Chicago Tribune Archives
Note: Rest of this article is on the next page.

Note: Beginning of this article is on the previous page.

Mother of Two Leads Drive on Dope in City [Continued from first page]

Dr. Lois Higgins, director of crime prevention bureau, discusses Chicago's mounting dope menace with Sherif John E. Babb.

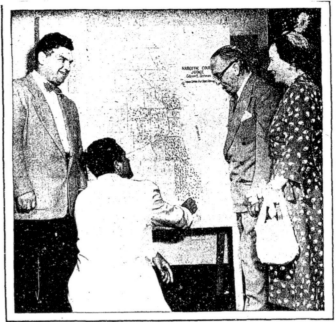

Dr. Higgins selects charts and films to illustrate one of lectures she gives on Chicago's narcotic problems.

Map in chambers of Judge Gibson E. Gorman of Narcotic court pinpoints new dope cases. From left are Assistant State's Atty. James Condon, assigned to Narcotic court; James Wakefield of crime prevention bureau, Judge Gorman, and Dr. Higgins.

Dr. Higgins talks with Judge Gorman in Narcotic court at recent hearing involving sale of dope in Chicago.
[TRIBUNE Photos by Robert MacKay]

Dr. Higgins relaxing with her niece, Lois McElheny (center); son, Frank Jr., and daughter, Mary Lois, in yard of new home at 3018 N. Menard av., into which family recently moved. Her husband is a Chicago building inspector.

Source: Courtesy of Chicago Tribune Archives

DOPE-OLOGY

ARTICLES and LECTURES
by

Lois Lundell Higgins, A.B., M.S.W., LL.D.

CRIME PREVENTION BUREAU
PUBLICATION

Source: Crime Prevention Bureau of Illinois

Dr. Higgins swings a scythe on marijuana found growing on Chicago's South Side.

Reproduced with permission of United Press Photo.

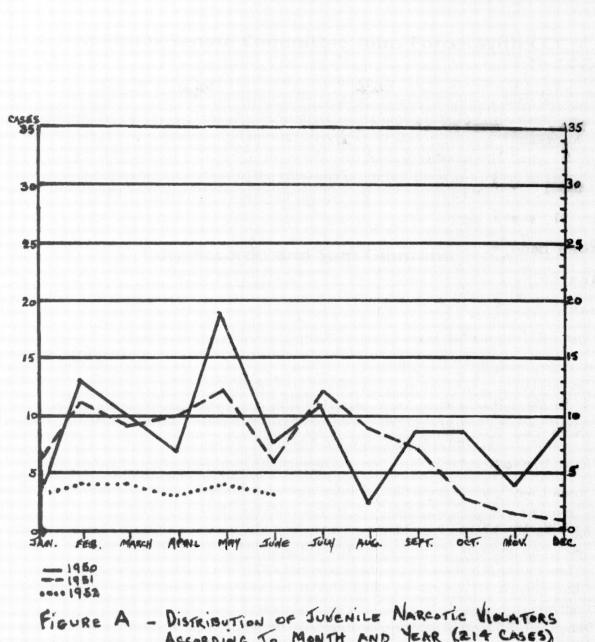

FIGURE A - DISTRIBUTION OF JUVENILE NARCOTIC VIOLATORS ACCORDING TO MONTH AND YEAR (214 CASES)

Narcotics Figures for Chicago

Source: Crime Prevention Bureau of Illinois

AGE	COLUMN 1 MALE NEGRO	COLUMN 2 MALE WHITE	COLUMN 3 FEMALE NEGRO	COLUMN 4 FEMALE WHITE	AGE TOTAL
12			1		1
13	2				2
14	10	3	5	1	19
15	24	7	10	3	44
16	100	13	13	3	129
17			19		19
SEX AND RACE TOTAL	136	23	48	7	214

FIGURE B — DISTRIBUTION OF JUVENILE NARCOTIC VIOLATORS ACCORDING TO AGE SEX AND RACE (214 CASES)

Narcotics Figures for Chicago
Source: Crime Prevention Bureau of Illinois

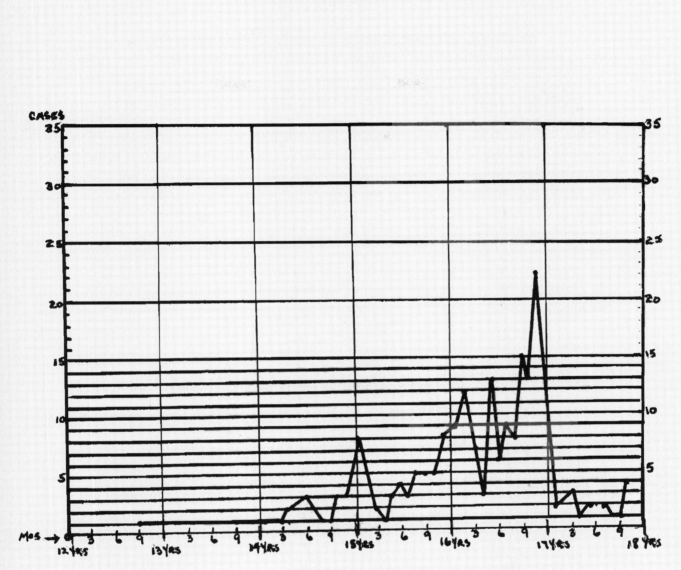

FIGURE C - DISTRIBUTION OF CHRONOLOGICAL AGE OF
NARCOTIC VIOLATORS   (203 CASES)

Narcotics Figures for Chicago

Source: Crime Prevention Bureau of Illinois

CRIME FOILERS FOR THE AVERAGE CITIZEN

THE EXPLODING HAT NET

BOOM
THWOOP

NET
EXPLOSIVE
HEAD SHIELD
COLLAR TRIGGER

Net, woven of extremely fine but strong synthetic fibers, is carefully packed into hat. When "victim" is grabbed at throat. special collar triggers an explosive device which sends net billowing out over both "victim" and "attacker." Since they are both trapped until help comes, "attacker" will not hurt "victim" and risk more serious punishment.

Note: The Chicago Crime Commission does not recommend this as a real safety device.

Reproduced with permission of the Chicago Police Department

Source: Chicago Police News Clips, August 4, 1993 booklet

1960

Chicago Police Department two-way radio system, 1961.

A police radio system supplied to the city of Chicago, Illinois, USA, was the largest Motorola had designed and produced to date. Twenty-two base stations, 34 dispatch consoles, and 885 vehicular two-way radios were provided.

1969

FRIEND

Sheriff Ogilvie (left) swears in Arthur J. Bilek as Chief of the Cook County Sheriff's Police.

Source: Arthur Bilek Collection

Arthur Bilek

Lieutenant Arthur Bilek, the then acting director of training for the Chicago Police Department, was appointed by Sheriff Ogilvie in 1962 to head the Cook County Sheriff's Police. As Chief, Bilek had the overwhelming job of cleaning up a highly corrupt department. Bilek established high entry standards for the department and discharged over 90 percent of the hold-overs from the prior administration. Within a short time, instead of an organized crime partner, the sheriff's department became a model law-enforcement agency and was studied and respected across the nation. The sheriff's police boldly and effectively began to target the Outfit in Cicero and elsewhere.

Although we are only able to highlight a few friends and foes for each decade, the Chicago Crime Commission reminds the public that there are many friends, and while perhaps not as famous as the criminals, they are courageous and far more impressive.

Larry Hoover

Source: Chicago Police Department

Latin King Graffiti

FOE

The Black Disciples, Gangster Nation, Black P Stones/Blackstone Rangers, Vice Lords, and Latin Kings Street Gangs

Although street gangs were not considered a major threat at this time, the 1960s brought about the beginnings of what would over time become "super gangs," highly organized street gangs that would become even more violent and more dangerous to society than the Outfit. David Barksdale was a Black Disciples founder; Larry Hoover was the Gangster Nation founder; Jeff Fort founded the Black P Stones/Blackstone Rangers; and Edward Perry was a founder of the Vice Lords. These early street-gang leaders often studied and then emulated the organization structures and criminal strategies of the well-established Outfit. The illegal drug trade became the primary crime business of these gangs.

"Super" Street Gangs Form In Chicago
"Super" Street Gangs Form In Chicago

Source: The Chicago Crime Commission Gang Book

During the 1960s, today's largest and most organized street gangs rose in power and strength. The Gangster Disciples Nation was founded in the early years of the decade when the Black Disciples led by David Barksdale united with the Gangster Nation led by Larry Hoover. The Black P Stone nation, (originally called the El Rukns or Blackstone Rangers) formed in 1959 and the Vice Lords formed in 1958 and was led by an intelligent and ruthless leader, Edward Perry. During the 1960s, these gangs grew to become more organized "super" gangs, some believe, because of their ability to show themselves as legitimate community organizations and thus receive significant federal and other funding, which, in turn, was put into development of their criminal activities. For example, the El Rukns received thousands of dollars in federal grants for inner-city development, but the money instead helped to finance gang recruitment, the purchase and sale of weapons, and a terror campaign aimed at the small business leaders of Chicago's Woodlawn community. The Vice Lords (as the Conservative Vice Lord, Inc.), around 1970, successfully applied for and received $275,000 in grant money from the Rockefeller Foundation, the foundation unaware that it was supporting criminal activity.

It is believed that Hoover, and likely other street gang leaders, studied Capone and the Italian organized crime operations in order to build these newly emerging criminal empires. However, unlike traditional organized crime, the sale of narcotics was the primary criminal pursuit and income for these street gangs.

Sheriff's Police Reformed & Professionalized
Sheriff's Police Reformed & Professionalized

Source: Jeffrey Thurston

In 1962, Richard B. Ogilvie was elected Sheriff of Cook County. Ogilvie, a former special assistant U.S. attorney who had successfully convicted Tony Accardo of income tax evasion, had campaigned for office on a program that he would spend the next four years fighting the Chicago Crime Syndicate. When Ogilvie was sworn in, his first act was to appoint Lieutenant Arthur Bilek, acting director of training of the Chicago Police Department, to head the Cook County Sheriff's Police Department (CCSPD). The sheriff's police had a long record as the most corrupt and unprofessional police agency in Cook County. The CCSPD had been long decried by CCC Director Virgil W. Peterson and the press as the police department that had allowed gambling, vice, and the Chicago Crime Syndicate to grow and proliferate throughout Cook County. Newly appointed Chief Bilek soon discovered that all of the members of the CCSPD had been appointed with political or Outfit sponsors. Chief Bilek also learned that there was no civil service in the department, few entry requirements, and little training. It had long been reported in the press that the sheriff's police were partners with the Chicago Outfit for forty years and were corrupt at all levels from patrol officers, sergeants, lieutenants, and captains up to and including the chief. Bilek established the highest entry standards of any police department in the state including a polygraph test, psychological evaluation, and written IQ examination. Over 90 percent of the former CCSPD officers of all ranks were discharged by Bilek. The Chicago Police Department offered to train the new CCSPD officers for free, and all new officers attended and graduated from the fifteen-week CPD recruit school. All new patrol cars were purchased. Michigan State University and the Northwestern University Traffic Institute provided professional assistance for planning and development. Bilek and Ogilvie went to Springfield and after hard-fought battles obtained the passage of legislation creating a merit system for the CCSPD. By the end of the fourth year, the police force was being used as a model not only for Illinois departments but for police departments around the United States. Over 1,000 gambling, prostitution, and tavern raids were made by the sheriff's police during the four years.

Sheriff's Police Take Over Cicero
Sheriff's Police Take Over Cicero

Source: Jeffrey Thurston

In the mid-1960s, finding that the Cicero police were unable or unwilling to close vice in that community, reform Chief Arthur Bilek of the CCSPD announced that his department will provide day-to-day policing on the streets of Cicero to shut down the persistent vice dens, some of which had been in operation for forty years. All gambling dens, strip clubs, and houses of prostitution were closed; all taverns were visited and inspected; and ultimately the Cicero police chief turned in his resignation under the pressure brought by the sheriff's police and the press.

Sheriff's Police Arrest Mob Chieftain Joey Aiuppa
Sheriff's Police Arrest Mob Chieftain Joey Aiuppa

Source: Jeffrey Thurston

In the mid-1960s, Donald Shaw, a new vice officer on the CCSPD was sought out by a former sheriff's police lieutenant, Jacob Bergbreighter, to arrange to put Shaw on the Mob's payroll. The ex-lieutenant offered to have Shaw meet with mob chieftain and boss of all gambling in Cicero, Joey Aiuppa. Shaw notified Chief Bilek and a secret operation was established involving the Illinois State Police, the Intelligence Division of the Chicago Police Department, and two hand-picked officers from the sheriff's police. They conducted a surveillance of the meeting between Shaw, Bergbreighter, and Aiuppa. A series of additional contacts were made, which included Bergbreighter giving Shaw a large sum of bribe money, all secretly observed by the special team. Ultimately, Aiuppa and Bergbreighter were indicted for bribery by the Cook County grand jury. The defense attorneys delayed the trial for a year until the Illinois Supreme Court, in an unrelated case, reversed its long-standing position on wiretaps. The court ruled that one-party consent to a wiretap was not legal and all-party consent was needed for a wiretap to be admissible in court. The defense attorneys immediately demanded a trial. In a bench trial in Cook County Criminal Court the judge threw out the tape recordings of the meeting between Shaw, Aiuppa, and Bergbreighter and the transcript from the tape recordings but found Bergbreighter guilty and sentenced him to the penitentiary. In the case of Aiuppa, the judge said he did not feel that he could find Aiuppa guilty on the officer's sworn testimony alone. Aiuppa was found not guilty.

Crime Scene Processing, Criminalistics & Evidence
Crime Scene Processing, Criminalistics & Evidence

Source: Chicago Police Department

From 1960 to 1962, the Chicago Police Department was reorganized and a new crime laboratory was built. The crime laboratory was divided into three divisions: 1) the crime scene processing section; 2) the criminalistic section; and 3) the evidence evaluation section.

Evidence technicians and mobile unit personnel were part of the crime scene processing section. Evidence technicians processed crime scenes for physical evidence looking at latent fingerprints while photographically documenting scenes. The technicians also conducted chemical breath tests to determine alcohol intoxication. Forty-seven evidence technicians responded to approximately 40,000 crime scene and traffic accidents annually. Mobile unit personnel processed homicide and death investigations such as suicides or sudden unexplained deaths. These officers also handled fingerprinting and the photographing of hospitalized arrestees, provided assistance to the missing persons unit by processing unidentified dead, and assigned one sworn member to the medical examiner's facility to recover evidence from autopsies.

The criminalistic section held four units. The controlled substance unit and the physical chemistry unit extended the field of crime detection through the use of sophisticated instrumental analysis and chemical tests of narcotics, and at times, arson, to not only identify a substance but to determine the source of the material. Infrared spectrophotometer, ultraviolet spectrophotometer, mass spectrometer, gas chromotography, liquid chromotography, X-ray fluorescence, and atomic absorption were instruments used to identify substances. The staff of qualified experts received about 22,000 cases annually and were often called upon to testify in court. The microscopy/trace evidence unit examined evidence such as wood, rope, glass, hair, fibers, soil, paint or plastics attempting to identify unknown trace materials and samples collected from arrestees or victims. This unit was also responsible for atomic absorption gun shot residue (AA-GSR) evidence. Through sample swabbing, the unit analyzed the presence of a specific metal in parts per million to determine if the same weapon discharge was on the hands of a victim or suspect. This process occurred within six hours after the shooting, prior to the victim or suspect bathing. The serology unit processed biological evidence usually consisting of blood and semen, and at times urine, tears, saliva, and perspiration, and submitted it to the crime laboratory to establish the source. A sample of blood as small as a single fiber long could be typed for three enzymes. The Vitullo rape kit, developed by the Chicago Police Department, was the standard evidence-gathering device used by all Chicago hospitals to ensure the proper collection of evidence in sexual assault cases. Illinois state law required each kit to be processed when submitted.

The evidence evaluation section was made up of the six units. The latent fingerprinting development unit searched and recovered fingerprints on objects that did not yield suitable impressions and were responsible for equipment maintenance and research in laser technology. Other units included: the document examination unit, the polygraph unit, the firearms identification unit, the comparative toolmark unit, and the forensic photography unit. Personnel in these units were experts in various forensic fields. The document examination unit examined the authorship and authenticity of documents by studying handwriting, ink impressions, altered documents, burnt, water-soaked or torn papers, and paper sources. The polygraph unit assisted detectives during investigations using instruments with electronic enhancements to measure blood pressure, pulse rates, respiration, and skin responses. Annually, the polygraph unit conducted approximately 1,000 examinations related to criminal investigations. The firearms identification Unit examined markings of fired bullets and, by maintaining a stock of ammunition for every caliber, compared the crime scene markings to their own markings to determine the weapon used in the crime. All firearms recovered by the Chicago Police Department, approximately 12,000 weapons annually, were sent to this unit and test fired. These bullets were then compared with the "open case file" bullets, bullets that had been recovered from the scenes of murders and shootings. The comparative toolmark unit identified tool marks recovered from a crime scene to determine what type of tool and how that tool was used. The unit restored serial numbers on metal surfaces and performed comparisons on footwear and tire-mark impressions. The forensic photography unit photographed evidence from the latent fingerprint unit, evidence technicians, mobile unit officers and other laboratory personnel, and developed all crime scene photos. The unit prepared evidence for the courts and investigating officers using lighting and equipment not available in the field. The unit annually printed and developed 100,000 five-by-seven-inch photographs, developed about 28,000 rolls of film, and photographed over 6,500 fingerprint lifts.

RICO: Racketeer Influenced and Corrupt Organizations Act
RICO: Racketeer Influenced and Corrupt Organizations Act

Source: RICO Act, Wikipedia, The Free Encyclopedia internet site

In 1962 the RICO Act came about and eventually became one of the most powerful tools criminal justice could use in bringing down the leadership of the Mafia, street gangs, and other organized-crime groups. In the context of organized crime, the target of the RICO Act is generally the leader or leaders and the racketeering criminal activities in which the criminal group engages which may include extortion, bribery, loan sharking, murder, illegal drug sales, prostitution, etc. Because these organized-crime groups have engaged in criminal acts for years, the actions can constitute a pattern. The government can prosecute the leader(s) under RICO even if he has never personally killed, extorted, bribed, or engaged in criminal behavior. The leader can be imprisoned because he operated a criminal enterprise that engaged in such acts. In addition, the victims or their families can sue the leader(s) civilly and recover the economic losses they sustained as a result of the organized-crime group's pattern of racketeering.

Omnibus Crime Control & Safe Streets Act
Omnibus Crime Control & Safe Streets Act

Source: Jeffrey Thurston

Science and technology began to play a big part in criminal justice as scientists and engineers were challenged to problem-solve. The movement toward enhanced technology in criminal justice brought about local and federal sources of support, which led to significant progress. Greater use of technology appeared when, in 1968, after nearly a century of debate, Congress passed legislation giving federal law enforcement agencies the authority to use electronic surveillance. Then, the same year, the Omnibus Crime Control and Safe Streets Act authorized the states to develop similar systems. It was concluded that billions of dollars would be necessary for the required research and development program on the many-faceted criminal justice problems.

Illinois Law Enforcement Commission
Illinois Law Enforcement Commission

Source: Jeffrey Thurston

A major portion of the Omnibus Act involved the distribution of massive federal funding to the states for the purpose of improving criminal justice on a local basis. Under the terms of the Act, as administered by the Law Enforcement Assistance Administration (LEAA), each state had to create a planning agency to receive the federal funds. Each state planning agency had to develop regional plans for their state for the improvement of law enforcement, courts, and corrections and distribute the funds throughout the state in accordance with the plans. In Illinois, the state planning agency was the Illinois Law Enforcement Commission (ILEC). Newly elected Gov. Richard B. Ogilvie appointed Professor Arthur Bilek, chairman of the criminal justice department at the University of Illinois at Chicago Circle, as the Commission's chairman and chief executive officer. During ILEC's first four years of operation, beginning in 1968, the Commission funded criminal justice projects throughout the state. Examples included equipping of all Chicago patrol officers with portable two-way radio transmitters for the first time in history, a new hi-level security lighting system for Grant Park and the building of a new Chicago Police Training Academy, which is still in use today. The ILEC also funded a special statewide project to provide all city and suburban police cars with a separate radio system called ISPERN, which allowed every police vehicle in the state to talk with every other nearby police vehicle regardless of what department or county the vehicles were from. ISPERN was used during high-speed police chases, manhunts, plane crashes, natural disasters, and serious emergencies, something never before possible because of the dozens of separate channels used by the city and suburban departments for their day-to-day operations. In its first four years, ILEC funded over 2,000 criminal justice projects across Illinois, which significantly upgraded the police, courts, and corrections.

Chicago Riots
Chicago Riots

Source: Chicago Sun-Times Almanac

Battle of Chicago. In the summer of 1968, a time of nerve-fraying domestic tension, 10,000 anti-war protesters flocked to Grant Park and Lincoln Park to protest during the Democratic National Convention, August 26-29. On the convention's third night, the so-called "Battle of Chicago" broke out in Grant Park sparked by protesters who taunted a tired and angry police force, calling them "pigs" and pelting them with garbage and human waste. The police had shown restraint, but now, for about twenty minutes outside the Conrad Hilton Hotel on Michigan Avenue, dozens of officers chanted "kill, kill, kill" and pummeled demonstrators savagely. One hundred and one demonstrators were hospitalized, and 192 police officers reported minor injuries. A national commission on violence headed by future governor Daniel Walker called it a "police riot."

Days of Rage. For about a week in October 1969, a radical group calling itself the Weathermen led thousands of angry young people in nightly rock-throwing sprees through the streets of Chicago's Loop and Gold Coast. Protesting the Vietnam War, police oppression, and as one speaker phrased it, "rich people," they wore helmets and goggles, carried sticks and clubs, and threw bottles. Windows were smashed in cars and businesses, and scores of civilians and policemen were injured. Two civilians were shot, and Richard J. Elrod, an assistant corporation counsel who later became Cook County Sheriff, was permanently paralyzed below the waist when he attempted a flying tackle on a running demonstrator. After a Weathermen bomb factory blew up in New York, the group's leaders, including Bernadine Dohrn and William Ayers, went into hiding. In time, most of the leaders were tracked down and arrested.

Police See Blackstone Guns Blaze in Assassination Bid
BERNARD JUDGE
Chicago Tribune (1963-Current file); May 10, 1968; ProQuest Historical Newspapers Chicago Tribune (1849 - 1985)
pg. A14

Police See Blackstone Guns Blaze in Assassination Bid

BY BERNARD JUDGE

Three members of the Blackstone Rangers were in Central Boys court yesterday charged with the attempted murder of the leader of a rival gang.

They were seized by three detectives of the gang intelligence unit.

The squad had stopped David Barksdale, 21, of 6424 S. Ashland av., a leader of the Disciples, and two of his gang members at 65th street and University avenue Wednesday night to question Barksdale about a fight outside the Criminal courts building between the two gangs earlier that day.

Tells of Kill Order

Barksdale told the three detectives that there "was an order out to Blackstone Rangers to kill me." When they asked him how he knew, he told them to follow him in their unmarked squad car.

Detectives Richard Peck, Sidney Clark, and Donald Foulkes trailed a block behind Barksdale's car.

Barksdale turned south in Ellis avenue. At 6526 Ellis, a dozen youths ran into the street firing into Barksdale's car.

The detectives said they seized Melvin Bateley, 19, of 1532 E. 65th st., in a gangway at 6512 Ellis as he threw away a .45-caliber automatic. On a porch at 6524 Ellis av., they caught Andrew McChristian, 19, of 7815 Woodlawn av., trying to unjam his .25-caliber automatic.

No One Is Hurt

When detectives brought the two to Barksdale's car, they found the three occupants of the bullet-riddled car untouched. Just then Edward Dinkins, 21, of 6647 Kenwood av., came up to the car and told Peck he couldn't arrest Bateley and McChristian.

Barksdale identified Dinkins as one of the assailants and police took all three to headquarters.

Peck described McChristian as a member of the Rangers' chieftain group known as the Main 21. Three of that group have been slain in gangland fashion. McChristian had check stubs in his wallet showing he was a $130-a-week supervisor for The Woodlawn organization, Peck said.

All three were charged with attempted murder, armed violence, and unlawful use of weapons.

Judge Arthur Zelezinski set bond at $50,000 and continued their cases until May 23.

Peck said Barksdale refused an offer of police protection. Peck said that what they initially wanted to ask him about was a report that he "worked over" the Rangers' Jeff Fort, 20, of 6230 Dorchester av., at the county jail, where both had gone to confer with Supt. Winston Moore about making peace.

2 Pedestrians Shot

Two youths yelling "Blackstone Rangers" shot two men walking last night along 61st street near Dorchester avenue.

The victims were Claude Connor, 22, of 1359 E. 62d st., and Ernest Mitchell, 20, of 8018 Langley av. Mitchell is on leave from the army.

Both men suffered minor pellet wounds. They were treated and released from Michael Reese hospital.

Source: Courtesy of the Chicago Tribune Archives

July 1961 – Police arrest a group of gang members from roving gangs around Harrison High School in Lawndale.

Source: Courtesy of Chicago Tribune Archives

July 1969 – The Blackstone Rangers gang after takeover of the Building Trades Council offices on Wells Street where 17 were arrested. Picture shows police searching one of those arrested.

Source: Courtesy of Chicago Tribune Archives

6 Disciples Get Jail for South Side Attack

Six members of the East Side Disciples, a south side street gang, got jail sentences yesterday for an attack July 8 on a parole officer.

One of those sentenced by Judge Arthur Zelezinski in Central Boys' court was David Barksdale, 21, of 6424 S. Ashland av., leader of the gang.

Barksdale was found guilty of aggravated assault and mob action. He was sentenced to six months in the Bridewell for assault and concurrently to 30 days for mob action.

Get Similar Sentences

Similar sentences were ordered for Hubert Burnett, 19, of 922 E. 62d st., and Verne Stevens, 18, of 6355 Maryland av.

Sentences of 30 days for mob action were ordered for Frank Holland, 19, of 6244 Ellis av.; Dwight Rankins, 18, of 105 E. 70th st.; and Minjo Shead, 20, of 6322 University av.

The attack on Baxter Burke, a parole officer, took place in a hall at 913 E. 63d st., where the Disicples and another gang, the Blackstone Rangers, were having a party to celebrate a truce.

Sees a Parolee

Burke said he was driving past the hall when he saw a parolee leaving and went into the hall to see if other parolees were there. He said he was ordered by Barksdale to leave, he refused, and the gang members threw chairs and stools at him. Burke fired four shots into the ceiling as he backed down the stairs.

Barksdale and the others denied the charge, saying they were not in the hall. Burke identified them as the ones who attacked him.

Source: Courtesy of the Chicago Tribune Archives

GANG MEMBERS FIGHT AS TWO CHIEFS PARLEY
Chicago Tribune (1963-Current file); May 9, 1968; ProQuest Historical Newspapers Chicago Tribune (1849 - 1985)
pg. C15

GANG MEMBERS FIGHT AS TWO CHIEFS PARLEY

Peace Talks Are Held at County Jail

Two street gang members had a fist fight outside the Criminal courts building yesterday while leaders of the two gangs, Blackstone Rangers and the Disciples, held a peace talk in the county jail with jail Supt. Winston Moore.

Moore said he invited Jeff Fort, 20, of 6230 Dorchester av., leader of the Blackstone Rangers, and David Barksdale, 20, of 5803 Carpenter st., leader of the Disciples, to a conference in his office in an attempt to end gang violence on the south side.

Spent Day In Court

While the three were conferring, t h r e e members of the Rangers, including Bernard Green, 20, of 6849 East End av., walked out of the Criminal courts building. They had spent the day in court as a jury was being selected for the murder trial of Eugene Hairston, 23.

Ten members of the Disciples stood at a car parked in California avenue just outside the building. T h e y confronted Green and the two other members of the Blackstone Rangers.

Insults were exchanged. Then Green and a Disciple, Orthell Champion, 20, started swinging fists.

Suffers Face Cuts

In a three-minute battle, Green wound up with cuts over both eyes, a cut lip, and a bloody nose.

Six Chicago p o l i c e cars pulled up in front of the building. The fight ended. Green and the other Rangers got in a car and drove away.

Fort and Barksdale, their meeting with Supt. Moore having ended, walked out. Fort walked away down the street, and Barksdale got in a car with the other Disciples. No one was arrested.

Moore said, "Nothing was accomplished."

Source: Courtesy of the Chicago Tribune Archives

Sheriff's Police Hope for "Reprieve"

★ ★ ★
DN-11-20-67
★ ★ ★

Bilek to Pick 190 Pledged To 'Honest Crime Fighting'

BY EDMUND J. ROONEY

Arthur J. Bilek Jr., 33, steps in Dec. 3 as the No. 1 symbol of Sheriff-elect Richard B. Ogilvie's attempts to fulfill an election campaign promise to "smash the local crime syndicate."

And it will be up to Bilek, as the new chief of the sheriff's police department, to assemble a 190-man force pledged to "honest crime fighting" from a group that has become somewhat notorious, historically, as a haven for political hacks.

"There will be absolutely no patronage appointments in my police unit," Ogilvie told reporters.

"I don't know what Chief Bilek's politics are," he said, "and I don't care because they're not important."

BILEK, a Chicago policeman since 1953, told reporters that he was an independent voter without a party affiliation.

Bilek totes a hefty packet of credentials as both one of Police Supt. O. W. Wilson's eggheads and as a detective with acknowledged street savvy.

"We're quite sorry to see Bilek take a leave at this time," said Col. Minor K. Wilson, a top aide to the superintendent.

"He's a first-class policeman and we regard him as one of the department's real comers. We wish him well, however."

BILEK, a native Chicagoan and son of a bank employe, earned a master's degree in sociology from Loyola University, and has two years in toward a law degree at the Kent College of Law.

His practical experience while serving with a special "syndicate intelligence" squad at the state's attorney's office in the late 1950s first brought him to Ogilvie's attention.

IN ADDITION, Bilek worked with two other detectives for 56 hours in 1957 to solve the murder of 14-year-old Mary Lou Wagner in the Rogers Park district.

"We're out to eliminate the syndicate here in Cook County," Bilek says. "We know who they are, too. There won't be any alibis from us on this. And, don't expect us to be ignoring letters from the Chicago Crime Commission on crime problems."

Sheriff-elect Richard B. Ogilvie (center) exchanges greetings with his two new aides, Edward J. Kucharski (left) appointed under-sheriff, and Arthur J. Bilek, chosen chief of the county highway police.

Source: Chicago Daily News, November 20, 1967
Reproduced with permission of the Chicago Sun-Times.

OGILVIE TO GIVE NEW SHERIFF'S COPS LIE TEST
Chicago Daily Tribune (1872-1963); Nov 20, 1962; ProQuest Historical Newspapers Chicago Tribune (1849 - 1985)
pg. 3

OGILVIE TO GIVE NEW SHERIFF'S COPS LIE TEST

Kucharski and Bilek to Be Top Aids

Sheriff-elect Richard B. Ogilvie announced yesterday that he would use lie tests to screen all members of his county highway police force.

He also disclosed at a press conference that he has selected Edmund J. Kucharski, a sanitary district trustee, and Arthur Bilek, a Chicago police sergeant, as his two top aids in the sheriff's office.

Kucharski has been an outspoken foe of corruption, waste, and mismanagement in the sanitary district since he was appointed to the board in January, 1961. His term as a district trustee will expire next month. Kucharski is a graduate of the University of Illinois and of John Marshall law school.

"Every man who applies for a job on the county police force will be required to take a polygraph examination on the questions he has answered on the application form," Ogilvie said. "The lie tests will screen my policemen f o r i ntegrity and honesty."

Expects to Replace Most

Ogilvie has vowed to replace most of the present 175 sheriff's policemen, whom he has described as "incompetents." He said he will pay for the lie tests from his personal funds.

New Sheriff and New Aids
(Story in adjoining column)

[TRIBUNE Staff Photo]
Sheriff-elect Richard B. Ogilvie (center), with two aids he selected yesterday. Edmund J. Kucharski (left), a sanitary district trustee, is to be undersheriff, and Arthur Bilek, a Chicago police sergeant, will be chief of the county highway police.

"It may come to a good sum, but it will be worth it," he said.

Kucharski, who is 46, will be undersheriff. Bilek, 33, will be chief of the sheriff's highway police.

Formal appointments will be made Dec. 3, when Ogilvie becomes sheriff. Ogilvie, a Republican and a former federal prosecutor, won the office in the Nov. 6 election.

Kucharski to Screen Aids

Kucharski, also a Republican, is the former 12th ward alderman, Superior court clerk, and county recorder. As undersheriff, he is expected to screen political appointments to the sheriff's staff, except for members of the highway police force, and to handle the routine administration of the sheriff's office.

With Kucharski in this role, Ogilvie will be free to take personal command of an organized crime squad of sheriff's policemen. This squad of 20 detectives is being organized by Ogilvie to crack down on crime syndicate rackets in Cook county, Chicago, and the suburbs.

Bilek Served Adamowski

Bilek now is a director of training for the Chicago police department. He was an investigator in the state's attorney's office during the regime of Benjamin S. Adamowski, former Republican county prosecutor.

Bilek is a World War II veteran and graduate of Loyola university.

Under Ogilvie's p r o g r a m, Bilek will have the task of reorganizing and training the sheriff's police force.

Source: Courtesy of Chicago Tribune Archives

In the mid-60s, Chief of the Cook County Sheriff's Police Arthur Bilek inspects some members of his new force, along with new cars and equipment.

Source: Arthur Bilek Collection. Reproduced with permission of Arthur Bilek.

Sheriff's Police Plan Cicero Patrol Today
Chicago Tribune (1963-Current file); Jan 9, 1964; ProQuest Historical Newspapers Chicago Tribune (1849 - 1985)
pg. D1

Sheriff's Police Plan Cicero Patrol Today

(Picture on back page)

Chief Arthur Bilek of the sheriff's police force said last night that, beginning this morning, sheriff's police will patrol the streets of Cicero "as if no Cicero police department existed."

Bilek made the announcement after he and other raiders of an alleged handbook at 5941 Roosevelt rd., in Cicero, were delayed by a series of locked doors they had to smash.

'It's Last Straw'

"This is the last straw," he said. "From now on sheriff's police will commence open patrol in Cicero. Starting at 8 a. m. uniformed sheriff's men in police cars and plain clothes detectives will begin to patrol the streets of Cicero."

Bilek said that for 10 years the Chicago Crime commission has been making complaints of vice and gambling in Cicero, and that raids have been made by sheriff's police, state police, and the state's attorney's police.

"Apparently the Cicero police department does not intend to take any action," he said. "Since they won't we will."

Keep Watch on Building

Bilek and several officers and men of the sheriff's police watched yesterday as persons went in and out of the two story building at 5941 Roosevelt rd., which formerly housed a tavern. Efforts to get an undercover man inside the place last week had failed.

When they decided to enter, they found the door padlocked and had to break it down with axes. Bilek said this took 25 minutes, and when he and his men reached the top of the stairway they found a locked door.

They smashed it down and wound up eventually in a kitchen, where they had to smash a third door to get into the gambling room.

Room Is Empty

The room was warm and cozy and showed signs of recent occupancy. There was a heavy haze of tobacco smoke in the room. There were gambling sheets, but the persons who had been observed entering the building were nowhere in sight.

Bilek said the patrons apparently reached the rooftop from a bathroom, and walked along the roof for half a block until they reached a ledge where they could drop to the sidewalk.

[TRIBUNE Staff Photo]

Detective James Dwyer using iron pipe as battering ram on locked door as another sheriff's policeman looks on during raid at 5941 Roosevelt rd., Cicero. Scratch sheets and other betting equipment were seized in building, but no patrons were found. *(Story on page 1, section 1B)*

Source: Courtesy of Chicago Tribune Archives

Cook County Sheriff's Police performed over 1,000 gambling, tavern and prostitution raids in a four year period.

Source: Arthur Bilek Collection. Reproduced with permission of Arthur Bilek.

Cook County Sheriff's Police make an arrest in Cicero.

Source: Arthur Bilek Collection. Reproduced with permission of Arthur Bilek.

Joseph Aiuppa
Source: Chicago Crime Commission Archives

Joseph Aiuppa
Source: Chicago Crime Commission Archives

Cops Turn Burglars! City Horrified
WAYNE THOMIS
Chicago Daily Tribune (1872-1963); Feb 23, 1960; ProQuest Historical Newspapers Chicago Tribune (1849 - 1985)
pg. 12

Cops Turn Burglars! City Horrified

Policeman Asks Thief for Favor; Scandal Ensues

(When he was arrested last July 31 after escaping a trap set by Evanston police, Richard Morrison, 23, boasted he was "the greatest burglar who ever worked in Chicago." He conceded, too, he probably was headed for forced retirement thru a long term in prison. But he made up his mind to blow the whistle on crooked policemen who had been his partners in crime. Honest policemen passed over his tale, not believing it. Then he told it to the state's attorney's office, and Chicago was rocked by its worst police scandal in decades: a scandal which brought about a search for a new head of the Chicago police department. The search ended yesterday when Mayor Daley appointed Orlando W. Wilson superintendent.)

BY WAYNE THOMIS

A SUMMERDALE DISTRICT policeman wanted golf clubs — and asked a neighborhood burglar to steal some for him. This was the start of a partnership between law and crime that exploded Chicago's worst police scandals in decades.

Horrifying evidence has been produced to show that a powerful, amoral, greedy segment of the city's basic law enforcement agency — patrolmen, detectives, precinct sergeants, and many higher officers — is made up of criminals who operate under the cloak of the law.

Instead of protecting citizens, these policemen prey on them.

And with the cover ripped off one corner of Chicago's rough, tough underworld, broader inquiries have disclosed, once again, the machinery of a long lived, well oiled, payoff system that provides big time crime syndicate protection.

Richard Morrison—he talked.

The city's policemen are the collectors. Politicians provide the "fix." Gamblers, gunmen, hoodlum union leaders, dope peddlers, and vice lords are the benefactors.

As a result of the police scandals, Chicago is getting a shocking, first hand glimpse of the kinky shadow-world everyone knows about, but the existence of which practically no one admits.

It is a world which THE CHICAGO TRIBUNE has been describing for years. It is a world in which wrong is right —in which all incentive for honor, justice, suppression of crime, and even fundamental discipline has disappeared from broad divisions of the police department, the courts, the all-pervading Democratic political party machine that has a strangle hold on Chicago proper.

Burglar-Police Scandals Disclose City's Underlying Corruption

The burglar-police scandals are bad enough, but they have touched off inquiries that have disclosed the deeper, underlying rot. Policemen who oppose "clout" and political interference with enforcement of the laws have made these disclosures.

Some have come forward with specific evidence on the sale in advance of answer sheets for written police examinations. Others have described in unmistakable terms how the police-political "fix" is operated. And some have come up with names and reports on police "bagmen," the collectors of graft and privilege money.

While all these disclosures were simmering and festering, even more startling evidence of organized and systematic police corruption was uncovered when a TRIBUNE reporter obtained admissions from four convicts in Stateville penitentiary that they stole more than $1,000,000 worth of furs and jewelry from Gold Coast apartments with active coöperation of detectives from the burglary detail and others.

Their police collaborators even warned them when special police task forces would be operating in areas where the gang planned robberies. The payoffs ran upwards of $20,000 a year.

The disclosures of the Summerdale police-burglar scandals and charges that policemen of the North Damen avenue station also were in collusion with burglars emboldened a number of merchants and business men to talk. They came forward with their own stories of systematic looting and harassment by police and other city agencies, including the courts.

The breakdown of policing in certain Chicago areas

The Summerdale district and location of police station.

has been so great that insurance underwriters refused to insure merchandise on store shelves or packed away in even the best constructed storage sites.

A Chicago Joke—Motorist to Cop: 'What's This—Ticket or Stickup?'

Chicago's desperate situation is epitomized by a joke told at bars and gatherings: A Chicago motorist was halted by a police squad on a boulevard late at night. As a policeman strode from the squadrol toward the citizen, the latter cranked down a window of his car and asked, "What's it to be—a ticket or a stickup?"

A brash, boyish-looking burglar, who didn't get the golf clubs his police associate wanted, caused all the furor. His name is Richard Morrison. He is 23, but appears to be closer to 16 when he is surrounded by policemen or strides

Mixed emotions. Mayor Daley (right) announces that Timothy O'Connor (left) is thru as police commissioner and Kyran Phelan is taking his place in an acting capacity. The date was Jan. 23. [TRIBUNE Photo]

into a grand jury room. By his own story, he "grew up in Summerdale district," an area once predominately German and Scandinavian, but now more polyglot. It is filled with small homes, many of them well kept, and is bounded by Lake Michigan on the east, Lawrence avenue on the south, Devon avenue on the north, and the north branch of the Chicago river on the west. The river boundary is 2800 to 3200 west of State street.

Morrison attended Swift Elementary school and Senn High school. He told police he began stealing when he was 15 years old. His first arrest was in May, 1953, when he was stopped by detectives while carrying a fine collection of burglary tools. For this, he drew a 10 day sentence in the county jail. A month later he was arrested with more burglary tools and got another 10 day county jail term. From these arrests, he said recently, his acquaintance with policemen began.

Morrison left Chicago in 1954 and returned in 1957. In December, 1955, he was sentenced to nine months in Los Angeles jail for burglary, serving four and drawing probation for five. A year later he was jailed for a month in Las Vegas, N. M., as a prowler. Back in Chicago in 1957, he served four months in the Bridewell for petty larceny.

Boasts He Has Many Friends Among Cops, Sent Yule Card to One

There is a strange affinity between some crooks and some policemen. Morrison boasts he has many friends among "the cops." He sent a Christmas card to one of the men who jailed him last July—the seizure from which the present scandals grew. He has not been free since that arrest, and is now in protective custody with his consent. But the police haven't got him; the state's attorney has.

This youngster called himself "Chicago's master burglar" when he was arrested last summer. He confessed 150 burglaries, saying his loot was worth over $100,000. That he profited is undeniable—he was driving a new Cadillac roadster when he was seized. And he has asserted that he "was ahead" an average of $500 to $2,500 each week. But let him tell his own story. It appeared exclusively in THE CHICAGO TRIBUNE last Jan. 20:

"I guess the place to start this story is when I was working for Wesley's pizza at 1116 Bryn Mawr av., because

Lt. John Ascher (left), demoted from chief of detectives, packs personal effects. Capt. Herman Dorf (right), involved in Summerdale inquiry, resigns rather than take lie test.

to the best of my knowledge that is where everything started with me and the police officers of the 40th [Summerdale] district.

"Delivery guys bringing supplies to the pizza joint had been having parking troubles, trying to get their trucks close to our place during the evening rush. Squads were giving them tickets, but after a while they were giving out so many our boss was calling in the policemen to eat free so they would let the truckers alone.

Source: Courtesy of Chicago Tribune Archives. *Article continues on next page.*

Article continues from previous page.

"Of course, he didn't let them all do it. Just the ones the sergeant detailed to that area. And, of course, the sergeant got his cut also. I know because I sometimes took his food to him at the station."

Tells State's Attorney He Tried to Go Straight After Jail Term

Morrison explained to state's attorney's investigators that he had just gotten out of the Bridewell and was "trying to go straight." He said he was holding two jobs, planning to be married, and trying to pay off his bills. Then he went on:

"Well anyway, getting back to the 40th district cops, I knew most of them because I lived in the district all my life and there were a few I went to school with, and at the time of June, 1958, I was on the bad side of them.

"Everything was going along fine until one day when I was walking down Berwyn avenue from Broadway and the policeman, Frank Faraci, came out of the corner saloon and says to me, 'Well, if it isn't the little burglar, Richie.'

"I knew Frank from the pizza place and I seen he was a little loaded so I just said, 'Hi, Frank, how are things with you?' and he said, 'Well, they would be a little better if you would cut us guys in on some of your jobs.'

"He said: 'You know Al Karras and some of the other fellows [policemen] and we'd go along with the show. After all, we like nice things, too.'

"I stalled for a month because I knew the cops from before. But they kept pestering me. Al Karras told me Brinn [Allan Brinn, a Summerdale policeman] wanted to know when I was going to steal some golf clubs for him. I was getting sick and tired of them asking. By 11:30 the night of July 31 [1958], I was pretty loaded myself and I was figuring that so long as the clubs were for a cop . . . so I drove up in Rogers Park. I was thinking that about 20 per cent of the new cars had golf clubs in them, so I was looking for new ones."

Morrison didn't find what he wanted and drifted into Evanston. He saw a station wagon with golf clubs in the rear and stopped to break into it. Unknowingly, he stepped into a trap. Evanston police, watching the car because of earlier pilferings, hailed him. Morrison jumped back into his Cadillac and gunned it toward Chicago. The policemen fired a number of shots. One of them punctured a tire, so Morrison abandoned the car.

It was found and traced to his home, then at 5556 Lakewood av., because it was registered in his real name. Early next morning, Summerdale policemen arrested him. In February, 1959, he was convicted in Criminal court of auto looting. Morrison's lawyer made a motion for a new trial, which is still pending.

"It was after this [his capture in 1958] I figured I might as well go in with the Summerdale cops since I was in trouble anyway," Morrison said. "I figured to collect a bundle to beat my Evanston rap.

"So, from day to day I met the cops in a restaurant at 1 a. m. and we set up jobs every night. From time to time I kept meeting more cops that were burglars, and from time to time I kept getting more cases in the Criminal court building and needed an awful lot of money for lawyers, bondsmen, and cops, as the ones I went on jobs with sometimes let their friends at D-3 [north side detective bureau headquarters] know I did it, but they wouldn't let them know about themselves.

"So I had to pay guys in D-3 to forget about the cases and it cost quite a bit, too.

"You see, the cop that let D-3 in on the business got a nice cut of my payoff to D-3, too. I didn't find that out until after I was arrested [again] July 30, 1959, and it was hard to believe that the same guys I went on burglaries with would also let their D-3 pals in on it so they could get a few more hundred out of the job."

Morrison's bitterness is understandable when it is known that he first told his story of the police partnerships in his burglaries to a central detective bureau interrogator in August, 1959. This man, Sgt. Robert Lynsky, relayed the report orally to Chief of Detectives John Ascher, both admitted. They said they completely discounted the story "because they just couldn't believe what Morrison said." No explanation was given for the failure to make an investigation. Lt. Ascher was demoted after the scandal broke.

In spite of Morrison's willingness to talk, no one in authority would listen until he was sent to the county jail in November, 1959, at which time he asked and got a hearing from the state's attorney's office. He told his story over and over again in a series of interrogations by lawyers and investigators and, as Frank Ferlic, first assistant state's attorney, has said repeatedly, "We were able to check out and support practically everything he told us." As a result, detectives under Lt. Ascher and state's attorney's police made simultaneous raids Jan. 14, 1960, on the homes of eight Summerdale policemen Morrison had named. Six truckloads of stolen merchandise were found in seven homes, all eight cops were arrested, and the scandal was out.

Morrison Tells Methods Cops Used to Help Him Carry Out Burglaries

How were these alleged burglaries accomplished? Let's get back to Morrison's own story.

"At first," he said, "my cop pals acted as lookouts.

"I'd gotten money from the place, when Frank spotlighted the window. Frank Faraci blocked off the detective bureau car that arrived half a minute later."

They sometimes drove round and round a block where I was pulling a burglary to see there was no interference. Sometimes they intercepted the private watch service guys who would be patroling. Sometimes they kept other policemen away from me.

"We decided a music store at Balmoral and Clark streets was a good 'case.' The night I broke in, Frank Faraci [one of the eight Summerdale policemen] was at the station and he heard the squad operator give out a radio call to cars on the street that a burglary was in progress in that store. He happened to hear this call and he happened to know it was me in the place.

"He shot down there in 207 [Morrison named the squad cars by number in much of his confession] and blocked the street and hit the window of the place [police procedure of shining spotlights from their cars into windows of stores where a burglary is suspected].

"I'd gotten the money from the place when Frank spotlighted the window. Frank Faraci blocked off the detective bureau car that arrived half a minute later. My other pals [also police lookouts on the job with Morrison at the time] came round the alley. I went out a back door, over the fence, and ran toward the street. My car was parked near and I took off."

Morrison said that later, in appreciation of Faraci's help, he gave the policeman all the money he had stolen from the music store—several hundred dollars. Time and again, in his statements, Morrison said he and his Summerdale police associates met in taverns and restaurants to talk about their burglaries, work out tactics, and laugh over their "take."

Morrison Tells How Private Guard Almost Got Shot During Burglary

Once, Morrison alleged, the cop-criminals almost shot a private watchman of the North Shore patrol.

"This particular night they [the policemen] wanted to hit a food store," Morrison related. They all had crowbars with them, and they'd picked out a place on Damen avenue and Bryn Mawr. I looked the joint over and said it was no good. They wanted food, tho, so I picked out a place at 1112 Thorndale av.

"There were five of these police officers and me, and we drove over to the place in squad car 207. I opened the door and they were all running around in the store getting this stuff. I happened to think, who is listening to the radio in the squadrol? I said I would.

"So I went to the car and I was sitting there. They were coming out with bacon and hams and everything you could think of in the store—real expensive foods. They kept filling the back seat of the squad car. Suddenly another car pulls behind us. It was a sergeant of the North Shore patrol.

"I figured if he sees me and all this stuff in the squad [car] everybody is dead. So I had to think fast. Anyways, I took off in the squad car and when I came back they [the five policemen] were still there. They said: 'Where you been?' They said: 'Jeez, we almost had a heart attack

"We all laid low in the store. But this guy was checking the door next door."

ourselves. We had our guns on him. We all laid low in the store. But this guy was checking the door of a place next door. He musta missed us completely. We might have had to drop him if he'd seen us.'"

Morrison said that later, talking over the night's incidents, his police accomplices offered to lend him a uniform to wear on "jobs." He said he "wouldn't go for it." He told them: "Too much trouble changing back and forth. Better to just stay out of sight."

After more than a year of police coöperation, Morrison reported, someone in his "clique" fired some shots at him one night when he burglarized a store on Lawrence avenue.

Begins to Watch Step for Fear He Would Be Killed by Cop-Pals

"It had to be somebody in that clique," Morrison continued. "I guess they were thinking I knew too much about them. Maybe it was just one guy's idea, so I began really watching my step with those fellows. They wanted me to open a meat market for them, so I was especially careful in picking the copper who was to keep watch. He was riding a three wheeler [motorcycle].

"He sat on his wheel while I got in and worked on the safe. I couldn't open it without blowing and didn't want to make the noise. But I picked up $1,300 in cash, from the register and drawers. Then I walked out and told my cop friend: 'The door's open. You can round up the guys and bring them in.'

"I went down the alley and hid on a garage roof. This guy called in almost every available vehicle in the district. They had all the three wheelers, and a paddy wagon, and the squad car. They had their lights on and they were loading up those squads and everything. Anyways, they cleaned out the whole meat market.

"I was eating some of the steaks taken out of there at their houses quite a few times in following mornings and, in fact, they were eating steaks every night. They had a ball with those steaks."

Once, Morrison related, when he was arrested in connection with one of his "150 or more burglaries" and locked up in a Summerdale cell, his "clique" moved sev-

[Continued on following page]

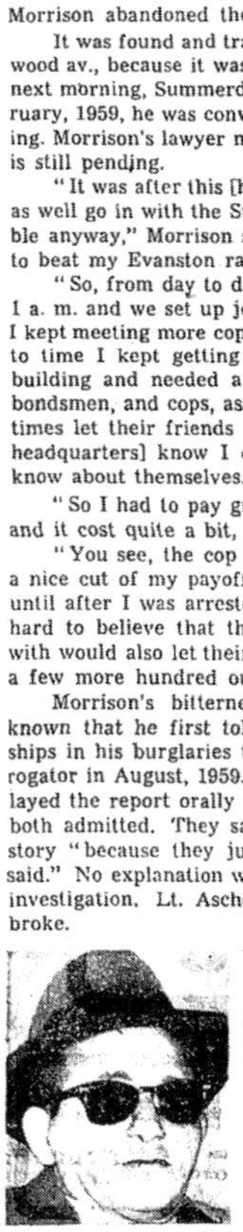
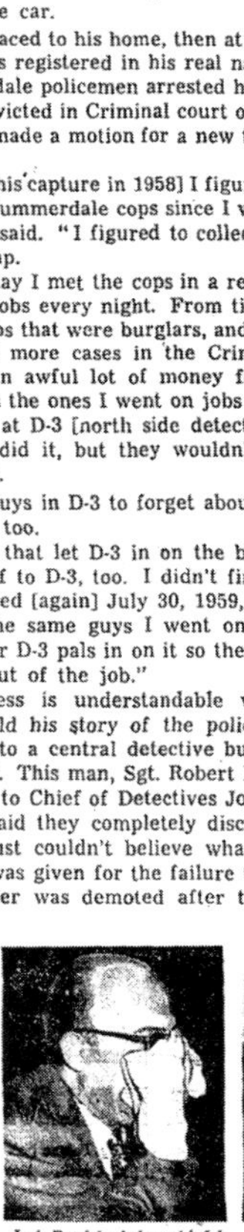
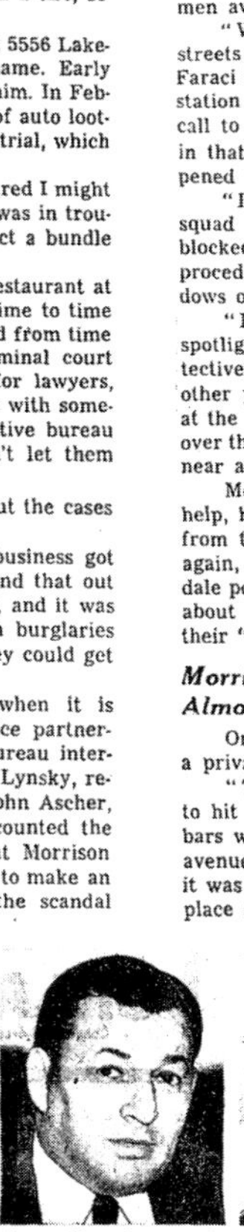
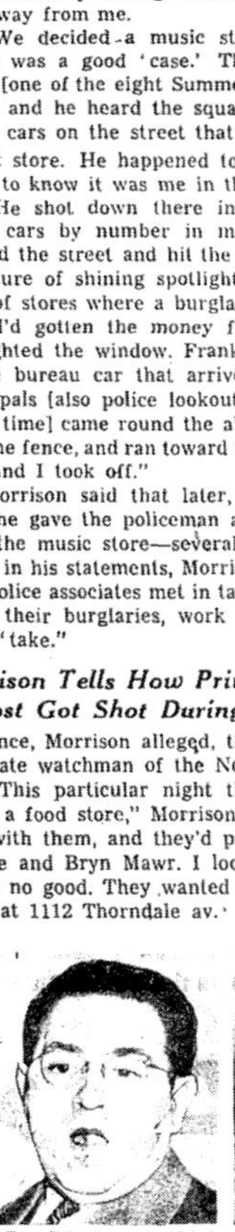
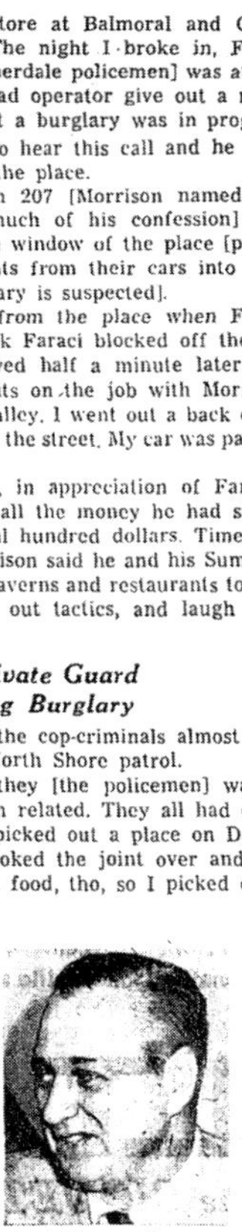
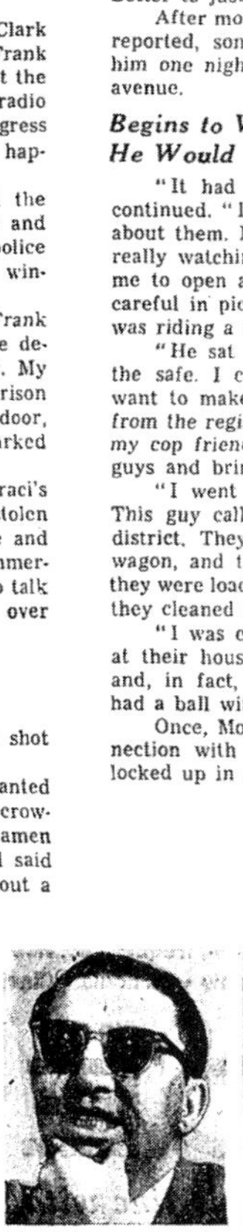
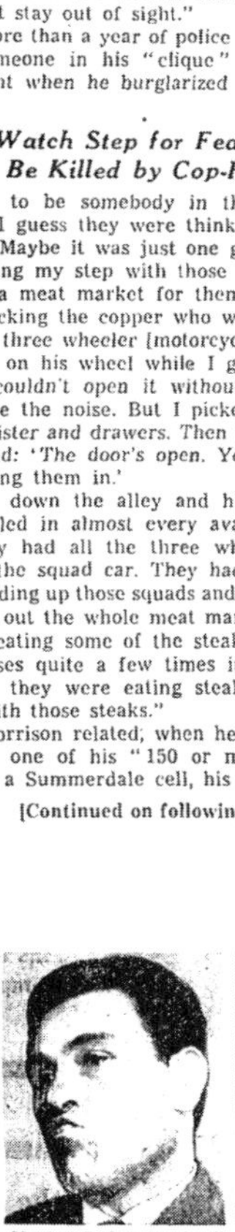
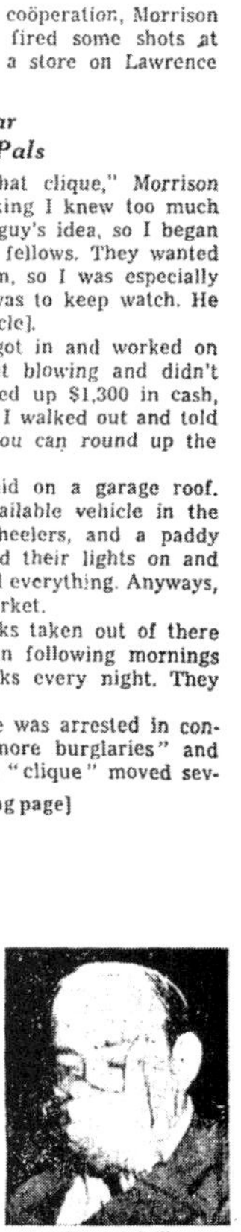

Sam Giancana — he affects dark glasses indoors.

Jack Patrick—he's a shy fellow at gambling inquiry.

James Allegretti—a man who handles cop contacts.

Ross Prio—he ranks high in syndicate circles.

Ralph Pierce—still a power in south side gambling.

Chuck English—active in two police districts.

Marshall Caifano—won't talk at Senate inquiry.

Fiore Baccieri dislikes being photographed.

Source: Courtesy of Chicago Tribune Archives. *Article continues on next page.*

Article continues from previous page.

Mob Wields 'Clout' Thru Politicians

[Cont'd from preceding page]

eral carloads of stolen radios, televisions, and other goods from his apartment "to prevent honest detectives from finding out what was going on."

The arrest came when two detectives found in Morrison's car some spark plugs that had been stolen a few nights earlier in a burglary which, Morrison said, had been committed in collusion with his police pals.

"When they [the detectives] took me over to the station," Morrison said, "I had most of the stuff from this place in my apartment and was keeping it for the cops. Now if they would have found out where I was living, if they had looked in my wallet and learned the address where I was living, they would have got the stuff.

"It was lucky the police officers I knew came. I got taken back into the back of the lockup and they come there and I gave them my keys. If they got rid of the stuff they would have a hard case to beat. They used the squad car—207 again—and drove over to my apartment and cleaned it out. I guess there was at least $5,000 worth of radios and televisions. They divided the stuff and hid it away."

'Squad Car Pushed Parked Auto When It Blocked Loading Area'

Illustrating how closely he allegedly worked with his police "clique" Morrison told of the looting of a tire and auto supply store at Carmen avenue and Broadway.

"We had a two hour delay," Morrison said, "because somebody had double parked a car alongside the loading dock at the rear. We didn't know if this person was going to come down and take it or not. We waited a couple of hours and this car was still there. I saw the squad with one of our fellows driving and I stopped him.

"I says: 'Listen, we got to get rid of this car somehow. It's been here for hours and it's delaying the job.' He said: 'I know, we've been waiting to go.' Anyways, they pushed the car. They put it on Broadway and says, 'To hell with the guy.' They pushed it with car 207. They gave me the signal then everything was okay. I said fine."

This place yielded tires, television sets, radios, electric shavers, shotgun shells, a variety of guns, and other expensive items, Morrison said. While the burglary was in progress, Morrison asserted, police associates in a squad car "circled the place every few minutes to see if everything was going all right, and they sent two or three of the paid-patrol service men away from this block during that time."

All policemen accused by Morrison have denied the charges.

The eight policemen charged with burglary are: Patrick Groark Jr., 28, of 1526 Norwood av., son of a late captain of police; Frank Faraci, 43, of 5121 Estes av., Skokie; Sol Karras, 26, of 1521 Ardmore av.; Karras' twin brother, Alex, 26, of 2631 Greenleaf av.; Peter Beeftink, 50, of 2049 Hutchinson av.; Allan Brinn, 30, of 5025 Sheffield ct., Skokie; Henry Mulea, 45, of 1521 Montana av.; and Alan Clements, 29, of 6565 Glenwood av.

Five other policemen were arrested on extortion or conspiracy charges in connection with Morrison's stories.

Five of policemen held in investigation of burglaries. Left to right: Sol and Alex Karras, Frank Faraci, Alan Clements and Allan Brinn.
[TRIBUNE Photo]

They are: Detectives George Raymond, 32, of 517 N. Albany av.; Robert Ambrose, 35, of 3243 Geneva ter.; and Jackson Whelan, 33, of 5669 N. Oconto av.; and Policemen John W. Peterson, 35, of 3111 N. Spaulding av., and Glenn Cherry, 33, of 4937 N. Tripp av. Peterson was identified by Paul Newey, chief investigator for State's Attorney Benjamin Adamowski, as "the fixer" at Summerdale station. Cherry was Peterson's partner.

The three detectives, Raymond, Ambrose and Whelan, were charged with accepting a $3,500 payoff from Morrison to suppress certain evidence in a burglary case against him.

At police headquarters; in Florida, where Mayor Daley was vacationing; in City Hall aldermanic offices, and in thousands of precinct political headquarters, saloons, and other gathering places the police scandal had a smashing effect. Chicago area citizens were indignant, apprehensive, disgusted, and more suspicious of the entire political and law enforcement machinery of Cook county and the City of Chicago than ever before.

Lie Tests Ordered for 130 Summerdale District Police

"Everywhere we go now people look at us as if we were lepers," one Loop patrolman reported that third week of January.

"The whole department is blackened," said Police Commissioner Timothy J. O'Connor. "The work of 10,000 good policemen is undone. It makes you heartsick."

Lie tests for 130 Summerdale policemen were ordered. Outside experts were assembled to conduct them.

On Saturday, Jan. 23, O'Connor resigned under fire. Kyran V. Phelan, who had been O'Connor's chief assistant, was appointed acting commissioner by Mayor Daley.

State's Attorney Benjamin S. Adamowski said: "This thing is a shocking indictment of the moral tone of law enforcement in Chicago. There are too many unsolved crimes. It is my opinion that the mayor better start looking thru the whole department."

Capt. Herman Dorf, who had been commanding Summerdale police station for a year, resigned rather than face a lie detector test. He said he had nothing to hide; that his 28 year career "spoke for itself." He added, however, that he felt it "too degrading and demoralizing to take the lie box." His resignation came less than two years before he would have been eligible for full retirement.

A number of honest policemen, sickened by their own situations, began appearing at the offices of the state's

Police Try to Cheat Lie Tests

Lie tests given policemen in connection with the burglary scandal have presented to Chicagoans the amazing spectacle of law enforcement officers trying to cheat on the same kind of test that many suspected criminals are asked to take. Some policemen took tranquilizers before going on the lie box. Some reported for the test after work, and some stayed sleepless for hours before the scheduled tests. But it was all in vain. Experts say skilled polygraph operators can tell when a subject is deliberately trying to "beat the box."

attorney or telephoning to Phelan's office with "reports of rottenness in the department."

Perhaps the most important disclosures, however, were those of the ex-policeman who wrote THE TRIBUNE on Jan. 28 and gave a city-wide blueprint of big time crime syndicate payoffs for protection. Over his own signature, he gave names, dates, and places. THE TRIBUNE, feeling that proper law enforcement agencies must investigate such charges, gave copies of the document to the state's attorney, the mayor, and the Federal Bureau of Investigation headquarters.

But here, with identifying material deleted, is what he charged:

1. One of Chicago's highest police officials permitted operation of the city's largest continuous dice game in his district, took his orders from a Democratic ward committeeman, and collected from gambling and vice.

2. Thirty-nine gambling rooms operated on a wide open basis in another police district under the same official and the take was collected by two bagmen, one for the police official and one for the ward committeeman.

3. Another high police official is part owner of a hotel where vice flourishes and a patrolman is maintained on duty at all times to see that no arrests are made and that no customer fails to pay for services rendered.

4. A police official who "investigated" several men involved in vice shakedown charges had used these same men as his collectors from vice joints thruout the city. The investigation, of course, was a whitewash.

5. A high police officer in a supervisory job was drunk at roll calls he conducted himself.

6. The same official hides his squad car while spending his time consorting with known hoodlums and prostitutes.

Charges Police Captain's Nephew Acts as Bagman for Officials

7. A police captain's nephew acts not only as his bagman but as the collector for several other captains. Both the captain and the nephew are constantly in the company of top syndicate hoodlums.

8. A prominent politician and office holder made a trip to Arizona to get a large sum of money put up by the crime syndicate to help make a well known lieutenant a captain.

9. A police captain takes frequent plane rides with Jimmy [The Monk] Allegretti, north side police payoff man for one gambling section of the crime syndicate.

10. James V. Rini, a syndicate hoodlum now in prison for coin machine terrorism and burglary, was protected by police officials by being booked only on minor charges whenever he was arrested at a north side syndicate operated tavern.

11. A lieutenant, recently a captain, watched the police message tapes for news of hoodlum arrests, then notified crime syndicate lawyers for a nice big fee.

12. A police officer collects from politicians who want their candidates to get police jobs or, if policemen, to be given certain assignments. He also gets a kickback from business men who sell equipment to the police department.

13. A police captain was "made by the syndicate for its personal use as a source of information for the crime syndicate." The same captain has minor hoodlums and some burglars as his employes in a private business he operates.

Among other currently active crime syndicate figures who were mentioned in the ex-policeman's letter were: Fiore [Fifi] Buccieri, a gambling boss and aid to Sam [Mooney] Giancana, one of the top syndicate leaders; Joe [Caesar] DiVarco, north side gambling boss; Frank [Hot Dog] Lisciandrella; Julius [Juju] Greco, vice and strip tease joint operator; Rini, and Allegretti.

THE TRIBUNE interviewed a number of police commanders, lieutenants, and veteran detectives subsequently and was told:

"Powerful Democratic politicians wield the clout within the department like a club. They have, in five years, almost wrecked the department. Examples follow:

"A patrolman who was Mayor Daley's campaign chauffeur became the unofficial and most powerful commissioner of police after Daley's election in 1955. This man, from an office in City hall, arranged transfers and appointments to virtually all levels of police jobs until he died in 1958.

Charles Nicoletti is quizzed in a slaying investigation.  | James Rini—now a prison guest of the state.  | Jack Cerone—he's on top in Austin district.  | Sam Cesario—he's a fixer and climber in syndicate. 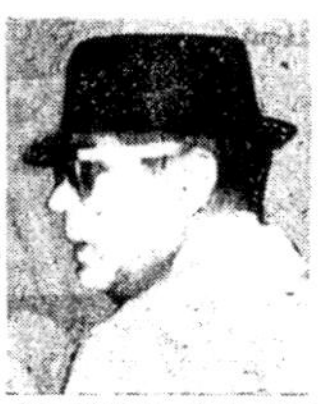 | Joe DiVarco—Rush street bows to his wishes.  | Jimmy Catuara—a reputed producer of bombs. | Sam Mesi—lost his job as supervisor of garbage. | Willie Aloisio—his word law in Shakespeare area.

Source: Courtesy of Chicago Tribune Archives.   *Article continues on next page.*

Article continues from previous page.

" A chief of detectives made the disgusted observation that sponsorship of a Democratic politician was essential before a policeman could be transferred to the detective bureau.

" Appointment of patrolmen to the rank of detective [plain clothesman] in precincts became a part of the Democratic city administration's political patronage. Sponsorship of a committeeman, an alderman or a party organization chief of some kind was mandatory before a patrolman could make the $600 a year jump in salary that goes with a detective rating.

" I can't make a detective or dump him," one captain told THE TRIBUNE, " and this means I have no control over my own men. They know it. A man doesn't have to give a damn about me. He listens to the politician who helped him get his rank."

Politicians, the policemen predicted, are not going to step out of the Chicago police picture because of the burglary scandal. The stakes in power and money are too high and the " fix system " is too well established by the crime syndicate that is willing to come up with a steady and substantial stream of dollars to get the protection it requires.

Chicago's crime syndicate operations are traditionally based on " cash clout "—that is the straight money payoff for freedom from interference. Sometimes this even includes the " pushing around " by policemen of citizens who want to cause trouble for syndicate gambling places, handbooks or slot machines, a veteran policeman told THE TRIBUNE.

" But in recent years," this police veteran added, " the syndicate has elected some of its own politicians—a regular syndicate bloc well known in the City hall and in the state legislature. They carry the syndicate ball at all times, but are not at all slow about getting into the collecting on their own. No matter what is said about crime organization—aside from the top level of it—practically everybody who is kinky is on the make for himself, and is not to be trusted with money or opportunity for shakedowns. This is what causes some of the hoodlum murders—fights right inside the syndicate for power or money."

The other side of the precinct " bag " operation is that of the crime syndicate. The same sources of information that named policemen as part of the politico-enforcement payoff machine named the following " mob " chiefs as the money payers in their respective zones of influence:

Ralph Pierce: An old-timer whose connections with the mob extend back into the Capone era. He is the man to see on gambling arrangements and payoffs in the Hyde Park,

Loot of burglaries, seized in homes of policemen arrested in burglary inquiry, occupies room in state's attorney's office in Criminal court building. [TRIBUNE Photo]

Woodlawn, Grand Crossing, and other south side police districts. Pierce has been pushed out of the 2d and 3d ward areas by Negro politicians and policy operators who have concluded more recent mob connections.

Ross Prio: A man whose appearance is deceptively like that of a middle-aged business man, but who has a reputation for indulging in his own muscle work. Prio's territory is that of the north side—an amorphous area extending from the Chicago river to Howard street and from the lake to the western city limits. Prio is high in crime syndicate councils, altho not top rank.

Frank [Strongy] Ferrara: A rising younger hoodlum who has taken over the Loop gambling supervision for the mob during the illness of Gus [Slim] Alex.

Louie Briatta: Brother-in-law of Ald. John D'Arco [1st] and manager of handbook layoff joints in the central district. These are big clearing houses for sizable bets and are used by bookies from all parts of town. Briatta's influence is confined to D'Arco's ward and is a secondary but highly profitable element in the illegal betting parlor network for Chicago.

Jimmy [The Owl] Catuara: Rackets manager for the syndicate in the Deering police district. Catuara has a reputation in the underworld as an accomplished bomb producer and tosser.

Chuck English: Former juke box chain operator who has made a deal with the syndicate for general gambling control in Brighton Park police district and in part of the Fillmore police district. In the latter, English pushed a powerful Democratic politician out of this job.

Jack Patrick: A syndicate muscle man for years, Patrick has the portion of Fillmore street gambling that is outside English's areas. In recent years, policy and some phases of take that started on the south side have become valuable to the syndicate in this area.

Sambo Cesario: The syndicate's fixer contact in Maxwell street police district. He is one of the youngest such liaison men and is jealously described by some of the fringe syndicate operators as an overrated punk.

Fiore [Fifi] Buccieri, syndicate gambling chief in the Marquette police district. He formerly ran the Greek dice games [barboot] in Maxwell street and farther north. Later he was identified with union rackets.

Jack Humphreys: Brother of Murray [The Camel] Humphreys who, in his late sixties, still is a major fixer and adviser to the top syndicate. Jack Humphreys is the gambling supervisor for the mob in New City and Lawndale police districts. He uses the name Jack Wright and has been busy in mob affairs—altho never a top man—since the 1930s.

Chuck Nicoletti: Warren avenue police district gam-

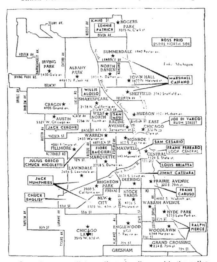

Legends on map link syndicate hoodlums with the police districts in which they control gambling and vice.

bling supervisor for the syndicate. Reputedly a killer himself, he has been active in recent years setting up handbooks and wire rooms.

Julius [Juju] Greco: Vice manager for the syndicate in Warren avenue. Greco has been a close associate and the mob payoff man for at least half a dozen different police captains. He is a specialist in handling stables of call girls, madams, and so-called stag shows on the west side.

Jack Cerone: Syndicate's top rackets man in Austin police district. Cerone once was driver and bodyguard for Tony Accardo, who is really a top drawer syndicate boss. Cerone got his job " strictly thru muscle," according to mob gossip. His spot formerly had been handled by gamblers and politicians who were shoved out when Cerone shot several and had some of his younger thugs slug others.

Sam Mesi: Racine avenue police district gambling supervisor. He comes from a family closely tied to mob operations for three generations. He is regarded as one of the newer, smoother hoods who still has a knack for violence if required. He was on a city payroll as a garbage truck supervisor—another indication of gang clout—but lost this job when exposed by THE TRIBUNE.

Marshall Caifano: Gambling manager in the Summerdale, Town Hall, and Sheffield avenue police districts. Reputedly a syndicate gunner whose trigger capacities often have been used outside his own areas. He is a playboy type who makes his headquarters in north side night clubs.

Joe [Caesar] DiVarco: Rush street syndicate boss for gambling, saloon supplies, vice, and some of the other illegal rackets offered in this rich night life area. DiVarco's gam-

---

bling sphere extends into the Summerdale police district and partly into Town Hall. He is senior in syndicate rank to most of the other precinct bosses.

Monk Allegretti: DiVarco's aid, who handles direct police contacts, payoffs, and beefs. Allegretti makes his headquarters in a quiet neighborhood saloon on Claremont avenue, south of Devon avenue, and DiVarco is frequently seen there. So are a north and west side police district bagman.

Lennie Patrick: Rogers Park syndicate gambling boss. A graduate of the old 24th ward Capone stronghold, where he was part of the mob muscle. Patrick reputedly was a murder expert, arranging for liquidation of various gamblers who resisted syndicate partnerships and other invasions.

Willie [Smokes] Aloisio: Gambling boss in Shakespeare police district and lately in northwest Cook county. Aloisio, who has a violent history as a muscle man and reputed killer, ran a quiet, lucrative gambling area in the Shakespeare district for years. His word was law with operators of slot machines, dice games, floating poker games, and the back room gambling houses and books in that area.

Frank [Skid] Caruso: The syndicate's man for dice, poker, and, above all, mob policy operations in the 1st ward end of the Prairie avenue police district. Caruso inherited the job from his father-in-law, Bruno Roti, who died in 1956. The mob invasion of this partly 2d and partly 3d ward area was marked by a number of murders for policy control.

Learn Twice A Month Payoffs Started by Syndicate in 1958

Best information available to THE TRIBUNE is that, since late in 1958, all syndicate payoffs in Chicago proper are on a fortnightly basis. Prior to that time, they had been made once a month. A number of greedy police captains and especially, according to the syndicate's side of the story, a pushing group of police lieutenants, commenced " fudging." They would arrange to raid various " protected " spots a day or two after standard payoffs had been made. The biweekly protection is supposed to cut any losses from such maverick raiding to a minimum.

" About this business," THE TRIBUNE was told by a police captain who does not command a district and for the moment is merely marking time in a clerical job where he " writes reports," " have no doubts that the regular syndicate payoffs are going right along while the scandals are on Page one.

" The syndicate is too big and too entrenched to be worried about a few stupid policemen who teamed up with a punk burglar. The syndicate payoffs are big time, involve the whole city enforcement system, extend into the courts and state legislature, and perhaps higher.

" Everybody who is anybody wants to ' forget the hysteria ' over the burglar scandals—but don't, for heaven's sake, upset any apple carts involving the real payoff."

A good deal of other information relating to police venality also has come to light. There was the case of the 150 question civil service sergeant's examination of last Oct. 31. A policeman delivered to THE TRIBUNE a copy which he said was circulated among policemen before the examination and offered to candidates for $100 to $500 a copy. James S. Osborne, commission secretary, verified the exactness of the copy.

Source: Courtesy of Chicago Tribune Archives.

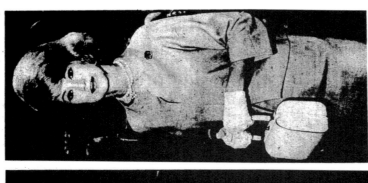

Humphreys Appears Before Grand Jury

[TRIBUNE Staff Photo]
Murray (the Camel) Humphreys in United States courthouse yesterday as he arrived to testify before grand jury investigating crime syndicate.

Singer Phyllis McGuire arriving at new Federal building to testify before grand jury investigating crime syndicate. *(Story on page 1)*

[TRIBUNE Staff Photo]

Quiz Phyllis McGuire in Crime Probe
ROBERT WIEDRICH
Chicago Tribune (1963-Current file): May 20, 1965; ProQuest Historical Newspapers Chicago Tribune (1849 - 1985)
pg. 1

Quiz Phyllis McGuire in Crime Probe

BY ROBERT WIEDRICH

(Pictures on back page)

Phyllis McGuire, a night club singer, and Sam (Momo) Giancana, a hoodlum, starred yesterday as witnesses before a federal grand jury.

They nad almost equal billing. Miss McGuire spent at

Sam. Giancana arriving in Federal building.

least an hour before the jury while her frequent traveling companion, Giancana, appeared for just a little less than that.

Reporters had the word of Murray [The Camel] Humphreys, aging mob political fixer for that.

Humphreys Awaits Call

Humphreys, who was waiting his turn to go into the jury, reported on what was going on when he left the new Federal building during a break for lunch.

"The girl was in there for about an hour and then Giancana and then that other fellow, the lawyer," Humphreys said.

The lawyer Humphreys referred to was Giancana's son-in-law, Anthony Tisci, who is also secretary to Rep. Frank Annunzio [D., Ill.]. It was the second trip into the jury room for both Giancana and Tisci. They first appeared last Friday.

Giancana lent Miss McGuire his two Washington, D. C., lawyers, Edward Bennett Williams and Thomas Wadden.

Williams tried to run interference later for Miss McGuire when she slipped out of a bank of elevators at the opposite end of the building, a block from the grand jury room.

At first Miss McGuire offered only a string of "no comments" to questions about her appearance.

But finally after she had again fled to an upper floor of the building and had run into the dead end of a corridor, she took Williams into a corner, held a whispered conversation, and then said: "I testified. O, yes I did."

But she persisted in her refusal to disclose whether she had invoked her constitutional rights against self-incrimination in response to any of the questions put to her before the jury by David Schippers, head of the justice department's organized crime unit, and his assistant, Sam Betar.

"I wish I could get out of here," Miss McGuire said. "I feel trapped."

Complains to Press

Then she complained about newspaper stories about her international travels with Giancana, operating head of the Chicago crime syndicate.

She refused to say whether she was breaking off her relationship with Giancana, but she said she wanted "O, very much" to continue her stage career.

"I don't know if all of this

hour before the jury and had claimed that she had testified, Giancana smiled.

Quiz Miss Clark Again

Miss McGuire was tanned, too. She looked trim in a tan two-piece silk suit and white shoes. Her sub blond hair was a contrast to the raven hair of Miss Bergit Clark, a secretary for the Central Envelope and Lithograph company, 729 Harrison st., Forest Park, the only other woman subpenaed by the jury.

Miss Clark was making her second appearance before the jury. She was a surprise witness last Friday. The envelope company is operated by relatives of Giancana.

Giancana Arrives Alone

Williams and Wadden had accompanied Miss McGuire when she arrived at the Federal building shortly before 9 a. m. Giancana, his usual surly self, arrived about an hour later without a lawyer.

But the attorneys split up after the grand jury session with Williams accompanying Miss McGuire and Wadden getting a taxi for Giancana. Williams' most recent hoodlum client was Felix [Milwaukee Phil] Alderisio, a mob enforcer convicted in Denver of extortion.

Giancana held down on his use of obscenities yesterday. On Friday he had freely cursed reporters.

He rode an elevator down to the second floor from the 18th floor jury room, walked a flight of stairs, and slipped into the lobby. But reporters spotted him.

When they told the heavily suntanned hoodlum that Miss McGuire had spent at least an

and cane be had carried several years ago when he appeared for questioning.

Stephen Anselmo, former Stone Park village attorney, took another bank of elevators to the building's 20th floor where he met his legal counsel for the day, Miss Anna R. Lavin. Then he rode down to the 15th floor and the grand jury.

Humphreys never did get to testify. He was told to go home and await another summons.

"Everybody frowns at you up there," Humphreys remarked as he left. The jury reconvenes at 10 a. m. tomorrow.

Bar Press from Floor

The 15th floor of the building, which houses the grand jury room and the offices of United States Atty. Edward V. Hanrahan, was closed to reporters by order of Judge Joseph Sam Perry of federal District court.

Perry late Tuesday granted a motion to that effect filed by Wadden in behalf of Giancana. Wadden said the order would prevent witnesses from feeling harassed.

The hoodlums and Miss McGuire, however, still had to pass thru the ground floor lobby where reporters stationed themselves.

Federal Jury Quizzes Phyllis McGuire

Singer Appears for an Hour in Probe of Mob

[Continued from first page]

[TRIBUNE Staff Photo]
Miss Bergit Clark arrives for hearing.

will hurt my career," she said.

Deals with Politicians

He is the onetime boss of the crime syndicate's labor rackets who now functions as the mob's emissary among politicians.

Humphreys appeared relaxed, asked reporters if they were in control of the elevators when one did not appear immediately, and thanked two newsmen who escorted him to the 15th floor.

He laughed when asked if he still had the black eye patch

[Continued on page 4, col. 5]

Source: Courtesy of Chicago Tribune Archives

The Mob: Who They Are...

If you're still with us, we think you'll be interested in today's excursion into the labyrinthine organization known as Chicago's crime syndicate. These daily readings started last Wednesday, two days after mob informer Lewis C. Barbe was bombed in his car parked outside the Criminal Courts Building and thus far we've summarized the views of an outraged citizenry and disclosed the Chicago syndicate's enormous take —an estimated $2 billion a year.

An expert task force of four veteran reporters has been assigned to bring readers of The Daily News the story of The Mob—who and what it is; how it corrupts and how it bleeds the community; what is being done (or isn't being done) to blast it into Kingdom Come. The reporters are M. W. Newman, Norman Glubok, Jack Lavin and Jack Willner.

Today The Daily News offers you an organization chart of the syndicate—a carefully documented rogue's gallery of The Mob's brass and an account of how they clawed their way to the top. Reporters Glubok, Lavin and Willner compiled the list from information supplied by law enforcement officials as well as underworld insiders.

And on Page 14 an editorial entitled "The Syndicate and You" spells out, eloquently and incisively, the awful price each of us in the Chicago area pays because we haven't found the will or the means to break the tyrannical grip of a handful of terrorists.

SAM GIANCANA
Chairman Of The Board

BOARD OF DIRECTORS

| Tony Accardo | Paul Ricca | Murray Humphreys | Gus Alex | Frank Ferraro | Ross Prio |

DEPARTMENT HEADS

| Ralph Pierce | Felix Alderisio | Fiore Buccieri | Jack Cerone | Sam Battaglia | Frank La Porte |

Source: Daily News, Chicago, February 1, 1964.
Reproduced with permission of the Chicago Sun-Times. Article continues on next page.

Article continues from previous page.

NOT LESLIE KR THE HOOD GAMBLER

Charles Nicoletti   Lester Kruse   Rocco Potenza   Charles English   Eddie Vogel

The table of organization of the Chicago Crime syndicate.

...And How They Got There

BY NORMAN GLUBOK, JACK LAVIN AND JACK WILLNER

They don't issue financial statements, publish annual reports or sell shares through the New York Stock Exchange.

But the directors of Chicago's most profitable business — the $2 billion a year crime syndicate—run an organization that rivals the efficiency of General Motors.

Its leaders got to the top through terror or brains or both. They'll stay on top only until somebody tougher or

---

Today's Chuckle

A gauge of success is not whether you have a tough problem to handle, but whether it is the same problem you had last year.

Atlantic Coast Line News

---

smarter comes along to push them out.

THERE'S NO democracy in Chicago's crime syndicate.

It's ruled by one man — Sam Giancana. His word is law.

He became board chairman because he didn't hesitate to kill or torture if it suited his convenience. He was arrested twice for murder before he was 20.

Giancana's directors a r e names that have been making headlines and rogues galleries for decades.

They include two of Giancana's predecessors, Paul Ricca and Anthony Accardo. They also include four other old timers—Murray Humphreys, Ross Prio, Gus Alex and Frank Ferraro. None is under 50.

THE DEPARTMENT heads —those who actually operate

the syndicate's far-flung enterprises—also are well known to police and to newspaper readers.

At the top rank are Ralph Pierce, Felix Alderisio, Fiore Buccieri, Jack Cerone, Sam Battaglia and Frank La Porte.

Just below are their lieutenants — Charles Nicoletti, Lester Kruse, Rocco Potenza, Charles English and Edward Vogel.

Police believe there are at least 250 men in the Chicago c r i m e syndicate. But those named above are the leaders.

IT MIGHT be worthwhile to see who they are and how they got to the top.

Board Chairman Giancana may well be the most powerful gangster in the United States.

He controls the entire Chicago area stretching from Milwaukee through Gary and

exacts profits from such far-off places as Las Vegas, St. Louis, Hot Springs and New Orleans.

HE IS believed to declare about $100,000 a year on his personal i n c o m e tax — but that's just what the government can prove he spends.

Giancana's actual income probably exceeds $100,000 a month—more than $1,000,000 a year. There's not a salaried executive in the United States who makes half as much.

Yet he lives modestly in a $45,000 bungalow at 1147 S. Wenonah, Oak Park, where he seldom attracts attention from the neighbors except when the police or FBI set up a surveillance at his doorstep.

BORN 55 years ago near Taylor and Halsted, Giancana

Source: Chicago Daily News, February 1, 1964. *Article continues on next page.*

Article continues from previous page.

...made his way up through the ranks from car thief to burglar to stickup man to moonshiner to crime syndicate boss.

During World War II Giancana escaped military service when his draft board found him to be a psychopath.

The description was seconded by one policeman who has trailed him for years. He describes Giancana as "a snarling, sarcastic, ill-mannered, ill-tempered, sadistic psychopath."

SAID THE veteran policeman:

"Giancana is the No. 1 snake in a pit of rattlesnakes."

Giancana, whose yearnings for respectability have advanced no further than a close friendship with singers Frank Sinatra and Phyllis McGuire, probably considers the title King Snake a compliment.

On Giancana's board of directors are Paul Ricca and Anthony Accardo. They both held the top spot until they were eased into retirement.

RICCA, 67, was a lieutenant of Al Capone during the 1920s. Born in Italy, he was twice convicted of murder before he stole another man's passport and sneaked into the United States in 1918.

Two years ago the government ordered Ricca deported. But so far some 80 countries have turned him down as undesirable.

While the United States tries to find a country willing to accept him, Ricca lives in luxury at 1515 Bonnie Brae in River Forest and helps Giancana run the crime syndicate. When Ricca went to prison in 1943, his lieutenant, Accardo, took over as boss. When Ricca got out in 1947 he found Accardo unwilling to step aside.

ACCARDO, who was Capone's onetime chauffeur, moved into a $500,000 mansion at 915 Franklin, River Forest.

He ruled the mob for more than a decade, married off two daughters in lavish style, set up a son in a travel business and gracefully retired to join Ricca on the board of directors.

Fellow director Murray Humphreys was a big man back in 1932 when Al Capone went to prison. In fact, he succeeded Capone as Chicago's Public Enemy No. 1.

AS DIRECTOR, Humphreys is the mob's master fixer and financial strategist.

Far from being the has-been he would like the authorities to believe him to be, Humphreys consults almost daily with other top mobsters, including Giancana and Accardo.

He maintains a lavish downtown apartment in Chicago and homes in Tucson, Ariz., and Key Biscayne, Fla. The Florida home cost Humphreys $250,000 and put him in trouble with the Internal Revenue Service.

BOARD MEMBERS Gus Alex and Frank Ferraro operate as a team.

They share command of the lucrative Loop with its dozens of profitable striptease joints, peep shows, sneak books and busy B girls.

FERRARO, 52, lives in the St. Clair Hotel under the alias "Mr. Frank." He shares a 16th floor suite with a redhead and a poodle.

Summers he sails Lake Michigan in his $40,000 yacht, the Heleda, and accepts the privileges that come to him as vice commander of the U.S. Coast Guard Auxiliary.

ALEX, 50, lives at 1159 Lake Shore Dr. He winters in the Alps and summers in Chicago where he looks after the syndicate's Loop interests.

Handsome and recently divorced from a beautiful blond fashion model, Alex has come a long way from his humble beginnings around 26th and Wallace on the South Side.

DIRECTOR ROSS PRIO is another poodle fancier. He walks his dog in Glenview near his $50,000 home at 1721 Sunset Ridge road.

Prio commands the North Side for the mob and sends such big name gangsters as Joe DiVarco and James Allegretti to run his errands.

A BALD, bespectacled, soft-speaking, suburban-looking man, Prio rose to the top by latching onto a series of winners.

While his mentors were being trussed up in car trunks, Prio managed to survive and prosper as he terrorized his competitors in the North Side dairy business.

Said one competitor of the dwarf-sized Prio: "He told me that if I didn't give up my dairy stops he'd put an ax in my head."

BELOW THE board of directors are a half-dozen executive department heads. They are:

Ralph Pierce, 60, of 7743 S. Merrill, who has controlled South Side gambling and vice for more than three decades, since the era of Al Capone. He looks like a banker and he travels under his own name.

Felix Alderisio, 51, of 505 Byrd, Riverside, who is Giancana's designated enforcer and boss of all illegal enterprises in the West Side and Near North Side districts. Alderisio has taken over at least a dozen "legitimate" businesses and is considered likely to succeed Giancana some day as boss.

Fiore Buccieri, 59, of 3004 S. Maple, Berwyn, rose from a muscleman in the embalmers' union in the 1930s to his position as West Side financier and gambling boss.

Jack Cerone, 49, of 2000 N. 77th Av., Elmwood Park, is Accardo's ex-chauffeur. A dapper, pint-sized hoodlum and syndicate golf champ, Cerone is a boss of West Side gambling and discipline.

Sam Battaglia, 54, who calls himself a farmer although he lives in the cramped suburb of Oak Park at 1114 N. Ridgeland. A convicted robber, Battaglia supervises west suburban gambling and specializes in gang murders.

Frank La Porte, of 1730 Cambridge, Flossmoor, is one of the mob's mystery men. His territory runs from Calumet City to Kankakee and from Chicago Heights to Joliet. Government agents have found him impossible to photograph and difficult to subpena.

MARSHALL CAIFANO, 52, has recently slipped from favor because of continuing legal troubles and bad publicity and his current role is in doubt. Caifano, born Marcellino Caifano, now calls himself Marshall.

JUST A STEP below the department heads are their lieutenants who make up the rest of the Chicago's mob leadership.

Lester Kruse, 57, of 5206 Oakton, across the street from Skokie's Village Hall. Kruse is a gambling expert whose missions for the mob range from far North Side overseer to diplomatic courier in the Caribbean.

Charles Nicoletti, 47, of 1638 Broadway, Melrose Park, served time in federal prison at Milan, Mich., for a narcotics violation. Two years ago Nicoletti was arrested with Alderisio in a "hit car" complete with hidden gun compartments. Nicoletti, a comer in the mob, is active on the West Side.

Charles English, 50, of 1131 N. Lathrop, River Forest, has a gangland history that includes counterfeiting phonograph records, muscling into the scavenger business and supervising illegal bookmaking at Cicero race tracks.

Rocco Potenza, 48, of 8857 Kildare, Skokie, supervises gambling on the Northwest Side and in the Northwest suburbs. For years he made his headquarters in a bookie joint in the 6500 block of Milwaukee Av. Lately he has been questioned in the bombings of the Sahara Inn.

Edward Vogel, 68, of 320 Oakdale, is a onetime gambling boss who has carved a new career as the syndicate's coin machine chief. Vogel's Apex enterprises stretch across the city—North, West and South.

A onetime slot machine racketeer, Vogel has branched into the distribution of legal machines — coin phonographs, cigaret vending and pinball games.

Source: Chicago Daily News, February 1, 1964

Zammuto, Ill.

Giordano, Mo.

Civella, Mo.

Balistrieri, Wis.

Lanza, Calif.

Cerrito, Calif.

Licata, Calif.

Colletti, Colo.   Civello, Texas

Giancana, Ill.   Zerilli, Mich.   Bruno, Pa.   Colombo, N.Y.   Bonanno, N.Y.

Source: Jim Flora Art LLC, published in Life magazine, September 1, 1967. Reproduced with permission of Jim Flora Art LLC.

Gambino, N.Y.

Genovese, N.Y.

Magaddino, N.Y.

Patriarca, R.I.

DeCavalcante, N.J.

Corallo, N.Y.

LaRocca, Pa.

Scalish, Ohio

Trafficante, Fla.

Marcello, La.

Lansky, Fla.

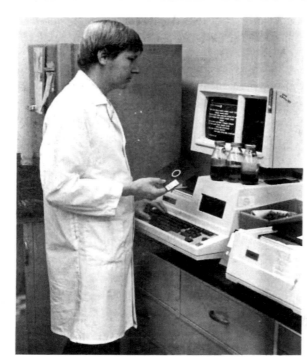

The gas chromatograph is also used in the Chemistry Section to determine the make up of unknown substances.

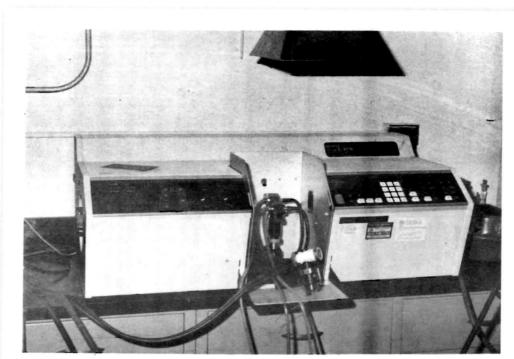

This is the Atomic Absorption Spectrophotometer which is primarily used for the determination of the presence of gun shot residue on a suspect.

Source: History of the Chicago Police Crime Laboratory by Mary Fitzgerald. Chemist, CPD Crime Laboratory Division. Reproduced with permission of the Chicago Police Department.

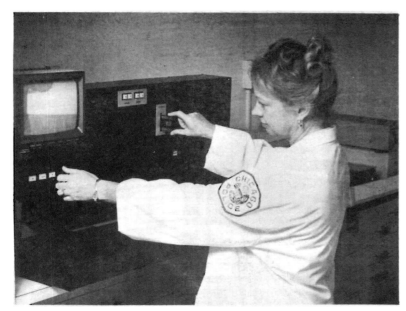

A bank check is examined to determine if it had been altered by the use of two different inks.

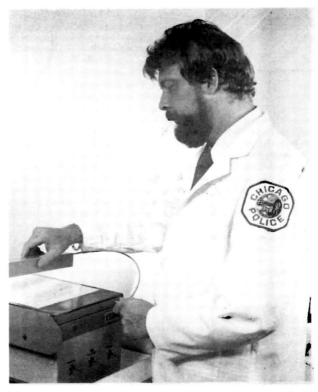

A document examiner prepares to examine a letter on a device that is used to make indented writing visible.

Source: History of the Chicago Police Crime Laboratory.
Reproduced with permission of the Chicago Police Department.

An expert in the photography lab and a view camera for a 1 to 1 comparison photograph.

Through the use of a fiber optic cable and dispersing lens, objects are checked for the presence of fingerprints by the use of laser light.

Source: History of the Chicago Police Crime Laboratory.
Reproduced with permission of the Chicago Police Department.

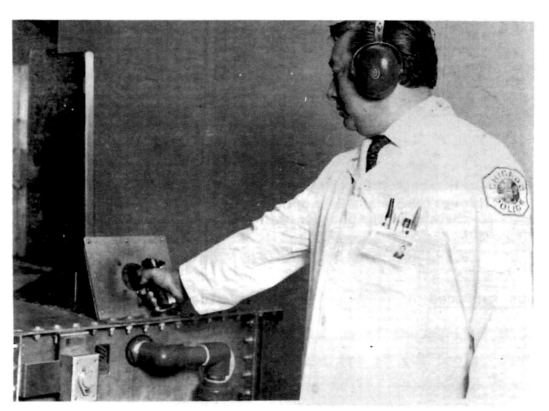

A technician test fires a weapon into the specially built bullet
recovery tank.

Source: History of the Chicago Police Crime Laboratory.
Reproduced with permission of the Chicago Police Department.

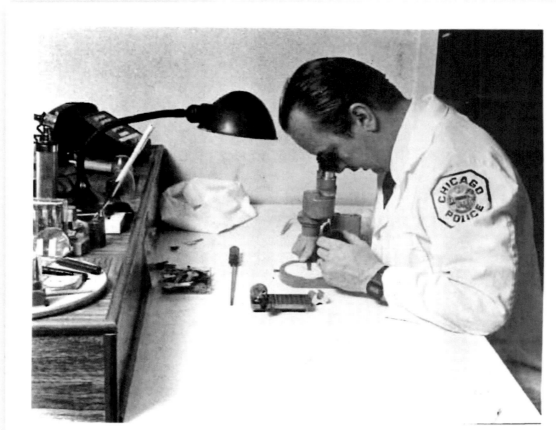

A toolmark examiner checks a piece of evidence for marks left during the commission of a crime.

Source: History of the Chicago Police Crime Laboratory.
Reproduced with permission of the Chicago Police Department.

Cops, Hippies War in Street
Chicago Tribune (1963-Current file); Aug 29, 1968; ProQuest Historical Newspapers Chicago Tribune (1849 - 1985) pg. 1

Cops, Hippies War in Street

Scores Hurt in Battle on Michigan av.

(Pictures on back page)

Michigan avenue was turned into a bloody battleground last night as police swung their sticks on anti-war demonstrators and anti-Democratic convention pickets in streets outside the Conrad Hilton hotel, the convention headquarters.

Scores were injured and thousands affected by tear gas fired on the demonstrators by police and Illinois national guardsmen.

Scores Are Seized

Scores were thrown into police vans and arrested. Late last night it was announced that more than 200 men and

---
'FORTRESS CHICAGO'
See editorial on page 20
---

women had been arrested since violence erupted during the afternoon in Grant park.

Plate glass windows on the Michigan avenue side of the hotel were shattered. Some shops in the hotel closed. The hotel itself was sealed off for a while to all persons, whether they wanted in or out. Guests in the lobby were advised to go to their rooms.

Mule Train Stalled

The principal clash of police and a portion of the 5,000 demonstrators still around the hotel area came around 8 p.m. when demonstrators blocked Michigan avenue at Balbo drive.

A Southern Christian Leadership Conference mule train—three covered wagons carrying poor people, each wagon pulled by two mules—was stalled in Michigan avenue after turning south at Jackson boulevard.

Police induced the demonstrators to clear a way for the mule train. It moved thru the intersection and the demonstrators closed ranks again. The Rev. Ralph Abernathy, head of the S. C. L. C., arrived, saw what was happening, and diverted the mule train from Michigan avenue.

Watch from Hotel

A few minutes later, police marched on the intersection. Big vans followed them to cart off prisoners. The police waded into the crowd.

Many convention visitors and others watched the battle from upper windows of the hotel. Many were appalled at what they considered unnatural enthusiasm of police for the job of arresting demonstrators. There were cries of "Cut it out . . . . don't hurt him . . . . how can you do this?" from hotel windows.

A woman stood on a curb, screaming at police, "Drop dead."

Some observers said the demonstrators were caught between two groups of police which, instead of pushing them back into Grant park, were squeezing the demonstrators between police lines. Neither of the police groups was aware of what the other was doing.

Police made a series of more than half dozen charges from the hotel side of Michigan avenue to chase the demonstrators into Grant park, opposite the hotel. The demonstrators came surging back. Police were the targets of rocks, bottles, business office staplers which showed up mysteriously, and even wooden saw-horse barricades.

Some demonstrators managed to reach the lobby of the hotel, where employes and security officers were kept busy pushing them back outside. A number of injured were taken into the hotel lobby.

People in the hotel dropped bags of water and tissue paper from windows. An ash tray came crashing into the street from somewhere high above the fighting.

The demonstrators finally were driven back into the park or into 8th street when national guardsmen, parking their vehicles south of 9th street, marched north, sweeping the demonstrators before them without any unusual incidents.

Conlisk Defends Police

Police Supt. James Conlisk Jr. defended his men against charges by convention delegates and others that his men had used excessive force in dealing with demonstrators.

"The police on the street have been faced with a difficult task," Conlisk said, "and they have performed it well. The force that was used was the force that was necessary to repel the mob, the mob which has sought to discredit the city of Chicago and the Chicago police department."

At the Amphitheater, Mayor Daley joined in defending security measures and the police.

"The security was needed to prevent violence," he said. "The same forces creating disorder outside the convention hall are creating it inside."

Asked if the police acted with restraint, Daley said, "Our police department is a great police department. They are all good and decent men and they don't respond with undue violence."

Just before midnight, the national guardsmen replaced police lines confining the hippies to the park across Michigan avenue from the Hilton.

At 12:30 a. m., two companies of guard military police, about 300 men, were dispatched to occupy the Old Town-Lincoln park area in relief of police. By that time 33 persons had been arrested in the area, police said.

Return to Hilton

Early today, hippies who had been chased around the Loop and north side after the battle in Michigan av. began drifting back to the area around the Hilton. The crowd once again swelled to 5,000.

Police told the demonstrators, as they did Tuesday night, that they would not be

[Continued on page 7, col. 1]

Source: Courtesy of Chicago Tribune Archives. *Article continues on next page.*

Article continues from previous page.

Police, Hippies Wage Pitched Battle in Michigan Av.

interfered with if they stayed in the park. The announcement was greeted with a cheer.

The demonstrators, who gathered in the park all day long and assembled 10,000 strong in midafternoon with the announced intention of marching to the Democratic convention site, the International Amphitheater at 43d and Halsted streets, were turned aside from their main objective.

The fighting began shortly after 3 p.m. when one man climbed the flagpole at the Grant park bandshell, pulled down the American flag, and hoisted a red flag. Police who charged in to seize him were surrounded by the throng, and more police formed a wedge to split the crowd and rescue those at the flagpole.

A tear gas bomb was thrown. Some said it was thrown by demonstrators into the ranks of police, who threw it back. Some said it was thrown by police. Police chased the demonstrators thru the park and demonstrators piled up bandshell benches to use as barricades from which they pelted police with rocks, bottles, and sections of tile torn from the floors of Lincoln park washrooms and filed until they had almost razor-sharp edges.

Two policemen were injured in the afternoon fighting. One of them was bitten on the neck by a woman. Five policemen were injured in the night fighting in Michigan avenue and at the edge of the park.

The nine demonstrators injured during the afternoon included Wolfe Lowenthal, 29, a Youth International party [Yippies] from New York, and Rennie Davis, 28, project director for the National Mobilization Committee to End the War in Viet Nam. It was the National Mobilization committee which originally planned and called for the rally in Grant park and a march from the park to the amphitheater.

Police and national guardsmen kept the demonstrators confined to the park, blocking them from crossing the railroad tracks that separated them from Michigan avenue. Demonstrators were herded north, where they found overpasses guarded by police and guardsmen. Finally they came to Jackson boulevard. No one was guarding the overpass, and hundreds of demonstrators crossed to Michigan avenue just as the S. C. L. C. mule train got there.

Wagon Train Escapes

The Poor People's caravan of wagons, mules, and about 100 persons, some of whom rode the wagons but most of whom walked, escaped the fighting. After they were permitted thru the intersection of Balbo and Michigan, they waited a block away until the Rev. Mr. Abernathy arrived. He was scheduled to deliver a speech in the street outside the hotel. He took in the situation and directed the caravan to leave at once. It returned safely with a police escort to its starting point, a vacant lot in the 1400 block of Adams street.

Late last night, several hundred demonstrators, many of them carrying rocks they had picked up in the park, invaded the Loop. As police would disperse them at one place, they would break up only to regroup a short distance away. The Palmer House and the Sherman House, along with the Hilton hotel and the amphitheater, had been selected by the National Mobilization committee as special targets.

Police guarded hotel entrances. Hotel security forces guarded the inner doors. Some demonstrators tried to get into the Palmer House but were seized and thrown out. Restaurants stationed employes at the doors to keep out demonstrators.

Rock Hits Woman

At Jackson boulevard and Wabash avenue a hippie-type demonstrator picked up a rock and threw it at a store window. His aim was bad. The rock hit a woman in the face. Demonstrators rushed across streets, yelling and overturning trash boxes and daring police to chase them, and the police did.

This was the way the day ended for both police and demonstrators — just about the same way it began. It started in the early morning hours, shortly after midnight, when police again used tear gas to clear Yippies and other demonstrators from Lincoln park, their chief congregating place. After daybreak, Abbie Hoffman, 31, a leader of the Yippies, was arrested in the coffee shop of the Lincoln hotel, 1800 N. Clark st., by police who said they received complaints an obscene word was written across his forehead. He told police his occupation was that of "a revolutionary artist."

Thirty-four persons were arrested in and about Lincoln park, including Richard Comerford, 23, of Madison, Wis. He threw a stone into the windshield of a police car at La Salle and Schiller streets. He was seen and arrested by Assistant States Atty. David B. Selig. Central district police arrested four in the morning hours, the warmup for the main events of the afternoon and evening.

[TRIBUNE Staff Photo: by Dave Nystrom]

Policeman arrests hippie in demonstration at Balbo and Michigan avenues and pushes him toward police squadrol.

[TRIBUNE Staff Photo: By Ron Pownall]

Young female demonstrator confronts line of national guardsmen who formed barricade to keep hippie demonstrators within Grant park.

[TRIBUNE Staff Photo]

Police and hippies clash in Grant park where thousands of demonstrators had gathered for march on Democratic national convention at International Amphitheater.

Source: Courtesy of Chicago Tribune Archives.

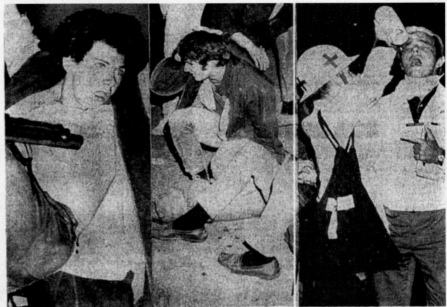

[TRIBUNE Staff Photos]

In Way of Police

Hippie demonstrators as well as newsmen covering Conrad Hilton demonstration came in path of police determined to clear the area. Demonstrator [left] is carried away, another hippie [center] is left injured on sidewalk, and newsman Thomas Thompson of Time and Life magazines is treated for wounds inflicted by police.

[Tribune Staff Photos By Don Casper]

Flames of Unrest

Police take demonstrator into custody during disturbance at Balbo and Michigan avenues. Flames from fire started by hippies burn at the feet of police who push demonstrator toward nearby squadrol.

[Tribune Staff Photo: By Walter Kale]

Taken Into Custody

Corps of policemen push demonstrators into squadrol at corner of Balbo and Michigan avenues after hippies attempted to break across police lines set up in front of Conrad Hilton hotel. Scores of hippies were arrested in fourth consecutive night of violence with demonstrators.

Source: Courtesy of the Chicago Tribune Archives

Members of the Chicago Seven.

The Chicago Seven, a group of protesters charged with inciting riots at the 1968 Democratic National Convention.

Source: As published in the Chicago Sun-Times.

105 SEIZED IN LOOP BATTLE
RONALD KOZIOL; WILLIAM JONES
Chicago Tribune (1963-Current file); Oct 12, 1969; ProQuest Historical Newspapers Chicago Tribune (1849 - 1985)
pg. 1

105 SEIZED IN LOOP BATTLE

Clash on La Salle Street

Police confront mob of demonstrators at La Salle and Madison streets in bloody battle in which scores of persons were injured.

[TRIBUNE Staff Photo by Walter Neal]

Officer subdues demonstrator in Loop after protesters hurled railroad flares and fought police with fists and chains.

[TRIBUNE Staff Photo by Walter Kale]

27 POLICEMEN ARE HURT IN FIGHTING SDS

National Guard Is Released

BY RONALD KOZIOL
and WILLIAM JONES
(Other pictures on page 2.)

A Loop march by 300 revolutionary Students for a Democratic Society ended in a bloody battle with police yesterday.

The demonstrators, using tire chains, clubs, railroad flares, and their fists smashed windows and fought a running battle with police in Madison street in the three-block area from La Salle street to State street.

The battle surged around buses, taxicabs, and autos.

Before it was over 105 demonstrators had been arrested, 27 policemen were injured, and two assistant corporation counsels were hurt, one of them seriously. More than 250 demonstrators have been arrested and more than 50 policemen have been injured since Wednesday.

After police cleared the Loop, 300 Illinois national guardsmen were called into the area to help police guard against further outbreaks of violence. At 7 p. m., Gov. Ogilvie said it appeared there would be no more trouble and released all 2,600 guardsmen who had been ordered into the city on Thursday.

Marchers Break Lines

The marchers, who had been expected to continue south in La Salle street to Jackson boulevard before turning east to their destination in Grant park, broke ranks on signal at La Salle and Madison streets.

They bowled over the thin line of policemen flanking the route of march and ran east, knocking aside pedestrians, as they smashed windows in 15 buildings.

With police in pursuit, other patrols fought the demonstrators in the intersections of Madison and Clark streets, Dearborn and Madison streets, and State and Madison streets.

Slash at Police

As the demonstrators ran, they drew weapons which had been hidden in their clothing. They used the sharp metal

[Continued on page 2, col. 2]

Source: Courtesy of Chicago Tribune Archives.   *Article continues on next page.*

Article continues from previous page.

[TRIBUNE Staff Photo by Walter Kale]

Police battle demonstrators during confrontation in Loop. More than 100 radicals were arrested.

105 Arrested as Cops Battle S.D.S. in Loop

[Continued from first page]

points of the railroad flares to stab at and slash policemen.

Richard Elrod, assistant corporation counsel, was struck in the head by a lead pipe. Brian Flanagan, 22, of New York City, was subdued and arrested in the assault.

Elrod was taken to Illinois Research hospital where doctors said he is paralyzed from the neck down.

Police Lieutenant Hurt

Police Lt. Joseph Healy of the criminal intelligence unit was struck in the head with a tire chain. Lawrence Chambers, and Terrence Corsentino, two other assistant corporation counsels, also were injured.

Some of the marchers threw cherry bomb firecrackers at police.

Four marchers were arrested in Haymarket Square before the protest parade began. Police identified them as among those who ran wild on the near north side Wednesday night, assaulting pedestrians and breaking windows of buildings and automobiles.

"Continue to Fight"

Before the marchers headed east on Randolph street to La Salle street, two speakers told them, "We must continue to fight."

After the battle along Madison street, a hundred marchers gathered in Grant park and shouted obscenities at police who stood guard nearby. Two more men were arrested, one for carrying a knife. The second was accused of mob action on the near north side Wednesday night.

Police restrain woman revolutionary demonstrator during Loop clash.

Source: Courtesy of the Chicago Tribune Archives

1970

Test vehicle nearly disappears in cloud of dust as driver slams on brakes during test at IACP's Technology Center.

1979

Stephen A. Schiller

Source: Chicago Crime Commission Archives

The Ad Hoc Committee on the Administration of Criminal Justice

In June 1974 the Chicago Crime Commission, the Chicago mayor and the Cook County board president called for the formation of the first joint task force of criminal justice leadership in Cook County. This ad hoc committee, coordinated by Crime Commission Executive Director Stephen A. Schiller, made significant progress in addressing crime issues of the day and criminal justice system improvements. It led the way for increased communication between law enforcement and criminal justice agencies on the local, state, and federal level.

FRIEND

FOE

Jerome "Shorty" Freeman, Black Disciples Nation King

Source: Chicago Police Department

Four Corner Hustlers and the Black Disciples Street Gangs

During the 1970s these two street gangs formed in Chicago and eventually would become dangerous, well-organized "super gangs" dealing heavily in the illegal drug trade and violent crime. Other street gangs also continued to act as public enemies.

The Outfit

Although untrue, many believed the Outfit to be of little concern in the 1970s. La Cosa Nostra Outfit hitmen were responsible for sixty-five gangland slayings during this decade.

Although we are only able to highlight a few friends and foes for each decade, the Chicago Crime Commission reminds the public that there are many friends, and while perhaps not as famous as the criminals, they are courageous and far more impressive.

Larry Hoover Incarcerated & Gangster Disciple Nation Splits
Larry Hoover Incarcerated & Gangster Disciple Nation Splits

Source: Chicago Crime Commission Gang Book

In 1973 Larry Hoover, leader of the united Gangster Disciple Nation (GDN), was sentenced to 150 - 200 years in prison for murder. While Hoover was still thought to be running the gang from behind prison walls, Jerome Freeman and several other GDN leaders severed ties and returned to the streets as the Black Disciples. Narcotics sales continued to be the primary source of income for the street gangs.

School Violence & Drugs
School Violence & Drugs

Sources: National Institute on Drug Abuse Household Survey, 1982
"Cost of School Crime Exceeds Half Billion Dollars Each Year," LEAA Newsletter, 1974

In 1971 it became publicly known that fifty-three of the nation's major cities reported a decrease in crime, and in 1972 armed robbery and major crimes against persons and property decreased by 27.5 percent. Crime in America's public schools, however, increased in the 1970s resulting in 100 murders committed on school property and costing around $500 million annually. From 1970 - 1973 school violence and vandalism increased at a devastating rate of 18 percent. Chicago high school seniors reported more marijuana use in 1978 than any other year between 1975 and 1995. In 1978, 37 percent of twelfth graders reported they had used marijuana in the previous month.

CCC, City & County Call For All
Criminal Justice Agencies To Join Forces
CCC, City & County Call For All
Criminal Justice Agencies To Join Forces

In June 1974 the CCC joined Mayor Richard J. Daley and the president of the Cook County board in issuing a joint statement asking that all major criminal justice agencies join forces to develop strategies to achieve security for the community and just treatment for all citizens. "To achieve this, we must foster cooperation between the community and the various law enforcement and judicial agencies that administer justice," CCC President Schooler said. It was unanimously agreed that the CCC's executive director Stephen A. Schiller would coordinate the newly formed joint committee, as the various agencies pointed to a lack of resources as the reason for the failure to cooperate.

This committee moved forward to address many concerns. A few of the subjects addressed included developing a system for providing criminal history information on suburban cases to a Circuit Court judge, developing a preliminary hearing rule that would streamline the process, a study of the service of warrants issued in forfeiture cases, the pretrial-diversion program, the random-assignment system, bond-forfeiture problems, career-criminal programs, problems of coordination between county law enforcement agencies, a direct indictment study, and victim-witness pamphets.

Justice Delayed — Justice Denied
Justice Delayed — Justice Denied

In 1979 the CCC released its study of delays in the processing of felony cases in the Criminal Division of the Circuit Court of Cook County. The study found that on average moving cases through the system took much too long, 352 days from arrest to disposition, and that the resources devoted to the system were totally inadequate to handle the number of cases assigned to it.

The Outfit Gangland Murders
The Outfit Gangland Murders

In the 1970s at a time when little attention was paid to Outfit activities, particularly with street-gang activity on the rise, the CCC tracked sixty-five gangland slayings from 1970-1979. The most Outfit slayings ever recorded by the CCC was seventy-five slayings in only one year – 1926.

Security: Silent Alarms and Housing Plans
Security: Silent Alarms and Housing Plans

Sources: "Security That Makes Sense," Chicago Tribune, April 20, 1979 and
"New Holdup Alarms Help Deter Crimes In Service Station," Chicago Tribune, December 9, 1971.

Crime-prevention security became important in this decade. In 1971 news of technological advancements in law enforcement broke when the first silent-alarm system was created. Among the first systems installed was the Chicago-area gasoline-station system. An attendant carrying a small transmitter in his pocket could push a button that would send a signal to a telephone in the gas station, then a tape-recorded message was sent over the phone to the central police station on 11th and State streets, to the nearest CPD station and to the homes of the station owner and manager. A second phone call to these locations would announce that a robbery was in progress giving the location of the station. The station alarm was also attached to money clips in the cash register and would go off when money was pulled from the clip. Soon after, alarm systems were installed in schools to cut after-hours crime. The school- and business-owner alarm system cost was between $100 and $500. In addition to security systems, homeowners were educated on how to prevent intruders. By adhering to simple lighting advice, keeping windows locked, and by keeping landscaping near entrances to a minimum, burglars, thieves, and vandals were kept at bay. Other considerations were shutters, fences, and walls.

Equipping Law Enforcement: Tools & Practices
Equipping Law Enforcement: Tools & Practices

In the latter half of the decade, Law Enforcement Alliance of America (LEAA) studies showed that many police departments in the United States were poorly equipped. Safety and prevention tools used by police included hazardous devices protective clothing to be worn during explosive episodes; automobile paint samples for investigating crimes involving cars; and high-speed, electric engraving pens to etch permanent identification on items that burglars are most likely to steal. Then, in 1975, the LEAA ensured that criminal justice agencies would receive objective and reliable consumer information on equipment. The National Advisory Committee of Law Enforcement Equipment and Technology, composed of criminal-justice officials and technical experts in the field of transportation, communications, weapons, forensics, and security systems tested equipment deemed most critical to enforcement and justice operations. This information helped criminal-justice agencies avoid unsuitable purchases. The LEAA also funded a grant in 1971 for the training of dogs to detect bombs costing over a two-year period approximately $33,000. Further recommendations were made in 1974 when the CCC suggested that local government agencies tighten fingerprinting procedures to prevent job applicants from concealing criminal records when screened for employment.

Metropolitan Enforcement Groups (MEGs)

Source: Chicago Crime Commission Gang Book

Metropolitan Enforcement Groups (MEGs) were authorized by the Illinois General Assembly in 1977 under the Intergovernmental Drug Laws Enforcement Act (30 ILCS 715-716), and are an important component in the collaborative effort to combat illegal drug traffic (and thus street gangs) throughout Illinois. In 2006 Illinois had nine MEG units covering nineteen counties with 21 percent of their personnel coming from the Illinois State Police and 79 percent from local and federal agencies. In February 2004 the MEGs received $1.17 million in state grants (63 percent General Revenue Funds, 29 percent Asset Forfeiture Funds and 8 percent from the Drug Traffic Prevention Fund).

Chicago Crime Commission Operation Crime Call

In the later part of 1973 Operation Crime Call, a telephone hot line that enabled the public to report incidences of criminal activity while remaining anonymous, received 140 calls. Knowing that 911 was to handle emergencies only, the Chicago Crime Commission created this public tool. Out of the 140 calls reporting narcotics, prostitution, burglary, threats and intimidation, fire code violations, and one shooting incident, the Chicago Police Department received seventy-one complaints, twenty-nine reports were forwarded to the Metropolitan Enforcement Group, a federally-funded organization of fifty-one trained narcotics agents, and one to the Cook County Sheriff's office. In its first fifteen months the hot line logged 1,441 calls and had nearly 600 arrests to its credit.

Two killers get 150-200 year terms
Charles Mount
Chicago Tribune (1963-Current file); Dec 11, 1973; ProQuest Historical Newspapers Chicago Tribune (1849 - 1985)
pg. A6

Two killers get 150-200 year terms

By Charles Mount

TWO LEADERS of a South Side gang suspected of dealing in narcotics each were sentenced to 150 to 200 years in prison yesterday for the murder of a dope addict.

Judge Frank Wilson of Circuit Court imposed the sentences on Larry Hoover, 23, of 121 E. 104th St., leader of The Family, a gang that operates in Chicago and Gary, and Hoover's lieutenant, Andrew Howard 26, of 6924 S. Bishop St.

Key evidence that helped convict the two was a deposition from a witness murdered before the trial began.

In the deposition, Joshua Shaw, of 1200 W. 79th St., told how he saw Hoover and Howard kidnap William Young, 24, of 7142 S. Parnell St., from 69th Street and Wentworth Avenue on Feb. 26, 1973, the day Young was shot to death.

William Oberts and Robert Smierciak, assistant state's attorneys, said Young's body was found in an alley behind 6814 S. Lowe Av. He was suspected of stealing narcotics from the gang's illicit supply.

Shaw had given his deposition describing the kidnaping at a preliminary hearing and was prepared to testify at the trial when he was slain Sept. 27.

A jury deliberated one hour Nov. 5 before bringing in the guilty verdicts.

Source: Courtesy of the Chicago Tribune Archives

BLACK DISCIPLES

GANGSTER DISCIPLES

Source: Chicago Crime Commission Gang Book

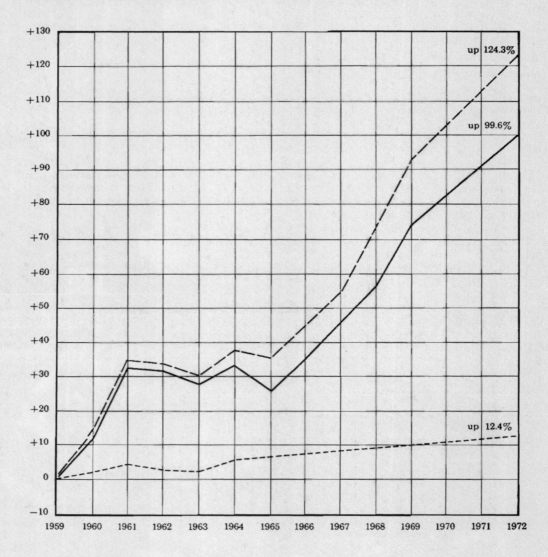

CRIME AND POPULATION IN ILLINOIS 1959-1972

up 124.3%

up 99.6%

up 12.4%

*Rate is based on 100,000 Inhabitants

— — — — Index Crime
———— Index Crime Rate
- - - - - - - Population

Source: Unknown

Agency of the Month

The U.S. Drug Enforcement Administration

The enforcement of laws prohibiting unlawful international and interstate trafficking in drugs or controlled substances has been a matter of special federal concern for half a century. The Federal Bureau of Narcotics was formed in 1930 as an agency of the Treasury Department and another Treasury agency, the U.S. Customs Service, had long handled criminal cases involving the illegal importation or smuggling of drugs.

Following a series of administrative changes, on July 1, 1973, the Drug Enforcement Administration was formed as an agency of the U.S. Department of Justice and was given the overall Federal responsibility for the suppression of domestic and foreign illicit drug trafficking.

The so-called "drug culture" of the 1960's and the changed attitudes of some Americans towards certain kinds of illegal drugs had created a massive illegal drug problem in the the United States. By 1973, it was clear that a massive effort would be needed to get matters under some semblance of control.

While no one in law enforcement today, least of all those in drug enforcement, would suggest that the problem has been solved, DEA can point with some justifiable pride to its accomplishments in seven years.

During the mid-1970's the flow of Mexican brown heroin into the United States had become substantial. The "Mexican mud," an opium by-product of relatively low purity, had replaced a flow of Asian and Middle Eastern white heroin that had been cut off when the so-called "French Connection" was broken in New York. By then, Chicago had become the hub and distribution point for the Mexican product. Most of the smuggling and much of the distribution was controlled by members of the

Herrara family of Mexico. At one time, Chicago area law enforcement agencies believed that as much as 90% of local distribution was controlled by the Herraras, who probably numbered as many as 2000 in the United States and Mexico. In early 1978 Jose Herrara was arrested and 24 pounds of heroin wàs seized. Earlier, another Herrara, Angel, age 31, had been arrested with 27 pounds of heroin. Neither was ever tried. Jose had posted $100,000 in cash to cover a $1 million bond; when Angel's bond was reduced to $250,000 he had no trouble finding the $25,000 cash required to obtain his freedom. Both fled to Mexico – but the back of the Mexican heroin traffic had been broken.

Meanwhile, in New York, on January 19, 1978, Leroy "Nicky" Barnes was sentenced in Federal District Court to life in prison on the charge that he had headed, in the words of the prosecutor, "the largest, most profitable and venal drug ring in New York City."

The successes against the Herraras in Chicago and Nicky Barnes in New York exemplify the enforcement techniques of the DEA.

In Chicago, the fight against drugs has achieved much of its success through a high degree of cooperative effort between federal, state and local law enforcement authorities. In the Chicago area a great deal of investigative expertise has been developed by state, city and county police who have long worked together cooperatively. In addition, members of some suburban police departments have gained useful enforcement know-how by virtue of participation in the Metropolitan Enforcement Group, a multi-agency unit formed to combat drug violations in the suburbs.

The Nicky Barnes case was prose-

cuted as a Continuing Criminal Enterprise under the Racketeer Influenced and Corrupt Organization Act of 1970 and imaginative use of this broad statute is being undertaken more widely as law enforcement and prosecutive familiarity with its complexities is developed. Under the law's provisions it is possible to achieve successful prosecutions against those who head drug trafficking operations but never personally come in direct contact with the drugs themselves.

Under the CCE statute as it relates to drug dealers, the government must prove that the defendants have violated the drug laws at least three times, that five or more people involved in the pattern of activity and that it has produced income. If found guilty, defendants face a mandatory minimum 10 year sentence without parole and may receive a sentence of as much as life imprisonment. Nearly as important a deterrent is the statute's forfeiture provision which allows the government to seize the proceeds of illegal enterprise. This can be – and has been in many cases – boats, automobiles, trucks, airplanes, cash, or even houses or businesses purchased with illicit cash. In addition to the Nicky Barnes conviction in New York, the law has been used successfully to prosecute the notorious "Black Tuna Gang" in Miami and the Hell's Angels in San Francisco. It was used for the first time in Chicago in 1979 to convict Green Smith, his partner Milton Kelly and eleven other defendants. Faced with the stiff penalties of the law, some of the lesser figures in the ring implicated the higher-ups. Smith was sentenced to 20 years in prison and Kelly to 15 years even though neither one ever been observed handling narcotics. Agents of the Internal Revenue Service formed part of the investi-

(cont. on next page)

Source: Chicago Crime Commission Searchlight

U.S. Drug Enforcement Administration

(cont. from previous page)

gative team because of their expertise in tracing the financial transactions of the gang. Most of the millions of dollars of assets acquired were forfeited to the government.

DEA remains deeply concerned about the volume of trafficking in highly potent South American marijuana and cocaine. They are also concerned about the appearance of the increasing quantities of high grade white heroin from such southwest Asian sources as Iran, Afghanistan and Pakistan. At the end of April, agents arrested a 38 year old Iranian, Mohammed Ali Bastanipour, who was attempting to smuggle 8.8 pounds of 78% pure white heroin through O'Hare's international terminal. The drug was concealed in gift wrapped cans of caviar with false bottoms and had an estimated street value of $10 million.

DEA works closely with officials of foreign governments to try to attack the drugs at their source. Part of the successful attack on Mexican heroin came about because of the cooperation of Mexican authorities. The political situation in Iran and Afghanistan together with the general political instability in the Middle East has resulted in the new influx of white heroin. However, in June, DEA administrator Peter Bensinger, while in Chicago for the Chicago Crime Commission's membership meeting, announced that French and Italian authorities had arrested a veteran of the old "French Connection" and had seized five illegal drug laboratories near Milan.

DEA is actively seeking modification of certain portions of the Tax Reform Act of 1976 so that agents of the Internal Revenue Service may play a more active role in tracking down the flow of cash coming out of illegal drug trafficking, especially in the Miami area. They are convinced that the added cooperation of the IRS and other federal, state and local agencies seeking convictions of top level drug dealers and financiers will produce more major successes in the future and will give the government a real chance to cut down the supplies of drugs in the United States.

DEA has a regional office located in Chicago headed by Regional Director William Olivanti and Deputy Regional Director Charles Hill. There is also a Chicago District Office headed by Special Agent in Charge Keith Fieger. They are headquartered on the 18th floor of the Dirksen Federal Building at 219 S. Dearborn Street.

Shown here are the upper-level bosses of the Chicago Outfit at a luncheon in 1976. Front and center is Anthony Accardo. The only surviving participant in this gathering is Joseph Lombardo who is standing at the back right. Law enforcement has oftened referred to this photo as the "Last Supper" since it is the only known photo of all of the top people.

Source: James W. Wagner Collection. Reproduced with permission of James W. Wagner.

GANGLAND-STYLE ASSASSINATIONS

Chicagoans who went away for a long weekend from July 22 until July 27 missed the biggest rash of gangland-style murders to occur since the days of the Al Capone, Frank Nitti and Bugs Moran era.

The shotgun slayings of former Austin Police District Commander Mark Thanasaurus early Friday morning and of Samuel J. Annerino, a nouveau riche underworld figure on Monday afternoon, sandwiched around the weekend discovery of the bullet-riddled bodies of four men in an elevator in suburban Park Ridge, capped a series of gangland-style assassinations that was worthy of headlines, even by old-time Chicago crime syndicate standards. As teams of investigators worked to find answers to the killings, Chicago area law enforcement officials met in an attempt to coordinate their efforts to make some sense of the 39 gangland-style slayings of Chicago crime syndicate figures that have occured in the last 3½ years. The shotgunning of Annerino in broad daylight on a busy street in suburban Oak Lawn was not only the climax to the long weekend of violence but also gave rise to widespread speculation as to how--if at all--the crimes might be linked.

The speculation began when the first news stories of the Annerino hit noted that he had been sought for questioning by police investigating the Park Ridge murders. Had he been silenced by the mob to prevent him from talking?

It was then noted that Thanasaurus, separated from his wife, shared an apartment with his brother in the same Oak Lawn apartment in which Annerino lived. Had there been something personal between the two and was Annerino punished for taking rash, independent action?

Prevention and punishment have long been established motives for crime syndicate killings. There is yet another motive--power--and this may be the most reasonable area of

speculation, particularly in light of the patterns in other recent killings. For instance, it was noted that when Annerino was killed, he was driving a $19,000 Mercedes and he had just left a furniture and appliance store after ordering items for a newly purchased house. Though only 35 years old, and never high in Chicago area mob circles, he had obviously come into some money. His role in recent years had been that of a muscleman and enforcer for Jimmy "The Bomber" Catuara, semi-retired syndicate boss of south suburban organized crime and a leading figure in Chicago "chop shop" operations.

Annerino's activities were not new to the Chicago Crime Commission. In September, 1973, the Crime Commission reported that Annerino and Samuel A. Sarcinelli were overseeing the management of the Bankers Building at 105 West Adams, the Oak Park Arms Hotel in Oak Park, and two residential apartment units on Briar Avenue. The Commission noted in its 1973 report that Sarcinelli had been indicted in 1972 in connection with the theft of $250,000 from the Metro Casualty Company and that he owned 15,000 shares of a company controlled by Kenneth Eto, a longtime syndicate hoodlum. Sarcinelli, together with Annerino, offered six million dollars for the Windemere and Allerton Hotels, though Annerino had declared himself a pauper in appealing an extortion conviction on February 8, 1973.

It has been speculated that Annerino may have been trying to "muscle in" on the highly lucrative business of stealing and dismantling automobiles and selling them one piece at a time. Because of the enormous profits in the "chop shops," organized crime has staked out the operation as a target for mob control. At least a dozen of the killings in the past year found victims who had been involved in auto thefts of "chop shops." It is in this area where it

seems clear that a struggle for control has been taking place.

On July 12, the nude body of Earl S. Abercrombie was found in a trunk of an auto parked at O'Hare Field. Abercrombie, who was last seen alive on July 6, had been involved with both drugs and stolen auto parts.

Richard Ferraro, the operator of Statewide Auto Wrecking Company in Calumet City, was reported missing on June 21. Ferraro's 1977 Lincoln was parked outside of his business with the keys in the ignition, but he has not been heard from since and is presumed dead. His wife has hired private detectives and has offered a $10,000 reward for "direct information" about his whereabouts. Ferraro was also believed to be a major dealer in stolen auto parts. He was an associate of William Dauber, an enforcer for Jimmy "The Bomber" Catuara.

A business associate of Ferraro's Joseph F. Theo was found shotgunned to death on June 15. Theo's body was found in a stolen car in the 1700 block of North Cleveland. He was reported to have been heavily involved in the stolen auto parts racket.

Norman Lang of Munster, Indiana, the operator of a Hammond used car lot, was shot to death in Calumet City on January 13, 1977. Authorities believe Lang's murder may be linked with other auto theft related killings.

On October 6, 1976, Steven H. Ostrowsky was killed by five rifle bullets fired from a van as he parked his car across the street from an auto parts shop he operated at 7370 S. Chicago. Ostrowsky operated several wrecking yards and was believed to have been a front man for the crime syndicate in the trafficking of stolen auto parts. People who have been in business with Ostrowsky have not fared well either. On June 6, 1975, Harry Holzer, a partner of Ostrowsky, was killed together with a woman friend, Linda Turner, at Holzer's home in Fennville, Michigan. An-

other former Ostrowsky partner, Harry D. Carlson, was killed in 1969 when a dynamite bomb exploded as he started his car. In addition, Robert Pronger, Jr., a stock car driver who had been associated with Ostrowsky, disappeared in 1971 and is presumed to be dead. Authorities believe that Ostrowsky himself may have been involved in one or more of these happenings.

In July, 1975, Jesse Richardson of Lombard was gunned down on a Cicero street in broad daylight. Richardson had been described as a "hillbilly mafia type" and was believed to have been involved in a west suburban hot car ring. An associate of Richardson, Ronald Munson, was also slain in 1975 while out on bond awaiting trial. It had been rumored that Munson was an informant.

The profits involved in "chop shop" operations are enormous. While

the car thief is usually satisfied with a few hundred dollars for the quick turnover of his hot product, the same car, reduced to virtually unidentifiable and untraceable parts will sell for thousands. This combination of high yield and low risk in an illegal activity presents an irresistible temptation to organized crime. It is typical of mob operations that they dislike competition or independent operations, unless, of course, these operators pay their tribute in the form of protection money. While other recent gangland killings in Chicago may have been related to juice racketeering or other forms of power struggles, revenge or protection, it now has become apparent that the syndicate's efforts to control "chop shop" operations have accounted for a substantial part of the casualty list.

Source: Chicago Crime Commission Archives

A Silent Trap To Catch a Thief

Vertical panel has a capacity for 450 numbered lights which tell officer where to send patrol.

Source: Chicago Sun-Times

As published in the Chicago Sun-Times.

Dramatic Reversal In Alexandria, Va.

Super Security Program In City Schools Cuts After-Hours Crime

Just four years ago, the Alexandria, Virginia, school district mirrored thousands of other school districts being assaulted by rapidly mounting school crime.

Arson, vandalism, burglary, robbery, and assault were common. The police department was being called on to investigate school crime with increased regularity. Vandalism and burglary losses jumped to $175,000 a year.

Today, losses have been cut to $50,000. Several vandals and burglars have been caught in the act. A potentially disastrous fire was detected so quickly it was extinguished before it could do extensive damage. The burglar who set it was caught.

"Our demonstration system is so successful," says L.W. Burton, Alexandria schools security director, "it has become a school security showcase for other school systems. If it emphasizes anything, it surely is prevention."

Mr. Burton was hired following a 1971 meeting in which concerned school officials discussed the district's crime problem with city police officials in an effort to develop an effective program to reduce crime. They decided to employ a security adviser and director of physical facilities to carry out the program and established a close working relationship with the police.

Security Director Burton designed

- Intrusion detection devices — including video, microwave, radar, ultrasound and infrared devices — were placed in areas that housed expensive equipment such as audio visual equipment rooms, science labs, music rooms, and business education equipment areas.
- A closed-circuit TV monitor and recorder system was installed in the main high school.
- A school security center was established at the main high school to monitor electronic equipment throughout the system after school hours. The center is operated by trained personnel who have a direct access line to the police department.

Other components of the security system include cameras, unbreakable polycarbon windows, UHF and VHF radio and "hot lines" to police and neighborhood reporting telephones, flood lighting, an evaluation of the school lock system, a neighborhood vandalism reporting system, and peer group hall monitors.

A precise system of reporting losses also is included in the program. The Alexandria system has been working with the National Association of School Security Directors to develop an exact, uniform system of reporting school losses and criminal incidents.

The program has saved thousands of dollars. Losses of $175,000 in 1971 were reduced to $59,000 in 1972, $56,000 in 1973, and $50,000 in 1974. With the cost of replacement equipment spiralling, the savings are even greater.

L. W. Burton, Alexandria School District security director, talks with city police on the direct access phone at the central security center. The center, which security personnel monitor after school hours, provides video coverage of certain school areas plus audio and electronic surveillance of all school buildings.

The dramatic turn-around, say school officials, can be credited to an LEAA-funded pilot security program that uses highly sophisticated equipment throughout the school district.

the system that incorporates these features:

- Public address systems in each school were adapted for use as audio monitoring systems.

In this article, school district security director talks with city police on the direct-access phone. The center provides video coverage of certain school areas after hours plus audio and electronic surveillance of all school buildings.

Reprint permission provided by Alexandria city public schools.

New Holdup Alarms Help Deter Crimes in Service Stations
THOMAS POWERS
Chicago Tribune (1963-Current file); Dec 9, 1971; ProQuest Historical Newspapers Chicago Tribune (1849 - 1985)
pg. N20

New Holdup Alarms Help Deter Crimes in Service Stations

BY THOMAS POWERS

A new holdup alarm system is being used by Chicago area gasoline station owners who have all-night service and are trying to prevent robberies in high crime areas.

Robert Ingersoll, business agent of the Gasoline Retailers Association of Metropolitan Chicago, said this measure, in addition to the exact change rule, appears to be successful.

The exact change rule which was put into use a year ago, is in effect from 10 a. m. to 6 p. m. in most stations. Signs are posted warning: "No Money; No Change." After receiving payment from the motorist, the money is dropped in a safe which can be opened only by the station manager or an armored car service.

Button Trips Signal

The new holdup alarm can be activated by an attendant carrying a cigaret pack-size transmitter in his pocket. A push of a button sends a signal to a hidden telephone in the gas station office.

A tape recorded message is sent over the telephone to the central police complaint room at 11th and State Streets, to the nearest Chicago police district station, to the home of the station owner, and to the home of the station manager.

After the message is delivered to each of the four locations, the telephone then places a second call to each of the four locations, repeating the message that a robbery is in progress, giving the location of the station.

Alarm in Register

The alarm also is attached to money clips in the cash register. It goes off when money is pulled from the clip.

"The alarm has brought police to the scene within minutes," Ingersoll said. "We've had very good cooperation from the Chicago Police Department. In really troublesome areas, police squads drive thru the station every half hour to discourage would be robbers."

Source: Courtesy of Chicago Tribune Archives

Protect your home
Stephanie Fuller
Chicago Tribune (1963-Current file); Apr 20, 1979; ProQuest Historical Newspapers Chicago Tribune (1849 - 1985)
pg. N_A1

Protect your home

Security that makes sense

By Stephanie Fuller

IN MEDIEVAL times, a castle owner didn't pull up the drawbridge after the enemy was inside his grounds. Today's homeowners shouldn't live in residences that invite intruders in through unlighted doorways, easily accessible windows, or massive planting around patios.

One way to make your home more secure is to remodel it with that objective in mind. The more difficult it is to enter a house unobserved, the less likely the house will be prey to burglars, thieves, vandals, and worse.

Although Chicago's property crimes dropped slightly in 1978, Chicago Crime Commission figures show 25,480 burglaries and 2,662 robberies in suburban Cook County in 1976, compared with 23,773 burglaries and 2,122 robberies in 1977.

URBAN PROBLEMS are becoming suburban problems as well. How does a man best protect his castle? First assess your home for security flaws. Consult experts such as architects, landscapers, and contractors. Suburban and city police departments will give free advice as to how you can make your home more burglar-proof.

"Design alterations are more effective than broken bottles on the top of a wall or lots of grates and grills," says Frederick (Rick) Phillips, Chicago architect.

Agreeing with him is A. J. Harmon, an architect from Southampton, N.Y., and Lake Worth, Fla., who has written a book, "Remodeling for Security" (McGraw-Hill, $14.95).

Regarding remodeling in general, Harmon warns there's a tendency to invest more than you can get out of a property if circumstances force you to sell. By "overimproving," you draw attention to your house as the most outstanding one on the block. It's an open invitation.

LIGHTING IS a key factor in both the city and suburbs. With the cost of electicity, Harmon suggests a combination of emergency spotlighting and low-wattage bulbs for continuous use. Put a panic switch in the master bedroom for the floodlighting, and use it only in an emergency. When you hit the switch, your neighbors will know something is wrong.

Use low-wattage lighting to chase away the shadows on driveways, front doors, garages, windows, and patios in the city and the suburb. Phillips says adequate lighting on the front porch of a city house enables a person to look out the front window and see who's there. You also might add a wide-angle peep hole to the door.

Interior electric lighting is effective in giving strangers the impression someone is at home. Lamps should be located near the front and back windows to enhance this impression further so be sure there are electric outlets in these areas.

THE FOCAL POINT of both city and suburban houses is the front entrance and everything else should be subordinate to it, according to Phillips, who says a back entry should blend with the house's design and be unobtrusive.

Next to lighting, landscaping can be the biggest deterrent to intruders. Dick Brickman of Theodore Brickman Co., landscape architects, says no tall plantings should be around a patio, masking it off. It's also easy for someone to hide behind massive evergreens at either side of a front door.

"Another prime spot for trouble is a massing of shrubs at the corner of a garage," says Brickman. "A person can hide there and follow

Continued on page 2

City home

- Replace garage with one that covers lot's width.
- Locate interior electrical outlets at front and back.
- Put up sturdy fence or brick wall on alley lot with no garage.
- Illuminate back yard and gangway.
- Close off side windows and entryways.
- Remove hiding spots. such as dense trees or shrubs.
- Replace recessed doorway with flush door; add side light.

Suburban home

- Light door, windows, driveway, and garage door.
- Eliminate evergreens at door, patio, and garage corner.
- Install an alarm system with activator in vestibule.
- Place emergency floodlight switch in master bedroom.
- Bolt window boxes under and in front of windows.
- Illuminate patio and create a no man's land between patio and lot line.
- Mark property line with fence—even a low one.

Tribune Graphics

Source: Courtesy of Chicago Tribune Archives

Sensible approaches to improved security

Continued from first page

your car right in when you open the door with an electronic release."

FOR A PRIVACY screen, Brickman recommends any thorny bush, such as a hawthorn or barberry. Especially in the city, don't plant anything by any door or access way. Any planting should be less than 2½ feet high so no one can crouch behind it, or more than 6 feet high with a trunk no one can hide behind.

In a city house, Phillips recommends closing up all the side windows and entries because the sides are the most vulnerable part of the house and many of the apertures look only into the next building. Interior, natural light can be provided from skylights and light wells, as well as the front and back exposures.

Harmon would cut down on the expanse of suburban house windows by subdividing them with 2 by 4s. This deters someone from bashing in a large window with a hammer and walking right in. A large glass area can be secured further by subdividing with 2 by 4s and reinforcing with industrial wire.

HARMON SAYS shutters correctly placed are of value. When used in a bedroom, enough exposed window should be left from top to bottom for a person to get out or signal for help in an emergency.

On the ground floor, shutters can be applied from the bottom of the window and ventilation space left open at the top. Window boxes place distance between a window and an intruder and make it more difficult for him to get into the house.

The front door of a city house should not be recessed or it will provide hiding space for an intruder. The door should be flush with the house and visible from all approaches.

"A CITY DOOR should be elevated from the sidewalk so you can see anyone who is at the entry from the ground," says Phillips. "In a lot of remodeling, people move the front door to the side. It should be maintained at the front for visibility."

Fences and walls are a touchy subject with some people. Harmon says he definitely would put a fence around a suburban home . . . even if it's a low fence just to define the property lines. Any stranger inside those lines is a trespasser and could be recognized as such by residents, neighbors, or the police cruising by.

Phillips, a preservationist, absolutely would not put up a brick wall or stone fence at the front of a house where it wasn't in character. He would stick with the traditional ornamental iron fence rather than foresake historic character for a blockade.

THE MOST SECURE city gardens are those with only one access — either a gate in a rear wall or fence or a door from a garage that covers the width of the lot. A home with an alley behind it should have a gate with a deadbolt lock, buzzer system, or both. A brick wall is the most psychologically forbidding type of fencing.

"A rear gate should be deemphasized and made to harmonize with whatever material is chosen for the wall or fence," says Phillips. "In some cases, a wood fence and gate are the best because the gate is less noticeable."

In this electronic age, audio alarm systems are playing a bigger and bigger part in security. These are especially popular in the suburbs, where they can be connected to a central security company headquarters or to the police or fire stations. Systems can be purchased or leased.

MIKE MORAN of American District Security Systems Co. says one of the more effective types is installed inside near the door of access and looks like a push-button apparatus on a telephone. You activate the alarm with your door key and have a certain amount of time in which to push your code buttons before the alarm goes off.

"We sell more systems in the suburbs because of the income levels and home values, but more and more people in the $30,000 income bracket are buying them now," says Moran, who estimates the company's business has increased 40 per cent in the last five years.

Harmon stresses the necessity of studying and obtaining an adequate system. He says to buy one costs from $600 to $4,500 depending upon how sophisticated it is, while leasing one costs from $300 to $1,000 for installation, with a monthly service charge from $20 to $80.

HARMON HAS gone further into security systems than even the sophisticated alarms. He has developed the concept of a "security room" for single persons or two elderly people living together. In his "security room," they can shut themselves off and never be seen by a burglar, who could take what he wanted but not harm them.

A criminal does not want to leave witnesses to identify him. At the first strange sound, a widow could rush into her security room and lock the door. It should be situated off the bedroom or in a bathroom.

Proper equipment includes a steel door and an alarm that turns on all the lights in the house and the floodlights. Walls should be of 4-inch concrete block or brick. A telephone, battery-operated lights and ventilation, a hand-cranked siren, any regular medication, and space to lie down should be available.

"People have safes for their jewelry, why not have safes for themselves?" asks Harmon. "There are people who live alone who are so frightened they don't sleep at night. They just catnap or watch TV until they can drift off at daylight. They're terrified. A security room is only for a certain segment of the population, but it's needed."

Source: Courtesy of Chicago Tribune Archives

Protective clothing demonstrated in hazardous devices course.

Source: National Law Enforcement Review

Dogs Sally and Brandy shown here just before they found a bomb aboard a TWA jetliner.

Source: National Law Enforcement Review

REPORT CRIME

Source: Chicago Crime Commission Archives

'Excessive' trial delays in county courts assailed
Storer Rowley
Chicago Tribune (1963-Current file); Aug 17, 1979; ProQuest Historical Newspapers Chicago Tribune (1849 - 1985)
pg. 3

'Excessive' trial delays in county courts assailed

By Storer Rowley

JUDGES AND defense attorneys in Cook County criminal courts often are guilty of "excessive" trial delays of up to several years, a study by the Chicago Crime Commission disclosed Thursday.

Based on a sampling of 442 criminal division cases disposed of this year, the average case was found to be 448 days old, about 15 months, compared with similar figures compiled by the commission in 1974, when the average case took 352 days for disposition.

The study showed the length of felony trials in the Chicago area lagging far behind four comparable metropolitan areas. In Detroit, the length was 230 days: in Los Angeles, 132 days; in the District of Columbia, 224 days; and in New Orleans, 102 days.

STEPHEN A. SCHILLER, commission executive director, blamed "unethical" l a w y e r s seeking continuances and judges who grant them routinely, a habit Schiller called "endemic" to the traditional environment of Cook County courts.

"If you [defense attorneys] want delay, if you seek delay, you get delay, that's all there is to it," said Schiller during a morning press conference at commission offices, 79 W. Monroe St.

Judge Richard J. Fitzgerald, chief of the Criminal Court, reacted to the study by saying: "We're concentrating on quality justice rather than quantity justice. We are now trying 25 per cent of the cases, where before we were pleading 90 per cent of the cases and trying 10 per cent."

Fitzgerald said there were now fewer than 5,000 cases on call as the courts continue to reduce a backlog at the rate of 1,000 cases a year. He said that as a result of more trials being held, rather than plea bargain cases, sentences have become much stiffer overall.

THE COMMISSION, a justice watchdog group, concluded in a 1974 brief.

before the United States Supreme Court that the average time it took to process a case in Cook County was too long and resources were limited.

The aftermath of that case brought an amendment to the Illinois Speedy Trial Act, limiting somewhat the extra time that continuances could draw out a trial. The law sets a limit of 120 days between the time of arrest and trial.

The commission wants to put pressure on judges to take more responsibility in limiting trial time by not granting as many continuances. It also is asking local bar associations to discourage "dilatory tactics" that delay trials unnecessarily.

THE NEW STUDY determined that since 1974, the time between arrest and arraignment has been cut back to an average of 58 days, compared with the 129 days it took five years ago.

However, between arraignment and the court's ruling, the median trial times have increased substantially: to 521 days now from 292 five years ago for

jury trials, to 346 days from 207 for guilty plea cases, to 396 days from 281 in bench trials, and to 387 days from 378 in other cases.

Indicating that the sample cases were representative of the whole county court system, Schiller released a "Five Most Wanted Dispositions" list, which he said would be a routine monthly offering of the commission in an effort to keep the problem publicized.

In addition to the list, which named five cases all more than three years old, Schiller also called for an Illinois Supreme Court omnibus hearing rule setting time limits for some court procedures, such as discovery, and a change in the Illinois Criminal Code requiring lawyers to submit sworn affidavits setting forth the reason when they request continuances.

Length of criminal cases in Cook County

Mean number of days between arraignment and conclusion of sample criminal cases

Jury trials
28 cases sampled
'74 — 292
'79 — 521

Guilty pleas
236 cases sampled
'74 — 207
'79 — 346

Bench trials
94 cases sampled
'74 — 281
'79 — 396

Other
85 cases sampled
'74 — 378
'79 — 387

Average time from arrest to conclusion of case
'74 — 352
'79 — 448

Source: Chicago Crime Commission

Tribune Chart

Source: Courtesy of Chicago Tribune Archives

1980

Pictured above (L-R): Nicholas Goodban, Chicago Tribune Charities, and Jerry E. Donovan, IBM Corporation, approve the installation of king-sized billboards on the exterior of CTA buses, which their organizations generously provided to spread the word about the "Report Crime" service.

1989

1984 – Terry Hake emerging after providing testimony.

Source: Courtesy of Chicago Tribune Archives

The Chicago Police Community Alternative Policing Strategy (CAPS)

Implemented in the 1980s, CAPS was a complete change in police philosophy, expanding it from one of enforcement to one of enforcement and prevention. CAPS brings into the Chicago police strategic-planning process the voice and resources of the community and works with multiple city departments to prevent crime before it starts.

Terry Hake

Disillusioned with what he found as he began his legal career in the Cook County courts, he told the FBI that he would pose as a corrupt attorney to expose the underworld that controlled the daily operation of justice in the county. He is an excellent example of the difference one person can make in ensuring justice. The Greylord Operation convictions were, in great part, a result of his willingness to work with the FBI.

Source: Chicago Crime Commission Gang Book

FOE ## New Breeds Street Gang

The New Breeds Street Gang, another developing super gang, was formed in this decade. It is heavily involved in the illegal drug trade and in violent crime activities. Other street gangs also continue as public enemies.

Convicted Individuals in the FBI Greylord and Gambit Operations

Eighteen judges, one state senator, one state representative, one alderman, fifty-seven lawyers, ten police officers, and twelve deputy sheriffs were convicted as a result of this FBI operation concentrating on corruption in the Cook County court system. It is atrocious to find those responsible for ensuring fairness, safety, and justice responsible for the opposite.

Although we are only able to highlight a few friends and foes for each decade, the Chicago Crime Commission reminds the public that there are many friends, and while perhaps not as famous as the criminals, they are courageous and far more impressive.

Gangs & Drugs: Chicago's Most Feared

Gangs & Drugs: Chicago's Most Feared

Awareness campaigns on crime and its prevention targeted the mainstream public during this decade. The Report Crime in Your Neighborhood hotline, previously known as Operation Crime Call, assisted police by averaging twenty to thirty calls per day, ranging from street-gang invasions to indecent exposure. Because of caller reluctance to report certain crimes to police for fear of retaliation or involvement, the hotline provided the public with another outlet. The need for the hotline was apparent; gangs, drugs and alcohol were spreading rampantly.

A 1987 meeting between Chicago Crime Commission members and two former gang members revealed a truly disturbing and frightening picture of some of Chicago's neighborhoods. Two year-olds knew gang signs, forty-two-year-old members were involving six-year-olds in the gang, non-gang member students were identified with a gang depending on what side of the school they exited, and there were "safehouses" in the suburbs for refuge from the police.

According to the 1982 National Institute on Drug Abuse Household Survey, the percentage of thirteen-year-old children who used marijuana in 1982 was 16 percent, up from 1 percent in 1962. The Institute for Social Research at the University of Michigan reported that the percentage of high-school seniors who had used cocaine in 1985 was 16 percent, up from 8 percent in 1975. In 1981, 22 percent of twelfth graders reported using drugs other than marijuana in the previous month. In Chicago, 73 percent of male arrestees tested positive for narcotics in 1987, an additional fact pointing toward the extensive drug problem. In 1987, Wesley S. Walton, CCC president stated, "There is no greater challenge facing this community than the eradication of narcotics in our neighborhoods. No business, family, or individual escapes its devastating impact. Narcotics cannot be viewed as a law-enforcement problem; the citizenry must accept its share of the responsibility." From 1986 - 1991, the Illinois Criminal Justice Information Authority received more than $125 million in federal funds for innovative programs to combat drug abuse and violent crime.

Narcotic Courts: Most-Wanted Dispositions List

Narcotic Courts: Most-Wanted Dispositions List

In 1979 the CCC's Most Wanted Dispositions list, an effort to draw attention to criminal court cases that had been unduly delayed, was created, and in 1985 the list was expanded to include suburban municipal districts, including Skokie, Niles, Maywood, Chicago Ridge, and Markham. In Markham alone, thirteen cases, three murder, three armed robbery, and seven rape cases, were discovered.

In 1986 the CCC noted, "the Report Crime in Your Neighborhood hotline has indicated that drug dealers are continuing to distribute narcotics at an alarming rate, despite the fact that they have been arrested." As narcotic problems in Chicago expanded, Narcotic Courts, first known as the Permanent Central Opium Board, officiated in 1925, were studied for efficiency and effectiveness. The study noted that over 1,000 felony narcotics cases were dismissed in 1984 because lab results were unavailable at preliminary hearings and according to official court sheets, 36 percent of 2,974 charges were dismissed because the arresting officer did not appear in court.

Operation Greylord & Operation Gambat
Operation Greylord & Operation Gambat

*Sources: Chicago Tribune articles, "Greylord's roots deep, intricate," December 18, 1993
and "Cooley, lawyer trade insults in On Leong cross-examination," July 3, 1991*

These two FBI investigations, focusing on corruption in the Cook County courts system, led to the conviction of eighteen judges, one state senator, one state representative, one alderman, fifty-seven lawyers, ten police officers, and twelve deputy sheriffs. Operation Greylord was launched in the early 1980s when a young prosecutor named Terry Hake, disillusioned with what he found as he began his career in the Cook County courts, told the FBI that he would pose as a corrupt attorney to expose the underworld that controlled the daily operation of justice in Cook County. The FBI, already well aware of the corruption, seized this opportunity to launch the massive investigation. Operation Greylord led to Operation Gambat (meaning "gambling attorney"). An admitted corrupt attorney and heavy gambler, Robert Cooley turned himself in to the United State's Attorney's office and then described his twenty-year history of bribing judges, assistant state's attorneys, public defenders, court clerks, sheriff's deputies, assistant corporation counsel, and aldermen. Cooley agreed to continue business as usual, but this time, from 1986 to 1989, he was wearing a wire.

Spilotro Brothers: Buried Alive?
Spilotro Brothers: Buried Alive?

Source: Wikipedia, The Free Encyclopedia Internet site

Anthony Spilotro, called "Tony the Ant," was a Mafia enforcer who worked for the Chicago Outfit in Las Vegas in the 1970s and 1980s. His job was to oversee and protect the Mafia's illegal casino profits. In June 1986, Spilotro, known to have been involved in a number of Outfit murders himself, was beaten and killed with his brother Michael after he got blacklisted from the casinos he was supposed to be controlling. He was also generating unwanted media attention through his jewel heists and broke the code of a "made man" by sleeping with an associate's wife. Two of the murder suspects were Albert Tocco and Frank "The German" Schwiehs. No arrests were made until April 2005. As a result of that investigation, "Operation Family Secrets," it is now believed that the Spilotros were murdered in DuPage County where they were beaten and strangled before being buried in Indiana.

Laboratory Accesses & Efficiency
Laboratory Accesses & Efficiency

In the midst of overwhelming shock brought about by Narcotics Court findings, Chicago leaders scrutinized the system to pin-point the source of the problems. The National Advisory Commission on Criminal Justice Standards and Goals advised in 1987, "Every police agency should immediately insure that it has access to at least one laboratory facility capable of timely and efficient processing of physical evidence and should consider use of a regional laboratory that provides more sophisticated services than that local laboratory, is situated within 50 miles of any agency it routinely serves, can process or analyze evidence within 24 hours of its delivery…" The recommendation, in addition to criticisms that local law enforcement didn't have the tools to gather evidence in the most serious criminal activities, but that criminals knew the departments' limitations, was taken seriously.

Electronic Surveillance: Wiretap Restrictions
Electronic Surveillance: Wiretap Restrictions

Source: Cook County State's Attorney News

One of the gravest law-enforcement obstacles stemmed from the Illinois Electronic Surveillance laws. The laws required that one party must consent to electronic surveillance and that the surveillance be monitored by the state's attorney and the criminal court. Law-enforcement goals to reduce narcotics sales and usage were unattainable, and frustration grew as Illinois wiretap laws remained the most restrictive in the nation. The state's attorney's office stated that they lacked the resources to penetrate organized crime and major narcotics operations and were too nervous to subject informants or investigators to the danger of wearing a wire.

CAPS: Community Policing
CAPS: Community Policing

Source: Chicago Police Department

Implemented in the 1980s was the Chicago Alternative Policing Strategy (CAPS), a philosophy that transformed the Chicago Police Department into a new, proactive agency preventing crimes before they occur. CAPS involved the forging of new partnerships with residents, business people, community leaders, clergy members, and all other city departments. Police and communities began to meet in formalized beat meetings and at district-area meetings in order to work together to address priority crime concerns and quality-of-life issues specific to their own neighborhoods. Police also had the opportunity to educate the community on how to better handle hate crime, domestic violence, and other types of crimes. Police and the community learned from each other. It is not surprising that it took some time for the community and for law enforcement to fully understand and embrace this new philosophy due to revised roles for each, but as these partnerships began to bring about results, both began to see the benefits of a strategy that combines their resources.

Spotlight

Members Encounter

On May 21st, members of the Commission's Inner-City Committee met with two former gang members. The meeting was designed to give committee members first hand information on the gang situation in Chicago and our suburbs. In a free-flowing question-answer session, members learned astonishing facts about street gangs and what it is like to be affiliated with one.

Q: How bad is the gang problem?

A: "It affects the newborn. It's that bad! It starts when he is two or three days old. This is my son. He will follow in my footsteps. At two years old they're already throwing up gang signs. It's serious. At 22, he'll have 20 years of gang experience."

"There is not a place in the city that is not affected by street gangs."

Q: Which areas of our City are affected by Gangs?

A: "There's not a place in the city that is not affected by street gangs. But there are six areas that are considered 'high risk': Cabrini Green, Humboldt Park, Pilsen, Little Village, Garfield, and Englewood. In my opinion, the whole city is 'high risk'."

Q: Are gang members primarily in their teens?

A: "Most of them are teenagers, but there are some members as old as 42

and as young as six or seven. The 'hard core' members use the six and seven year olds to hold their guns and drugs when the police drive down the street. They figure the police won't suspect the little kids and even if they do get caught they don't get in as much trouble."

Q: How many gangs are in the city?

A: "There are lots. Some cover an entire neighborhood, some only cover one block."

Q: How are they organized?

A: "Basically, the city is divided into two rival groups, the People Nation and the Folk Nation. Every gang falls under one of these two Nations. For instance, the Vice Lords and their affiliates make up the People Nation and the Disciples and their affiliates make up the Folk Nation."

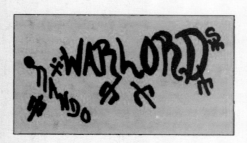

Q: How are gangs able to distinguish a member of the Folk Nation from one of the People Nation?

A: "On the street you can tell the nations apart by the signs they throw

up and the way they dress. The People are always wearing things on the left side, like earrings and left sleeve rolled up or hat tilted to the left or the left shoe lace tied and the right untied. The Folk do all those things on the right side. But, a lot of break dancers and punks will dress this way even though they are not affiliated with a gang. So, the only sure way of telling is by the gang signal they return to you."

Q: How bad is the gang problem in the public schools?

A: "It's bad and a lot of school officials won't admit it. There's one high school on the Northwest Side that falls right on the border of People/Folk territory. Kids in this school that aren't even affiliated with a gang are considered a People or Folk by which side of the building they enter or exit."

"Today, most gang leaders are in prison so they are not only controlling prison life but they are still giving orders to the guys on the streets."

Q: Is it true that gangs control prisons?

A: "Yes. Gangs usually gain control by recruiting new members and threatening those who won't join. Today, most gang leaders are in prison so they are not only controlling prison life but they are still giving orders to the guys on the street. In fact, Jeff

Source: Chicago Crime Commission Searchlight

GANGS Face to Face

Fort, who's spending time in Texas, is still controlling the Vice Lords here in Chicago."

Q: What are safehouses?

A: "Safehouses are places where a gang member will go if the heat is on him. When the cops are looking for you or you are wanted on the street then you hide out in one of these places."

Q: Where are these safehouses?

A: "Most of them are out of the city. They're usually somewhere in the suburbs like, Evanston, Rockford, Springfield, and University Park. Sometimes guys in Humboldt Park are even sent back to Puerto Rico."

Q: Are there gangs in the suburbs?

A: (Laughter) "Yeh. Some parents think if they move their kid out of the city then they won't get involved in a gang, but a lot of times the kid is already in a gang. So their kid will start inviting his gang friends to the suburb to start recruiting and staking new

territory. They may start this by putting their signs up, painting graffiti on walls and get kids in the neighborhood to start hanging with them."

Q: How did you get involved in a gang?

A: "I began hanging with the wrong people at an early age and then I started making a lot of money dealing drugs and started going to school less and less. Next thing I knew all my time was being spent with the gang and hanging on the corner."

"A lot of girls are forming their own gangs and they are just as violent as the guy's gangs."

Q: What made you decide to leave?

A: "I was doing time for dealing drugs and I started thinking that it really wasn't worth it and all the buddies of mine that I had seen get killed cuz of it. When I got out I decided to go back to school and get my GED and try and find a job."

Q: Was it difficult or life threatening for you to break your affiliation with the gang?

A: "I just slowly stopped going to the street corner and started going to night school so I think they realized I was just getting out of it and I wasn't going to bother them so they just let me be."

Q: Are girls involved in gangs?

A: "Some girls help out by hiding drugs on them or carrying weapons. They figure the police won't harass the girls as much. But, a lot of girls are forming their own gangs and they are just as violent as the guy's gangs."

Q: How can businesses in the city co-exist with gangs?

A: "Work with the guys. Talk to them. Treat 'em with respect and they'll respect you in return, and leave your place alone. But, the minute you begin to talk down to them, the gangs react very strongly to that."

SEARCHLIGHT July 1986 — 5

Source: Chicago Crime Commission Searchlight

GANG ORGANIZATION STRUCTURE

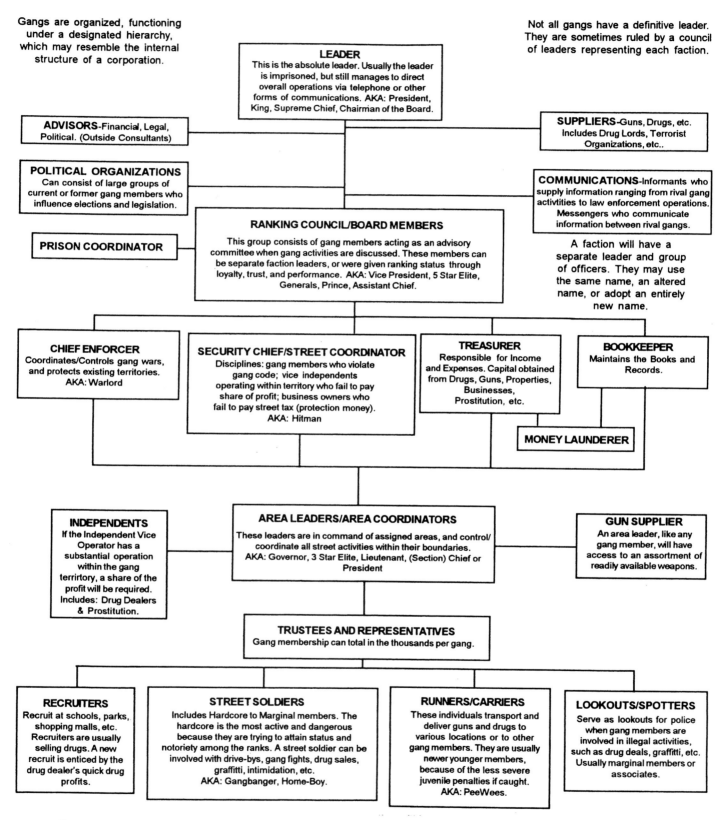

Gangs are organized, functioning under a designated hierarchy, which may resemble the internal structure of a corporation.

Not all gangs have a definitive leader. They are sometimes ruled by a council of leaders representing each faction.

LEADER
This is the absolute leader. Usually the leader is imprisoned, but still manages to direct overall operations via telephone or other forms of communications. AKA: President, King, Supreme Chief, Chairman of the Board.

ADVISORS-Financial, Legal, Political. (Outside Consultants)

SUPPLIERS-Guns, Drugs, etc. Includes Drug Lords, Terrorist Organizations, etc..

POLITICAL ORGANIZATIONS
Can consist of large groups of current or former gang members who influence elections and legislation.

COMMUNICATIONS-Informants who supply information ranging from rival gang activtities to law enforcement operations. Messengers who communicate information between rival gangs.

PRISON COORDINATOR

RANKING COUNCIL/BOARD MEMBERS
This group consists of gang members acting as an advisory committee when gang activities are discussed. These members can be separate faction leaders, or were given ranking status through loyalty, trust, and performance. AKA: Vice President, 5 Star Elite, Generals, Prince, Assistant Chief.

A faction will have a separate leader and group of officers. They may use the same name, an altered name, or adopt an entirely new name.

CHIEF ENFORCER
Coordinates/Controls gang wars, and protects existing territories. AKA: Warlord.

SECURITY CHIEF/STREET COORDINATOR
Disciplines: gang members who violate gang code; vice independents operating within territory who fail to pay share of profit; business owners who fail to pay street tax (protection money). AKA: Hitman

TREASURER
Responsible for Income and Expenses. Capital obtained from Drugs, Guns, Properties, Businesses, Prostitution, etc.

BOOKKEEPER
Maintains the Books and Records.

MONEY LAUNDERER

INDEPENDENTS
If the Independent Vice Operator has a substantial operation within the gang territroy, a share of the profit will be required. Includes: Drug Dealers & Prostitution.

AREA LEADERS/AREA COORDINATORS
These leaders are in command of assigned areas, and control/coordinate all street activities within their boundaries. AKA: Governor, 3 Star Elite, Lieutenant, (Section) Chief or President

GUN SUPPLIER
An area leader, like any gang member, will have access to an assortment of readily available weapons.

TRUSTEES AND REPRESENTATIVES
Gang membership can total in the thousands per gang.

RECRUITERS
Recruit at schools, parks, shopping malls, etc. Recruiters are usually selling drugs. A new recruit is enticed by the drug dealer's quick drug profits.

STREET SOLDIERS
Includes Hardcore to Marginal members. The hardcore is the most active and dangerous because they are trying to attain status and notoriety among the ranks. A street soldier can be involved with drive-bys, gang fights, drug sales, graffitti, intimidation, etc. AKA: Gangbanger, Home-Boy.

RUNNERS/CARRIERS
These individuals transport and deliver guns and drugs to various locations or to other gang members. They are usually newer younger members, because of the less severe juvenile penalties if caught. AKA: PeeWees.

LOOKOUTS/SPOTTERS
Serve as lookouts for police when gang members are involved in illegal activities, such as drug deals, graffitti, etc. Usually marginal members or associates.

Gang structures vary from gang to gang. Structure depends on size of membership and the extent of illegal activity with which the gang is involved. The above structure depicts a well organized street gang.

Source: Chicago Crime Commission Gang Book

Chart 1

**Percentage of 13-Year-Olds
Who Have Used Marijuana,
1953-1982**

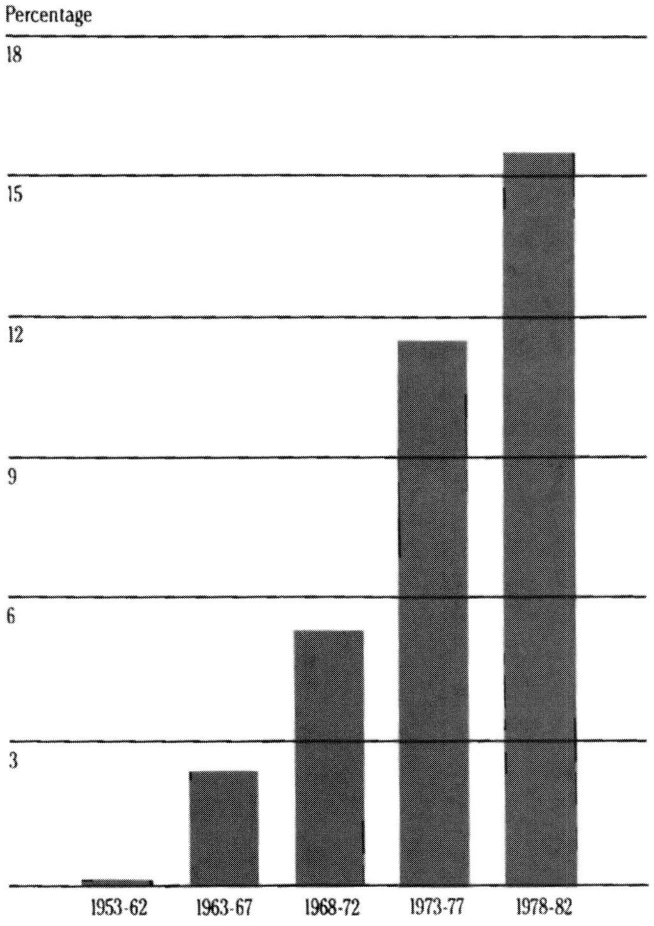

Percentage

18	
15	
12	
9	
6	
3	

1953-62   1963-67   1968-72   1973-77   1978-82

Source: National Institute on Drug Abuse Household Survey, 1982.

Source: National Institute on Drug Abuse Household Survey, 1982
as published in "What Works: Schools Without Drugs" by the U.S. Department of Education

Chart 2

**Percentage of High School
Seniors Who Have
Used Cocaine**

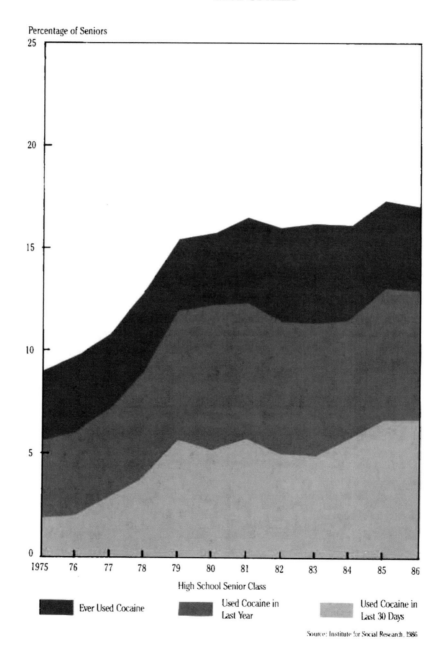

Percentage of Seniors

High School Senior Class

Ever Used Cocaine   Used Cocaine in Last Year   Used Cocaine in Last 30 Days

Source: Institute for Social Research, 1986

*Source: Monitoring The Future Study, Institute for Social Research. University of Michigan, 1986,
as published in "What Works: Schools Without Drugs" by the U.S. Department of Education*

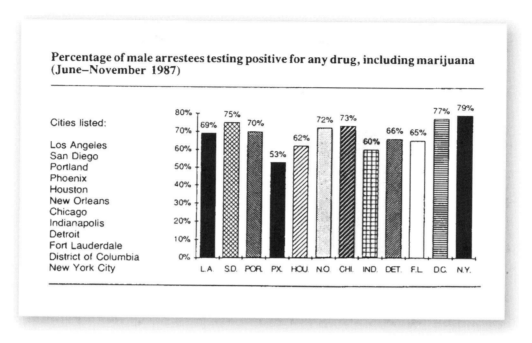

Percentage of male arrestees testing positive for any drug, including marijuana (June–November 1987)

Cities listed:

Los Angeles
San Diego
Portland
Phoenix
Houston
New Orleans
Chicago
Indianapolis
Detroit
Fort Lauderdale
District of Columbia
New York City

Source: National Institute of Justice Reports/SNI 208 March/April, 1988

COURT CALL SUMMARY
Branches 25 & 57
4/27/87 - 5/8/87

CASE DISPOSITIONS FOR FELONY NARCOTIC PRELIMINARY HEARING COURT
APRIL 27, 1987 — MAY 8, 1987
CASES ON THE CALL: 1,684

Finding of Probable Cause:	163	Continuances: 487	Pleas: 1
Finding of No Probable Cause:	198	Motion to Supress Nolle: 29	Drug School: 46
Overnighters:	307	BFW: 115	Waive Right to Preliminary Hearing: 2
FMPC to Detain:	56		

CASES DISMISSED

	ARRESTING OFFICER NOT IN COURT		NO LABORATORY RESULTS @ PRELIMINARY HEARING		NEGATIVE LABORATORY RESULTS		BOND FORFEITURE		OTHER		
	M/S NOLLE	B/F NOLLE	M/S NOLLE	B/F NOLLE	M/S NOLLE	B/F NOLLE	B/F NOLLE	B/F NS	M/S NOLLE	M/S SOL	M/C NS
	88	17	54	10	45	7	36	4	33	10	32
TOTAL	105		64		52		40		75		

Source: Chicago Crime Commission Searchlight

The CCC released a 1987 report revealing that 2,974 felony narcotics charges were dismissed during the first six months of 1986 for reasons the CCC considered unacceptable.

Commission Probes Narcotics Courts

On February 2nd 1987, Commission President Wesley S. Walton, held a press conference to release the findings of a Commission study on case processing in the felony narcotic preliminary hearing court. Official court sheets revealed that 2,974 felony narcotic charges were dismissed during the first six months of 1986, "for reasons the Commission considers unacceptable," said Walton.

The study was a follow-up to a similar Commission study conducted in 1986 which found over 1,000 felony narcotic cases dismissed in 1984 because lab results were unavailable at preliminary hearing. Following the initial study the Commission made several recommendations, none of which have been adopted.

The recent study examined charges dismissed from felony narcotic hearing court for one of four reasons: the arresting officer was not present in court, the defendant failed to appear and an arrest warrant was never issued, the crime lab report was unavailable at preliminary hearing or the State dismissed the case for no cited reason. According to the official court sheets, 36 percent of 2,974 charges were dismissed because the arresting officer was not in court and 53 percent were dismissed by the State's Attorney for no cited reason. The Commission also found 6 percent of the charges dismissed because the defendant failed to appear and an arrest warrant was not issued. The court sheets reflected that only 5 percent of the charges were dismissed because a lab report was unavailable.

These findings were presented to the Chicago Police Department, Cook County State's Attorney, the acting presiding judge of the First Municipal District and the specific judges who heard cases.

The Police Department disagreed with the judge's court sheets in a majority of cases where the grounds for dismissal were, "no arresting officer in court." The Police Department stated that their pay records indicate officers were paid for court appearances in many of these cases. "However, the judges who heard these cases are in disagreement with the Police Department and have clearly stated that their court sheet entries are accurate," said Walton.

The State's Attorney also disagreed with the 1,569 charges recorded as dismissals for no apparent reason. The State claimed these charges were dismissed for several reasons including, the lack of a laboratory analysis at preliminary hearing and the arresting officer's failure to appear. Official court sheets, however, contained no such explanations.

The Commission did not attempt to determine whether police officers were in fact in court or whether the State's Attorney's Office had valid explanations for these dismissals. "The Commission did find it very distrubing that court, police and State's Attorney's records are either contradictory or incomplete with respect to the dismissal of such a substantial number of felony narcotic cases," claimed Walton.

The findings of this study give credence to the Crime Commission's initial contention, the felony narcotic preliminary hearing court is presently acting as a quasi-screening unit for felony narcotic cases. The Commission believes that these cases merit the attention of the State's Attorney's Felony Review Unit or a screening unit of its own.

During his press conference, Walton offered several recommendations to improve case processing in the narcotic preliminary hearing courts. His recommendations included establishing a felony screening unit to review narcotic cases, adding a third preliminary hearing court to relieve the volume of cases being heard in the two existing courts and adopting the color/crystalline examination to ensure that lab results are available for preliminary hearing.

He also recommended relocating the crime lab's chemistry unit, the unit that analyzes narcotics, to the criminal courts building at 26th and California and examining the present record keeping methods of the Police Department, State's Attorney and Judiciary to provide uniformity.

"Our overriding objective," claimed Walton, "is to improve the prosecution of drug cases and ensure that drug pushers are put away."

Outgoing President, Joel D. Gingiss, admires a distinctive bronze plaque commemorating his three terms of outstanding leadership as he officially "passes the baton" to newly elected Commission President, Wesley S. Walton.

SEARCHLIGHT March, 1987 — 3

Source: Chicago Crime Commission Searchlight

Greylord's roots deep, intricate

Janet Cawley; William B Crawford Jr
Chicago Tribune (1963-Current file); Dec 18, 1983; ProQuest Historical Newspapers Chicago Tribune (1849 - 1985)
pg. 1

Greylord's roots deep, intricate

By Janet Cawley
and William B. Crawford Jr.

IN THE WINTER of 1978, Randall Lamar Jordan, an FBI case agent assigned to the Chicago office, was investigating a minor case involving charges of corruption in the Chicago Police Department. In the course of that probe, Jordan stumbled across an unrelated lead that planted the seeds for an undercover investigation of suspected corruption in the Cook County court system.

Last week the investigation, unprecedented in the annals of federal law enforcement, bore its first bitter fruit. Two Cook County judges, a former judge, three lawyers, two court clerks and a policeman were indicted by a federal grand jury on charges ranging from racketeering and conspiracy to extortion and mail fraud. U.S. Atty. Dan Webb has promised that he will seek more indictments before the investigation is finished.

The investigation, code-named Operation Greylord, first made headlines in August, and there have been scattered reports since then of what the elaborate, 3½-year probe entailed. Much more remains to be known. But now, in the wake of the first round of indictments, some of those involved in its inception have provided a fuller account of how Greylord came into being.

JORDAN, 40, a 12-year veteran agent currently assigned to the Birmingham, Ala., FBI office, said in an interview: "In 1978, I was a case agent investigating charges of police corruption, and as a spinoff of that investigation, I guess you could say, I came across allegations of corruption in the state court system."

Jordan said he contacted Thomas Sullivan, then-U.S. attorney for the Northern District of Illinois, and "for the next two years, we planned how we were going to go forward, and during the early phase, I directed the under-

Continued on page 22, col. 1

Source: Courtesy of the Chicago Tribune Archives

From Page 1

Greylord

Continued from page 1

cover operations. It was an interesting investigation, t say the least. And I will also say this: It was the most closely guarded investigation, the most closely monitored investigation I have or ever will work on.

He said he could not comment on the specifics of the case, but "it went to the very top. We were in constant contact with [FBI chief William] Webster and to officials from the Justice Department from the very beginning. Information was shared among us on a need to-know basis.

"I ALSO BELIEVE that without Tom Sullivan, we may never have been able to sell the investigation to Washington. Had I tried it alone, it never would have gotten off the ground. But Mr. Sullivan is a bright scholarly lawyer and when he went to Washington and presented his argument, he was able to sell it.

Jordan was not the only person to stumble across apparent wrongdoing in the court system about this time. In 1979, a pair of young prosecutors in the U.S attorney's office and another prosecutor in the state's attorney's office approached officials independently with stories of wrongdoing involving lawyers, judges and the fixing of cases.

Chuck Sklarsky and Daniel Reidy, now two of the top prosecutors in Webb's office, went to Sullivan with information that corruption "had become a way of life among certain lawyers and judges in the state courts," according to one prosecutor later closely associated with Greylord.

Terry Hake's important role

Sklarsky, a bright, bespectacled and scholarly looking young lawyer, had joined the office less than a year before. Before moving to the Dirksen Federal Building, he had spent six years as a prosecutor in the Cook County state courts and was able to provide valuable initial information about certain judges and lawyers he suspected were involved in the payoff scheme.

AT THE SAME time, Terrence Hake, a member of the state's attorney's staff who had passed the bar only two years earlier, went to his bosses with similar allegations of wrongdoing that he had seen during his time in the courts.

Hake, described by friends as "the all-American boy" and an up-and-comer at the state's attorney's office, had grown increasingly disillusioned about things he saw daily, particularly around the Narcotics Court, that he believed were tainting the judicial system.

Unlike others who had seen the same thing, he decided to take action.

"He did something, that all of us talk about," said one veteran prosecutor. "But something that most of us had the guts to do."

He volunteered to put his reputation and his law career—and possibly his life—on the line and work undercover to bring dishonest members of the court system to justice.

JORDAN, REFLECTING on the sequence of events in the investigation, said: "Terry Hake entered the picture later [after the onset of the probe]. But his presence certainly represented a turning point in the investigation. He gave us an invaluable boost. . . ."

From the outset, the unprecedented probe was faced with imponderables and fraught with roadblocks.

Fly Catcher to Greylord

Sullivan was about to step down as U.S. attorney. State's Atty. Bernard Carey, who also had been brought into the investigation, faced an election that summer. He subsequently lost to his Democratic opponent, Richard Daley. And, as Webb acknowledged later, the highest judges in Cook County's court system were neither consulted nor

Webb   Lockwood   Hegarty   Daley   Carey

he said later.

Lockwood said he became involved in Greylord after he went to the Justice Department in Washington with information on corruption in Chicago's courts.

"By virtue of that, they put me in touch with Operation Greylord," he said. "I agonized for a year on whether to join them." He finally did, and remained "wired" until last summer, when the undercover portion of the project ended.

According to the indictments returned Wednesday, Operation Greylord was in full swing by 1981.

Thomas Kangalos, an assistant corporation counsel assigned to Traffic Court between April, 1976, and October, 1983, was charged with soliciting and receiving more than $3,710 in bribes between August, 1981, and April, 1982, in payments ranging from $50 to $1,200 to influence the disposition of cases. Five of the seven incidents cited involved payoffs from a David Ries.

Lockwood said last week he had initiated a friendship with Kangalos during his stints in Traffic Court and had secretly recorded conversations with him that he considered incriminating.

ALAN KAYE, a former Holiday Court bailiff, was charged with soliciting a $30,000 bribe in or about October, 1981, from Ronald Elder, an undercover FBI agent using the name Ronald Johnson, which was to go to a judge in Divorce Court to influence the outcome of a divorce proceeding to be filed on behalf of the agent. Ronald Elder's name also crops up in connection with a $2,000 bribe to Kaye on or about Dec. 3, 1981, and a $1,000 bribe on or about Dec. 10, 1981.

Ira Blackwood, a 25-year veteran of the Chicago Police Department, allegedly took 10 bribes totaling $4,400 from December, 1981, to May, 1983, to influence the disposition of cases in Traffic Court, where he was assigned. All the payments came from David V. Ries and one concerned an case involving a "Gary Copeland," a pseudonym of an FBI agent posing as a criminal that turned up in "manufactured" cases.

Big step: Bug is planted

During the same approximate period, the indictment against Olson alleges, the judge was accepting payoffs from Costello: a total of 21 totaling more than $9,630 from June, 1980, to Feb. 10, 1981. According to the indictment, Olson and Costello had an arrangement in which Costello paid Olson half of all cash bond refunds, usually signed over by defendants as reimbursements for legal fees, that he earned in connection with cases referred to him by Olson.

IN LATE 1980, an apparently unprecedented step was taken in the probe. A court-ordered electronic eavesdropping device was planted in Olson's chambers, reportedly inside a picture, for two months in late 1980 and early 1981. Sources close to the inquiry said the chambers of a Divorce Court judge also were bugged but that nothing untoward was heard.

Nevertheless, Operation Greylord slowly but surely took on momentum. Besides Sklarsky and Reidy, Webb added at least three other assistants to work on the case. They were Candice Fabri, John Podliska and Scott Lassar.

White Knight listens

Hake, who later would be code-named the "White Knight," for his role in the probe, was equipped with electronic eavesdropping equipment to record conversations as he went about his working day in the Narcotics Court presided over by Judge Wayne Olson. Hake began transforming his image from an earnest, honest young lawyer to a sleazy attorney on the take.

Another "mole" also entered the case. Again, officials are reluctant to release dates, but at some point probably in late 1979 or early 1980, David V. Ries, an FBI agent who also is a licensed attorney, began posing as a corruptible defense attorney, identifying himself as D. Victor Ries.

AS THE CAST expanded, so did the number of undercover agents and the schemes involved. Authorities began "manufacturing" criminal cases to be put through the court system. According to former Chicago Police Supt. Richard Brzeczek, the manufactured cases began with less serious traffic cases, then misdemeanors, then felonies including narcotics cases. At the outset, he said, about one bogus case was introduced into the court system each week. "But it was so easy we began putting more and more through," he added. At the height of the 3½-year inquiry, he said, 73 bogus cases were in the system.

The first record of a manufactured case to surface in the indictments returned Wednesday alleges that on Sept. 29, 1980, Harold Conn, a deputy court clerk,

Payoffs to judge charged

Associate Judge John M. Murphy, who was assigned at that time to Belmont Avenue Police Court, was charged with taking payoffs ranging from $200 to $400 from either Hake or Ries seven times between January, 1982, and May, 1983. On April 12, 1982, his indictment charged, Murphy received about $400 from attorney David Ries to influence the disposition of People v. Gary Copeland, who was charged with breaking into a car that apparently also belonged to another undercover agent.

Former Associate Judge John J. Devine, among other counts of mail fraud, racketeering and extortion, was charged with receiving three bribes totaling $450 from Hake on three occasions between July 7, 1981, and Feb. 3, 1983.

BUT OPERATION Greylord also had its setbacks, including a phony robbery that went awry in March, 1982. Two agents staged the robbery outside Water Tower Place. The "robber" took off running after snatching an attache case. The "victim" pursued the thief and tackled him as police arrived. Police soon discovered phony identification and FBI credentials stuffed in the suspect's pockets and socks, leading them to believe the FBI had staged the incident to expose wrongdoing by police.

But despite the occasional blunder and ensuing rumors that drifted through police and legal circles, Greylord apparently remained in place until last summer. At that time, sources close to the case said, a police officer who served as a Traffic Court bailiff was confronted by the FBI, refused an offer from federal prosecutors to become a Greylord informant and then began to tell others about the probe.

Greylord came to an abrupt and unscheduled end and reports of the investigation were public by early August.

Sources close to the case predict that besides the nine indictments returned last week, as many as 20 other people may be charged before the probe ends—and with appeals, that could be years from now.

The 'hillbilly' mole enters

LOCKWOOD, WHO says he believes himself to be the first judge involved in such an undercover investigation, cultivated a "hillbilly" image complete with country twang as he moved through the courts. Frequently, he said, he would sit down and swap stories with some of the individuals under investigation.

"I liked them but I didn't like what they were doing,"

Source: Courtesy of the Chicago Tribune Archives

Chicago Tribune, Thursday, June 27, 1991

U.S. says informant bribed 20 judges

By Ray Gibson
and Matt O'Connor

Federal prosecutors have told defense lawyers that former Chicago attorney Robert J. Cooley, the government's chief witness in several public corruption and organized crime investigations, paid bribes to fix court cases with as many as 20 judges, according to lawyers familiar with the case.

The prosecutors have outlined Cooley's past deeds in court documents provided under federal trial rules to defense lawyers who are preparing to cross-examine Cooley when he takes the stand as a prosecution witness in the ongoing Chinatown federal racketeering and gambling case.

Attorneys familiar with the documents said among the disclosures are the names of 20 judges with whom Cooley dealt, including at least one judge already convicted in Operation Greylord, an earlier federal probe of court corruption.

In addition, the government disclosed that it paid as much as $71,000 in gambling debts run up by Cooley during the time he was working for the government.

Cooley began cooperating with federal investigators in 1986 and for the next three years he secretly recorded conversations with judges and politicians about fixing court cases ranging from murder cases to partnership disputes with judges and politicians as well as recording organized crime figures discussing gambling operations.

The cooperation of the attorney led to last December's federal indictments on corruption charges of then-Ald. Fred Roti (1st); three powerful 1st Ward political figures; and David Shields, former presiding judge of the Cook County Circuit Court Chancery Division, as part of what federal prosecutors dubbed Operation Gambat. The defendants have all pleaded innocent and are awaiting trial.

Next week Cooley is expected to make his first public court appearance since his role as an undercover informant was disclosed when he testifies at the trial of 11 businessmen accused of operating a gambling enterprise through a Chinese business organization known as the On Leong Merchants Association.

He is expected to testify that he got $75,000 from the businessmen's organization and gave the money to Roti and 1st Ward Democratic secretary Pat Marcy Sr. to fix a 1981 China-

See Judges, pg. 7.

Judges

Continued from page 1

town murder case being heard by former Cook County Circuit Judge Thomas J. Maloney. Maloney's attorneys have denied the judge ever received any payments from Cooley.

Cooley has also cooperated in a federal investigation of Maloney and William A. Swano, a prominent criminal defense attorney.

Barbara Lazarus, a spokeswoman for the U.S. attorney's office, refused to comment Wednesday on news reports that Swano was secretly indicted last week on charges stemming, in part, from his alleged payment of $10,000 to $20,000 to Maloney to fix the outcome of a 1986 murder trial involving two El Rukn gang members. The supposed payment was allegedly returned by the judge who subsequently sentenced the two gang members to death.

But a high-ranking federal lawyer said an announcement about indictments is imminent.

Swano and his attorney, Gregory Schlesinger, did not return repeated phone calls, but Schlesinger has described last month's testimony of Rukn gang member Earl Hawkins, who outlined the alleged bribe, as "absolutely incredible, the desperate act of a man facing the death penalty."

Hawkins and a co-defendant were found guilty by Maloney, who later sentenced them to death.

The Gambit Operation

Source: Courtesy of the Chicago Tribune Archives

2   Section 2   Chicago Tribune, Wednesday, July 3, 1991 N   ★

Cooley, lawyer trade insults in On Leong cross-examination

By Matt O'Connor

Robert J. Cooley fended off often personal attacks on his credibility by defense lawyers Tuesday as he detailed alleged mob ties to 1st Ward political figures in his second day of testimony in federal court.

Cooley said he believed that former Ald. Fred Roti (1st) and 1st Ward Democratic secretary Pat Marcy Sr.—both close associates of Cooley's when he was bribing judges and other court officials for almost two decades—were connected to La Cosa Nostra, the U.S. counterpart to the Sicilian Mafia.

Cooley, the central government witness in a wide-ranging corruption investigation, said he also believed that Roti and Marcy controlled Chicago's Chinatown.

Roti "had bragged he controlled the Chinese," Cooley testified at the On Leong racketeering and gambling trial.

On Monday, Cooley said he passed $75,000 from two On Leong officials to Roti and Marcy in 1981 to fix a Chinatown murder trial. Cooley said he kept $25,000 for himself.

Roti and Marcy have pleaded innocent to bribe-taking charges and are awaiting trial.

Until the Greylord judicial probe became public in the mid-1980s, Cooley routinely paid bribes to judges, lawyers, police officers, court clerks and others "to go along with the program," he said Tuesday. "Everything had a price."

In often combative exchanges with Cooley, defense lawyer Pat Tuite sometimes grew testy as he bore in on Cooley during several hours of questioning.

At one point, Tuite barked, "I'm

Robert Cooley says that when he was sworn in as a lawyer, he knew he would violate his oath.

disgusted to be a lawyer in your presence."

When Cooley said he had gone over "my bad acts" in conferring with federal prosecutors before the On Leong trial, Tuite quipped, "That took an awful lot of time, I bet."

At the end of another exchange, Tuite, standing in front of Cooley, said, "I doubt if you'd know an ethical lawyer if you saw one."

"That makes two of us," Cooley responded under his breath.

Tuite spun around, pointed a hand at Cooley and shouted, "I resent his comment to me."

Cooley, who admitted gambling extensively, disclosed that he went

to John DiFronzo, one of Chicago's top organized-crime figures for help in getting bookmakers to quit pressuring him to pay off his gambling debts of $150,000 to $160,000 in February 1986.

DiFronzo, whom Cooley referred to as "Johnny," contacted the bookmakers, who then informed Cooley that he could pay off his gambling debts "at my own leisure," Cooley said.

Cooley indicated he was also friends with reputed mob figure Marco D'Amico, whom he identified as his gambling partner. "I placed bets with him and for him," he said.

On cross-examination, Cooley denied he began cooperating with federal authorities in March 1986, the month after he contacted DiFronzo, out of fear for his safety because of his huge gambling debts.

Cooley admitted that when he traveled to Springfield with some family members to be sworn in as a lawyer in 1970, he knew full well he would violate the oath he took that day as soon as he started practicing law in Chicago.

"Were your fingers crossed when you took the oath?" Tuite asked.

"I knew what the system was in Cook County and that I'd be breaking my oath," said Cooley, who testified he had taken bribes of $25 to $50 about a dozen times from Traffic Court lawyers when he was a Chicago police officer in the 1960s.

Cooley, under protective custody since his undercover role became public in 1989, confirmed he still has a law license, but that he isn't practicing law.

Cooley agreed to go undercover to secure evidence in the Gambat Operation.

Source: Courtesy of the Chicago Tribune Archives

CHICAGO SUN-TIMES, Monday, June 30, 1986

FBI finds witness to Spilotro burial

He describes scene at Indiana cornfield

By Art Petacque

An eyewitness in federal custody has told authorities that he saw a group of men burying reputed mob boss Anthony Spilotro and his brother Michael.

The brothers, who disappeared on June 14, were savagely beaten and buried in a northwest Indiana cornfield two days later. Their bodies were discovered in a grave last Monday.

The eyewitness has been placed under extraordinary security measures, and the FBI has tried to keep even his existence secret. He has not yet picked out pictures from mug books, sources said.

The witness told authorities he had been traveling along a road at about dusk on June 16 when he came upon the cornfield and heard men's voices. He then saw several men digging the hole from which the bodies were recovered.

Sources close to the investigation said informants have named Chicago mob chieftain Joseph "Joe Nagaul" Ferriola as the man who or-

Source: As published in the Chicago Sun-Times. Article continues on next page.

Article continues from previous page.

dered the slayings and might have even participated in them.

The FBI's prime suspects, sources added, are Ernest Rocco Infelice and Wayne Bock, two Ferriola loyalists; Frank James Calabrese, a lieutenant of Angelo LaPietra, and Frank Schweihs, a soldier for Joseph "Joey the Clown" Lombardo who might have switched allegiance to Ferriola.

At stake, the sources said, were control of the mob's Las Vegas operations, some $10 million in cash that Anthony Spilotro reportedly had hidden, and the outcome of a longstanding feud between Spilotro and Ferriola.

Authorities believe that the Spilotro brothers were lured to a supposed peace meeting with Ferriola, taken to one or more locations in the O'Hare Airport area and beaten until Anthony Spilotro revealed the hiding place of his money, gleaned from casino skimming, extortion and fencing stolen goods.

Michael Spilotro was taken along, sources said, probably because if he were beaten, his brother might have talked more readily.

The money's hiding place, authorities feel, was probably near the burial cornfield, since the brothers had frequented that area. The Spilotros were driven there, and after Anthony pointed out where he'd hidden the money, they were beaten again and thrown into a single grave.

One investigator said it made no sense—except for the money—for the slayers to take the Spilotros 60 miles by car and then kill them. "There's no reason to carry the electric chair in the car with you," he said.

The bad blood between Anthony Spilotro and Ferriola began in 1971, when Spilotro killed Ferriola's brother-in-law, Sam "Sambo" Cesario. The killing was done on the orders of imprisoned mob leader Felix "Milwaukee Phil" Alderisio, whose girlfriend had married Cesario.

The feud grew worse when Lombardo and LaPietra were imprisoned for their part in attempted bribery, and Lombardo tried to continue his mob rule from prison, through Anthony Spilotro. But Ferriola had assumed effective control.

Finally, during Spilotro's recent trial, government wiretaps were played, on which Spilotro could be heard ridiculing Ferriola's ability to run the mob.

The Spilotro brothers knew they were on thin ice when they agreed to the meeting with Ferriola on June 14. As they left Michael's west suburban house, Michael told his wife, Ann, "If we're not back by 9 o'clock, we're in big trouble, and you might not see us again."

Meanwhile, Ferriola's lieutenants already are taking over the Las Vegas operations that Spilotro had run. In charge is Frank "The Horse" Buccieri, the reputed Palm Springs, Calif., rackets boss.

Buccieri is a college graduate who does not have a criminal record and can thus operate openly in the Nevada city.

His behind-the-scenes associates are Donald Angelini, known as "The Wizard of Odds," and Dominic Cortina.

Source: As published in the Chicago Sun-Times

CHICAGO CRIME COMMISSION
OUTFIT HIT LIST FOR 1980-1990

Since the Chicago Crime Commission began keeping count, in 1919, the Syndicate has been assigned responsibility for 1,102 slayings in Chicago. In the last decade, as the following list shows, there have been 33 mob murders:

July 2, 1980: William Earl Dauber, a chop-shop enforcer facing federal gun and cocaine charges, was shot with his wife Charlotte while enroute to a court appearance. Killer unknown - although Jerry Scalise is a suspect.

November 28, 1980: Eleftherios "Nick" Valentzas, a restaurant owner who testified in a federal extortion case, was shot to death in an Elmwood Park parking lot. Killer unknown.

March 14, 1981: William "Butch" Petrocelli, mob overseer, was found on West 25th Place with his throat cut, face burned with lighter fluid, mouth taped shut — death was by asphyxiation. Killer unknown.

May 6, 1981: Fiore Forestiere, an ex-con, was found in a van in River Grove, shot five times. Killer unknown.

May 18, 1981: Sam Farruggia, jukebox firm operator, was found in River Forest, wrapped in a rug in a station wagon. He had been stabbed at least five times, and his throat was cut. Killer unknown.

August 5, 1981: Charles Monday, drug dealer, was found in the trunk of a car on West Schubert, beaten to death. Killer unknown.

August 7, 1981: Anthony Legato, drug dealer associate of Monday, was found beaten to death in a car trunk. Killer unknown.

September 13, 1989: Nicholas D'Andrea, who reportedly dealt in drugs and gambling, was discovered in the trunk of a burning car. Killer unknown.

October 3, 1981: Samuel Guzzino, mob associate, was found in a ditch shot in the head and with his throat slit. Killer unknown.

June 3, 1982: Robert Hayden Plummer, once indicted for interstate gambling, was beaten on the head and left in a car trunk. Killer unknown.

October 8, 1982: Leo "John" Manfredi (aka Leonard Corfini or John DuBois), a gambler, was found in the basement of a Berwyn pizza parlor, shot in the head four times. Killer unknown.

January 11, 1983: Robert P. Subatich, suspected of "chop shop" involvement, was discovered shot once in the head and left in a car trunk. Killer unknown.

January 20, 1983: Allen F. Dorfman, union racketeer awaiting sentencing on federal conspiracy charges, was shot eight times in a hotel parking lot. Killer unknown.

March 2, 1983: Michael G. Chorak, an auto wrecker suspected of chop shop involvement, was shot in the back of his head in his car. His former employee Joe Radisch, a criminal escapee, was convicted of the homicide.

Source: Chicago Crime Commission Outfit Hit List For 1980-1990

July 14, 1983: John Gattuso, a deputy sheriff who had operated syndicate honky tonk taverns, was found wrapped in plastic and placed in the trunk of his Volvo, which was parked on Pebblewood Lane in Naperville. He had been stabbed and strangled, possibly in a torture session. Killer unknown.

July 14, 1983: Jasper Campise, was discovered stabbed to death and laid beside Gattuso. Both were implicated in the bungled hit attempt of gambling kingpin Ken Eto. It is believed that mob bosses, angered at their failure, had the pair slain to prevent them from talking. Killer unknown.

December 16, 1984: Anthony V. Crissie, a former bank director who became enmeshed in underworld financing deals, was shot several times. He had recently been quizzed by federal agents about his knowledge of mob affairs. Killer unknown.

January 10, 1985: Leonard "Lennie" Yaras, a syndicate sports betting boss, was gunned down in front of one of his businesses. Killer unknown.

February 9, 1985: Charles "Chuckie" English, a top mob lieutenant who at one time controlled all gambling activitiy on the West Side and in Cicero, was shot several times, once between the eyes. Killer unknown.

February 12, 1985: Hal Smith, one of the country's most successful bookmakers, who had been cooperating with a government probe into mob rackets, was found in his car trunk, tortured and beaten to death. Killer unknown.

July 26, 1985: Patrick "Patsy" Ricciardi, boss of the syndicate's lucrative pornographic film business, and a government informer, was shot once and left in the trunk of a stolen car. The car was eventually towed to a police auto pound. When the owner came to claim it, he noticed something dripping from the trunk. Killer unknown.

January 13, 1986: Michael S. Lentini, shot to death in his car. Killer unknown.

January 27, 1986: Richard N. DePrizo, about to be indicted for fraud in city construction contracts, was shot twice in the head. Killer unknown.

March 16, 1986: Giuseppe Cocozza, a heavy bettor, was shot to death in a parked car. Killer unknown.

June 22, 1986: Anthony J. and Michael Spilotro were discovered buried in a shallow grave in Northwest Indiana. Michael was under indictment in Chicago on federal extortion charges. Anthony was described by the government as the overseer of the Chicago syndicate's Las Vegas operations. Killers unknown.

September 14, 1986: John A. Fecarotta, a former labor organizer, was gunned down in his Riverside home. Killer unknown.

November 13, 1986: Thomas B. McKillip, was found shot and stabbed in the back of a Chevy Blazer. Killer unknown.

September 23, 1987: John Castaldo, owner of two River Forest Beauty salons, was found riddled with bullets in a River Forest alley. Killer unknown.

August 14, 1988: John E. Pronger, was shot twice as he stood in the doorway of his Springhill Drive home. Killer unknown.

Source: Chicago Crime Commission Outfit Hit List For 1980-1990

November 22, 1988: Philip Goodman a 73-year-old Las Vegas bookmaker and former Chicagoan, was found beaten to death in a motel. Killer unknown.

December, 1989: Robert "Bobby" Hartidge and Michael Oliver, both reputed mob killers, who reportedly had been slain in the late-1970's, were unearthed in a mob burial ground in south DuPage County. Killer unknown.

May 14, 1990: James Pellegrino age 31 of 122 Thomas Court, Mokena, Illinois was found by two men canoeing down the Des Plaines river. The victim had been wrapped in a tarp after being tied hand and foot and shot once in the back of the head with a 25 cal. slug. Killer unknown.

July 2, 1990: Victor Lazarus, an 86-year-old Chicago and Las Vegas bookmaker, was found shot to death in the trunk of his car in a North Side parking lot. Killer unknown.

Source: Chicago Crime Commission Outfit Hit List For 1980-1990

CHICAGO "OUTFIT" & ASSOCIATES

ANTHONY ACCARDO
Chairman

SAM CARLISI
Street Boss

JOHN DIFRONZO
Under-Boss

GUS ALEX
Political. Liaison

JOSEPH AIUPPA
JOHN CERONE
ANGELO LAPIETRA
JOSEPH LOMBARDO
ALFRED PILOTTO
Advisors/In Prison

JAMES MARCELLO
Driver

ALBERT TOCCO
(In Prison)
Chicago Heights

CHRIS PETTI
California and
Las Vegas Contact

ERNEST INFELISE
Lake County &
Enforcement

Harry Aleman
Robert Bellavia
Sal Delaurentis
Gary Gagliano
James Inendino
James LaValley
Louis Marino
Frank Panno
Mike Posner
Robert Salerno

VINCENT J. COZZO
Grand Avenue

James D'Antonio
Frank Derosa
Tom Forliano
Mike Malmenato
Frank Schweihs
Albert Vena

VINCE SOLANO
North Side

Frank Demonte
Roland Ignoffo
Charles Parrilli
Louis Parrilli
Leonard Patrick
Joe Petitt
Larry Petitt
Mario Rainone

MARCO D'AMICO
Elmwood Park

Joe Andriacci
Dom Basso
Mike Biancofiore
Mike Carioscia
Mike Castaldo
Virgil Cimino
Joe Difronzo
Peter Difronzo
Willie Messino
Carmen Migliore

DOMINIC CORTINA
West Side

Donald Angelini
Joe Grieco
Joe Pascucci
Joe Spadavecchio
Ray Tominello

JAMES LAPIETRA
26th Street

Carmen Bastone
Sal Bastone
Sam Bills
Wayne Bock
Frank Calabrese
Mike Gurgone
Joe Lamantia
Gino Martin
John Monteleone

Source: Chicago Crime Commission Outfit Organized Crime Chart published in 1990

Glossary: electronic surveillance

bug: an electronic device placed in a room (not connected to a telephone or telegraph instrument) which enables the overhearing of communication.

consensual overhear: current Illinois law permits electronic eavesdropping for 10-day period where one party consents, where the state's attorney approves, and where the consensual overhear order (COH) is signed by a criminal court judge.

electronic eavesdropping: a general term which includes both "wiretapping" and "bugging."

forfeiture: legislation enacted into law Jan. 1982 allows law enforcement officers in Illinois to seize money found in the proximity of illegal drugs; the law also stipulates that certain other properties are forfeitable subsequent to a conviction in a narcotics case.

minimization: a legal limitation placed on the electronic surveillance order which confines the area of information which can be overheard.

pen registure: an electronic apparatus which is connected to a telephone that determines the destination of a wire communication from a telephone (but does not intercept the contents of any communication).

privileged communications: physicians, licensed lawyers, practicing clergy, and places used primarily for habitation by a husband and wife are privileged; special provisions are made in electronic eavesdropping laws to protect the integrity of these relationships and professions.

probable cause: the provision of reasonably trustworthy information that a crime has been committed enabling a court to issue an electronic surveillance order (or warrant or indictment).

Title III: legislation enacted by Congress in 1968 enabling federal law enforcement agencies the authority to use electronic surveillance; the law also authorized the respective states to develop similar electronic surveillance for their law enforcement agencies.

trap: a device which is connected to a telephone that determines the origin of a wire communications to the phone but does not intercept the contents of any communication.

wire: a generic term for a recording device used for electronic surveillance.

wiretap: an electronic device which connects to a telephone or telephone line enabling communication to be overheard.

State's Attorney News is published by the Cook County State's Attorney's Office. Your questions, comments and criticisms are invited.

State's Attorney News
Room 406, Daley Center
Chicago, Illinois 60602

Editorial: 443-5690
R. Harvey, editor
Circulation: 443-5598
Bill Bresnahan,
circulation director

Source: Cook County State's Attorney News

Reproduced with permission of the Cook County State's Attorney's office.

Under the Chicago Alternative Policing Strategy (CAPS),
community volunteers and police personnel serve as co-facilitators for beat-community meetings

Source: Chicago Police Department

Reproduced with permission of the Chicago Police Department.

By attacking the underlying conditions to crime, such as abandoned autos and dilapidated properties, the CAPS philosophy has shown that a positive impact can be made on overall incidents of crime

Source: Chicago Police Department

Reproduced with permission of the Chicago Police Department.

Motorola Syntor X9000 mobile two-way radio, Chicago, 1985.
© 2007, Motorola, Inc. Reproduced with permission.

Motorola Centracom Series II Communications Control Center, Chicago, USA, 1986.

© 2007, Motorola, Inc. Reproduced with permission.

Public Safety two-way radio users. Chicago, Illinois, USA, Crica 1985.
© 2007, Motorola, Inc. Reproduced with permission.

1990

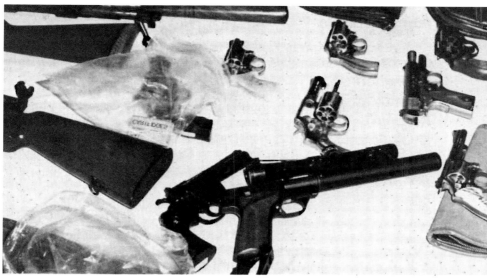

Weapons seized by the Chicago Police Department's Gang Crime Section

2006

Source: Chicago Crime Commission Archives

Source: West Chicago Police Department

FRIEND

FOE

Superintendent Philip Cline

Chicago Police Superintendent Philip Cline, building upon the good work begun under Superintendent Terry Hillard, developed numerous highly effective and cooperative strategies for dealing with street gangs, gun violence, and drugs in the city of Chicago. In the 2000s, Cline led the way for increased partnerships between the CPD and suburban police departments. Operationally, Cline has developed creative ways to more effectively use limited resources and – has significantly improved criminal justice information – sharing.

Community Leaders

There are many community leaders who have led local, grassroots efforts in high crime and other areas. These individuals, while too many to name, deserve to be recognized. Often, by taking a stand against the gangs, drugs, and guns on their streets, they put themselves in danger. They extend themselves to help children find healthy opportunities. They work to rebuild community areas. They have many roles and their communities are fortunate to have them.

Sureno 13s Street Gang

While many powerful street gangs continue to act as public enemies and should also make this "foe" list, the Sureno 13s, during this decade, began to establish themselves throughout the suburban Chicago areas with the general population generally unaware of their existence. This street gang, an immigrant Mexican gang, has direct ties to Mexican organized crime and thus could bring about even greater drug distribution in the suburban areas. Immigrant gangs are violent, have little fear of law enforcement, and are of great concern to local, state, and federal agencies. Their knowledge of moving illegal goods over the border could become an even greater threat if they decide to expand their criminal activities to include human trafficking.

Although we are only able to highlight a few friends and foes for each decade, the Chicago Crime Commission reminds the public that there are many friends, and while perhaps not as famous as the criminals, they are courageous and far more impressive.

Making Room For Justice
Making Room For Justice

In 1996 the CCC released its report focusing on the overcrowding of our criminal justice system, particularly courts and prisons, due to misdemeanor drug cases. The report notes, "Drug offenders who are guilty only of possession of minor amounts of drugs with no intent to distribute or other criminal activities should be diverted to the misdemeanor court system where legal sanctions can be quickly coordinated with treatment for drug dependence. As the findings in the report show, a shocking number of one gram/simple possession cases are clogging our court system. The concentration of our police, courts, corrections and other forensic resources against the lowest level drug charges deludes the public into thinking that we are making progress in fighting crime by overwhelming us with minor cases. Accordingly, the Commission recommends that felony courts, jail cells and other resources be focused against the most serious felons, including drug abusers who are guilty of other felonies or who are likely to be engaged in drug dealing."

The Chicago Crime Commission *Gang Book* Released
The Chicago Crime Commission Gang Book Released

Street gangs are the greatest concern of law enforcement in Chicago and increasingly in the suburbs during this time period. Fueled by increased gang activity, the number of murders in the forty-seven largest suburban towns in northeastern Illinois has increased each year since 2002 from sixty-four in 2001 to ninety in 2005. Immigrant street gangs, specifically the Sureno 13, are moving quickly to make Chicago suburbs their own, and with their first line connection to Mexican drug dealers, this could result in increased drug trafficking in our communities. In addition, Chicago gang activity has developed beyond the traditional violence and drugs; one recent Vice Lord case involved $80 million in fraudulent mortgages.

In 2006, ten years after the CCC released its 1995 *Gangs: Public Enemy No. 1* book, the CCC brought the knowledge of the Chicago Police Department, Illinois State Police, eighty-one suburban police departments, Drug Enforcement Administration, Federal Bureau of Investigation, HIDTA, Alcohol Tobacco Firearms & Explosives (ATF), the U. S. Attorney's Office, Cook County Sheriff's Department, Chicago public schools, and numerous others together in the most comprehensive but concise overview of Chicago gangs ever produced, *The Gang Book*. The report provides law enforcement, educators, parents, and others with needed information on fifty Chicago-area street gangs, gang maps, suburban gang activity, gang crime, e.g. homicide, theft, illegal drugs, mortgage fraud, identity theft, etc., organizational structure and gang leader photos, gangs in prisons, probation and parole, girls in gangs, political, organized crime and terrorism links, dog fighting, gangs in schools, gang identifiers—colors, graffiti, and slang terms, communications methods, law enforcement strategies and response, gang behavior and the media, recommended strategies, policy and legislation, getting out of the gang, and a directory for assistance.

2006 CCC Suburban Gang Activity Survey
2006 CCC Suburban Gang Activity Survey

Eighty-one suburban police departments from around Chicago responded to a Crime Commission survey about street-gang activity. A full reporting of the results from this survey are in the 2006 CCC publication, *The Gang Book.*

Survey results show that gang activity is wide-spread and that in most cases police have contact with multiple gangs. Thirty-one departments out of eighty-one reported an increase in gang activity in the past three years. In some cases the problem is quite large with some suburbs reporting the estimated number of gang members at between 1,500 and 3,000.

In the northern suburbs, the Latin Kings have the largest presence, with the Gangster Disciples and the Surenos 13s coming in a somewhat distant second. The Latin Kings also have the greatest presence in the western suburbs, followed by the Gangster Disciples, the Latin Counts, the Surenos 13s and the Vice Lords. The Gangster Disciples and the Latin Kings are both widespread in the south suburbs, followed by the Vice Lords, Four Corner Hustlers and the Two Six gang.

The Surenos 13s are by far and away the most prominent of the newly emerging gangs both in the northern and western suburbs. This is of even greater concern given their direct connection with the Mexican Mafia and Mexican drug dealers. The *13* in their name is based on the fact that *M* is the 13th letter in the alphabet. The *M* represents the Mexican Mafia. Members of the Surenos 13s are generally illegal immigrants.

Most suburbs report an increase in illegal drug distribution, including cannabis, heroin, crack, cocaine, methamphetamines, and other types of drugs. It appears, however, to be increasing at a greater rate in the southern and western suburbs than elsewhere.

Law Enforcement Strategies Fine Tuned & Effective
Law Enforcement Strategies Fine Tuned & Effective

Source: The Chicago Crime Commission Gang Book

The Deployment Operations Center (DOC) is the backbone of all the Chicago Police Department efforts. DOC analyzes crime incidents in real time and makes deployment recommendations based on data, intelligence, and information from the community.

Chicago Police District gang teams work under the direction of the area deputy chief within their areas to arrest street narcotics dealers. Officers arrest the street drug dealers, then pose as dealers to arrest and seize the vehicles of customers who come into the community to buy drugs. Officers also trace guns and go after offenders who illegally sell guns to criminals.

In the *Main 21 Initiative*, officers work with representatives from the U.S. Attorney's office, State's Attorney's office, Drug Enforcement Administration, Federal Bureau of Investigation, U.S. Department of Alcohol, Tobacco Firearms and Explosives, Illinois State Police, Illinois

Department of Corrections, and the Cook County Sheriff's office. The top twenty-one gang leaders are targeted with emphasis on those most involved with narcotics and violent activity.

The City is utilizing thirty high-visibility surveillance cameras (pods) to prevent violence before it occurs. Pods, marked with flashing blue lights and the CPD logo, are mounted on city light poles and are equipped with the ability to capture criminal activity blocks away.

The Chicago's Drug and Gang House Ordinance, 8-4-090 of the Municipal Code of Chicago, "Drug and gang houses, houses of prostitution and other disorderly houses," provides, in laymen's terms, that when there are two or more offenses of any nature upon a particular premise within a six-month period, or any one felony offense, the premise shall be deemed a "public nuisance." Once so declared, an owner must take appropriate abatement measures; failure to do so may result in fine, incarceration, or forfeiture of property.

Project Safe Neighborhoods (PSN) is a highly effective, cooperative effort between federal, state, and local law enforcement and the Chicago Crime Commission (as Community Engagement Partner) that seeks stiff federal prison time for felons who are in possession of firearms and works with parolees on job training and education so they won't re-offend. There are also strong PSN media and juvenile programs in place. Pilot Chicago PSN areas showed a 38 percent drop in their homicide rates.

To combat street gang members who are illegal immigrants, law enforcement has begun to work even more closely with Imigration and Customs Enforcement (ICE).

Narcotics Continues As Major Problem
Narcotics Continues As Major Problem

Source: The Chicago Crime Commission Gang Book

It is estimated in 2005 that Chicago street-gang narcotics sales is more than half a billion dollars a year. This kind of money would put a legitimate organization into the Fortune 500. The Chicago Police Department estimates that 68,000 gang members control Chicago's street-level sales of narcotics. In 1999, 83 percent of male arrestees tested positive for use of any drug within the two days before their arrest. Drug cases, 19,580 in 1995, amounted to more than 50 percent of all felonies charged in Cook County and more than all felonies charged in any year prior to 1998.

From 1990 to 2002, according to the Drug Abuse Warning Network (DAWN), cocaine in Chicago rose from 5,000 mentions in 1990 to over 16,000 mentions in 2002, greater than in any other city in the United States. The level of violence associated with cocaine, especially crack cocaine, exceeds all other drugs. Marijuana had around 1,400 DAWN mentions in 1993 and rose to over 5,000 mentions in 2000, and then slightly dropped in 2002 to about 4,500 mentions. Most law-enforcement sources in the Chicago metropolitan area in 2006 felt that marijuana distribution was again on the rise. Heroin-related hospital ED mentions in Chicago rose from about 2,000 in 1990 to over 12,000 in 2002. Chicago is unique among American cities in that heroin from all four source areas is available on a regular basis. Methamphetamine trafficking changed dramatically in the 1900s when Mexican drug cartels started operating super labs. This resulted in a significant increase in the supply of the drug.

New Faces of Organized Crime
New Faces of Organized Crime

Coupled with the crime originating from street-gang and traditional organized crime, the Chicago Crime Commission's report, *New Faces of Organized Crime*, released in 1997, noted increasing organized crime activity from other criminal groups. These groups include Asian, Eastern European, Nigerian, Polish, Colombian, Yugoslavian, Albanian, Croatian, and Serbian crime groups. These new organized-crime operations prey upon vulnerable members of their own groups, as well as the general public and operate in the Chicagoland area. During this time, although the number and variety of organized-crime groups was growing, law-enforcement resources and intelligence organizations devoted to defeating these organizations were being downsized.

Asian organized crime groups have been involved in murder, extortion, kidnapping, gambling, fraud, counterfeiting, prostitution, weapons trafficking, drug trafficking, money laundering, alien smuggling, and armed home invasions. A complex and fluid relationship exists between the Triads, Tongs, street gangs and American-Chinese organized crime groups. Eastern European organized crime travelers commit crimes that include ruse entry, burglary, home invasion, store diversion, home-repair systems, insurance fraud, fortune telling scams, welfare fraud, credit-card and check fraud, shoplifting, and the pigeon drop. Nigerian organized crime groups are active in drug trafficking, money laundering, check fraud, credit-card fraud, advance-fee fraud, financial fraud, mail-order scams and telemarketing scams. Polish organized crime groups are known to have been involved in auto theft, insurance scams, drug smuggling, counterfeiting, bank fraud, money laundering, robbery, forgery, bombings, and extortion.

Russian organized crime includes extortion, bribery, fuel tax scams, kidnapping, murder, auto theft, racketeering, money laundering, nuclear-weapons trafficking, drug trafficking, healthcare fraud, insurance fraud, telecommunications fraud, credit card fraud, prostitution, weapons trafficking, and counterfeiting. Yugoslavian, Albanian, Croatian, Serbian organized crime crews have been involved in commercial burglary, counterfeit indentification, narcotics trafficking, arson for profit, extortion, and money laundering.

"Family Secrets"

"Family Secrets"

Source: James W. Wagner

The "Family Secrets" investigation of the Chicago Outfit culminated on April 26, 2005 when the United States Attorney (USA) obtained a nine-count indictment of fourteen Chicago organized-crime members and associates. This landmark indictment charged a racketeering conspiracy involved in eighteen murders, spanning a time period from 1970 to 1986 and including some of the most infamous "hits" committed by the Outfit, such as Spilotro brothers' murders in 1986. The CCC provided archival background information, which assisted the investigative efforts leading to this indictment.

Two defendants, Frank Schweihs and Joseph Lombardo were not located and arrested immediately, but were tracked down by the FBI and taken into custody at the end of 2005 and the beginning of 2006. One murder in particular was very brutal. Joe Lombardo has been identified as a participant in the killing of Daniel Siefert. Siefert had been scheduled to be a witness against Lombardo and others and was shotgunned to death in front of his family. This prosecution should graphically and dramatically show that the Chicago Outfit is still a force to be very concerned about, particularly since they continue to resolve conflicts with murder.

Technology Connects Law Enforcement & Criminal Justice Systems

Technology Connects Law Enforcement & Criminal Justice Systems

Sources: "The Compiler, Fall 1995 Winter 1996: Illinois Criminal Justice Information Authority,"
The Chicago Crime Commission Gang Book, and
"Walking Prisons: The Developing Technology of Electronic Controls," CJ The Americas, Vol. 7, No. 1

At this time in history, law-enforcement professionals were challenged to keep pace with new technology. Information systems, electronic devices, and computer equipment and software had infiltrated the criminal justice system. In 1997, the Criminal History Records Information System, costing $4.5 million, enabled officers to file reports and get court and criminal information by computer. Officers were able to type in a suspect's physical description, method of operation, or geographical patterns to generate a computerized lineup of mug shots. This high-tech progress not only curbed searches for criminal rap sheets, it also decreased Chicago police officers' handwritten case reports by 3,500 documents a year. Technological advancement generated 1.4 million documents a year and reduced the time from thirty minutes to thirty seconds to identify an offender via fingerprints. The technologically advanced information system, ALERTS (Area-wide Law Enforcement Radio Terminal System), was the first system to link dozens of police agencies together for the collection and sharing of information and to coordinate crime-fighting. In 1992, 105 law-enforcement agencies in eight Illinois counties were part of the ALERTS network.

In 1994 an additional high-tech enhancement increased the efficiency of how law enforcement officers utilize information. Forensic image processing, with its ability to clarify blurry and jumpy images, hit the courtroom, revolutionizing evidentiary videotapes. Once slow frame rates with poor quality optics, the security camera market ballooned. Law-enforcement equipment benefited from the new technology. Foams, Sticky, and Fog, were used for peacekeeping operations in Somalia and in U.S. prisons. New strobe-and-goggle technology was designed to darken when officers were exposed to bright light and to blind and disorient subjects during drug raids or assaults. The Magic Wand, or the Fingerprint Visualization System, allowed investigators to lift and develop prints from non-porous surfaces at the scene of the crime within seconds and to apprehend suspects quickly. Tracking devices for offenders were created early in this decade in hope of decreasing incarceration costs. Incarceration initial cost was $100,000, additional years were about $25,000 per inmate. The Electronic Supervision Program participants wore an anklet transponder electronically linked to a monitoring station. This program allowed criminals to work, attend school, or participate in job-skills programs. Some believed that house arrest would encourage rehabilitation because inmates reside in a family setting unexposed to other criminals.

Alcohol Tobacco Firearms & Explosives (ATF) operates an on line process, the F-TIP System, which is unique to Illinois and allows police to trace guns to the original purchaser. ATF also provides a national Integrated Ballistic Information System (IBIS). IBIS equipment allows firearms technicians to acquire digital images of the markings made by a firearm on bullets and cartridge casings; the images then undergo automated initial comparison. If a high-confidence candidate emerges, firearms examiners compare the original evidence to confirm a match, thereby allowing law enforcement to discover links between crimes more quickly.

CCIJIS & IIJIS
CCIJIS & IIJIS

The tragic events of September 11, 2001 serve to underscore the need to link justice systems and close dangerous loopholes in overburdened systems. The Cook County (CCIJIS) and the Illinois Integrated Justice Information Systems (IIJIS) are both plans for exchanging critical information between public-safety decision-makers in a complete, accurate, and timely manner, which will improve decision-making and the quality of justice while enhancing public safety. CCIJIS and IIJIS partners represent justice agencies spanning the full spectrum of the justice enterprise, including law enforcement, prosecution, defense, the judiciary, corrections, the Chicago Crime Commission, and other relevant non-justice agencies at city, county, and state levels.

An IIJIS survey of 130 Illinois police departments, thirty-one circuit court clerk's offices, twenty-nine probation departments, twenty-seven sheriff's offices, and twenty-two state's attorney's offices clearly illustrates the need and critical importance of this work. A few of the many findings of this survey are as follows: 1) of the 1,139 types of information exchanges between criminal-justice agencies documented in this study, 91 percent were paper-based; 2) of the eighty-six different categories of information surveyed, only twenty-four of the data types accounted for seventy percent of the information transferred; 3) certain subject identifiers and arrest charge data were redundantly entered, as many as fifteen times, into several different systems.

In 2005, IIJIS: 1) worked to develop a privacy policy that is being utilized on a national level as a model; 2) developed the concept of operations for an Illinois Homeland Security scenario; 3) released an electronic newsletter and held an IIJIS summit; and 4) identified orders of protection and warrants, booking and rap sheets, and standard police reports as priority integration areas and began developing business plans for each. IIJIS advocates the use of a recently accepted national XML global language. The use of this global language will enable systems on a local, state, and federal level to connect to each other in time.

In 2005, ICLEAR, a system developed jointly by the Chicago Police Department and the Illinois State Police (ISP) and supported by IIJIS was announced. The Chicago Police Department and the ISP developed a partnership that will leverage the existing financial, technological, and human resources of the CPD and the ISP to develop a system for the collection, maintenance, and dissemination of criminal-justice data in Illinois. This system builds on the power of CPD's existing CLEAR system and the ISP's LEADS System to create one integrated technology solution to serve all law enforcement in the state.

Computer Chips: New Theft Target
Computer Chips: New Theft Target

Source: Elizabeth Van Ella

Law-enforcement officials were not the only ones benefiting from technology, however. In the mid-90s street gangs and organized-crime groups were stealing computer chips costing the United States $8 billion a year with an expected increase to about $20 billion by the year 2000. Most of the downloading of stolen information and software produced untold damage and disaster, and it continues to do so today.

Computer Crime, Identity Theft & Terrorism
Computer Crime, Identity Theft & Terrorism

Source: Chicago gets FBI lab tuned to computers by Christine Tatum, Chicago Tribune, February 10, 2003

In 2003, computer crime rates exploded as conspiracies involving forty or more computers with victims from all over the world became common, and attacks on hundreds of thousands of computers worldwide became possible. Fear of global terrorism spread and the need to monitor and control shared global information became practical, prudent, and sensible to identify conspirators. Chicago examiners, expert in navigating computer operating systems, recover data from damaged, deleted, or encrypted files, while collecting, preserving, and examining digital information from crime scenes. In March 2003, Chicago was tapped by the FBI to gather evidence from hard drives, cellphones, and handheld devices to become part of a national network of crime labs dedicated to computer forensics. A $2.3 million, 15,000-square-foot facility on Canal Street, one of three labs, investigates global terrorism, identity theft, Internet attacks, and trafficking of child pornography technology. Gathering evidence from technological devices has become as important as dissecting a crime scene or interviewing a suspect.

Internet Web Sights & Software Inform Chicago's Citizens
Internet Web Sights & Software Inform Chicago's Citizens

Source: _Crime data is a mouse click away_ by Frank Main, Chicago Sun-Times, September 28, 2000

In 2000 the Citizen ICAM Website was created. It identifies crime hot-spots by using a colored map to categorize burglary, theft, and damage to property. By typing in a home address, users are able to pinpoint where a crime took place, when it took place, what classification of crime it was, and for police officers, who committed the crime. In 2002, sex offenders on probation began having Cyber Sentinel software, originally developed to record chat-room conversations so that parents could monitor their child's activity, installed on their computers. The software alerts the offender's parole officer via email if the offender goes to a prohibited Website, uses sexually explicit language, or uses phrases common to online predators. Citizens can also access information through the Chicago Crime Commission Website www.chicagocrimecommission.org and the Chicago Police Department Website.

Thursday, February 2, 1995   **Daily Herald**

.each passing day.   gar said.   torney who has represented the ...

Gangs are everywhere

Crime commission report targets 'public enemy No. 1'

BY JIM ALLEN
Daily Herald Staff Writer

From the decaying neighborhoods of Elgin to the bucolic countryside of Harvard, street gangs are infiltrating virtually every suburb, according to a Chicago Crime Commission report released Wednesday.

Gangs, with membership ranks swelling toward 100,000, are so threatening to society that they have earned the title of "public enemy No. 1," said Chicago Crime Commission President Donald G. Mulack, resurrecting the words once used to describe Prohibition-era crime boss Al Capone.

But today's gangs make Capone seem tame, Mulack said, because these merchants of drugs, guns and death don't hesitate to embrace the young. And where the criminals of yesteryear often operated in the shadows, today's gangs are working the playgrounds and broad lawns of suburban subdivisions.

"There is no suburban town that is immune from gang activity," Mulack said, pointing to how the new report had found that virtually every Chicago area police department acknowledged seeing criminal activity involving at least one street gang.

The new report, designed to be used as a guide for community groups, identifies 116 gangs

> ## "There is no suburban town that is immune from gang activity."
> — Chicago Crime Commission President Donald G. Mulack

operating in the region, ranging from neighborhood organizations to motorcycle clubs. Included in the report are photos of young convicts—displayed in the same spot the Crime Commission formerly saved for the aging dons of organized crime operations.

The report covers hand signs, graffiti logos, colors, affiliations and other details of gang organizations, including how they are typically structured, what names they use and what warning signs parents should observe.

The report also lists different police contacts and organizations that parents can call.

Yet for all the concern for suburban gangs, Mulack conceded that of the reputed membership, most of the "30,000 to 40,000 hard-core" gang members reside in the city, and most of the "wannabes" or fledgling groups are in the suburbs.

Notably, the report openly identifies different gangs by name, which marks a major change for police and media, which for more than a decade operated with an unwritten code of avoiding the public mention of gang affiliation.

The fear was that gangs would only thrive on publicity and increase their bloody conquests to in the name of infamy.

Mulack said the commission began compiling the report at the

Graffiti is only one sign of gang presence in the suburbs.
Daily Herald file photo

Crime Commission targets gangs

With the exception of tiny Bannockburn in Lake County, the Chicago Crime Commission says police are reporting gang members or gang activity in every suburban community. Some of the more surprising sites and the number of gangs identified were:

Town	Gangs contacted or identified by police
Barrington Hills	6
Wheaton	2
Lincolnshire	6
Naperville	6
Glencoe	2
Geneva	4
Hawthorn Woods	8
Lake in the Hills	4

Source: Chicago Crime Commission
Daily Herald Graphic

Growth and impact of gangs*

- 100,000 gang members in Chicago metropolitan area (30,000 to 50,000 "hard-core" members)
- 125 different gangs
- 129 gang-related murders
- 177 drive-by shootings
- 8,842 drug-related offenses by gang members

*1993 figures

behest of Chicago police Chief Matt Rodriguez, who cited the growing number of gang-related crimes in the city in 1993, including 129 homicides, 177 drive-by shootings, 533 robberies, 3,221 beatings and shootings, and 8,842 drug offenses. "Gangs, drugs and guns were the three main factors behind the 930 murders in 1994," Rodriguez said.

In a letter included in the report, Rodriguez endorsed the

idea of revealing the gangs: "The compilation of information and photos of these identified gang members ... will go a long way in helping to eradicate this criminal element."

Mulack said another reason that the issue needs to be addressed is that the gang members are beginning to seek political power.

Mulack cited the aldermanic candidacy of convicted felon and former gang member Wallace "Gator" Bradley. A former enforcer for a gang, Bradley admits he remains in contact with the imprisoned reputed leader of the gang, Larry Hoover.

But Bradley maintains that he is not involved in a gang, has rehabilitated himself and deserves a chance to serve the public.

INSIDE

Parents can help stem gang tide

Local experts agree that most parents do not know if their children are gang members, but they note that being aware of subtle warning signs can help them to identify the problem and work to solve it — Page 9.

Should gangs be identified?

Among the recommendations made by the Chicago Crime Commission's attack on gangs is a policy to identify gangs by name and other characteristics. That about-face from current policies, however, has met with mixed opinions — Page 9.

The media reports on information provided in the CCC's 1995 *Gangs: Public Enemy No. 1* report.

Source: Daily Herald, Chicago. Reproduced from the February 2, 1995 issue by permission of The Daily Herald, Arlington Heights, IL.

Article continues on next page.

Article continues from previous page.

Gangs in our communities

Labeling street gangs as "Public Enemy No. 1," the Chicago Crime Commission has identified about 125 gangs that operate in Chicago and the suburbs. Below is a listing of the number of gangs reported by local police to be currently active or occasionally present in each town.

Northwest Suburbs

Arlington Heights	10
Barrington	5
Barrington Hills	6
Bartlett	6
Buffalo Grove	2
Des Plaines	8
Elk Grove Village	9
Hanover Park	10
Hoffman Estates	11
Mount Prospect	7
Palatine	7
Prospect Heights	8
Rolling Meadows	3
Schaumburg	7
Streamwood	4
Wheeling	4

Lake County

Antioch	2
Bannockburn	0
Deerfield	5
Fox Lake	4
Grayslake	4
Gurnee	7
Hawthorn Woods	8
Highland Park	2
Highwood	1
Kildeer	4
Lake Forest	3
Lake Zurich	5
Libertyville	2
Lincolnshire	6
Mundelein	3
North Chicago	8
Round Lake Beach	4
Vernon Hills	4
Waukegan	10
Zion	6

DuPage County

Addison	8
Aurora	11
Bensenville	5
Bloomingdale	6
Carol Stream	6
Downers Grove	7
Elmhurst	9
Glendale Heights	6
Glen Ellyn	8
Hinsdale	1
Itasca	4
Lisle	7
Lombard	8
Naperville	6
Oak Brook	6
Oakbrook Terrace	7
Roselle	7
Villa Park	4
Warrenville	4
Wheaton	2
West Chicago	6
Winfield	2
Wood Dale	2

Fox Valley

Algonquin	4
Batavia	6
Carpentersville	7
Cary	4
Crystal Lake	3
East Dundee	3
Elburn	2
Elgin	7
Fox River Grove	2
Geneva	4
Huntley	1
Lake In The Hills	4
McHenry	4
St. Charles	6
South Elgin	3
West Dundee	3
Woodstock	6

Source: Local police departments, Chicago Crime Commission

Gang report available
For a copy of the Chicago Crime Commission's report, "Public Enemy Number One — Gangs," call the commission at 312-372-0101. A nominal cost plus postage and handling will be charged.

Daily Herald Graphic

gangs in the workplace

60% of 75 Chicago area corporations that responded to a CCC survey are aware of a gang presence in their geographical area, 24% have noticed graffiti or strange markings inside or outside their facility, but only 3% of those surveyed reported having a Zero Tolerance Policy regarding gangs.

It is not a myth... gang activity has surfaced in major institutions and corporations in the Chicago area. Consider the following examples of true stories:

Case one. When a national company based in Chicago discovered missing computers valued at up to a half million dollars, an investigation revealed that known gang members had been hired by the company for the M.I.S. department and shipping/-receiving department. The stolen computers were being fenced at a local store front. It was also determined that these same gang members were selling drugs to their fellow employees.

Case two. The leader of a notorious street gang was admitted to a Chicago hospital after being shot. Members of a rival gang, who had been hired by the hospital for legitimate positions, began to threaten the patient. Members of the wounded leader's gang attempted to enter the hospital to protect him. Quick intervention by hospital security prevented a potentially deadly situation with many innocent victims.

In conjunction with the National Gang Crime Research Center, the CCC's White Collar Crime Committee surveyed 500 Chicago area corporations to determine the extent of gang infiltration in the corporate sector and to determine the level of awareness concerning gang activity. This is the first step to the committee's strategy to promote awareness of gang problems in the corporate workplace and to educate businesses on how to avoid these problems. Seventy-five surveys have been returned. Results are listed in the highlighted area on this page.

These results, which indicate minimal awareness in the corporate sector are not surprising. Street gang infiltration is an emergent trend, however most businesses are unaware of the problem and its implications. Thus, the CCC will strive to better inform the business community in areas such as gang-related policies and procedures for large and small businesses. This effort was begun in 1996, when the White Collar Crime Committee presented a Gangs in the Workplace Seminar at the Chicago Chamber of Commerce Small Business Expo.

"A business leader has a civic obligation to deal with crime. It is the most serious threat to our freedom."

Chamber of Commerce Leader

Gangs in the Workplace Survey Results

The CCC White Collar Crime Committee & the National Gang Crimes Research Center surveyed 500 Chicago area corporations regarding street gang awareness and activity. 75 corporations responded. The results indicate:

▶ 15% report that employees have been victimized by gang crime in the last year;

▶ 10% of respondents are aware of street gang activity within the company;

▶ 7% are aware of employees who are members of a street gang;

▶ 24% have noticed graffiti or strange markings inside or outside their facility;

▶ 76% of security personnel and 89% of key management staff have not had training in gang identification and awareness;

▶ 81% of respondents perform background checks; of those companies, 65% of the staff responsible for performing background checks have not been trained in gang identification and awareness;

▶ In 23% of companies who responded, an active gang member would be eligible for employment;

▶ 81% of companies who responded do not have a dress code prohibiting gang colors or symbols;

▶ In 70% of the companies who responded, flashing gang signs while working would *not* be in violation of written employee policies;

▶ 91% of companies do not have a written Zero Tolerance Policy regarding gangs.

Source: Chicago Crime Commission Action Alert

Hi-Tech Crime: The Dope of the 90s

by Elizabeth Van Ella
Chair, CCC White Collar Crime Committee

For street gangs and organized crime groups, computer chips have become the dope of the 1990's. Small, portable, easily concealed and legal in one's possession, they are worth more money by weight than drugs. The Engineering and Safety Service group reports technology-related crimes cost up to **$8 billion** a year and are expected to increase to **$200 billion** by the year 2000. The FBI's computer crime division estimates the average technology theft cost at $450,000. These parts can be stolen through shipping and receiving, warehouses, in mail rooms, from trucks in transit and customs shipments, and are easily concealed in a lunch thermos, trashbins, etc. Any office that uses electronic equipment can be a target.

Once stolen, they are almost untraceable. Of the 80 million "486" computer chips currently in use, fewer than 2% have serial numbers, a fact that has attracted organized crime groups. After all, it is not a crime to walk around with a suitcase full of central processing units. One million dollars worth of chips fits in the back of a van. A hard drive, once the size of a Volkswagen, is now no thicker than a wallet. Additionally, within the span of 72 hours, stolen chips, memories and other components can change owners as many as 18 times. After these transactions they begin to gain a paper history and the appearance of legitimacy. One customs official reports chasing a single shipment across three states and two countries within eight hours.

Hi-tech crime is a global problem. The computer chip is the most valuable commodity on the international market. In 1995 alone, there were armed robberies or thefts in plants in Scotland, France, Ireland and Malaysia. When five bandits blew through the front door of Top Line Electronics, they knew exactly what they wanted. Brandishing shotguns and semiautomatic weapons on their way towards the computer assembly room, the thieves were after flecks of processed silicon the size of a baby's thumbnail.

These gangs generally work with someone on the inside, a security guard or temporary employee, who directs them to the computer chips. In excess of 50% of full high-valued component thefts have been traced to "inside jobs" conducted by gangs successfully masquerading as temps. High-tech thieves send in scouts, job applicants, employees or temporary workers to learn floor plans and storage areas and to help demobilize alarm systems. Inside theft can extend over a long period with few or no deterrents. One company took a write-down on missing inventory each month, until it extended beyond $50,000 monthly. Inventory shortages are not insurable. Sun Microsystems lost $5 million in two chip thefts. They believe it was an inside job.

The potential for disaster from component theft is great. Often, components are stolen out of storage bins containing rejects and flawed devices before they can be destroyed. These flawed components can end up in airplanes, medical equipment and automotive equipment, potentially causing untold damage or disaster.

The other issue here is trade secrets, the lifeblood of American industry, with potential losses far exceeding the actual value of the components. The United States spends ten times more in Research and Development than any other country and U.S. companies have become the prime target of foreign entities looking to short cut the R&D process. Theft of proprietary information has increased 260% since 1985. At Imogen, an employee stole the source code, changed identifiers and sold secrets abroad. In 1995, an Intel employee fled to Argentina and sold identifiers to a competitor. This employee actually videotaped Intel's screens because he was unable to download from home.

Remarkably, there is no federal trade secret statute. FBI Director, Louis Freeh is proposing one to Congress. In the meantime, lawyers must rely on old statutes.

Source: Chicago Crime Commission Action Alert

METAMORPHOSIS
justice improvement

Although the criminal justice system has expanded over the past five years to meet the challenges of a growing crime problem, much of this expansion has not addressed the threat of serious and violent crime. Limited personnel and resources are being depleted by relatively minor cases which will choke the system unless our efforts are redirected. The CCC's *Making Room for Justice: New Priorities for the Criminal Justice System* released in March 1996, focuses on solutions which will greatly increase the effectiveness of our law enforcement efforts.

Drug offenders who are guilty only of possession of minor amounts of drugs **with no intent to distribute and no other criminal activity** should be diverted to the misdemeanor court system where legal sanctions can be quickly coordinated with treatment for drug dependence. A shocking number of **one gram/simple possession** cases are clogging our court system. The concentration of our police, courts, corrections and other forensic resources against the lowest level drug charges deludes the public into thinking that we are making progress in fighting crime by overwhelming us with minor cases. As one corrections official told a CCC member, "You will never punish hard until you punish smart." Accordingly, the CCC recommends that felony courts, jail cells and other resources be focused against the most serious felons, including drug abusers who are guilty of other felonies or who are engaged in drug dealing.

There is an urgent need to expand the number of criminal courts. In a system where only the defense can appeal a finding on the merits, society will best protect itself with a professional and adequately staffed trial court system. If due process is sacrificed because of overwhelming caseload, judges may attempt to limit appeals by issuing more lenient sentences. If courts do not have adequate time to hear cases, the balance of power in plea negotiations will shift to the defense. If the courts are overwhelmed, society - not the criminal - is the loser. To assure that justice will best be served, the CCC proposed the four major steps as outlined in the highlighted box on this page.

The CCC is working to implement these recommendations. Since the release of the report, **legislative options and strategies** have been discussed with Illinois State Senator *John Cullerton* (D), Illinois State Senator *Judy Biggert* (R), Illinois State Senator *Kathy Parker* (R), and *Matthew Jones* – Legal Counsel for the Judiciary Committee of the Illinois State Senate. **Courts needs** have been studied further with *Mary Griffin* – Chief Coordinator, Bureau of Public Safety and Judicial Coordination (Cook County), and *John Stroger* – President, Cook County Board of Commissioners. *William Quinlan* – Chairman, Judicial Advisory Council and *James O'Rourke* – Executive Director, Judicial Advisory Council have met with the committee to discuss **funding issues.** Also reviewed in greater depth, is the issue of **intermediate sanctions and alternatives to incarceration.** This was discussed with *Nancy Martin* – Chief Probation Officer, Adult Probation and *John Prinzi*, Public Information Officer, Adult Probation.

Thomas B. Kirkpatrick, CCC Executive Director, **testified on November 15 at the Cook County Board Budget Hearing** on court facility needs and has been appointed by President Stroger to a committee to review and recommend court facility needs.

Courts Committee Report proposes:

1 The Illinois State Legislature should reclassify simple possession of small amounts (1 gram or less) of cocaine and heroin, **with no intent to distribute and no other criminal activity,** from a Class 4 felony to a Class A misdemeanor (a volume of cases which is equivalent to eleven full-time felony courts). The purpose is to utilize resources to fight more violent criminals.

2 The Cook County Board should increase the number of felony courtrooms (including personnel and other resources) currently available from 48 to 69 (if #1 is implemented) or to 80 (if #1 is not implemented), and plan for annual incremental increases.

3 The Illinois State Legislature and the Illinois Supreme Court should encourage the expansion and utilization of **intermediate sanctions** for appropriate non-violent and non-threatening offenders. It is also essential that crucial pretrial and pre-sentencing information regarding defendants be made available to the court in a timely manner.

4 The Cook County Judicial Advisory Council should review the hodge-podge, patchwork quilt of state, county and city funding of the court system, and recommend systematic improvements.

NOTE: The Legislative Committee is assisting the Court's Committee to implement these recommendations.

The report has received the endorsement of:

The Illinois State Bar Association (in concept) and the Chicago Bar Association.

Source: Chicago Crime Commission Action Alert

Source: Chicago Crime Commission New Faces of Organized Crime

Spring/Summer 1997

Chicago Crime Commission
ACTION ALERT

A Not For Profit Citizen's Organization Combatting Crime In The Greater Chicago Area Since 1919

New Faces in Organized Crime
– CCC Report To Be Released In August –

In August, the Chicago Crime Commission will release its long awaited report *New Faces in Organized Crime*. The 120 page report provides both a conceptual overview of organized crime and specific, although not comprehensive, information on many of the organized criminal groups currently preying on businesses and residents in the greater Chicago area.

New Faces:
The modus operandi and analysis of the development of emerging organized crime groups, including Asians, Eastern European Criminal Travelers, Nigerians, Polish, Russians, South American groups and YACS (Yogoslavian, Albanian, Croatian, Serbian) organized crime groups.

These groups range from highly sophisticated international criminal organizations involved in corporate

"The report was designed not only as a tool for businesses and individuals seeking to protect themselves from becoming a target of organized crime, but also to be a resource for law enforcement," said Donald Mulack, Chairman of the CCC.

kidnaping and extortion, murder-for-hire, and drug trafficking to local burglary rings.

The report considers the dramatic shifts in social, political and economic systems around the world, as well as extraordinary advances in communication technology and transportation, which have opened new markets for organized criminal activity and new methods of operation. Over the last few years, several major trends in organized crime have emerged, which apply to both traditional and emerging organized crime groups, including street gangs:

- Organized crime is no longer confined to neighborhood, or even national boundaries. Nearly every organized crime group now operates to some degree on a worldwide scale.

- Organized crime groups are forging alliances with one another to capitalize on the strengths of each.

- Organized crime groups are exploiting increasingly sophisticated new markets that jeopardize international and corporate security, including selling nuclear weapons to rogue nations and infiltrating sensitive computer networks.

- More than ever before, organized crime groups are investing their

ill-gotten resources in legitimate businesses as a means to launder large sums of money.

What has not changed is how these groups secure their power. Organized crime cannot exist without the protection provided by corrupt public officials and without tainting our political processes and public institutions. For a price, these organizations ensure that their gambling enterprises remain untouched, their businesses get special treatment on regulatory issues, their associates and families can draw public paychecks for little or no work, and that mob-friendly judges are elected to fix their cases.

Source: Chicago Crime Commission Action Alert

TUESDAY, AUGUST 2, 2005 **Daily Herald** SECTION 3

Suburban Living

New charges dust off old skeletons of THE MOB IN THE 'BURBS

By Robert McCoppin
Daily Herald Staff Writer

Chuck Fagan has seen the effects of organized crime, and they aren't pretty.

As a deputy for the Lake County Sheriff's Office, Chuck Fagan looked into an attempted mob hit in 1982.

The victim, Nicholas Sarillo Sr., was driving in Wauconda when an explosion flattened his van and sent it off the road.

The blast imbedded a heavy coil spring in the victim's neck. Sarillo was injured, but survived. Though suffering and his face covered in soot, he remained silent.

Detectives suspected the explosion was mob-related, but Sarillo didn't want to talk about it.

"It looked like a cartoon face, all in black," remembered Fagan, now chief of police in Antioch. "But when you try to talk to these fellas, it's like talking to a wall. Even in that pain and agony, they've got nothing to say."

A recent round of federal indictments describes such an incident, though it does not identify the victim.

The indictments turn the soil on buried memories of the heyday of the mob. The charges demonstrate again that the Outfit has had a home in the suburbs since long before TV's Tony Soprano moved to New Jersey.

Of the 18 murders charged in the federal "Family Secrets" investigation, four occurred in the suburbs.

Of 11 defendants, six lived in the suburbs, including the alleged leader of La Cosa Nostra in Chicago, James Marcello of Lombard.

The murders occurred between 1970 and 1986. While the indictments have received a lot of media attention, they only touch the surface of the history of organized crime outside Chicago.

A litany of mob-related stories has gone down in the suburbs — murder at the Rouse House, allegations of mob activity at Sam Giancana's Villa Venice and a vendetta to the death between rival gang members.

A quick look back shows organized crime has always gone where money can be made through gambling, sex, juice loans or illegal substances — even in the quiet, leafy subdivisions of suburbia.

Capo Capone

Even before Fox Lake was incorporated in 1907, the village was known as a destination for drinking and gambling, according to the Chicago Historical Society.

After reform in Chicago moved vice to suburban roadhouses, business flourished during Prohibition in the Roaring '20s.

Al Capone spent time at the Mineola Hotel in Fox Lake, which still displays his hat in a glass case in the lounge. Capone's rival, George "Bugs" Moran, supplied booze to Lake County, according to news accounts from that time.

In 1930, a year after the St. Valentine's Day Massacre in Chicago, five people were shot and three killed in a

From left, mobsters Michael Spilotro, Anthony Spilotro, Al Capone, Sam Giancana and Ernest Rocco Infelise all lived, died or did business in Chicago's suburbs.

mob-related hit at the Manning Hotel in Fox Lake.

The Fox Lake Massacre was the worst incident of Prohibition-era gang violence in Lake County. And the crime was never solved.

The Manning Hotel still stands, but is now a home next to the KK Hamsher Funeral Home on Pistakee Lake.

Terrible Touhy

Capone's reign didn't go unchallenged, according to mob historians. Roger "The Terrible" Touhy, son of a Chicago cop, stood up to Capone, but paid the price.

As crime author Richard Lindberg tells the tale, Touhy lived in Des Plaines, and bootlegged beer and slot machines across the Northwest suburbs during Prohibition.

He refused to reduce his price when Capone claimed his kegs were

See **MOB** on **PAGE 3**

Before Sam Giancana's Villa Venice near Wheeling burned to the ground in 1967, the Rat Pack played a command performance there.

The Rouse mansion near Libertyville was the scene of a domestic double-murder before it became a mob casino and scene of a hit. It burned down in 2002.

The Roman House, on Milwaukee Avenue near Lincolnshire, once featured nude dancers. It's been demolished and the site is now near a

HERALD FILE PHOTOS

Source: Daily Herald, Chicago. Article continues on next page.
Reprinted from the August 2, 2005 issue by permission of The Daily Herald, Arlington Heights, Illinois.

Mob: Villa Venice club somehow somehow got top talent

Continued from Page 1

leaking.

In retaliation, Capone used his influence to set up Touhy, Lindberg said.

In 1933, John "Jake the Barber" Factor, the brother of cosmetics czar Max Factor and an acquaintance of Capone, claimed to be the victim of a kidnapping and fingered Touhy.

Touhy was sent to prison in Joliet, and busted out at gunpoint in 1942, but was caught and sentenced to 199 years.

Years later, a federal judge concluded Factor had fabricated his own kidnapping and freed Touhy.

In 1959 — just 23 days after getting out — Touhy was gunned down in Chicago, presumably by a Capone gang member. His dying words, according to The People's Almanac, were, "I've been expecting it. The (expletive deleted) never forget."

Villa Venice

In the 1960s, mob boss Sam "Momo" Giancana ran a restaurant and nightclub on Milwaukee Avenue in Wheeling called the Villa Venice Supper Club.

Located where Allgauer's Restaurant now sits, near the Des Plaines River, the Villa Venice had a boat landing with Venetian lanterns on the banks, where patrons could ride in a gondola.

For an out-of-the-way club, the Villa Venice somehow got top-flight talent, including Frank Sinatra, Sammy Davis Jr. and Dean Martin, and then-popular singer Eddie Fisher.

Sinatra's daughter Tina wrote in her book that to repay Giancana for help getting the union vote for John F. Kennedy in 1960, her father brought the Rat Pack to do several shows at the Villa Venice.

One of the shows is still available on a CD, "The Rat Pack — Live at the Villa Venice."

In 1967, the theater and restaurant burned down in a mysterious fire.

Bill Hein, a member of the Wheeling Historical Society, was at the Rat Pack show. He said the club was gorgeous, with satin ceilings and tapestries, and the show was fabulous.

Hein, a former volunteer firefighter in Wheeling, was also there the night Villa Venice burned down.

"I've never seen anything go up so quick in my life," he said.

Giancana was shot and killed while cooking in his basement kitchen in Oak Park in 1975.

In the years Villa Venice was open, according to crimemagazine.com, the FBI estimated the supper club and gambling at the nearby Quonset Hut grossed over $3 million.

Lake corruption

By the 1970s and '80s, mob influence peaked in Lake County, in particular, according to investigators like Bob Schrader, who became head of the Lake County Sheriff's first organized crime unit.

Mob watchers attribute the rise in crime to expansion and corruption.

The stage was set in 1975, when then-Sheriff Orville "Pat" Clavey and former Lake County Board Chairman Ronald Coles were charged with taking payments from nude dance clubs.

Clavey went to prison, and Coles got probation.

In ensuing years, the Joseph Ferriola mob crew expanded to take over all vice in Lake County.

One of the crew's more colorful characters was Salvatore DeLaurentis of Inverness — known as "Solly D" — a stylish businessman who ran a liquor store, bowling alley and pizza parlor in Island Lake.

According to federal prosecutors, DeLaurentis worked for Ernest "Rocco" Infelise, underboss for the Ferriola crew.

According to court documents, Infelise said he bribed someone in the Lake County Sheriff's Department to notify him in advance of raids.

Under his oversight, card and dice games were played in bars, and juice loans charged 10 percent per month or week.

Prostitution ran out of two notorious strip joints, federal prosecutors said: the Roman House on Milwaukee Avenue near Lincolnshire, and The Cheetah on Half Day Road, as well as Businessman's Consultants adult bookstore in Mundelein.

All of those businesses have long since closed.

Investigators estimated that the Ferriola crew ran gambling in Lake County from 1974 through 1988, with profits of more than $10 million.

Much of the money was hidden in real estate, including condominiums in Addison, investigators say.

The Rouse House

Gambling and much worse took place in one particularly cursed home, known as the Rouse House.

It all began on June 6, 1980, when Darlene and Bruce Rouse were killed in bed in their man-

Article continues on next page.

Source: Daily Herald, Chicago.

Article continues from previous page.

sion located on Milwaukee Avenue north of Libertyville.

The murders went unsolved for 15 years, until their son, Billy, confessed, in one case that was not mob-related.

In the meantime, the house was home to another murder involving a different family.

By 1982, prosecutors said, the mob had bought the house and turned it into a casino, with fixed craps and blackjack. They allegedly raked in more than a half-million dollars in two weeks.

When independent book-maker Robert Plummer, who was not connected to the games at the Rouse House, refused to give a cut to the mob, William Jahoda, a federal informant, testified that he lured Plummer inside the Rouse house.

Jahoda said he heard Plummer cry out and saw him pinned against a wall by mob members. Plummer's body was later found in the trunk of a car at a Holiday Inn in Mundelein.

Infelise and DeLaurentis were later convicted in the case and sent to prison, where DeLaurentis remains and Infelise died just last month.

Ferriola died in 1989, though his operation continued.

In 2002, though the house was vacant, the rambling, 13-room, $600,000 "Murder Mansion" burned to the ground.

Playboy Hal Smith

Hal Smith was known as the playboy of Prospect Heights after the IRS found $600,000 in gambling proceeds in a raid on his pillared mansion in 1983.

After the raid, according to federal court documents, DeLaurentis stepped up efforts to get a piece of Smith's book-making.

When Smith refused and responded with a string of ethnic slurs, DeLaurentis warned him he'd be "trunk music," according to federal prosecutors.

In 1985, Jahoda, the federal informant, met Smith at a bar and brought him back to his house on Hilltop Road in Long Grove.

Jahoda testified that he last saw Smith slumped on the floor with Infelise and others around him.

Smith's body was found in the trunk of his car at the Arlington Park Hilton. Smith had been strangled, beaten, cut and had his throat slit.

The Spilotros

Tony "The Ant" Spilotro handled the Chicago mob's business in Las Vegas, but after Outfit leaders were convicted of skimming money from the casinos, Tony and his brother Michael disappeared in 1986, federal prosecutors said.

Their badly beaten bodies were found in a cornfield in Indiana, where the coroner said they had been buried alive.

The infamous incident became the basis for a scene in the movie "Casino," in which Joe Pesci played a role similar to The Ant.

Now the story has changed slightly to have happened in the suburbs, according to the recent federal indictment.

An FBI agent testified that a mob informant said James Marcello had brought the Spilotro brothers to a basement near Bensenville, by Route 83 and Irving Park Road, under the ruse that they were to be elevated in rank within the mob.

In the basement, the Spilotros were jumped, beaten and strangled — and then buried in the cornfield.

That was then ...

All these crimes go back almost 20 years or more.

The mob's low profile since then raises the question of how much of it remains.

The FBI said the latest indictments put a "hit" on the mob, so the organization remains alive, but smaller.

Sports and video gambling make big money, and unions and political connections provide jobs and benefits.

Most recently, the FBI alleges the mob is trying to get a piece of the proposed casino in Rosemont, a charge village officials strongly dispute.

The most dangerous aspect of the mob, according to former Chicago Crime Commission investigator Wayne Johnson, is its corruption of government through contributions, bribes and sponsored judges.

With investigators' attention focused on past crimes, homeland security, community policing and street gangs, Johnson worries, "Nobody is looking at these guys anymore."

• *The Daily Herald relied on interviews, newspaper accounts, court documents and information from Illinois Police & Sheriff's News and organized crime watchdog groups for this account.*

The Cheetah II in Wheeling was destroyed by arson in 1982. It was the successor strip club to The Cheetah in Half Day, which was the scene of two attempted bombings before being converted to an MRI center.

Source: Daily Herald, Chicago

WEDNESDAY, JUNE 28, 2006 • CHICAGO SUN-TIMES

ON THE PULSE

48% of Americans today say the federal government should be involved in promoting moral values, down from 60% in 1996. –GALLUP.COM

TO REACH US: letters@suntimes.com

CHICAGO SUN-TIMES
AN INDEPENDENT NEWSPAPER

John Cruickshank • Publisher
John Barron • Editor in Chief
Steve Huntley • Editorial Page Editor
Don Hayner • Managing Editor

Regional cooperation needed to fight gang problems

If anyone still thinks of street gangs as a problem unique to the inner city, a new report from the Chicago Crime Commission should disabuse them of that notion. Included in the commission's report on area gangs is a survey of local police departments that found that the street gang problem is widespread, on the rise and in some cases quite large. With the exception of a few affluent or outlying suburbs, almost every department in the survey reported street gang activity.

That isn't news to suburban police, of course. Some of the larger suburbs have been fighting gangs for years, and many already cooperate to solve the problem. But the survey is a useful primer for anyone who doesn't already know the area's gang landscape, and it can only help police coordinate their efforts from suburb to suburb.

The survey found that 31 of the 81 departments that responded reported an increase in gang activity, including large suburbs such as Naperville, Wheaton, Evanston, Mundelein and Cicero, and smaller ones such as Woodstock, Stickney and Lynwood. Most suburbs that reported gang activity said they have encountered more than just one gang in their communities. Gangs bring crime with them — most frequently drug activities but also violent crimes that go hand in hand with drugs. As gangs take root, their activities "become broader and more sophisticated" — and police had better be prepared for the growth, the survey warns.

The report's authors say the suburban migration is fueled in part by the destruction of Chicago's public housing high-rises and also a perception among gang members that police in smaller towns can't handle them as well as Chicago police can. A similar process in under way in northwest Indiana, where efforts to fight gangs in Gary have pushed gang activity into other areas. As one Chicago gang member who moved to Indiana said in an Illinois Issues article reprinted in the report: "Everyone I talk to is looking for a small town. The small towns don't know the tricks yet."

Not every suburban department is undermanned, but when suburbs were asked the biggest obstacles to combatting the problem, the most frequent ones cited were a lack of resources, poor cooperation by victims and witnesses, and a lack of solid information on gang activities. They cited community education, creation of special police units and cooperation with other agencies as among the best strategies for taking on the gangs.

The fact that gangs don't stop at the state line or a suburban border points to the need for police departments to cooperate on tracking gangs and sharing intelligence about them. It's a regional problem that requires a regional solution.

This represents the consensus of the Sun-Times News Group of 100 papers in metro Chicago.

Media sources highlight the 2006 *The Chicago Crime Commission Gang Book.*

Source: As published in the Chicago Sun-Times.

CHICAGO GANG-MOTIVATED MURDERS BY LOCATION — YEAR 2005

Location	Total	Percent
CHA Property	7	4.2%
Private Residential Property	13	7.8%
Alley	7	4.2%
Street	90	53.9%
Automobile	35	21.0%
Miscellaneous Outdoor Locations	12	7.2%
Commercial Location	3	1.8%
Total	167	100.0%

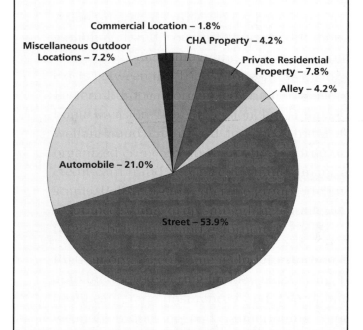

Source: CPD Detective Division Homicide Database query on Feb. 10, 2006.

Note: Location Type refers to the location where the body was found. This may or may not be the location where the murder occurred.

Note: Private Residential Property includes the following residential categories: Apartment, Hallway, House, Vestibule, Gangway, Porch, and Yard.

Note: Miscellaneous Outdoor Locations include the following categories: School Yard, Park Property, Parking Lot, and Vacant Lot.

Note: Commercial Locations include the following categories: Restaurant, Retail Store, and Gas Station.

CHICAGO GANG-MOTIVATED MURDERS BY WEAPON — YEAR 2005

Weapon Type	Total	Percent
Bludgeon/Club	3	1.8%
Firearm	158	94.6%
Stabbing/Cutting Instrument	3	1.8%
Burn	1	0.6%
Other	2	1.2%
Total	167	100.0%

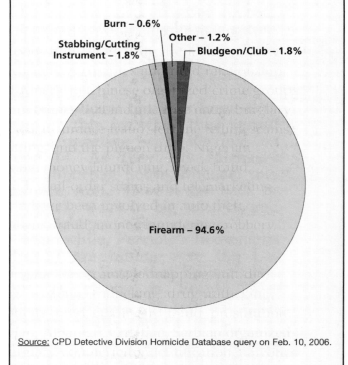

Source: CPD Detective Division Homicide Database query on Feb. 10, 2006.

Source: A page from the 2006 *The Chicago Crime Commission Gang Book.*

LEADERSHIP OF CHICAGO AREA GANGS

Source: Chicago Police Department

BLACK DISCIPLES

Jerome Freeman
Nation King

MANIAC LATIN DISCIPLES

Francisco Garcia
Institutional Leader/Prince

RENEGADE VICE LORDS

Henry Gaston
Nation King

GAYLORDS

William Giles
Institutional Leader

LATIN KINGS

Raul Gonzalez
Nation Leader

LA RAZAS

Jose Gutierrez
Nation King

AMBROSE

Peter Guzman
Nation Leader

POPES

Michael Hamilton
Nation Leader

CICERO INSANE VICE LORDS

Anthony Harris
Nation King

MAFIA INSANE VICE LORDS

Wesley Hawkins
Chief

GANGSTER DISCIPLES

Melvin Haywood
Nation Leader

INSANE UNKNOWNS

Ruben Hernandez
Institutional Leader

Source: A page from the 2006 *The Chicago Crime Commission Gang Book* highlighting some of Chicago's gang leaders.

GANG TATTOOS

Source: Illinois Department of Corrections

EBONY VICE LORDS

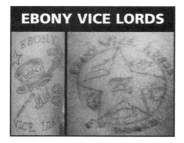

IMPERIAL INSANE VICE LORDS

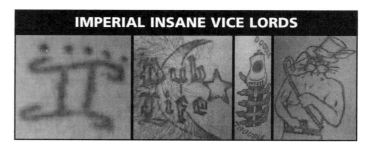

INSANE VICE LORDS

MAFIA INSANE VICE LORDS

RENEGADE VICE LORDS

TRAVELER VICE LORDS

Sureno 13s Photos provided by the West Chicago Police Department.

SURENO 13S

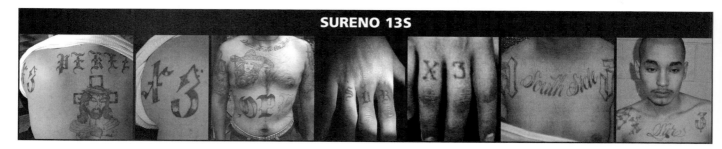

Source: A page from the 2006 *The Chicago Crime Commission Gang Book* showing some gang tattoos.

GANG HAND SIGNS

Source: Illinois Department of Corrections

AMBROSE

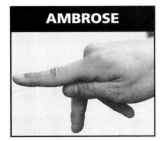

BISHOPS

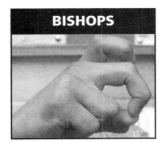

BLACK DISCIPLES

BLACK GANGSTER LLL/NEW BREED

BLACK P STONES

BLACK SOULS

C-NOTES

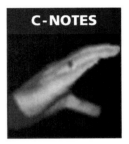

CAMPBELL BOYS (MANIAC & INSANE)

DRAGONS (INSANE, LATIN)

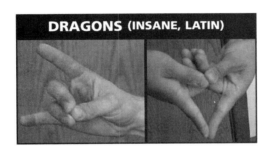

GANGSTER DISCIPLE NATION

GAYLORDS

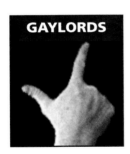

(ALMIGHTY) HARRISON GENTS

IMPERIAL GANGSTERS

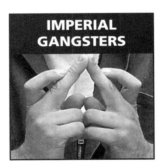

POPES (INSANE, ALMIGHTY)

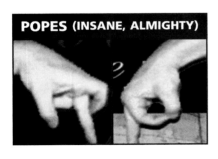

INSANE UNKNOWNS

LA RAZA

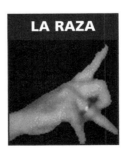

LATIN COUNTS

Source: A page from the 2006 *The Chicago Crime Commission Gang Book* illustrating some gang hand signs.

GANG GRAFFITI

LATIN DRAGONS

LATIN EAGLES

LATIN JIVERS

LATIN KINGS

LATIN LOVERS

LATIN PACHUCOS

LATIN SAINTS

LATIN SOULS

LATIN STYLERS

MANIAC LATIN DISCIPLES

MICKEY COBRAS

MILWAUKEE KINGS

Source: A page from the 2006 *The Chicago Crime Commission Gang Book* illustrating some gang graffiti.

TABLE 1
CCC Suburban Gang Survey 2005 — Gangs (Top Three and Emerging) by Area

North
(Top Three Gangs)

	# Of Suburbs Reporting Gang as a "Top Three" Gang
Acros	1
Black P Stone	3
Dragons	1
Gangster Disciples	11
Insane Deuces	1
Insane Unknowns	1
Latin Counts	1
Latin Disciples	1
Latin Kings	26
La Razas	2
Pachucos	1
Renegade Disciples	1
Russian (Ad Hoc)	1
Satan Disciples	3
Spanish G. D.'s	5
Sureno 13s	11
Surenos Locos Tres.	1
Vampires	1
Vice Lords	3
Fourteens	3
Four Corner Hustlers	1
Thirteens	2
Two-Six	2

South
(Top Three Gangs)

Ambrose	2
Arabian Posse	1
Aryan Brotherhood	1
Black P Stone	1
Gangster Disciples	12
Goon Squad	1
Insane Vice Lords	1
Latin Counts	3
Latin Kings	11
Outlaws	1
Satan G. D.'s	3
Vice Lords	5
Four Corner Hustlers	4
Two-Six	4

West
(Top Three Gangs)

Ambrose	1
Gangster Disciples	9
B. G. D.	1
Imperial Gangsters	4
Insane Deuces	1
Insane Dragons	1
Insane Popes	2
Latin Counts	7
Latin Disciples	1
Latin Kings	24
Latin Saints	1
La Razas	1
Maniac Latin Disc.	2
Maniac Sureno 13s	1

Pachucos	1
Satan Disciples	1
Simon City Royals	2
Sin City Boys	1
Sureno 13s	6
Vice Lords	6
18th St.	1
Fourteens	1
Four Corner Hustlers	2
Thirteens	1
Twelfth St. Players	1
2-2 Boys	1
Two-Six	3

North (Emerging Gangs)

	# Of Suburbs Reporting Gang as an Emerging Gang
Acros	1
Black P Stones	1
Bloods	1
Boxwood Boys	1
Brazers	1
Latin Counts	1
La Raza	1
Norteno 14s	2
Renegade Disciples	1
Russian (Ad Hoc)	1
Skin Heads	1
Sureno 13s	6
Sureno Locos Tres.	1
Vampires	1

South (Emerging Gangs)

Goon Squad	1
Hells Angels (bikers)	1
Insane Vice Lords	1
Lithuanians	1
Lockport Thugs	1
Outlaws (bikers)	2
Mickey Cobras	1
Satan Disciples	2
True Players	1
Vice Lords	1
14th St. Posse	1
Four Corner Hustlers	1

West (Emerging Gangs)

G Unit Girls	1
Insane Dragons	2
Imperial Gangsters	1
Insane Popes	1
Latin Counts	1
Latin Saints	1
Maniac Sureno 13	3
Original Crew	1
Sin City Boys	1
Sureno 13s	5
18th St.	1
4th Gen. Messiahs	3

Source: Chicago Crime Commission survey results.

SUBURBAN GANG CRIME

As Reported By 82 Suburban Police Departments in the Chicagoland Area

Crime Type	Number of Northern Suburbs Reporting This As Gang Activity (30 Suburbs Responding)	Number of Southern Suburbs Reporting This As Gang Activity (20 Suburbs Responding)	Number of Western Suburbs Reporting This As Gang Activity (32 Suburbs Responding)	TOTAL All Suburbs (82 Total)
Drugs	18	16	20	54
Homicide	6	3	6	15
Sexual Assault	3	3	3	9
Aggravated Assault	16	4	12	32
Robbery	13	7	13	33
Theft	16	9	13	38
Burglary	15	8	13	36
Motor Vehicle Theft	10	7	13	30
Arson	4	3	5	12
Gun Trafficking	6	3	5	14
Mortgage Fraud	0	0	0	0
Kidnapping	3	0	2	5
Identity Theft	1	3	1	5
Illegal Immigration	8	0	2	10
Counterfeiting	0	1	2	3
Dog Fighting	2	2	3	7
Prostitution	1	1	2	4
Human Trafficking	0	0	0	0
Money Laundering	1	0	2	3
Terrorism	0	0	0	0
High Tech Crime	0	1	1	2

Source: Chicago Crime Commission survey results, 2005.

Project Safe Neighborhoods (PSN)

PSN is a highly effective, cooperative effort between federal, state and local law enforcement, and the Chicago Crime Commission (as Community Engagement Partner) that seeks stiff federal prison time for felons who are in possession of firearms and works with parolees on job training and education so they won't re-offend. There are also strong PSN media and juvenile programs in place. Pilot Chicago PSN areas showed a 38% drop in their homicide rates. Also, only 4 percent of parolees went back to prison for new crimes after attending PSN parolee meetings. But more than 22 percent of parolees from the same neighborhoods who did not attend those meetings wound up getting arrested again. For more information, visit the CCC-hosted PSN website at www.psnchicago.org.

Drug Enforcement Administration

DEA is mandated to target and disrupt the highest-level drug traffickers in the world. As a result, DEA investigates the primary sources of supply for the street gangs that distribute illegal drugs on the streets of Chicago. In fact, it is at this critical juncture—between the sources of supply and the street gangs— where investigations are most effective in disrupting drug distribution. For many years, DEA Chicago has been working aggressively with its law enforcement counter-

parts in targeting Chicago street gangs through a variety of initiatives, such as the Top 21 Initiative, and through the use of task forces. For example, DEA Chicago currently has dedicated four enforcement groups at the Chicago High Intensity Drug Trafficking Area (HIDTA) Task Force to target and dismantle both the highest-level drug traffickers in the street gangs and their sources of supply.

Source: Chicago Crime Commission Gang Book

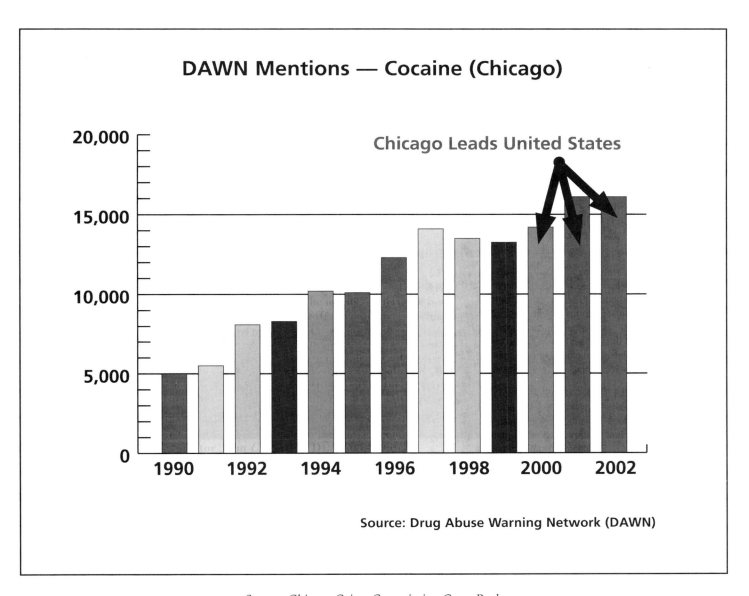

Source: Chicago Crime Commission Gang Book

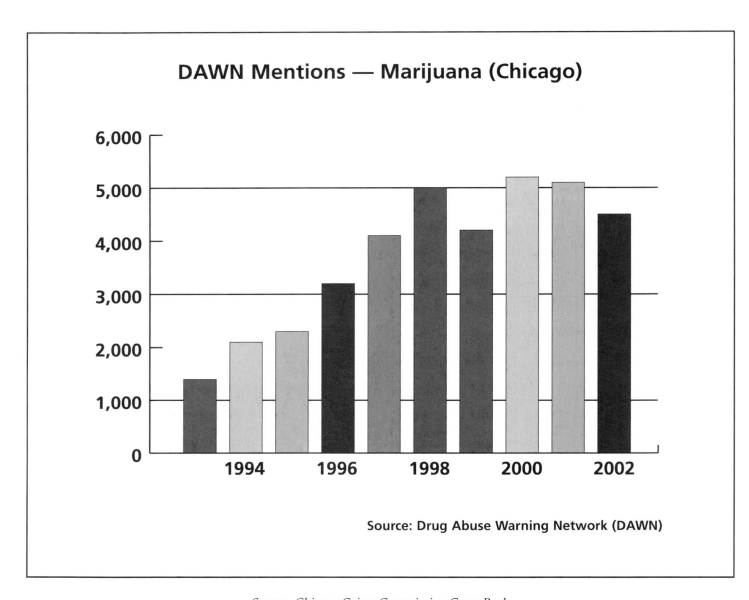

Source: Chicago Crime Commission Gang Book

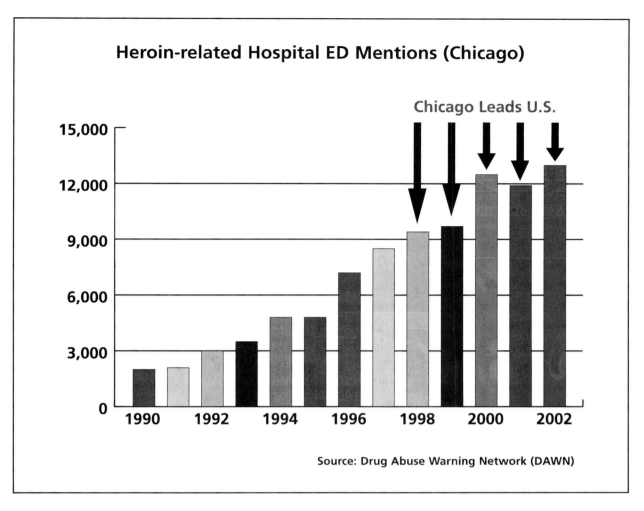

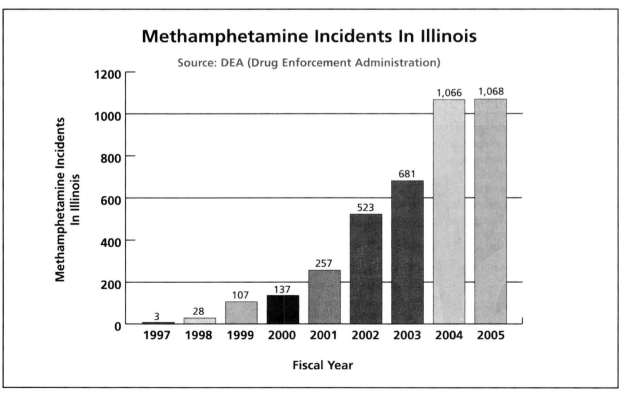

Source: Chicago Crime Commission Gang Book

Police Systems

Over the past year, the Authority expanded its ALERTS mobile computer system beyond the Chicago area and into parts of the state where such technology was previously unavailable.

The Authority develops and operates a set of technologically advanced, yet affordable, information systems that are helping dozens of police agencies, large and small, to collect and share information and wage a more coordinated fight against crime. Without the Authority's help, most of these agencies, particularly the small and medium-sized ones, simply could not afford the information systems they now rely on.

Over the last year, the Authority expanded its police information systems well beyond their base in the Chicago metropolitan area and into parts of the state where such technology was previously unavailable. Experience in places such as Champaign and Sangamon counties suggests that jurisdictions statewide could benefit from the Authority's unique police information services.

Mobile Data Systems. ALERTS, the Authority's in-car computer terminal system for police, continued to experience phenomenal growth over the last year. With more than 800 terminals on its statewide network, ALERTS in just three years has become the nation's largest user of mobile data technology for law enforcement.* The system currently processes more than 3 million messages a month—on-the-spot inquiries about motor vehicles, wanted or missing persons, and other national, state, and regional crime information.

What makes ALERTS unique, and popular, is that it is a cooperative venture among local law enforcement and the Authority. Most other mobile data systems are built and operated for only a single agency. But ALERTS (which stands for Area-wide Law Enforcement Radio Terminal System) is designed to be a network of user agencies. The Authority is responsible for research and development, and it operates and maintains the central computer hardware and telecommunications equipment. User agencies procure their own in-car terminals, and they pay the Authority a user fee for operating and maintaining the system. This arrangement allows individual agencies to keep their costs down, while gaining access to a dynamic, state-of-the-art system

As of June 1, 1992, 105 law enforcement agencies in eight Illinois counties were part of the Authority's network. ALERTS users include some of the state's largest law enforcement agencies, as well as some of the smallest. In fact, more than one-third of the law enforcement agencies using ALERTS have 10 or fewer full-time sworn officers.

The number of ALERTS agencies has more than doubled in the last 18 months, as the system continued to expand in the Chicago area—and into Champaign and Sangamon counties as well. Seventeen agencies in Sangamon County, including the sheriff's police and the Springfield Police Department, use ALERTS. So do six agencies in Champaign County. Officials there hope to implement ALERTS countywide over the next year. In the six-county Chicago area, where ALERTS was first introduced in 1989, the system has more than 80 user agencies.

* Source: Motorola, Inc.

Units hailed as lifesavers

A computer terminal in a police car can sometimes protect an officer's life as well as a weapon can.

Shortly after the police department in Richmond, in McHenry County, joined the statewide ALERTS computer system, Patrol Officer Jerome Volstead got curious about a parked car and its driver.

Volstead first sought information the old way, by radioing the county sheriff's department. But its computer was down.

Turning to his terminal, the officer quickly learned that the driver was "armed and dangerous—Do not approach." He summoned other officers.

Volstead was pretty sure the suspect had noticed him. As he waited for help, he saw the man bend over and straighten up, as if pulling something onto the car seat.

When Volstead's backup arrived, the officers drew their guns and talked the driver out of the car.

On the front seat they found a duffel bag with the handle of a loaded .357 magnum poking out.

Richmond Police Chief Kevin Bays said, "In talking to [the suspect], I'm convinced he intended to shoot the officer."

ALERTS also has saved the town money. Working mobile phones into the system, the department has been able to eliminate dispatching, saving "a minimum of $80,000 a year," Bays said. —*Gary Wisby*

Reprinted from *Chicago Sun-Times*, June 9, 1991

Law enforcement officials are discovering that ALERTS can "sometimes protect an officer's life as well as a weapon can."

Source: Illinois Criminal Justice Information Authority annual report
Reproduced with permission of the Illinois Criminal Justice Information Authority.

CJ the AMERICAS

Volume 7, Number 1

February-March, 1994

Page 21

CORRECTIONS

Walking Prisons: The Developing Technology of Electronic Controls

by Max Winkler

Tracking devices, such as anklets, bracelets, and implants, could let low-risk criminals be put safely on the streets instead of in prison.

The cost of incarcerating criminals in America has steadily spiraled upward. Maximum-security incarceration now requires an average of $25,000 per year per inmate, with an initial cost of $100,000 to construct a one-inmate cell. The costs of local detention and jail units are also on the rise, now averaging $18,000 per year per inmate. Such massive costs provide a compelling reason to shorten prison terms or to reserve incarceration for the most dangerous and threatening of criminals.

Alternatives to imprisonment are increasingly being offered, but humanitarianism alone is not enough to justify releasing prisoners for good behavior, conferring leniency on first-time offenders, or offering work-release or other such programs where the offender is supervised in the community.

One revolutionary alternative for controlling criminals is a system known as the Electronic Supervision Program. It may prove a precursor of felon-supervision systems in the new millennium. The Electronic Supervision Program is now a popular system for managing offenders by means of electronic monitors. The system enables law-enforcement agents to keep better track of released prison inmates.

Drive-By Tracking

The Electronic Supervision Program's home-detention system is based on current technology available from a variety

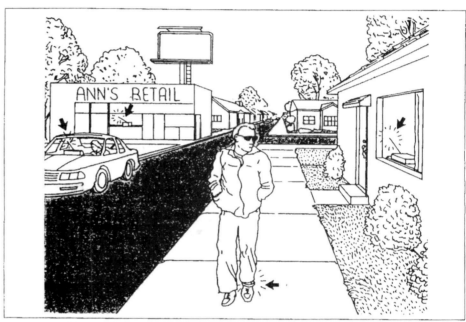

Invisible Prison: first generation. **A modem signals that an offender with an anklet transponder is leaving his home. Drive-by units can continue to track the signal. The store in the background uses the system to alert security personnel when an ankleted shoplifter enters.**

of national and international corporations. This first-generation system consists of an anklet transponder electronically linked to a telephone modem. Its purpose is to alert a central monitoring station when the offender moves outside of a 100-foot radius around the modem. The system also periodically checks the offender's location. Attempts to leave the specified location or to tamper with the transponder are relayed back to the monitoring station automatically.

The system also allows law enforcement officers with "drive-by" units to check on offenders at their workplace, home, or other authorized locations. The officer's car has a portable electronic receiver that displays the frequency code of the nearest transponder unit. Often, drive-by units get signals from unexpected locations, such as city jails or locations with reported crimes in progress.

Chicago Sun-Times

Crime data is a mouse click away

Neighborhood stats on Net

BY FRANK MAIN
CRIME REPORTER

Starting today, Chicagoans should be able to type their home addresses into a new police Web service and instanay- see the crime hot spots in their neighborhoods.

The Web site, Citizeiu, ICAM, is the outgrowth of a computer system launched in 1993 that until now was for police eyes only.

"Those of us interested in the community policing concept are more apt to know where to focus our efforts," said Sandy Campbell, 62, an Uptown resident who saw the system demonstrated last week.

Citizen ICAM can be reached through the city Web site, *www.eityof chic-a-go.orgcaps,* at noon today, city officials said.

The system is easy to use. A citizen chooses a street address, intersection or police beat, and a radius of up to one mile. One can search for all crimes or only certain crimes.

Source: As published in the Chicago Sun-Times

1943: Assistance of the States Attorney's office in conducting raids on gambling establishments was secured after Cook County highway police staged fake raids. Grand jury action was requested when the gambling equipment seized in those raids disappeared from the custody of the highway police. The grand jury was appointed, voted numerous indictments of police and gambling figures in Cook County and Chicago, and three convictions were finally obtained. The Commission exposed the sale of police reports by officers in the Accident Prevention Division of the Chicago Police Department. The police and sheriff's committee met with the Mayor on this matter and reports were subsequently made available to any individual upon request.

Source: John Binder Collection

1944: Commission investigations disclosed that liquor licenses were issued to persons with criminal records and taverns were managed by ex-convicts in violation of the Tavern Code. Also, as the result of the 1943 efforts of the Commission and the Grand Jury action on gambling disclosures, seven police captains were discharged by the Civil Service Commission.

1945: Commission investigations established irregularities in the handling of deceased persons coming to the attention of police. Conferences with the coroner, public administrator's office, and police officials led to the establishment of procedures, which would ensure the proper handling of deceased persons and the disposal of the property of the deceased.

1946: The Commission undertook a study of rackets preying on Chicago citizens and businessmen. Ten thousand businessmen were contacted by letter with a request to furnish the Commission with information on known rackets and the type of law enforcement prevailing in their districts. The Commission published a manual of criminal law and procedure by E.W. Puttkammer for use by police and other law-enforcement officials.

1948: After the Commission questioned the validity of police department statistics, a survey was undertaken by the FBI at the request of the Police Commissioner of police reporting and statistics. This resulted in numerous changes in the statistical division of the police department.

1952: A distraught tobacco wholesaler turned to the Chicago Crime Commission for help against competition that was undercutting prices by using phony cigarette tax stamps, therefore not paying the tax. A Commission investigation found the Capone mob in the tobacco business and reported the findings to Illinois Gov. Adlai Stevenson. On May 3, the first guilty verdict was handed down by a criminal court against Max Dolgin. Twenty-two people went on trial at a later date for tax-stamp fraud.

1955: The Commission's rigorous investigations exposed an auto-towing racket that revealed collusion between police officers, towers, and garages. As a result, the Commissioner of Police created a new bureau, headed by a police captain, to eliminate the abuses.

1956: Federal authorities were investigating what was believed to be an attempt by hoodlums to take over Chicago's wholesale tobacco business, which grossed an estimated $125 million a year. The Commission helped in the investigation.

1957: The Commission led the fight at a closed session of the Illinois State Legislature to defeat legislation that, if enacted, would have seriously hampered law enforcement. Senate Bill #1389, which would have legalized pari-mutuel betting on jai alai, opened the door to other forms of legalized gambling and would have added to an already increasing crime problem. House Bill #215 would have hindered police work, virtually eliminated questioning of suspects in murder, kidnapping, and other serious crimes, prevented opportunity for victims to view and identify suspects, and would have aided only the criminal element.

1959: A letter was sent by the Commission to the United States Attorney General calling attention to the magnitude and strength of organized crime. After the Attorney General's favorable reply, a special unit was set up in his office to coordinate the activities of all federal agencies.

1960: Studies by the Commission of organized crime operations throughout the nation were turned over to federal prosecution and investigative agencies, providing substantial assistance in fighting syndicate operations. Commission staff members played important roles in the work of both the Kefauver and McClellan committees investigating organized

Source: John Binder Collection

crime and rackets. Much of the evidence obtained at hearings of these committees was predicated on data furnished by the Chicago Crime Commission.

1963: The Commission announced that it was solidly behind the police reform program of Police Supt. O.W. Wilson. It also stated its opposition to House Bill #298, which would sanction police unions. The potential danger in such a bill is the opportunity it may ultimately provide for union strikes by the police and consequently a complete breakdown of law enforcement.

1966: In its continued attack on organized crime, the Commission announced a seven-point legislative program designed to bolster police and prosecution officials in their attempt to improve law enforcement.

1968: The Commission focused public attention on organized crime. In October 1967 a twenty-page booklet entitled, "The Chicago Crime Commission Spotlight on Organized Crime – The Chicago Syndicate" was prepared and given wide distribution. Listed in this publication were 214 individuals with criminal syndicate affiliations or associations and forty-two business firms having direct or indirect connections with crime syndicate figures.

Source: James Wagner Collection

1971: The Commission and the Illinois Institute of Technology Research Institute released "A Study of Organized Crime in Illinois". The six-month project studied the nature of organized crime in Illinois, its history, a theory of its operations, and its impact on the state.

1972: Operation Crime Call was set up to give the public an open line to help combat crime. The special Commission phone number allowed a victim to report a crime without revealing his/her identity.

1973: A Commission study of the Cook County Department of Adult Probation charged the agency in failing to protect the public from criminals by failing to properly supervise its 17,000 probationers. The study reported that probation officers were in short supply, undertrained, overworked, and often not qualified. The report charged that probation officers had little idea of what was going on in the lives of the convicted criminals under their supervision.

1974: The Commission adopted a resolution supporting a bill calling for the elimination of the requirement of grand jury indictments in felony cases. The Commission stated that the state's urban areas were literally choking on the backlog of criminal cases.

1975: The Commission proposed legislation to permit the revocation of the release on bail of offenders who commit crimes while awaiting trial. The proposal was in direct response to the problem of serious crimes committed by offenders on bail.

1976: With an awareness of community-based organizational interest in combating crimes, the Commission's Inner City Committee established a communications network whereby neighborhood organizations in the Chicago area could share and explore methods of assisting criminal justice agencies in the war against crime.

1977: The Commission released a comprehensive statement, "Principles Underlying a Sound Correction System." This principles statement considered the subject of deterrence, detention prior to trial, sentencing, probation, the prison system, rehabilitation, and parole.

1978: The Commission initiated the idea for establishing a system for crime-pattern analysis for use in Cook County and the five-county metropolitan area.

1979: The Commission played an active role in shaping criminal justice legislation in the 81st General Assembly. The Commission focused on three areas where reform was needed. These issues involved the right of the state to demand a jury trial, the abuse of continuances, and the availability of electronic surveillance to law enforcement in Illinois.

1984: The Commission sponsored a gang crimes training seminar and workshop in which training sessions were held on gang identification and structure, intelligence and investigative techniques, and legal issues for prosecutors. The conference was a proactive measure designed to curb the spread of gangs throughout Cook County. The Commission hoped to assist communities in the control and suppression of gangs before they gained a foothold in the community.

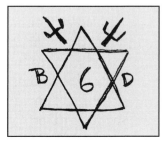

Source: Chicago Crime Commission Gang Book

1985: The Commission launched a full-scale project to evaluate Criminal Court judges who were seeking re-election. The Commission's research and recommendations offered citizens a unique management tool to objectively measure judicial performance. It served as a valuable and urgently needed public service so that only qualified judges would serve on the bench.

1986: The Commission released a year-long study of the Chicago Police Department's crime laboratory recommending a new facility and different procedures for collecting and analyzing evidence. The study also recommended that no less than four procedures in the narcotics preliminary hearing courts be changed to ensure the quality of felony narcotics cases before they proceed to the trial level.

1987: The Commission conducted a study of the processing of drug cases in the preliminary hearing courts. Official court sheets revealed a large number of felony narcotics charges were dismissed for one of four unacceptable reasons, such as, the arresting officer was not present in court, the defendant failed to appear and an arrest warrant was never issued, the crime lab report was unavailable, or the state dismissed the case for no cited reason. Recommendations were presented to various public officials and many were implemented.

1988: A seminar was held in Washington, D.C. on organized crime and drug enforcement by the FBI, DEA, the National Association of Citizens Crime Commissions and the Commission.

1989: Commission leaders provided written information and oral testimony before the U.S. House of Representatives Sub-Committee on Criminal Justice urging Congress to support the retention of the federal organized crime strike forces throughout the United States.

1990: The appointment of self-admitted organized crime associate John Serpico as the Chairman of the Chicago Port Authority was vehemently opposed by the Commission.

1991: The Chicago Police Department studied the Commission's recommendations regarding community policing. The result was a five-year effort of the Department to fully adapt what is now referred to as the Chicago Alternative Policing Strategy (CAPS). Also, in conjunction with Fox-TV, the CCC started airing a segment called *Chicago's Most Wanted*.

Source: Chicago Police Department

1992: In response to the gambling issue, the Commission published the *Analysis of Key Issues Involved in the Proposed Chicago Casino Gambling Project.*

1994: The Partners in Safety Network, comprised of over 300 community groups, was established to help concerned citizens reduce crime.

1995: The Commission released *Gangs: Public Enemy Number One.* Over 40,000 copies were distributed. The Commission co-sponsored the National Summit of Urban Coalitions for Public Safety & Violence Prevention. After holding focus groups on community-based crime problems, the Commission established training workshops, programs, and resource guides on the issues of crime breeding properties, youth alternatives to crime, gang awareness, and small-business crime concerns.

1996: After working with key officials in the criminal justice system, the Commission released *Making Room For Justice: New Priorities For The Criminal Justice System.*

1997: The Commission filed an amicus curiae brief supporting the City of Chicago asking the Federal Court for the Northern District of Illinois to minimize the provisions of the 1983 consent decree limiting the Chicago Police Department's ability to investigate organized crime, street gangs, and terrorists. A 120-page report, *The New Faces of Organized Crime* was released. This report redefined organized crime and for the first time in America spotlighted new organized-crime ethnic groups as a threat along with the traditional Mob. The Commission also formed the Business Assistance Network comprised of 150 local chambers of commerce.

1998: The first campus gambling conference in the Chicago area was co-sponsored by the Commission, DePaul University, and the Illinois Attorney General's Office. The Commission's community youth program, a pilot program for redirecting first-time juvenile offenders, was developed by the Commission and its many partners, including the Chicago police, Cook County State's Attorney's office, Chicago public schools, DCFS, the Boys & Girls Clubs of Chicago, and Allstate Insurance Company.

1999: The Commission released the 90-page *Girls Behind the Boys: Girls in Gangs* report and an *Analysis of Video Gaming* report. The Commission testified before the Cook County Board's Committee on Courts for the 21st Century to advocate for an increase in the number of courts and judges. It also hosted a three-day National Association of Citizens Crime Commissions meeting, a Russian Organized Crime & Money Laundering Conference and a Campus Gambling Conference.

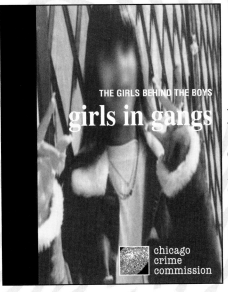

Source: Chicago Crime Commission

2000: The Commission released a special *Gun Violence* report covering twenty-five different facets related to gun violence in the Chicago metropolitan area. The Commission was an active partner in the Chicago Department of Public Health's Prevent Violence Chicago effort, the State's Attorney of Cook County's Commission on Juvenile Competency and the Bureau of Alcohol, Tobacco and Firearms LPS Program designed to introduce high-school students to careers in law enforcement and criminal justice. The Commission released a list of more than fifteen corporate sponsors of the web pages of Chicago's most violent street gangs and called upon them to exercise greater responsibility in choosing where to spend their advertising dollars and with whom to associate their name. Also, the Commission highlighted thirty fugitives on the televised *Chicago's Most Wanted* program resulting in the capture of five fugitives. The Commission reviewed the needs of five Cook County Court facilities and provided resulting recommendations in its testimony to the Cook County Board of Commissioners, while also calling for the formation of a task force on the Re-codification of the Illinois Criminal Laws. The Commission also continued its efforts to combat any existence of organized-crime involvement in the proposed casino in Rosemont.

2001: The Commission's Community Youth Program, a pilot program to redirect first-time juvenile offenders, began. A conference on Anti-Terrorism, Threat Assessment and Vulnerability Analysis for High Rise Structures was held. The Commission explored and reported on the ease with which terrorists or criminals might be able to secure false identification over the Internet. The Commission's chief investigator researched the state of

Source: Chicago Crime Commission

homicide investigation in Cook County which resulted in a number of recommendations for improvement. The Commission's chief investigator provided detailed testimony and information to the Illinois Gaming Board regarding questionable associations of individuals involved in the proposed Emerald Casino deal. The Commission began its effort to inventory and estimate the deterioration of its eighty-two-year collection of valuable organized crime records in order to explore options available for digitizing the collection.

Source: Project Safe Neighborhoods

2002: The Commission was selected to be the Project Safe Neighborhoods (PSN) community engagement partner. PSN is a gun-violence reduction program involving numerous law enforcement and criminal justice partners. The Commission's Community Youth Program provided data to the Chicago police on the assessment and service linkage of first-time offenders. The Commission also became the lead agency in piloting the Neighborhood Restorative Justice Mediation Program in Cook County, a conflict-resolution program providing an alternative to juvenile court. The Commission's Administration of Justice Committee reviewed the *Report of the Governor's Commission on Capital Punishment – Recommendations Only* and released its endorsement of most of its content and its comments on other items. The Commission held a conference for finance–related industries on Cyber Crime.

2003: The Commission formed the first inclusive task force addressing child exploitation – the Coalition Against the Exploitation, Prostitution and Trafficking of Children. The Commission joined the Illinois Integrated Justice Information System Implementation Board and committees in an effort to enhance statewide information-sharing and quality between law enforcement and criminal justice agencies. A Presentation on Financial Statement Fraud, a seminar on Protection From Business Fraud and a presentation on Espionage & Conspiracy: Robert Hanssen were held. The Commission met with the chairman and administrator of the Illinois Gaming Board to express its concerns regarding the Emerald Casino settlement agreement.

2004: The Community Youth Program process evaluation was completed and work was begun on the outcomes evaluation of the program. A one-day conference for 300 individuals was held on Child Prostitution and Exploitation. Research for *The Gang Book* was begun. The Commission and the Cook County State 's Attorney's office worked together on RAV2 – Reduce Animal Violence, Reduce All Violence. RAV2 educates criminal-justice and law-enforcement personnel on the links between human violence and animal cruelty and on new animal-cruelty legislation that may (when appropriately used) be a tool to confront gangs, guns, and drugs. Gang Education Training was provided to students from twenty Chicago schools and to other agencies. Again, the Commission provided testimony to the Illinois Gaming Board in regards to the Emerald Casino situation. How to Avoid Identity Theft recommendations were provided to thousands through the Commission's *Action Alert Newsletter* while Avoiding Employee Theft was detailed for over 200 chambers of commerce through the Commission's *Business Assistance Bulletin.*

2005: The Commission continued in its partnerships. It reduced gun violence through *Project Safe Neighborhoods* and worked to enhance information-sharing among criminal-justice agencies through the Illinois and the Cook County Integrated Justice Information Systems Partnerships. It worked through its Coalition Against the Exploitation, Prostitution and Trafficking of Children and its Community Youth Program to save exploited children and redirect troubled first-time juvenile offenders. It advocated for the separation of juvenile corrections from adult corrections. The Commission surveyed over 200 suburban police departments on street-gang activity. It also made a presentation on Identity Theft to corporate employees.

2006: While continuing the activities noted in 2005, in June 2006, the Commission released its nationally acclaimed *The Gang Book* – a concise but detailed guide developed in partnership with local, state, and federal law enforcement, the Chicago public schools and others. *The Gang Book* received media attention from most every newspaper, radio station, and television station and has spurred the introduction of legislation and new partnerships between law enforcement, particularly in regards to suburban gangs. In September, the CCC launched its new anonymous public corruption web-based and automated telephone crime reporting system specially designed for government employees and citizens. The well-received www.888eyeongov.org website and 1-888-Eye-On-Gov hotline receive allegations of corruption from throughout the United States.

Source: Chicago Crime Commission

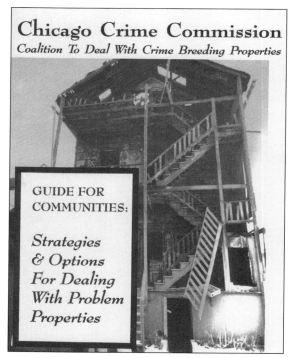